THIS BOOK IS NEITHER FICT NOR FACTION

IT IS BOTH FRICTION AND FRACTION

IT IS SHORTER BECAUSE I HAD LONGER

IT IS WORSE BECAUSE I AM BETTER

drif's guide

the

drif

field

guide

to

the

secondhand

and

antiquarian

book

shops

of

britain

by

drif

field.

---

p u b l i s h e d   b y   d r i f   f i e l d   g u i d e s

l o n d o n

1 9 9 1

ISBN 0-9510005-3-5

Published by drif field guides
Omnibus Workspace, 41 North Road, London N7 9DP

Dedication

This book is dedicated to the bookshop owner in Vermont whom I had telephoned whilst searching for a bóok. He was the most polite and helpful bookshop owner I have ever encountered. At the end of the conversation he asked me my name so that he could send me a catalogue, when I said "drif field" he asked in a voice close to quaking, "Are you thee *Mr Driffield?" I had to admit that I was. There was then a silence that lasted thirty seconds. It was the most pleasant response that I have ever had from a secondhand bookdealer.*

C O N T E N T S

D I S - C O N T E N T S

*I have never worked out which one I am supposed to be.

THIS BOOK WOULD NOT HAVE BEEN POSSIBLE WITHOUT THE ASSISTANCE OF THE FOLLOWING PEOPLE:

INVOLUNTARY

Carol Watkinson
Alan & Ludi Kipping
Leslie Cole
Judith Mansfield
Bill Heyward
William Hoffer
John Martin
Raymond Carver

VOLUNTARY

Scott Thompson	Photographer
David Mann	Layout Artist
Alan Scaife	Bookshop counter
Leighton Printing	Printers
Raymond Carver	Chauffeur

AS I WAS SAYING BEFORE I WAS SO RUDELY INTERRUPTED

The number and quality of the secondhand and antiquarian bookshops of Britain is in serious decline. The main part of the responsibility for this state of affairs must rest with the bookshop owners themselves, but it is also true that they have been ably assisted by external forces, namely: The bookfairies, the popular image of bookselling, and the docile customers. If nothing is done soon, when you see the sign "Rare Bookshop" it will mean the bookshop is rare, not the books.

In 1987 when I last published this guide there were over 1,000 places that could possibly have been classified as secondhand bookshops, approximately 900 of which I recognised as being such (and I am not exactly renowned for my high standards.

There are currently 803 places that stock second hand books in Great Britain, of which 618 now meet my definition, which some people would say has also seriously declined.

The bookshop owners like to blame several other factors: high rents, the business rate, the lack of books and too many other shops. I find it extremely reassuring that they should blame others for their fate. It shows that my doubts as to whether booksellers are human are unjustified, for it is a perfectly human characteristic to blame everybody else when things go wrong. I do it all the time myself. After all, what are other people for?

If a bookshop is unable to afford the rent then it should not take the premises. There is no reason why bookshops should be subsidised. Bookshops are in the leisure industry, not the culture business. If you wish to be in the culture business and have something to do with books, I would humbly suggest that you go and become a librarian. The same argument applies to the 'business rate', if you cannot afford it then you should not open. It is a purely business decision. If the rents of bookshops are subsidised what happens is that it is the people who are best at getting the subsidies who get the shops, as has happened in the Charing Cross Road. The shops that are currently there are keeping the others out, because they the occupants are subsidised and there are no spaces left for anybody else. The rents of those shops that are to let are disproportionately high because the subsidised ones have used up all the good will and the space.

Another argument that bookshop owners use in their defence of the decline of the shops is the lack of books. It says, something about the sense of humour of most bookshop owners that they can say this and keep a straight face. Last year, in Britain 60,000 titles were published. This total increases every year, this is titles, not books. A secondhand book is just that - a second hand book. There is nothing special about it, other than the price. There are few shops in Britain that solely deal in antiquarian books, but the argument remains the same, even with vanity publications there is somebody that wants them. Too often, in Britain, the bookshop owners have a fixed idea about what people should buy, collect and read. If a book was published at a fixed price then it stands to reason that there must be people who would pay a lesser price for it.

What bookshop owners really mean when they say there is a shortage of books, is that the number of people willing to sell them books at the price they wish to pay is declining and this is indeed true. For years bookshops in Britain have been surviving by "stealing" books, from private call outs. The amounts they offer bears no relation to the amounts they sell the books for. Those shops that prospered in the seventies and eighties paid derisory amounts for the books they bought. The shops were often filled with the near unsaleable residue. It still goes on, and I do not doubt that it will go on in the future, but the number of opportunities for it to happen are less and less.

When bookshop owners say there are too many other shops, what they really mean is that they think they should be the only shop in the area. It is true that several entirely inappropriate people have opened shops in bizarre areas which had no natural catchment of customers, but it cannot be that there can be too many bookshops. Secondhand bookshops are a labour intensive occupation, the problem is not that there are too many shops, but that the wrong people have been opening them and that the books they have put in them are entirely inappropriate. The sad news about this is that it tends to be the sensible shops that close down and the bad shops that stay.

One of the reasons for the opening of entirely inappropriate shops is that antiquarian book dealing is such a high status profession. It has the cache of being a doctor, a professor or a solicitor. It has the income of a nurse, a student or an articled clerk. Thus it is, that people who have already made money at other professions are exceedingly keen to come into it. They are not in it for the money, they are in it for the status, and it is these people who are keen that it should be part of the culture industry.

One of the major reasons for its high status is the reverence and adulation that the media give it. Journalists love writing about books, the amount of space given to books is absurdly out of proportion with the number of people who buy them. When they run out of ideas about new books, journalists move on to the secondhand, primarily because they are always trying to sell their own. From the newspapers and magazines is where the television picks up its notions. There is now a lady who has written a book about a bookshop that she has never been in. At least, she was more honest than most journalists. This bestselling book was made into a film, which gets shown on television. Television, which is the main social influence in Britain today is obsessed by image. The words Antiquarian Bookseller conjure a whole host of images for the television folk. There is but one shop in Britian that actually predominantly sells antiquarian books. (Vanbrugh Rare Books, Museum Street, London) all the others sell secondhand books. Most of the books on sale in British secondhand bookshops are Post War, but it does not sound quite as good when you say "I am a Post War secondhand dealer, bugger the truth think of the image; I am an antiquarian book dealer.

In a survey by the Bookseller Magazine, which is devoted to new books, it was discovered that less than 4% of the population ever goes in a bookshop. The bad news about this statistic is that W.H.Smith was defined as a bookshop. Nobody has ever done a survey to find out what proportion of the population ever goes into a secondhand bookshop, but I would not be surprised to hear that it was less than 4% of those who go into new bookshops. At best it means that at least 96% of the population has never been in a bookshop, let alone in a secondhand one.

It is supposed to be that the customer can never be in the wrong, but whoever said this had not encountered bookshop owners or the customers of bookshops. For most ordinary customers going into a bookshop is a nerve racking experience. I have great difficulty persuading bookshop owners of this notion, but I maintain that I have greater experience than they. I have sat outside innumerable bookshops talking to potential customers, who often fled when the shop did eventually open. Bookshop owners only ever see the people who do go into bookshops; this cannot be more than 4% of the population (see above). One of the reasons, people do not like going in shops is that the owners are so unwelcoming and so unhelpful. I am not judging this on how they behave to me. I looked upon it as a compliment when one bookseller told me I had the hide of a rhinoceros, after he had all but physically attacked me and I asked him if there was any chance of a lift to the station. I seldom buy new things, but when I do I go over the top.

When a bespoke shoe maker held a sale in Jermyn Street I was there at 9 a.m. to purchase a pair of shoes that had been marked down from £440 to £120. Unfortunately, I was not there early enough, there were several other skinflints in the queue in front of me. The shop did not open until 9.30 a.m. and then allowed only one person at a time in. I did not get in until 11 a.m. All the time, I kept examining the feet of the people in front of me, but I did not think they had feet as big as mine or the pair of shoes that were on sale.

At eleven, those shoes and I were still there. At 11.01 am we were joined in holy pedlock. When I went into the shop, the assistant treated me as if I was the only customer he had seen all morning. He politely enquired as to what it was I wanted and complimented me on my choice (I don't think there were another pair of shoes big enough for me in the whole shop). He helped me on with them and omitted to comment on the state of my socks. The shoes were wonderful, it was like walking on butter. He instructed me in how to clean them, how to care for them and how and where to have them repaired. When I enquired as to why the reduction in price was so great, he explained to me the economics of 'boot building'. When I handed over the money he did not react as if I was some loathsome barefoot who had strayed in off the street. He certainly had been dealing with customers all morning and he must have been tired, but not once did he express this idea, I don't doubt that he had worked in that shop for a considerable time, but he was not in the least bit "off hand" about my inane questions. As I left this shop, he thanked me for calling, as if I was the only customer he had ever had. There was a queue of about thirty people outside. As I walked down the road in my new 'rhinoceros-hide' shoes, I wondered why I had never seen any such behaviour in a bookshop. Not once, have I ever seen anything close to the politeness that that man gave me as a matter of course.

Many of the ex-customers of secondhand bookshops have voted with their feet. In wine bars, they have a happy hour - the secondhand bookshop equivalent is different , it is called the surly hour and it lasts all day.

The Bookfairies are the AIDS of the book business, they are the carriers of a disease for which no cure has yet been discovered, and the prognosis is bad unless some way is found of solving this problem.

They started in the late '60s as a collection of provincial bookdealers hiring a venue in London in an attempt to attract more custom. A wholly admirable aim but now they have mushroomed into a vast hydra headed monster. The PBFA has a membership of 750, almost the same as the number of secondhand bookshops.

The main reason why the Bookfairies are bad news is that they do not produce any new form of life. At a typical bookfair there is a hardcore of bookdealers who have much experience of which book does sell and which does not. (This is especially true of the London Bookfairs). They are experts in such subjects as Childrens, Modern Firsts, Art Reference or Antiquarian. When a non-expert dealer, or even one with not as much experience as they, arrives and sets up his stall, they are ready to pounce and buy up anything which is grossly underpriced. That which is merely slightly underpriced they advise the new dealer to increase the price of it. There is nothing wrong in this and it is completely natural, but what is wrong and what causes the problems is that during the lulls in business - and Bookfairs are the ultimate in Being and Nothingness - the new dealer goes round the other stalls and sees the book he arrived with at £5, marked up to £45. They never make that mistake again. Either their pride is wounded, or their wallet, but it does not happen a second time. From then on the newly pledged bookdealer charges £45 for everything and reduces it when he has seen it on somebody else's stall for less. This is why when you go round bookfairs you can see several copies of the same book at similar prices. Emulation is the name of the game. Every book starts at its level of unsaleability.

You may say that the same thing happens in street markets and bookshops, but there are crucial differences. Firstly when something is bought at either of the former it is often taken elsewhere to be sold, and thus the original seller does not find out the price, but secondly, and much more importantly, anybody can turn up and buy at a street market or bookshop. There are no entry qualifications, all you have to do is be there and be faster than everybody else.

At Bookfairs, only those people who are already exhibitors are allowed to buy before the market officially opens - in the city this is called insider dealing - thus those people who are the selectors of the new exhibitors are able to select the most saleable stock, and because they are familiar with the regular customers at the bookfairs they know how much the potential customer will pay - which has very little to do with the market price.

If somebody opens a market bookstall or a bookshop then those customers who are in the right place at the right time are able to buy the books at what they consider to be bargain prices. The bookshop owner seldom gets to hear of how much a particular customer may value that book. He slowly learns that there is a wide variety of books that that particular customer will buy, and although the prices will rise slowly, everybody gets an equal chance. All you have to do to be a customer in a bookshop is be there, you do not have to belong to the PBFA or any other organisation. This element of serendipity actively encourages customers.

As the bookfairs began to grow in size and number the exhibitors were forced to find new sources of stock. They began to frequent the secondhand bookshops in even greater number. They bought the books which they knew were sure to sell at bookfairs - an extremely small range given how many books there are in the world, and because the shop owners saw these people spending money they too began looking for the type of book sought after by the bookfairies, and this attracted more bookfairies. But the more bookfairies that were attracted, the less the range of books got to be. Soon there was not a subject in which the bookfairs did not have an expert and within minutes he or she would have a neck breathing emulator.

An author or a subject would be declared 'hot' and the next month, books by/on that author/subject would appear at egregious prices. In the early '70s it was possible to tour the secondhand bookshops of Britain and make a living. I know I did it, but I could not do the same today. Not because I cannot compete against the bookfairies but because there are so many of them. Each one has the shop in his county staked out, there are more bookfairies per bookshop than there are other customers. In the early '70s I used to meet collectors, now I only shun bookfairies.

This is the acquired immune deficiency that bookfairies suffer from, or rather we suffer from. Those arseholes have no idea of their sickness and keep spreading it. The only books they care about are the ones the experts buy. All prices rise towards the level that the experts charge. No new blood is ever brought in, and no customer was ever borne at a bookfair.

The reason that the bookfairies have to haunt the bookshops is that they have no natural source of buying books. An ordinary customer is not allowed to turn up at a London bookfair and attempt to sell books to the so called bookdealers. Bookshops by their very presence encourage people to sell books to them. It may be the first time a person ever goes into a bookshop when he or she attempts to sell books, but because they have seen the shop there over a number of years they will think of it and enquire when they next go by. When the shops do buy the bookfairies are ready to pounce and thus ensure that no ordinary customer can ever accidentally buy a book too cheaply (in their eyes). It is the number of bookfairies which it is impossible to compete against. In the same way as it is possible to put up with some locusts but not an entire swarm so it is possible to put up with some bookfairies.

After being assiduously schooled by the bookfairies large numbers of shops have closed down to run away and join the circus with this bunch of clowns. It is no accident that the Surrey sweep from the Thames round to Croydon that used to contain the largest number of bookshops outside the Charing Cross Road now contains almost as few shops as East London.

If you look in the PBFA membership list, Surrey contains the greatest number of members (that's what I call a scientiffic survey).

By its very presence a bookshop is encouraging people to take an interest in books. A bookshop does a lot of its best business when it is closed, this is why bookshop owners should attempt to make the window interesting. It may be years before a passer by goes into a bookshop, but nobody but nobody ever started collecting books at a bookfair.

You occasionally see the residents of hotels stray into a bookfair, within minutes they are suffering from shell shock. No normal person can take an interest in any single subject for more than twenty minutes. To the human beings, a bookfair is one subject: old books.

This is why the books outside of a bookshop are so crucial, not to make money out of them now, but to encourage the customers of the future. There is not one collector in the world who ever started by buying the most expensive books. All the biggest customers began by buying books at ten pence a time. When first shown a book that costs £5 they throw up their hands in horror, and that is the sign of the sure collector, they are trying to avert their eyes from temptation.

No matter how many thousands a bookfair spends on advertising it is only ever advertising a single venue. By just being there a bookshop is only advertising itself.

The hordes of bookfairies buying from hordes of bookfairies at hordes of bookfairs may look as if they are at the head of secondhand bookdealing, but they are like the head on a glass of beer. It is the first part you notice and it draws comment, but essentially it is just froth. Without the liquidity underneath it could not exist. That is what sustains it. It is possible to make the glass consist of nothing but froth, but who wants to drink that?

The bookshops can fight back by declining to stock the frothy books that bookfairies go in for. They should put more books outside the shop at even lower prices if only for the joy of seeing a bookfairy throw up his hands in horror at the sight of a book for ten pence. There is no money to be made from the books that are outside - and in some ways it deters customers from buying more expensive books which they are now unable to carry, but the seed thus planted stands more chance of flourishing than that which has never been planted at all.

The bookfairies do nothing to encourage new customers, they live off the ones that have already been created, what the bookshops should do is try to encourage customer loyalty by being friendlier and more open. The books themselves are almost irrelevant. It is not the job of a secondhand bookdealer to tell the customers what he should collect, it is his job to find the books that the customers want to buy. This is a concept totally beyond the bookfairies, because their heads have become clouded by imbibing nothing but froth.

At the risk of furthering my reputation as a Reactionary Fascist I hope that no cure is found, that they continue to swirl round in a cess pit of their own making, and that they die in agony. I don't doubt there will always be a few who will continue regardless, for me they will be like the drunks in the street, a deterrant to drink.

Lest the picture, I am attempting to draw should appear too gloomy, I would like to say that I find secondhand book dealing interesting, sustaining, exciting, but above all fun. This is why I am so keen for the secondhand book trade to thrive. Never again, do I wish to return to work. It is a time I remember with loathing. It was tedious, draining, pathetic, but above all unremunerative. In all the years of book dealing, I have never had a time as bad as when I worked, it was the worst fortnight of my life.

* * * * * * * * * * * * * * * * * * * *

HOW TO USE THIS GUIDE

This guide, like its compiler is split. The first section is geographical and works on the assumption that the user is going to visit all the secondhand bookshops in Britain. It begins in London and follows the tube and rail lines round the capital in a clockwise direction. It then continues with the rest of England starting at Newcastle and follows the rail lines in a clockwise direction round the country. It finishes with Wales, Northern Ireland and Scotland. Neither I, nor the Irish Government count Eire as being part of Britain.

The second part is alphabetical by town. It works on the assumption that the reader is a sensible person who neither wishes to visit all the shops nor read the compilers inane remarks.

Specialist shops and non-book bookshops are listed in the town section. .

The subject index refers both to those shops in the main sequence and to those in the town index.

WHAT IS AND WHAT IS NOT A SECONDHAND BOOKSHOP

The question, what is and what is not a secondhand bookshop, is almost as difficult to answer as what is and what is not a secondhand book. I define a book as anything that appears in the British Library Catalogue. The British Library takes about 10,000 words to define what a book is. Even then, it omits a lot of things that appear in secondhand bookshops.

The most important part of a bookshop, is that it should be open. I do not accept that places that open less than three days a week are bookshops. At three days, I am prepared to give it the benefit of the doubt, if it is good, but I maintain that there is little point in having a shop if you are not going to open it at least four days a week. To open a shop, less than four days a week is to stack the odds against the collector or dealer who have to make a special journey, just to visit the shop. In most cases, it is just not worth it. A place that opens less than four days is a hobby or a warehouse, it is not a bookshop.

When I use the term new bookshop, I am referring to those shops which primarily sell new books, but also have a small stock of secondhand books. I am not referring to newly opened secondhand bookshops.

I do not consider it necessary that a shop should be on a High Street, nor do I consider it necessary that it should be on ground level, but I do not accept country houses as being bookshops. Even if the book part is seperate, it is not possible to go into them without drawing attention, and then having to justify yourself.

In the case of those places which are solely secondhand bookshops, there is no minimum size requirement, but in the case of those places which sell new or remaindered books the criterion is, is it worthwhile? This is when things start becoming problematical.

Shops that sell trashy paperbacks, otherwise known as pulp literature, are included, if they are close to serious bookshops. Comic shops are excluded on the grounds that most comics are in fact, periodicals. It is also a feature of these shops that they mainly sell posters and tee-shirts. Market stalls are included where they are close to significant bookshops. In brief, therefore, anywhere I say is a secondhand bookshop IS a secondhand bookshop. Anywhere I say is not a secondhand bookshop is NOT a secondhand bookshop. Some people may have other opinions, but with that spirit of tolerance for which I am renowned I always say that the man who thinks there is two sides to every opinion is the man who is in the wrong.

The name of the bookshop is as it appears on the fascia, no account is taken of the denizens of those shops which are convalescent homes for book fairies. Those shops without names or simply called bookshop, have been given a name by me, hopefully an appropriate one. The best possible name for a secondhand bookshop is the name of the place where it is. By taking the name of the place, you will remind people of your presence everytime that place is mentioned. It also makes it easier for people to find your bookshop. Giving the bookshop the name of the people who run it is a dreadful mistake. It is true that you cannot take the name with you when you move, if you call it by the place name, but I am only taking into consideration the method of improving the accessibility of the shop, and if the bookshop is successful, you will not have to move. The more easily recognisable the name, the more likely it is that customers are going to come to you.

I have excluded the phone numbers from this main section, which is meant for people who genuinely travel round bookshops or wish to read interesting things about them. In my experience phoning a bookshop is a hopeless task, whatever British Telecom may claim on the contrary. Firstly, you will have difficulty finding a phone when you are on the road. Secondly, asking a bookshop when it is open or whether it has a particular book or not is like asking a poker player what hand he has. Most bookshops will do everything to get you into their bookshops, when they want you, but the crucial point is that it is not possible to browse down the end of a phone. I am attempting to encourage people to go to bookshops, not discourage them - although several people seem to doubt this.

The address of the shop is not always clear, especially in the High Streets of towns, this is one of the reasons it is often better to look for the fascia or a sign. Quite why shops, and not just bookshops think you will not need to know the number is hard to imagine.

The name of the town is more problematical than you might at first believe. Most people accept Richmond as being a part of London, but it is in fact a seperate town in Surrey. The Hayes Bookshop is in Ickenham, which is in Middlesex according to the Post Office, but Middlesex as a place does not exist on any map. The Hare and Hounds Pub Bookshop is in a place called Waytown. There are no other houses of any kind in Waytown. Marston Green is in the West Midlands, but you would be unlikely to go there unless you were going to Birmingham, which is where I include it.

THE OPENING HOURS OF SECONDHAND BOOKSHOPS

I try hard to get the hours of secondhand bookshops right, but the reason I make mistakes is that I have no confidence in the hours as they are told to me or as they are displayed in the window. Unless you are a single minded fanatic such as me there is little point in knowing the actual hours, what you need to know are the days.

If a secondhand bookshop says it will open at 9 a.m., then usually it will open at 9.30 a.m. If you are standing outside at 9 a.m. you are likely to get some very strange looks from the owner when he does deign to turn up. The majority of shops now open at 10, officially, but all that has happened is that they now arrive at 10.15.

The shops that open at 9 tend to close at 5, officially, in reality they attempt to get rid of any customer at 4.45. There is a growing trend for shops to open later in the morning, that is at 11.00, but there has not been a growing trend for them to close later in the evening.

The question I would like to ask is, apart from the maniacs such as myself, stood there with stop watches, who do these shops expect to have as customers?

The number of adults who are free between the hours of 9 and 5 must surely be fairly limited, and of those that are free, how many have the money to spend their time in such places as secondhand bookshops. Even in these days of high unemployment, the number of people who are working is 33 million, as most of them are working during the day, they have little chance of going into bookshops? Who do the bookshops want as their customers? Indeed, do they want customers at all?

The old style bookshop, the one before the advent of television, used to rely on knowledgable collectors, people who had some grounding in the subject they collected. People who had some understanding of the history of English literature and European culture, but there are no such people any more. They also relied on what was known as the carriage trade, who did not so much buy books, as buy decorations for their homes, but most of these people are long dead and their offspring now try to emulate what they fondly believe is working class culture.

People such as these have ceased to exist. The major customers for bookshops fall into three groups. The passers by and those who live locally; the collectors and the dealers.

The passers by are often indifferent to which book they buy, they are simply looking for something to read, for them it is more important that a shop should have variety, turnover and a pleasant atmosphere. Thus, to fail whilst running shops in the Charing Cross Road where there are more passers by than anywhere else in Britain is nigh impossible, but it has been done. These same passers by are put off by the unwelcoming shops of Cecil Court, which they already consider to be in the hinterland. To open a shop where the local population is less than can support a bookshop is total madness. To not open that shop at convenient times is incurable lunacy. It is noticeable that they do the greatest proportion of their trade at lunchtime.

READERS, COLLECTORS, DEALERS

The description of the stock is on average. Any shop can have a good book once, the crucial question is what does it have consistently. I do not accept reserve stocks which are not on show as being part of the stock. Only those books which can be easily seen are included.

It is a sign of ignorance of most British book dealers that they are unable to tell the three different types of customers, Readers; Collectors and Dealers. If a bookshop owner takes more than two fifths of a second to tell to which group a particular customer belongs, he is in the wrong business. And most British book dealers are in the wrong business.

READERS: As readers are usually extremely nervous about going into a bookshop - when they do summon up the courage to buy a book they spend a lot of time outside looking in the window. This is why shops should put their cheapest books in the window. Better still, they should put cheap books outside to show how cheap a bookshop can be. Most ordinary people have no comprehension of how the price of a secondhand book is arrived at and they assume that anything which is old is going to be expensive. Readers always turn the handle of the door with extreme trepidation, this is how the dealer can tell them. Unfortunately, most dealers are far too dim to comprehend this. They only ever see the people who make it into the shop and not the vast majority who don't. Readers are usually lost in bookshops and it is indeed sensible to ask them if you can help them, but not in such a way that it intimidates them. Readers often display signs of confusion and say such things as "Is this a library?" or "I could spend hours in a bookshop." (the only thing they do spend); Or "Is this a bookshop?"

I was in a bookshop talking to three other dealers when a very attractive young lady came in and asked this very question. One of the other dealers said "No, this is a male brothel!" She looked at the thousands of secondhand books, then looked carefully at us and said "It is not for me then."

COLLECTORS: Collectors try to enter a secondhand bookshop looking confident in an attempt to obscure their trepidation. They try to look as if they know where everything will be to mask their confusion. They look at all the books and try to work out where to start. To ask them what they are looking for is to increase their nervousness. Collectors often have a far greater knowledge of books in their subject than a dealer ever can. They are interested in one subject, dealers are interested in them all. When collectors look at books they lean forward, when dealers look at books they lean back. Collectors do take out books which at first would not appear to be in their subject, thus some Crowley collectors ask for books on mountaineering, because Crowley was a mountaineer. Some collectors are extremely nervous of saying what subject they are interested in, because they fear it will put up the price. Unless they ask there is no point in saying anything to a collector, that way their confidence will increase and they will come in again.

DEALERS: It should take a bookshop owner the same length of time to spot a real dealer as it does for the dealer to get through the door, one fifth of a second. It is the determination with which dealers come through the door that marks them out. Those who go in for fancy cards and long conversations before starting on the books are frauds. In the second fifth of a second, a real dealer has already read the bookshop. They have scanned the shelves looking for the sections that are likely to interest them. They move round the shop in a methodical fashion leaning back to take in as much information as possible. They only take uncommon books that they have not seen before from the shelves. If they do take a common book it is to try and work out what the price scale is. To a dealer the most important part of a book is the one part an author has no connection with, the price.

THE SUMMER SICKNESS

Several shops all over the country have been affected by what I call the Summer sickness. Instead of having genuine secondhand books they have taken to selling what are euphemistially known as publishers returns. One would have more faith in the truth of this statement if it were not for the fact that many of the books have not even been offically published. What is in fact happening is that major publishers are already breaking the Net Book Agreement by the simple device of turning a blind eye.

Publishers genuinely sell off books which have been returned by new bookshops and which tend to be slightly damaged. What happens with the Summer sickness is that many books are going out of the back door and are being sold to the secondhand shops as being slightly soiled. When I publicly complained about this, the publishers began marking the books on the fore-edge with a line, so that they were indeed damaged.

This whole operation is controlled by one man, which either says much for his industry or a lot about the lethargy of the publishers. My objection to this is that these books swamp out the genuine secondhand books. It is a booksellers job to sell varied secondhand books, not hundreds of copies of the same one. I strongly object to traipsing all the way to North Wales in search of a newly opened "secondhand bookshop" to discover that is in fact a remainder shop. These books encourage apathy on the part of the book dealers. It is a secondhand book dealers job to show taste and discrimination, not to stock publishers rejects. It is possible to do this with books that cost £1.00 as it is possible with books that cost £100.00. At least fifty thousand titles a year are published in Britain. This means that there are at least fifty thousand books to choose from. Just because the publishers are a bunch of wallies, it does not mean that secondhand book dealers have to be.

RC writes:
Bloody hell, you notice the swine does not have the courage to name the perpetrator, this is because the last time he did so, the bloke rang up and the prop was having to duck every time he spoke.

PRICING

The opinion as to the prices is on average. The most expensive shop can have books which are cheap and the cheapest shop can have books which are over-priced. The mystery of pricing is something that confuses readers and collectors. The price of a book is an opinion. There is no such thing as the right price. This is the main thing that makes going round secondhand bookshops worthwhile. It is to be expected that specialist shops will charge more for rare books, but it should be remembered that specialist shops often charge a lot less for common books.

DISCOUNTS AND DISCUSSIONS

Most secondhand bookshops give 10% discounts to book dealers. Some bookshops prefer dealers to announce themselves before they start looking at the books. Some like to see a card when the books are being paid for. This is why several collectors/dealers have such cards. There is no central authority that issues these cards; it is simply a question of having them printed.

If you ever see a collection of these cards what strikes you is how unattractive they are. It is strange that people who are dealing in printed matter all the time cannot produce something more collectable themselves, but then these cards are largely useless and a waste of money.

If a bookshop owner cannot tell the difference between a collector and a dealer he should not be in the business. As most books are priced at less than £5 making 50p the difference between buying the book or not is equally pathetic.

Most dealers simply build the discount into the price (this is why you often see books priced at £5.50 or £11). A far more useful piece of information to know is whether the bookshop owner will negotiate or not. It is supposed to be that everything is negotiable, but whoever said that had never met book dealers. Some take massive and seemingly genuine offence that you should question their opinion as to how much the book is worth. Others regard the price as simply a starting figure. The rule tends to be that the more expensive a book the more it is open to negotiation. This is why the people who fight for discounts on 50p books are so irritating, they are training the dealer in how to resist blandishments from those people such as me who seriously want a book which is priced at £100, but for which they are only prepared to give £5.

DIRECTIONS

The main purpose of the directions is to help me. I am always getting lost, even when I have been to a bookshop several times, I often cannot find it again. This is partially due to the fact that the high streets of Britain are now all identical, but it is mainly due to the fact that I am so dim. This is why I believe I am the ideal person to write this guide, there is nobody who needs more instruction than me.

Most towns in Britain have railway stations and these are usually signposted for the benefit of motorists. Stations also tend to be in the poorer parts of town, which is often where the bookshops are.

When it says OOS (Out of Station) turn right it means if you are standing at the station door, not at the bottom of the driveway. These directions only apply if you are walking. It is not possible to help motorists, one way streets change more often than bookshops.

If lost, the thing to remember is that bookshops tend to be in secondary streets and are often close to Health Food shops. It is invariably a mistake to ask people the way, especially in London. Where most people know the way to work, the way to the West End and the way home after that, they tend to think of everywhere else as being where unfortunates live.

In London it is vital that you should have a map. It is irritating and impertinant to expect everybody else to provide you with directions.

Other than in London the nearest shop is given in a clockwise direction as near as possible to the quarter hours of the clock. Only general shops are so listed, and only sensible ones that is those that are open more than three days a week.

LONDON TOWN INDEX

KEY TO THE TOWNS IN MAIN SEQUENCE

I am sorry this is in the wrong place, but I had to ditch the alphabetical index and all the maps.

RC writes
It never occurred to him to ditch the text.

ABBREVIATIONS AND TERMINOLOGY

A brief explanation of the abbreviations and terminology used in this book is given below. A fuller explanation is given when they are first used in the text. This is why the main section should be read as a work of fiction, as many people claim it is.

ABBREVIATIONS

AB above

ACAD academic/student/scholarly

ANTQRN antiquarian
(it depends on the book, modern first dealers mean before 1500)

ARS arts related subjects

ASTRL astrology
(the belief that the stars control our lives, its always nice to blame somebody else.

AV average

AWYW asks what you want.
(essentially what I am looking for in bookshops is their mistakes, i.e. a book worth thousands of pounds, priced in pennies. However, it is considered undiplomatic to give this answer when asked this question by a bookshop proprietor. I also object to telling people what I am actually looking for on the grounds that I do not want them to put up the price the next time they buy it. The only answer is to lie. I usually tell people I'm looking for books to read, as most people know I'm a dealer this completely fools them)
The book I would like is one I can sell for a million pounds, falling that I would like bookdealers to stop asking me stupid questions

BGNS bargains
(bargains can be found in the most unexpected bookshops, only those that consistently have them are so listed.

BIB bibliography

BKS books

BKSP bookshop
(for the purposes of this guide a bookshop is defined as anywhere which has more second hand books than other stock, is open more than three days a week, and is somewhere where you do not have to ring a bell and give a reason for wanting to look at the books. I do make exceptions when I like the people, but this is rare.

BKRM	book room
BKST	book stall
B&MC	book & magazine collector
BL	below
BR	british rail
BSMT	basement
BSN	bibliographically sub-normal.
BTA	better than average
BTR	best to ring
BYERS	passers by/through
C(s)	collector(s)
CAL	calibre
CLSD	closed
CND	condition
D(s)	dealer(s)
DIFF	difficult (usually refers to parking)
DISC	discussions (in the same way as taking a statement is the one chance a British policeman gets to use his imagination, so writing the price is the one chance a bookdealer gets to lay down the law.)
EC	early closing
EMPHON	emphasis on (which means that they have significant numbers of books in that particular subject.)
ESPEC	especially
ETF	easy to find
ETGOW	easy to get on with (See also NETGOW and VETGOW)
FARTS	follows around recommending the stock
GOB	grand old bore
GIOPOC	gross incompetence on part of compiler
HSF	hunting, shooting and fishing

ILL	illustrated
IMPOSS	impossible
INT	interesting
KUTI	keeping up the image (I.e. looks erudite and is kind to customers)
L	lunch
LG	large
LIT	literature
LT	London Transport
LTHRWR	leather ware
MED	medium (the size of a stock applies only to those books you can see)
MOD 1STS	modern first editions
NAST	not a short trek (i.e. it takes at least twenty minutes to walk it.)
NAT HIS	natural history
NETGOW	not easy to get on with
NFDA	no further details available
NIMS	not in main sequence
NO NO.	no number
NPIOTCI	not previously included owing to compiler's incompetence
NRLY	nearly
NSOC	not strong on condition
NV	not visited (Unless otherwise stated all the secondhand bookshops listed in the main geographical sequence have been visited by me in 1991. It is one of my more confirmed prejudices that you can only learn about secondhand bookshops by visiting them. Those bookshops that have not been visited have been relegated to the TIN section, not necessarily through any fault of theirs, but because I had not the time to visit them, this year. I have indeed, been to many of the bookshops so dismissed, but as an

	eternal optimist, I believe that they could have changed radically since I was last there.
OPP	opposite
OOS	out of station
OOSH	out of shop
OOTZ	out of travel zone
OWOWS	oversupplied with one way streets (I don't know who it was that invented one way streets, but I'd like to meet him and remove one eye, one ear, one leg and one testicle. I don't think any woman could have been that stupid.
P.POSS	parking possible This does not mean that there is parking right outside the door, it means that a sensible person should be able to find a legal parking space within five minutes walk of the shop. Please see Scottish section to read why I no longer travel in motor cars.
PBKS	paperbacks
POCS	proliferation of charity shops
POSS	possible
R(s)	reader(s)
REL	reliable
RES STK	reserve stock
S/F	science fiction/fantasy
S/H	second hand
SIOL	shop is on left
SIOR	shop is on right
STN	station
STK	stock
SPEC	specialising/specialist
T	trade
TC	tank commander
TIN	town index
TOPOG	topography

TWC trade with card (some shops only give discounts if you have a card)

UNINT uninteresting

UNR unreliable

V very

VETGOW very easy to get on with

WAD worth a detour

WAP worth a pilgrimage

WEBCOC was expecting a better class of customer

WYLAH watches you like a hawk

TERMINOLOGY

ANORAKSIA NERVOSA
Named after Mr Rolph of Lowestoft, a shop where despite the warmth of his personality cold war lives on.

A SAMUEL BECKET SPECIAL
A bookshop which is often covered in dust that theatre designers would give fortunes for and which when you look at the books makes you wonder why you are here? Why are you book collecting? What is the purpose of these books? Are they genuinely for sale? Who would want to buy them? Seldom is there any conversation in these places, instead there is a stream of words that are not meant to make sense. When you do leave, it is in silence.

B&MC SPECIAL A book and magazine collector special. A bookshop where they have difficulty working out the difference between books and records.

BOOK DEALER SPECIAL
A bookshop where it is hard to decide which is more dead, the owner or the stock. Named after the weekly trade periodical, but usually called the Tombstone Gazette. The editor only notices book dealers when they are dead and most of its advertisers are cowboys.

BOOK FAIRIES People who exhibit at book fairs.

DOGS Books that nobody can get rid of.

DRIF SPECIALS A shop so low key, most dealers loathe it, but one where I am convinced there are lots of bargains to be had.

A HELEN HANFF SPECIAL

A bookshop which looks great from the outside, preferably 3,000 miles away. The owner is usually very good at talking and writing, but the books are terrible. The good news is that these shops soon go out of business. The bad news is that it does not stop people writing about them and reinforcing the Hollywood image of what book dealing is like. The unforgettable book, whose name no American can ever remember is constantly being quoted in the press as the way book dealing is. Miss Hanff is one of those people who would not go to the toilet without informing the press first. The end result is the same, a dark smear on a clean sheet.

A HOSAIN SPECIAL

A shop which claims to specialise in a particular subject, but knows nothing about that subject, whose prices display its ignorance to other specialists, and invariably is never open.

LIBRICIDE Valuing books for the number of plates that can be torn out of them. Most plate book dealers claim they do not do this themselves, that it is the people they sell them to who are responsible. This is true, the reason they do not do it is that they would have to pay VAT as print dealers, whereas book dealers do not.

THE LITERACE Sellers of flash books. They usually know quite a lot about books, but they know even more about marketing. The books they sell always look good, require little effort to be appreciated, but above all attract the attention.

NATURAL AND UNNATURAL ROUTES

Most bookshop owners are so egotistical that they think when a collector or dealer turns up at their shop, that it is the soul reason why the collector or dealer is in that area. That to get into most bookshops you have to have a computer to work out when they are officially open and the luck of the Irish to actually find them open, never occurs to them.

NEB Not enough books. This largely or smally applies to inclusion in the main sequence and occurs with specialist shops. Unless a specialist shop has enough books or enough calibre to make travelling to see it from most places in Britain, it is not included. Indeed, there are several places that claim to be specialist shops which have no books at all. These are regularly listed in the Shepperd Press directory and the Skoob directory, but when you actually turn up there are no secondhand books. One such is the Wholefood bookshop in London. There is no Wholefood bookshop at this address, what there is, is a shop selling wholefood, which has the usual dreadful new books, but no secondhand books are on display. I am not exactly certain what a bookshop is, but it is my personal opinion that if it had no secondhand books on display, then it is not a secondhand bookshop.

NON BOOKSHOPS Bookshops without books. At first this may seem a contradiction in terms but this is not a problem that seems to bother other directories. There are no other guide books. They list any shop which tells them it stocks secondhand books, without bothering to check if this is true or not. Both the current Skoob directory and the Shepperd Press directory list a place called the Wholefood bookshop in London as being a secondhand bookshop. There are no secondhand books in this shop. It primarily sells organic vegetables and has done so for the last twenty years. Similarly with J.H. Allen in London which is supposed to specialise in horse books. There are no secondhand, or antiquarian books in this shop. My ire is aroused, not only by the fact that I have to go and look at these places and many more, but also by the fact, that if I do not mention them, people assume that I do not know about them. I realise it may be considered naive on my part, but I consider that to be called a secondhand bookshop, you must have secondhand books on the premises and to further assuage my anger, I consider that they must be visible.

I have often thought of setting up entirely imaginary bookshops, but as both Skoob and Shepperds are already filled with imaginary book dealers, there would be little point.

RC this gentleman claims to be my biographer and chauffeur.

MR SALTEENA SPECIAL

A shop where the owner is partial to young ladies. I have no doubt there are shops which are partial to young men, indeed, it is one of my ambitions to write an essay entitled, Homosexuality and Modern First Editions, but I have never found a book dealer who was at any time partial to me. Therefore, I am unable to include shops which are partial to young men.

THE STURMINSTER NEWTON EXCLUSE

No shop that closes on a Tuesday or a Saturday will be allowed in the main sequence. Tuesday is almost the one day that dealers can guarantee to get into the most number of shops, without having to use a computer. To close on a Saturday, is to show such utter contempt for people who work, that I am almost keen on it, but it does make life bloody annoying. The shop in Sturminster Newton does both.

SUMMER SICKNESS

A secondhand shop which has new books masquerading as secondhand.

l o n d o n

t h e   l i t   c i t

THE LIT CIT CAP IT ALL OF THE A TO Z

A light hear for the tour divorce, and

B prepared for a small ear quake, come and

C how it should be dunces

D light in the heavy league heavy in the light d.

E gregeious to eroic ephemeral to ever last ting

F oughtlessly from our nose grove to the 7 pillars of Willesden.

G o logical Jeeves to the 'T'ravels for the Thai.

H bombed in Achne,

I see all for the mee generation, but don't forget the groan ups.

K tass trophies avoided by the following party lines.

L evated we are not, this is the city of the under ground.

M barrassed with riches, bitches and pitches.

N trancing always: no more scum days: no more blank holidays.

O ver the top and un der the skin

P brained bookdealers are podded.

Q's avoided, give us credit. We stand a loan.

R philosophy is Cap it all pun ishment for e

S O'teric and his fiend O'cult. but

T is never censored, weave eves without leaves.

U V W ? sheep car cases remain out of the M25 ring but

Y'Z to avoid the dogs outside for there is nothing like our men.

LONDON TRANSPORT REGRETS

London Transport's greatest regret is the passengers; they will keep trying to use the system. They try to get to work, they try to get home and they try to go out in the evening. Why ever cannot they emulate the management of London Transport and do absolutely nothing. If only the passengers would stay away London Transport could spend all its subsidy on designing bright new buses which look wonderful at Press Functions. It could install yet more gates and turnstiles everywhere. It could install piped music in all its stations and it could keep the trains lovely and clean. It would not have to think about cooperating with British Rail but best of all there would be no complaints.

That is the real trouble with the public they will keep complaining. They expect such outrageous things such as being able to get to work on time! And being able to get home in the evening! This is the thin end of the wedge, if you give into that sort of nonsense they will start wanting transport at all hours of night and day.

London Transport! The very name is a lie. It should be called London Stationary. Its greatest asset is the patience of its potential passengers. You will spend more time waiting for its services than you will using them. The greatest difficulty you will face with the London Bookshops is getting to them. Motorists cannot find anywhere to park. Buses never arrive. The Underground is crowded and smelly and cyclists do not survive.

For the purposes of this guide London is defined as anywhere within the M25 motorway. This mote, this ring of death, this ultimate clanger is even now being redesigned. There are suggestions for narrowing the lanes and getting more traffic in. There are suggestions for widening the lanes and getting more traffic out. There is a suggestion that another motorway should be built on top so that the lower deck would be for clockwise traffic and the upper for anti-clockwise. This is clearly not going far enough. What should be done is to build a spiral motorway starting at Piccadilly Circus and going up and up and up round and round and round on and on like the topless tower of Illium. The motorists would love it. They would queue up. We could charge them fortunes just to get on to it. The more they paid the further it could go. Only a lunatic would drive in London and only lunatics do.

The main deterrant to cycling in London is not the potholes but the other cyclists and motor cycle messengers. The cycopaths who believe in death before braking, who think that traffic lights are for decoration and that Zebra Crossings are to match their apparel, and that one way streets are solely for their benefit. These morons who are so brainless that they have not heard that trousers with flies have been invented, have made life so impossible for all other cyclists that sensible cyclists use the potholes as bunkers to get away from them. They are the messengers of death.

LONDON BUSES

Follow the example of the management of London Transport and avoid the buses. The reason you see so many young and elderly people waiting for buses is that in a war there can only be two sides. The middle aged have all surrendered. Unless you start young you have no hope of getting a bus. By the time the bus arrives you will look old. The idea of queueing has been lost. There is now one long straggle for about fifty yards around the bus stop. This is because the would be passengers know that if the buses do come they will be in groups of at least three. What London Transport should do is have one long chain of buses and make doors in the front and back and the passengers could walk to their destination.

The one man buses are aptly named, they exist almost solely for the benefit of the driver. He is enabled to spend time chatting up any pretty girl who comes along, give histories of London to American tourists and complain about having to give change for the fares. The buses themselves were designed by someone who had a special admiration for the sixties. He was especially keen on a dance called The Shake and has incorporated this feature in the buses. This is also one of the reasons the drivers never smile; they have to maintain the centre of gravity.

The upper deck of a London bus is the only known place where the underclass comes out on top. They come prepared with all the smells of the slaughterhouse. They insulate themselves with personal stereos. Should you inform them that their stereo is not working properly, i.e. you can hear it, you will be informed (if you are male) that you are of the opposite sex (and if you are female) that you should indulge in sexual intercourse. However it will not be put quite like this.

London Transport does recommend you get a bus pass. This statement should be taken literally. It is however the most sensible thing to do on the Underground which is the least awful alternative. An All Zone Travel Card is valid for almost all the London bookshops listed, and where it is not, most of the stations are unmanned.

On the Underground you will have a splendid opportunity to meet the Londoner in his natural habitat. They are easy to spot - they are the ones who try to walk straight through you when you try to get off the train. A Londoner is unaware that there are any other people in the world.

On the platform you will be able to see Britain's most successful export; the Great British yobbo. To help train these London Transport has installed several machines which claim to sell chocolate. They may have done so at one time but now their purpose is to train GBY in the art of kicking the life out of anything he sees. It was very sensible of London Transport not to waste money changing the lettering as most GBY's cannot read.

To make life more fun, London Transport has installed information machines which can only tell lies. When the "Matrix Dot Indicators" say a train will arrive in two minutes, it means 90 seconds on the Piccadilly Line and four minutes on the Northern. On the Circle line if a train is more than seven London Transport minutes away the machine does not work.

London Transport claims that it has too many passengers on the Underground. What it certainly does have is too many passengers who do not bathe. What it should do is install showers at the entrance to the tube stations in the same way as is done in swimming pools.

At the exit you will see blackboards with notices saying what it is London Transport Regrets today. One way of doubling productivity would be to have the blackboards already printed with these words rather than having to write them afresh every time.

London starts with the best shop and continues down the book - collectors line, the Northern which goes through Charing Cross Road and continues on to Wimbledon. The rest of London is then done by starting at each tube in a clockwise direction.

EDGWARE via CHARING CROSS to WIMBLEDON

T H E   N O R T H E R N   L I N E

THE TWO JAYS Edgware
14 Whitchurch Lane, Edgware, Middlesex
Tue, Wed, Fri, Sat 10-5.30. V.Rel.
Med Lg R/C stk ab av cal. Av cnd, bl av prices. This is by far the best general bksp in Britain. It is open sensible hours and is reliable about those times. The stk is varied and int and turns over fast. The prices are on average cheap and several bgns are known. And they are etgow. It does nothing to diminish their achievement to say that these things should be fairly obvious but it is surprising how rarely they are done. Other dealers complain because I rate this shop so highly. This is because they are lazy buggers. Most dealers are looking for a bksp that has Audobon's Birds of America, in first edition priced at £50.00 and preferably close to the West End. Anybody considering opening a s/h bksp should be made to study this place in detail and I am glad to see that the owners have gone into consultancy on the next listed shop. Tube Edgware. OOS turn left and cross main Edgware Road into Whitchurch Lane and shop is on right.

BOOKMARK Edgware
67 High Stret, Edgware, Middlesex
Tue, Thur, Fri, Sat 10-5.30 Rel.
Newly opened R/C stk, av cal, cnd & prices. Emphon S/F and Football. T. OOS turn left and left at Edgware Road which is the High Street and not the one by the station. If you continue down for another 200 yards there is London's second best grease cafe, the best is in lovely lovely Leyton. In Colindale there is a pbk shop which is not much good but does have the wonderful name: BUY A BOOK AND BANISH BOREDOM.

KEITH FAWKES Hampstead
1-3 Flask Walk, Haverstock Hill, London NW3
Mon-Sat, 10-5 Rel.
Med size R/C stk of far from singular boringness. If this bksp is a reflection of the customers then it has deterred me in my ambition to become an intellectual when I grow up. This type of shop damages what few brain cells I have left. TWC. Tube Hampstead. OOS turn left down Hill and first left.

VILLAGE BOOKSHOP Belsize Village
41 Belsize Lane, London NW3
Mon-Sat, 11-5 Unr.
This is the bksp as victim of Arterial Schlerosis. The stk has now expanded so much that it is impossible to get into this shop, not that you would want to. The piles of books are as unstable as the owner. A Helen Hanff Special. Tube Belsize Park. OOS turn right and left at Ornan Road (more appropriate known as Onan Road) which becomes Belsize Lane.

PRIMROSE HILL BOOKS **Chalk Farm**
154 Regents Park Road, London NW1
Mon-Sat, 10-6, Sun 12-6.
New bksp with bsmt stk of R books, Acad orientated. Some C books upstairs. Av cnd, cal and prices. TWC but worth going to for the cafe next door, there is also an antique shop with books towards the station on opp side, see TIN.

WALDEN BOOKS **Camden**
38 Harmood Street, London NW1
Thur, Sun 10.30-6.30 Rel.
Med size R/C stk, av cal, cnd and prices. This is the bksp as messianic cause. I went in here one Sunday morning and the place seemed much neater and tidier than usual. I asked the lady behind the counter if it had perhaps changed hands. "What do you mean changed hands?" "I just wondered if there was a new owner?" I said. "What's wrong with the current owner?" I said nothing but what is wrong with the owner is that he claims to represent the ideas of Thoreau. I remember reading that book and this shop is nothing like it. Why is it that bksps that espouse causes are always so gloomy? Tube Chalk Farm. OOS south towards Camden Town and left. There are also some stalls in Camden Lock market on Sundays but they are not very good.

CAMDEN TOWN

Nobody sane has ever made it out of Camden Town tube station. All those demented people you see standing around outside are the ones who tried to follow London Transport's directions. Those who think they have survived have taken to wearing mourning in memory of lost friends. That is why they sell nothing but black clothing in Camden Lock market.

Trains leave Camden Town's Northern line in four directions. To board the train you want it is imperative that you reach the right platform. To help you London Transport has installed an Indicator Board at the bottom of the escalator. It will tell you the four destinations to which Northern line trains go. It will also tell you how many minutes you will have to wait for each train. It will NOT tell you which platform the train will be on. The reason that this particular piece of information is omitted is that the platform is always changing. The only way to find the platform is by trial and error.

One day I was in Camden Town tube and the Indicator Board said that all the southbound trains were going to Charing Cross, my destination. After I had tried the other three, I found the right platform. The Indicator Board there said that the Charing Cross train would be along in four minutes. I settled down to read the last 200 pages of Anna Karenina. (London Transport has publicly admitted that a minute on the Northern Line is at least 90 seconds.) An announcement came over the tannoy saying that all Bank line trains would leave from platform four. I checked to ensure that I was not on platform four. By the time the train came in I had got to the best bit of the book where the heroine is contemplating suicide. I got on the train and sat rivetted until we got to Kings Cross when I realised that I was on the wrong train. I got off and went in search of the supervisor. I told him the train indicator said Charing Cross, the platform indicator said Charing Cross and the tannoy left me with the impression that the train would go to Charing Cross, but the train went to the Bank. He looked at me and put on his voice that he used for talking to five year olds and said "But did you look at the front of the train?" There, he had me, what a fool I had been to assume that if three indicators said the train would go to Charing Cross, that I did not have to check the fourth. If Anna Kerenina had tried to commit suicide at Camden Town she would never have made it past the mourning wear.

To ensure that you continue on the Charing Cross Branch, board the train at Chalk Farm even though Camden Town is closer.

THE MARCHMONT BOOKSHOP Bloomsbury
39 Burton Street, London WC1
Mon-Fri, 11-6.30 Rel.
Med size C/D stk, emphon ARS. T. Tube Euston. OOS cross main road to left of church and right.

COLLINGE AND CLARKE Bloomsbury
13 Leigh Street, London WC1
Mon-Fri, 11-6.30, Sat 3.30.
Med size C/D stk, specialist in Private Press, Printing and Art History. Ab av cal, cnd and prices. It is one of those shops where you walk in and feel that you are not quite the sort of customer they are looking for. TWC. From Marchmont Bksp continue south, turn left, turn right at curved street (in English Crescent) and continue.

WORLD OF BOOKS Bloomsbury
39 Bloomsbury Way, London WC2.
7 days a week 11-7 summer, -6 winter. Rel.
Med/lg R/C stk av cal, cnd and prices. TWC. As the sign over the door proudly proclaims "formerly of Sackville Street" - which closed about five years ago but the books are identical, they just look as if they have been hibernating. The shop is redolent of school dinners, what is served up is sustaining but in your stomach you know there must be better than this. There are the occasional visits from the headmaster who declares the odd chip to be haute cuisine, and that he has never tasted better, which is possibly true and that is what makes it so awful. He then departs for the more important business of writing a panegyric in the Antiquarian Book Monthly Review. I suppose it is churlish to complain that the torture does not go on for long enough but why does a bksp in central London have to open so late in the morning. When you officially open at 11 nobody is going to believe that you will actually be ready before half past. Most of the shops in central London do their business in the lunch hour but the idea of a shop is to extend the number of customers by encouraging them to visit at other times. The one good point is that it is open on a Sunday which means that you do not have to use up the time that could be spent in more interesting shops. Tube Euston. OOS turn right into Eversholt St. and cross Euston Road and continue. Nearest tube Russell Square OOS turn left and right at main junction (none of the streets round here have any names).

DILLONS Bloomsbury
82 Gower Street, London WC2
Mon,Wed,Fri 9-7, Tue 9.30-7, Thur 9-7.30, Sat 9-6. V. Rel.
New bksp with lg C/D stk very acad. Ab av cal, cnd and prices. This shop nails the lie that chains of s/h bksps do not work. All it takes is proper management. TWC. Tube Goodge St. OOS turn left into Tottenham Court Rd and right into Torrington Place, and ahead.

L O N D O N

SEE BLOOMSBURY ON THE CENTRAL LINE

C H A R I N G C R O S S

As you emerge lava like from the dormant Vesuvius that is Tottenham Court Road tube station and attempt to fissure your way through the ticket machines, an acrid smell will permeate your nostrils, keep sniffing, this is the direction you will have to take and it is a harbinger of things to come...

In this tunnel beneath the icon to self aggrandisement and conspicuous consumption lie the victims of the consumer society. This is where the Heritage Industry meets begging. It is a scene from Dore's London or the nineteenth century picture of miners tunnelling beneath the homes of the rich.

These maladrous minors know how to dig money out of pockets, their entire lives have been spent learning the wiles of the advertising industry. They have placards declaring they are homeless. They have brightly coloured blankets the better to draw your attention (and to hide their expensive trainers). They have mattresses, should you imagine that they are just sitting there by choice.

You may avert your eyes, but nothing will rid you of the smell, mainly of guilt. For who among those emerging from Tottenham Court Road is rich enough to give to all these beggars. For them, like the advertisers whose techniques they have so assiduously studied, we are all customers. No notice is taken of the fact that most of the passers-by are struggling to work and in many cases have less money than the beggars. It is noticeable that this tunnel is now used almost solely by tourists. Habituees would rather risk life and limb than face the carrion.

Having shrugged off this web of deceipt and begun to walk down the Charing Cross Road you will be importuned by another group who will ask you if you are against or for Peace in The Middle East. It is not until you have signed up that they will ask for a donation. It is hard to decide which is more repugnant, those who have no money and ask for it or those who already have money and ask for more.

The other side of the road now seéms suddenly more attractive but only if, like most people you have learned not to look. For here you will see the real failures of our society; the people being cared for in the community. Westminster Council has provided dustbins to help with their nourishment. The restaurants that advertise on these bins are beyond the dreams of the users, but are frequented by the blanketted ones who hold demonstrations should the management dare to refuse them entry.

By the time you reach Cambridge Circus the ticket touts outside the theatre will seem like the last living exponents of capitalism. The last descendants of Samuel Smiles as eagle eyed for profit as for the police. Why they, and not the beggars, should be harrassed is hard to understand until you realise that the beggars - some of them - have the media on their side whereas ticket touts are the bogeymen of the entertainment industry.

What exactly is the difference between buying books at £5 and selling them for five times that amount. If the management of the theatres are unable to work out a sensible pricing system, why do they get upset at the people who can?

It is the self proclaimed guardians of the entertainment business who have brought about this state of affairs. When you go in the bookshops of the Charing Cross Road you will notice a curious feature. All previous price labels of books have been snipped off or obliterated. This has been done by the dealers who rate a book without a price tag as being damaged. The reason for this is that the dealers are fed up with people coming up to the counter and asking "How come this book is now £5 when it was only £1 when it was produced." Some dealers lose their temper when asked this question but the sensible thing to say is: "I will sell you that book at the price it was when it was produced if you will sell me your house at the price it was when that book was produced."

Close to the till of capitalism you will always find the religious fingers. On the corner of Lichfield Street charming exotic young ladies offer a service you do not expect. They are allegedly holding a survey. They do not come up to everyone but only those to whom they are directed by a supervisor who stands across the other side of the road. I am so unattractive that it took me several attempts before I got one of these young ladies to ask me the questions. The first question is: "What is the cause of all the world's problems?" I knew the answer to that one straight away. "It is other people!" I said. The young lady claimed that it was not the right answer and that I had got it very wrong and she refused to ask me any further questions. If this was a genuine survey there surely must be alternative answers to these questions but the truth is it is not genuine - for these young ladies are in fact Moonies, whose branch office is in Lichfield Street. It is hard to decide who is more lost, the pathetics they stop or these young ladies on their fortnightly holidays in Europe.

As you approach Leicester Square tube station you will see them. They start as inarticulate students using body language to communicate their message. Later they become braver and more brazen. Some lose all inhibition and begin shouting words they would not normally mutter. They bang their own drum enthusiastically and try to embarrass those not of a like mind. Further along they become despondent. They become sullen and begin to grunt, desperate now for any punter they behave unexpectedly. Soon they are holding perfectly logical conversations with themselves. They should not be confused with the more acceptable denizens of the Charing Cross Road: the students trying to get you to attend a language school; the drunks trying to browbeat you into giving them enough money for a can of special brew; the drug pushers indifferent to their own safety; the shizophrenics being cared for in the community. The people I am talking about are a far more obnoxious band. They believe they speak on everybody else's behalf. They are the official charity collectors.

The difference between the smug official collectors and the other importuners is that they gulp in one day what it takes the less sleek months to acquire, savour and experience.

They also have official sanction which grants them immunity from persecution by the police.

What the beggars of the Charing Cross Road should do is come up with their own flag preferably one that looked like everybody else's. People would give them money for this flag in the hope that it would grant them immunity from further persecution by both the officials and the unofficials. Perhaps as Charing Cross leads to Soho the picture of a bum being pinched would serve the purpose.

One day outside of Leicester Square tube I saw an 'official' beggar collecting on behalf of the 'homeless' whilst at the bottom of the steps there was a homeless person but he would have been classified as unofficial. The official homeless collector, who looked like the type of person who had two homes, was doing a lot better than the unofficial homeless person who genuinely did not look like he had a home to go to. As an ardent supporter of unofficial activities, and a well known shit stirrer, I went and told the unofficial but actually homeless beggar that if he was prepared to start a demarcation dispute with the official homeless collector I would give him, some money. The purpose of my aim was beyond the comprehension of the actually homeless person but another person whom I had not seen because he looked like he had a home, came up to the unofficially homeless one and said "See, I told you this was a good pitch so why don't you give me some money for it?" I did not know that even if you are homeless there is no immunity from persecution by other beggars.

As you approach Charing Cross Station more scientifically organised begging does indeed take place. Here the punk rockers who ensure that they cannot get a job by spending all their time in the toilets massaging their hair into place have deputized dogs and young ladies to do the begging for them.

Why I have gone on for so long about the beggars of the Charing Cross is not in order to deter you from coming but in an attempt to explain why it is that many of the habituees of this area are so aggressive. They have had to adopt this posture in order to withstand the beggars, drunks, drug addicts, shizos and maniacs who inhabit the road. If you ask the way they will think that you are asking for money, if you smile they will think that you are trying to sell them a strange substance. People who live and work in Charing Cross invariably take the long secret way round to avoid the local fauna. The beggars have used all the good will that may have existed in Charing Cross.

And this is before you have got into the shops.

FOYLES Charing Cross
119 Charing Cross Road, London WC2
Mon-Sat, 9-6, Thurs 7pm.
New bookshop with R stk at C prices. The only thing that moves slower than the books is the staff. TWC.

FOYLED AGAIN

Foyles is proof that the most important thing for a bookshop is the right position. No matter how bad you are, and you would have to be pretty bad to be worse than Foyles, if you have the right location, you can succeed. It would be hard to have a worse stock than Foyles and yet they are proud members of the Antiquarian Booksellers Association who exhibit every year at the Park Lane Hotel Fairs. They are like a great turtle (most of their better stock is hidden beneath the carapace of Beeleigh Abbey in Essex) they are not quite of this world but nor are they quite of the next. As long as the ABA is pleased to have shops of this appalling ilk in its membership it is never going to succeed in encouraging people to buy books.

JOHN RHODES Charing Cross
Earlham Street, London WC2
Mon-Fri but erratic.
The worlds only fruitarian/occult bkstl WAD just for the owner. There are also two other stalls in this street which mainly deal in magazines. Earlham Street is off Cambridge Circus.

MURDER ONE Charing Cross
71-73 Charing Cross Road, London WC2
Mon-Sat, 10-7.30.
New bksp specialising in detective fiction, with a lg section of true crime, crime fiction and Sherlock Holmes. Despite being a new bksp it seems to have more s/h detective books on display than anywhere else in Britain. WAD.

The most interesting thing about detective fiction and true crime is how many people read it, but how little attention it gets in the papers and on TV. True they do have crime sections and series but given how many titles are published and bought you would think that the subject merited more attention. Crime fiction is about the only subject I have seen that bookdealers read - but as usual not the ones who deal in it - however if you talk to lots of other bookdealers they all seem to have a favourite crime fiction author. I am not sure why this is and it certainly does not fit my theory that the reason most people buy crime fiction is that in the end the baddies always get their come uppance, whereas in real life only seven per cent of crimes are ever cleared up. The reason this shop is alone on the West side of the Charing Cross is that detective fiction is the only subject which is profitable enough to sustain the rent. Almost all the other s/h bksps are subsidised in some way and have to stay on the side where their lords and masters decree.

ANY AMOUNT OF BOOKS Charing Cross
62 Charing Cross Road, London WC2
Mon-Sun, 10.30-7.30

Med sized R/C.D. stk, av cal cnd, and prices. The sister shop of the Charing Cross Road Bksp. The main reason it is kept open is that the owner, Mr. Nigel Burwood, is terrified that any other bookdealer who might be serious competition might take it over. This is what happens when you have subsidised rents. T.

HENRY PORDES **Charing Cross**
58-60 Charing Cross Road, London WC2
Mon-Sat, 10-7 Rel.
Med/Lg R/C stk, emphon remainders, av cal, cnd and prices. The apotheosis of a sensible shop. T.

THE CHARING CROSS BOOKSHOP **Charing Cross**
56 Charing Cross Road, London WC2
Mon-Sun, 10.30-7.30.
Med/Lg R/C/D stk, av cal, cnd and prices. Bgns known. This is the best general bksp in the Charing Cross Rd, mainly because the others are all so bad. The first thing that it does better than any of the other shops is that it actively promotes books. Its window changes frequently, this encourages regulars who in turn encourage passers by. At night the population of the Charing Cross changes dramatically, and even though these nightclubbers do not buy s/h books at the moment, they will remember when their passing interest changes. A s/h bksp gets a lot of its best custom when it is clsd.

This shop is easy to go into, or rather it is not difficult, too many bksps make going through the door a trauma by rushing forward and asking what you want and then asking why you want it, as if somehow you had to justify yourself. Customers may be forced to put on a brave face once but the second time they do not go in the shop. Because bookdealers only ever see the people who do go in shops they assume that that is all the customers there are.

One factor that does encourage people to go into bksps is if they see other people already inside. An empty bksp actively discourages customers, this is why bksp owners should be grateful to deadbeats such as myself, who to the ordinary customer look like an ordinary customer. (It is true that this has disadvantages, I once cleared this shop in three seconds after a "discussion" with another dealer.

Another factor in encouraging customers is that the staff are behind bars, a position they adopt in their spare time and in their musical interests. In most s/h bksps staff are something to beat the customers with.

One major advantage this shop does have is the absence of the owner. The customers in this establishment can be seen nervously trying to work out who is in charge and being extremely relieved when they find out the answer is no one.

The bks change frequently, which encourages regulars, which encourages passers by. The owner likes to believe that it is his selection of the bks that causes this turnover, but in truth it is the other way round. He is forced, much against his will to spend money on new arrivals to keep the shelves full.

One peculiar feature of the shops of the Charing Cross is that most of the customers are from the suburbs. How I know this is that during a recent rail strike this shop was almost completely empty.

QUINTO Charing Cross
48a Charing Cross Road, London WC2
Mon-Sat, 10-9.30, Sun 12-8.
This is the Alcatraz of s/h bksps. At first it seems like a wonderful site and worthy of better things but in truth it is subject to sudden mists, deep fog, dangerous currents and freezing waters. Not one inmate has ever escaped and lived to tell the tale. The ones in the window are due for release but close inspection reveals that they have endured years of sensory deprivation. Getting in is deceptively easy, getting out is an altogether more diff proposition, especially for the inmates. The tiers and galleries are arranged so that only one convict at a time can go down them. There is a policy of no fraternization. The first thing that strikes you is how remarkably young they all look, it is the pallour which is old. Upon conversing with these outcasts it soon becomes apparent that they have experienced every deprivation known. They live, if that is the right word, sealed off from every day experience. Their unspoken fear is the governor, a presence seldom seen, but he has the power to transfer them instantly and these ghostings happen every three months or so. This is the only hope of variety otherwise they would rot in their cells. True there are visitors from outside but they can do nothing, the tariff of the inmates is far too high. The prison officers do their best but they have been rejected by every other place in this country. The only power they have is sending the inmates to the cooler in the bsmt, a fate from which no inmate has ever recovered. There is also a maximum security block next door but the only real difference is that the inmates there are serving an even higher tariff.

ANN CREED Charing Cross
22 Cecil Court, Charing Cross, London WC2
Mon-Sat, 10-7 V.Rel.
Med/lg spec shop in Art Reference, emphon 20th C design. Ab av cal, cnd and prices. Well WAD.

Well WAD is putting it mildly: It should be compulsory for anybody who claims to run a spec shop. This is the best organised spec bksp in Britain and there is some stiff competition from places like John Randall in Pimlico, Taikoo in York and John and Judith Head in Salisbury. Why this shop wins is that at the same time as being a spec shop it encourages non-specialists. From the outside it says that it does Art books. Not just the words on the fascia, but the display and the whole look of the place. It has been carefully thought out. It has been designed. It says this is art. When you go in, it is not intimidating, it encourages people by its non-aggressive layout. Therefore what this shop is doing is encouraging those people who would normally never go into a bksp - a mere 96% of the population - that bksps are interesting places.

Once inside there is none of that atmosphere that somebody is going to suddenly pounce. The books are displayed in a readily comprehensible manner, and there are lots of them. This does not mean that everything that is an art book has been piled on the shelves without thought, the books have clearly been carefully chosen. Whoever chose these books was able to read beyond the cover.

This shop, and others like it, is the reason why it is grossly unfair for other shops to claim that they specialise in a particular subject. The Charing Cross Road Bksp claims that it specialises in Art. This is a lie. It is true that they do have art books and it is true that they are more eager to buy art books than other subjects but this is because they sell. Thus they will stock any book on Michelangelo or Bauhaus Design, but there is no real expertise behind these books. It is the difference between mass catering and haute cuisine. It is the difference between a common prostitute and a lover. I don't doubt that they will claim that there is no difference, that the end product is the same, but this is because they have no taste.

The crucial element about a spec shop is that when you go in - will they know what you are talking about? Only the naive and journalists are impressed by numbers. What counts is taste. It is not possible for any shop to have all the books on a subject as vast as art, but you cannot claim to specialise in a subject unless there is more than a fifty percent possibility of having the books you claim you deal in.

It is unfair to shops such as this one that those people who know nothing of the subject which they claim to specialise should appear in the same index. In most cases of the shops that specialise in Art they have no idea of what you are talking about. I see no reason why I should promote the lies that they believe. This is why the index of this book is so short. It is not simply lethargy on my part. It is that in the case of most shops they are not worth going to. They are not worth ringing, but above all, they are not worth thinking about. They are using up the time that could be better spent in places such as this.

Another int feature of this shop (you can tell I am keen can't you?) is that it seems to attract customers I have never seen before. It is possibly true that these people have more taste than to mix with me, but I also suspect that they are attracted by the catalogue that this shop issues. Too often spec shops open and expect the customers to come rolling in, without thinking that they have to do anything else. *RC: You can tell this lady is a veggie can't you?*

REG & PHILIP REMINGTON Charing Cross
18 Cecil Court, Charing Cross Rd, London WC2
Mon-Sat, 10-5.
Med size spec in Travel & Topography, ab av cal, cnd and prices. T.

MARCHPANE Charing Cross
16 Cecil Court, Charing Cross Rd, London WC2
Tue-Sat, 11-7.
Med size spec in Childrens and illustrated. Av cal, cnd and prices. TWC

PAUL HILTON Charing Cross
14 Cecil Court, Charing Cross Rd, London WC2
Mon-Sat, 10-7.30 Rel.
Newly opened med size R/C/D stk, slightly roast beef but does look promising. Av cal, cnd and prices. TWC

JOHN ADRIAN'S BOOKSHOP Charing Cross
12 Cecil Court, Charing Cross Rd, London WC2
Mon-Sun, 8-10 Rel.
Lg R/C stk, av cal, cnd and prices. Emphon Golf, Cricket, Wodehouse, Giles. A Book & Magazine Collector Special.

In some way I feel partially responsible for the prices in this shop. One Sunday morning I was down Club Row market when a man with a barrow appeared and unveiled about 500 books. These books were a lot better than the average books you see in Club Row and within seconds a half dozen other deadbeat bookdealers appeared out of nowhere.

"Nobody is allowed to touch these books until seven o'clock", said the barrow boy. He had to repeat this a few times in more demotic English as this is the only language that bookdealers of the club ilk understand. We all stood there trying to work out which were the best books to grab when the cock crowed at seven o'clock. (This was in the days when they sold pets at Club Row). We had all got it vaguely sorted out who was entitled to what, when at seven o'clock the barrow boy suddenly announced "All these books are fifty pounds each". Even the antique dealers who carry round fifty pound notes like bags of confetti were impressed enough to come over and have a look, but nobody actually bought anything. We all stood there awaiting developments. After fifteen minutes the barrow boy announced "Right, all these books will be £25 at half past seven, and from then on they reduce by £5 each half hour. We all were desperately trying to work out how long it would be before they were free. By the time eight o'clock came the worm of bookdealers had formulated a plan that nobody would buy any books until 9.00. The thought of having to spend one hour in the company of bookdealers was not one I relished, but I agreed, however at 8.30 I pulled out the 3 books I really wanted and walked off.

For weeks afterwards I was telling everybody who would listen about this man's brilliant marketing technique. I omitted the part about walking off with the 3 books at 8.30.

This man did not know about books. He also knew that he did not know about books. He was using our expertise and greed to get the best possible price for the books. The only person who listened to this story was Mr. Adrian. He has now adopted the same policy in his shop, much to the ire of the other bookdealers in the Charing Cross Road. Many of the books in this establishment start at £120, but eventually come down to £18, if you can wait that long.

THE CLEARING HOUSE Charing Cross
10 Cecil Court, Charing Cross Road, London WC2
Mon-Sun, 9-9 Rel.
Med size R/C stk all priced at £1.50 or less. This is what happens to the books Mr. Adrian cannot sell in the other shop (see above entry).

PLEASURES OF PAST TIMES Charing Cross
11 Cecil Court, Charing Cross Road, London WC2
Mon-Fri, 11-2.30 & 3.30-5.45 V.Rel, some Sats.
Med size spec in Performing Arts and ephemera. Ab av cal, cnd, av prices. The best part of this shop is the window. Not only is it carefully thought out, changed frequently, it is a joy to behold. the owner has understood the lesson that

a secondhand bookshop does most of its business when it is clsd. People who would normally never go near a bksp pass this window at three in the morning and this shop is not just advertising itself but the whole world of s/h bks. It is promoting bks to people who would never normally see them. It is encouraging people to go into bksps, not necessarily its own but all s/h shops. This is the one area where bksps can always win over the Bookfairies. They have to advertise every event that they hold and no normal person is ever going to remember that a bookfair is going to be held on the 2nd Sunday of the month. But a bksp is advertising itself just by putting books in the window. It is not even necessary to have as grand a display as this one, all that is needed is something which says "This is an interesting place". This is one of the crucial differences between Bookfairs and shops, bookfairs are for people who are already interested in books, bksps encourage people to read bks and buy them.

THE TRAVELLERS BOOKSHOP Charing Cross
25 Cecil Court, Charing Cross Road, London WC2
Mon-Sat, 10-6.30 Rel.
Med size spec in Baedeckers and some other travel books, as well as new books. Very high cal, av cnd and prices. Etgow. This is one of the few spec bksps where it does not need nerves of steel to turn the handle of the door.

H M FLETCHER Charing Cross
27 Cecil Court, Charing Cross Road, London WC2
Mon-Fri, 10-5.
Med size R/C/D stk, av cal, cnd and prices. This shop is a Bookdealer special par excellance. It is an old established shop, which from the outside looks remarkably dull. Inside the books are solid roast beef, but the real business is conducted with the stk that is in the bsmt. How you obtain a look at these books is beyond my comprehension. They do not seem to be interested in having new customers and they work on the basis that all the customers who count will know about the type of books they deal in anyway. The only sleepers in this shop are the staff.

ADELAIDE BOOKS CENTRE Charing Cross
9 Adelaide Street, London WC2
Mon-Sat, 12-7.30 Unr.
Med size R/C stk at strange prices. NSOC. The owner of this shop is a major contestant in the "How many bksps can I close down league". So far I make it 7, and I thought this one was going to close but the rumour is that it will reopen as a mini bookfair. I could really like this shop, it is beautifully situated and is positioned between two of my major interests in life: Vegetarian restaurants and Public toilets. The stk of this establishment resembles the contents of my stomach after I have been to one and not yet got to the other. Tube OOS at Saint Martin in the Fields exist & right.

You are now entering South London where they think literature is something you drop in the street.

NATIONAL THEATRE BOOKSTALLS

Outside the National Theatre, overlooking the river, there are some s/h bkstls, sometimes. The owners of these stalls are all delicate flowers, despite behaving like cactuses. They abhor rain, but like warm weather and gentle winds. Hardy perennials they are not. Their delicate leaves seem unable to withstand constant exposure. The dedicated can occasionally spot them just before the theatre opens in the evening. BR. Waterloo, follow the signs for the Royal Distressful Hall.

BOOKS Waterloo
29 Tenison Road, London SE1
Mon-Sat, 10.30-6.30.
Med size R/C stk, emphon remainders, av cal, cnd and prices. And where exactly is Tenison Road, you may well ask? This minor bksp has one of the greatest assets in the world. It is right next door to Waterloo station. Even if you have an Atlas of London, it is almost imposs to find Tenison Road. The best name for a bksp to have is the name of the area it is in. When people are telling one another about it they are already giving the address. Every time somebody else mentions Waterloo station a book person will think of this shop, and this one certainly needs all the help it can get.

secondhand BOOKS **Waterloo**
20 The Cut, London SE1
Wed,Sat 11-7.
Med size R/C stk emphon Remanders. Av cal, cnd and prices. A Samuel Beckett Special. Minimal name for shop, minimal shelving, minimal books, minimal effect. Rare reviews in the Guardian. Tube and BR Waterloo. OOS by Imperial War Museum exit, turn right down ramp and left back on yourself in market. There is also a curious ephemera shop (it mainly sells hardware) nearly opp.

MY BACK PAGES **Waterloo**
Elephant and Castle Shopping Centre, London SE1
Mon-Sat, 10.30-6.30
Med size R/C stk primarily pbks (see next entry). Tube Elephant & Castle (this is not strictly on the Charing Cross Branch but it is easiest to do this way) OOS into the ultimate shopping mall for the maladjusted and find the W H Smith. Bksp is alongside.

MY BACK PAGES **Waterloo**
8&9 Balham Station Road, Balham, London SW12
Mon-Sat, 10.30-5.30 Rel.
Med size R/C stk remaindery. Av cal, cnd and prices. Bgns known. I wish this shop well but I also wish that it would change its name. Maybe the disease of giving bksps the wrong name is endemic in South London. The best poss name for a bksp is the name of the area in which it is located or a landmark that is well known. S/h bksps need all the extra help they can get. If you call a shop by the most prominent local feature it will encourage people outside of the area to come to your shop. That it may be diff to find is neither here nor there, you have to get them to make the attempt, having got to the area they will then set about the problem of actually finding the place. Balham is famous for sellers and byers to Wimbledon. If this shop was called the Balham Station S/h Bksp every time Balham was mentioned book people would think of this shop.

Nor is there any point in calling your shop by a joke name. The ultimate in folly was a S/F bksp called: "Small they were and Golden Eyed". They had to employ a person who could keep a straight face and answer the telephone at the same time. In the end they would simply answer the phone with the words "Bookshop"!

Tube.....see you do not even need to know what tube it is, no more directions are necessary.

BOOKS AND LYRICS **Wimbledon**
Unit 6 The Apprentice Shop, Merton Abbey Mills, Sth Wimbledon London SW19
Tue-Sun, 11-6 Rel.
Med/Lg R/C stk. Low key NSOC but bgns known. WAD. The books are a bit chaotic but I am all in favour of this. In fact I am in favour of piling more and more in. There is a definite shortage of shops in London just filled to the roof with books. A shop that just has everything and piles it high and sells it cheap. T & Disc. Tube Colliers Wood. OOS turn left and right at the roundabout. It is equidistant from South Wimbledon Tube OOS and turn left and right. But

here you meet a curious sign which says "No Pedestrians!" This cannot possibly be legal. You are allowed to walk anywhere on the Queen's highway (a motorway is not the Queen's Highway - but this is not a motorway despite the fact that the motorists treat it as such). I have walked along this bit of road several times, but so far have not attracted any police attention but several motorists have gone berserk.
There are two other stalls in this complex. See TIN.

NICHE **Wimbledon**
5 Hartfield Crescent, London SW19
Mon-Sat, 10-4 Unr.
A charity bksp with an extremely boring stk which does however produce several bgns. No T. BR & Tube Wimbledon. Note South Wimbledon which is on the Northern Line. OOS turn left along main road and right at Safeway Supermarket. Street not signposted. Wimbledon is notable for its amazing number of charity shops. Currently there are nine, excluding this bksp. For me it is only eight, as I am barred from one. I went in and saw a beautiful Expresso Coffee machine. When the lady saw me taking an interest in it she came over (it was a slow day and she was looking for new gossip) and began to explain to me how this thing was made, and all the different parts and how well they fitted together. How well it would make me a cup of coffee first thing in the morning - a lot of the people who work on charity shops seem to have trained at the Harvard Business School. I told her that everything fitted extremely well except the price, but the truth was I was extremely keen on this thing, and eventually I succumbed to buying it. She went away and got a beautiful bag and I got out the £9 to give to her. There was some confusion whilst they worked out how they were going to take the money. She then asked me how I was going to pay, I said with the cash I had on the desk. "But what about the rest of it?" she expostulated, just refraining herself from screaming. "The rest of what?" I said. "The money." "This is the money" I said, waving a ten pound note. "This coffee pot is £90.00." I had read it as being £9, and even that I was chary. "For ninety pounds I could get a nice young lady to make me coffee every morning." I said. "Not round here you couldn't" she said. The ladies in Wimbledon are beyond price.

HIGHGATE

THE THREE PENNY OPERA

The three shops in Highgate are all keen to put on performances, but they can't decide which one it should be. The lady in Ripping Yarns is keen on anything as long as she is the Prima Donna. The gentleman in Fisher & Sperr refuses to acknowledge her existence and is hanging on to the libretti. The gentleman in Bonaventure has lost patience with the whole project and is on the verge of giving up. The lady in RY is keen to stage something that children will be interested in but unfortunately it is not children who buy the tickets and the adults who pay this piper are extremely demanding but not quite as demanding as the gentleman in Fisher & Sperr. (F&S could strike him as being the invasion of modernism). He wants to be director, designer, conductor and lead violin. For want of anything better to do the gentleman in Bonaventure has taken to designing the set. Samuel Beckett would be proud of him. As so often in Opera nobody is bothering about the audience.

RIPPING YARNS **Highgate**
366 Archway Road, Highgate, London N6
Mon-Sat, 10.30-5.30, Sat -5pm, Sun 11-4.
Med/Lg R/C stk, av cal, cnd not strong, adventurous prices. Keen on childrens bks. Tube Highgate OOS, up steps to right and cross road and turn right.

BONAVENTURE **Highgate**
259 Archway Road, Highgate, London N6
Wed-Sat, 10.30-6.00
Med size R/C stk, av cal, NSOC, av prices. A Samuel Beckett Special. TWC. Tube Highgate OOS up steps, cross road and turn left.

FISHER AND SPERR **Highgate**
46 Highgate High Street, London N6
Mon-Sat, 10.30-5.30, Lunch 1-2
Med/lg R/C/D stk, av cal, cnd and prices. AWYW and then lights up the room where it is. A Bookdealer Special.

THE ONLY ONE NOT IN JULIAN'S DICTIONARY:

THE ANGEL ISLINGTON

BOUTLE & KING Angel
23 Arlington Way, Islington, London EC1
Mon-Sat, 10.30-5.30
Med size R/C/D stk, av cal, ab av cnd and av prices. This shop is a coalition between the Workers Revolutionary Movement at rest and the Yuppies in retreat. Tube Angel OOS to crossroads turn left and first right and first left. Directly behind the Sadlers Wells Theatre.

LEFT BOOK CLUBBING

The one who looks like he could run the policy book for the mafia in the South Bronx, he used to be the leader of Haringey Council, the one who looks like his bodyguard, bootboy and runner, he used to be his bootboy, bodyguard and runner on Haringey Council. When the "Lead" was deleaded in a left wing coup, the pair of them decided to continue their endeavours in the recycling industry of bookdealing.

The "Lead" did not hold it against the bodyguard that he had failed to see the knife coming because he was engaged in a far more important task at the time: polishing his principals of non violence. There is of course the other possibility that the "Lead" thought the bootboy would always be so slow that he had no danger of being knifed in the back by him. Whatever the reason, together they entered the gloom of non party life. For those of us who think Gengis Khan was a leftie, the flutterings of the wings of the Labour Party are not easy to spot at a single glance, however if you are genuinely interested the pair of them will expound the history and philosophy with a vehemence and determination that would be much admired by the mafia, if they applied it to debt collecting.

The part that really interests me is the large number of secondhand bookdealers who were once prominant in Left Wing Politics. I don't mean the supporters of the Labour party - if indeed that can be described as being left wing - I mean people who were holders of political positions: Mr. Louis Bondy used to be on the GLC. Mr Paul Minet wrote a book on the European Community and the Left. Mr Brian Lake, of Jarndyce Books was a Labour Councillor in Hampstead, Mr. Tom Jackson of Ilkley used to be head of the Post Office Union, which the pair above have informed me must mean he was a supporter of the Labour Party, but I fail to see the connection. Mr. Richard Booth used to dabble in Left Wing Politics before he decided to nominate himself King of Hay on Wye - A far better title would have been Tsar of all the Mushers.

There are also many other bookdealers not quite as famed, but equally fervent in their espousal of the left cause. I am not trying to claim this as an in depth survey of the voting habits of secondhand bookdealers, but I am hard put to come up with a similar list of conservative supporters.

The left predominance also seems to stretch to the collectors. You are much more likely to see a Labour Politician in a secondhand bookshop than you are a conservative one.

The interesting part about this is that secondhand bookdealing is an exclusively capitalist enterprise. It consists solely of buying a book at X pounds and selling at 3X pounds. There is nothing else to know. Nothing is manufactured other than the price. No greater wealth is created other than that which already exists. It is true that bookdealers are supplying a service but you do not have to be in the book business long to discover that books rise to the level that a customer can afford to pay. When the lefties in the book business first discover this, they throw up their arms in horror, but they soon lower them when you are not looking and change the old prices.

Most Left wingers start off as book collectors - as do most other bookdealers - with the exception that they feel they are furthering the cause, by buying Left Wing books. Then something happens, either redundancy, marriage break up or sheer boredom with the life they are leading provokes them into a new career, and secondhand bookdealing looks like something where they can promote the cause by other means. That they have failed to promote the cause by direct means often acts as an added impetus. They usually start off with a stall either at a bookfair or in a street market (the soft Left go for the bookfairs, the hard left go for the street markets), and for the first few weeks they are a roaring success, because they are using their own books.

In the years when they have been book collecting for themselves they have also purchased things which were obvious bargains, quite often they were doing this whilst they were officially at work, but in fact were out exercising the expense account. It is not the Left wing books that sell but the ones on Big Game Hunting, which they find philosophically repugnant, and usually sell cheaply to get rid of it as it is lowering the tone of their stall.

But they soon learn, oh how soon they learn, there is nothing more voluble than the Left Wing bookdealer who discovers that an agent of the capitalist classes has purchased a book from him, made an egregious profit and is now able to grind down the working classes even more, (instead of seeing it as a valuable lesson). They speak of it as a moral duty that they should stop the exploitation and in an effort to help the working classes they raise the prices.

They also soon discover that selling secondhand books is remarkably easy, if you have the right ones. All the effort and skill in bookselling is in acquiring the right ones. This is when they begin to cost their time and see how valuable that expenses account from the Council really was. There is no expense account in secondhand bookdealing. You either make a profit and survive or make a loss and go under. This is capitalism at its crudest.

Soon they exhaust their resources and one of two things happen, they either become belligerent and attempt to force the customers to buy the books they think are worthwhile, at the prices they feel are morally justified, or, they begin to deal in highly saleable books at highly saleable prices.

You should see the ones who become belligerent, or rather you should try to avoid them, they would terrify the living daylights out of the mafia. There is one in London known as "The Inurbane Guerrilla". When I first met him I was certain he must have been sponsored by the Conservative Party to give lefties a bad name. There is not a bookdealer in London with whom he has not had an altercation. Being a socialist he divides his belligerence equally; 50% of the people he meets have physical scars, and 50% have mental ones. Should some innocent interloper (nobody would attempt it knowingly) encroach on his territory he takes action that makes the Five Families War in New York look like Toytown tantrums. He is not in this guide book despite the fact that he has a bookstall outside of a North London Labour Party Headquarters. I only include people whom I have seen, and I would not go within five miles of him.

There is a rumour that he is no longer there, but I am prepared to wait another five years before I check it out. There is a small possibility that the stock might have changed by then, and if inflation continues at the same rate and he does not change his prices (some hope) I may just be able to afford a paperback edition of the Communist Party Manifesto. However I am nervous of doing even that. It is hard to decide which upsets him more, a dealer buying a book from him, or not buying one.

The second path, which I am pleased to say Boutle & King have taken - in part inspired by the 'Inurbane Guerrilla' - is that of becoming extremely efficient booksellers. They have that quality so noticeably lacking in the people they used to represent; industriousness. They have also acquired the most crucial trait for a successful bookdealer, they are able to spot who is going to spend the money and value them accordingly.

The pair of them have an eye for business that would impress the mafia, they have not yet learnt how to be quite as ruthless, but give them time.

The only thing that I can think of which makes bookdealing attractive to Lefties is the backstabbing. Maybe they have more experience.

There is a subtle method of spotting Leftie bookdealers for use by those of us who are so dim that we had to ask whether Tom Jackson used to be in the Labour Party. Most bookdealers you meet go on "Buying Trips", but not Leftie bookdealers, they go on "holiday". Most bookdealers do not take their 'Holidays' in places where you can meet the working class. You are not going to tell me that anybody else in the world goes to Colne for a 'holiday' or Hexham? Not only do they go on 'holiday' they are always going on 'holiday'. The only people I have ever heard of who go on more holidays than them are the people who are involved in what the Sun Newspaper describes as Sex Scandals. Not even I am so credulous that I could believe you could have a Sex Scandal in Colne. And it is not as if they go off together, the only time they seem to meet is to arrange holidays.

THE PICCADILLY LINE

Sniff in our nose grove, breathe New Worlds in Museum Street, Bad Breaths forthe South Worst Ones, Winded up from Aus to Ley, Blow out on the way to the air o plane.

DENIS CAINE Arnos Grove
343 Bowes Road, Arnos Grove, London N11
Mon-Sat, 10-5 Rel.
Med size R/C stk, av cal, cnd & prices. TWC. Tube Arnos Grove, almost opp station (rumoured to be closing).

WHETSTONE BOOKS **Whetstone**
368 Oakleigh Road North, London N20
Mon-Fri, 10.30-3.30, Sat 10-5.
Small R/C stk, av cal, cnd & prices. T. Tube Arnos Grove, OOS turn right and continue past roundabout. NAST. 1 mile +.

CROUCH END BOOKSHOP Crouch End
60 Crouch End Hill, London N8
Mon-Sat, 10-6
New bksp with small s/h R/C stk, av cal, cnd & prices. TWC. Tube Finsbury Park, and get one of the only reliable bus services in London. This is because they only try to cover short distances.

SKOOB BOOKS Bloomsbury
15 Sicillian Avenue, London WC1
Mon-Sat, 10.30-6.30.
Lg R/C stk, emphon Literature and Acad bks. The ultimate Helen Hanff Special. T & Disc. Tube Holborn OOS and ahead turn left, about fifty yards.

SEE ALSO BLOOMSBURY ON THE CENTRAL LINE

BERTRAM ROTA Covent Garden
9-11 Langley Court, Long Acre, London WC2
Mon-Fri, 9.30-5.30
Med size spec in modern 1st eds and literature, ab av cal, cnd & prices. TWC. Tube Covent Garden OOS turn right into Long Acre and into alleyway on left.

THERE ARE ALSO SOME BKSTLs in Covent Garden Market on Mondays.

ALIGHT AT LEICESTER SQUARE FOR CHARING CROSS ROAD. See Northern Line.

SOTHERANS Piccadilly
2-5 Sackville Street, London W1
Mon-Fri, 9.30-5.30, Sat am
Lg C/D stk ab av cal, cnd & prices. Emphon Nat His, English Lit, Bindings and sets. Despite recent upheavals, from which they have not quite settled down this is still one of the most pleasant upmarket bksps to be in, Trade ABA only. Tube Piccadilly Circus, OOS into Piccadilly and turn first right.

THOMAS HENEAGE ART BOOKS St James's
42 Duke Street, London SW1Y 6DT
Mon-Fri, 10-6, Sat 10-2
Lg Ars spec, ab av cal, cnd & prices. New bks mixed with old, but superlative quality stk. TWC. Tube Green Park, OOS into south side of Piccadilly turn right at St James St, left Ryder St (see also Sims Reed in TIN).

PICKERING AND CHATTO St James's
17 Pall Mall, London SW1
Mon-Fri, 9.30-5.30
This establishment bears as much relationship to an ordinary s/h bksp as its owner Sir William Rees Mogg does to an ordinary person. Its purpose is to provide him with an acceptable image. It convinces the establishment that he is one of them. It convinces television producers that he is a cultured person. It convinces newspaper editors that he will know how to write, but above all it convinces Sir William that he is a human being.

If you are powerful, rich, famous or known then this shop will welcome you with open arms. If you are a television crew then this shop will lay out the red carpet. If you are a journalist it will encourage you mightily, but if you are an unknown book collector you will have to ring the bell, and possibly, a never snotty nosed member of staff may deign to open the door. He or she will then ask you what you are looking for and in most cases they will tell you that they do not go in for those bks. And this is indeed correct they do not go in for bks, what they are there for is image.

Some people have described Sir William Rees Mogg as being hydra headed; this is nearly true; he would be better described as hydrated. For years the establishment in Britain had had to train separate public school wets to run the country, edit the newspapers and head the legal system. With the invention of the rees mogg model all you had to do was add the right amount of water. A quick sprinkle and he becomes head boy, a swig at the bottle and he is head of the Oxford Union, a tumbler full and he is editor of the Times, half a bottle and he is head of the BBC, a whole bottle and he is head of the Arts Council, a gallon of the stuff and he is head of the Broadcasting Standards authority. Now that he is a complete wet we have to put up with him as an antiquarian bookdealer.

What irritates most about these worms is that they are everywhere, despite their smallness they contaminate everything that they wriggle into. And they are always right! They were right about the poll tax, they were right about the guilt of the Birmingham six, they were right that Guinness was an excellently run company, they were right about our television being the free-est in the world (that must be right because they are the only ones that regularly appear). They are always right!

It may be claimed that I have a chip on my shoulder: THIS IS NO CHIP IT IS AN ENTIRE FOREST. I am fed up with these prats telling me what I may and may not do. Why don't the few of them go to a lesser place where there is a gold standard, where there is no nudity before 9pm, where everyone can write subjunctive clauses. I don't know why I bother, you can spit venom at these buggers all day but it will have no effect, because they have no feelings: THEY ARE NOT HUMAN.

As long as these pathetics are involved only in trivial matters such as government, law and the media, I am prepared to be indifferent but I am not prepared to tolerate them when it comes to something important - such as books.

I have a fantasy that one evening I shall go to the opera and midway through the first act, two Great Brittish Yobboes will rush in, one carrying a sawn off shotgun and the other shouting "fire", and then one of the bow, but never tongue, tied brigade will stand up and say: "I think I can speak on behalf of everybody here when I say that you should make your language more explicit, in short do you mean, 'fire the gun'? or do you mean that 'the building is on fire'?" In the background there will be mutters of "Hear hear" "Bad upbringing" "Wrong family" "No education" and the two yobboes will be speechless with incomprehension. Whilst all this is going on I shall have crept away claiming to be going to ring the police or the fire brigade, but in fact I shall stand outside cheering wildly as the whole house and all its occupants are burnt to a cinder.

Lest you should think that I am in someway opposed to Sir William Rees Mogg and his ideas, I would like to say that I share some of his views. Not least that abortion should only be allowed on extreme medical grounds: In the case of Sir William I say, abort now.

RC: Don't take any notice of the prop; the real reason he cannot stand Moggy is that he writes in The Independent every Tuesday and this is the day they have all the sex problems. The prop is desperate to read about them but can't bring himself to buy the paper when Moggy is in it. Also the prop is hoping that when he dies that the Independent will take some notice. And he does stand a chance, there are some very strange people die in the Independent; they don't die anywhere else. The curious thing is that you have not heard of them before you read the obituary and you have never heard of them after you have read it.

HEYWOOD HILL **Mayfair**
10 Curzon Street, London W1
Mon-Fri, 9-5.30, Sat 9-12.30
Med sized R/C/D stk general bks. Av cal, cnd and prices. Tube Green Park, OOS into Piccadilly turn right towards Hyde Park Corner and right.

THE OLD EPHEMERA & NEWSPAPER SHOP **Knightsbridge**
37 Kinnerton Street, London SW1
Mon-Fri, 10-4.45, Wed -8pm
Spec Ephemera shop, unique. I am not keen on ephemera, mainly because I always lose it, after placing it safely in a book, but I am keen on this ephemera shop because I can always remember when it is open; on Wed nights until 8. It does also open during more normal hours but to open late like this means that I can get to other shops during more normal hours. I am pleased to see that more and more shops are opening after six especially in London, but those that have not taken the plunge could do worse than emulate this one by opening one evening a week. The second thing this shop does and this is even more crucial to the success of opening in the evening is that it brings out its new stock on that open evening. This has the effect of attracting all the deadbeats in London, such as myself.

At first this may not seem a great advantage until you realise that nothing attracts more customers into a shop than seeing customers already there. It is unlikely that a byer could be worse dressed than one of the scruffy anorak and beige trouser brigade and the sight of them in somewhere as daunting as a s/h bksp is likely to encourage him or her in their belief that if those scruffs can go in so can they.

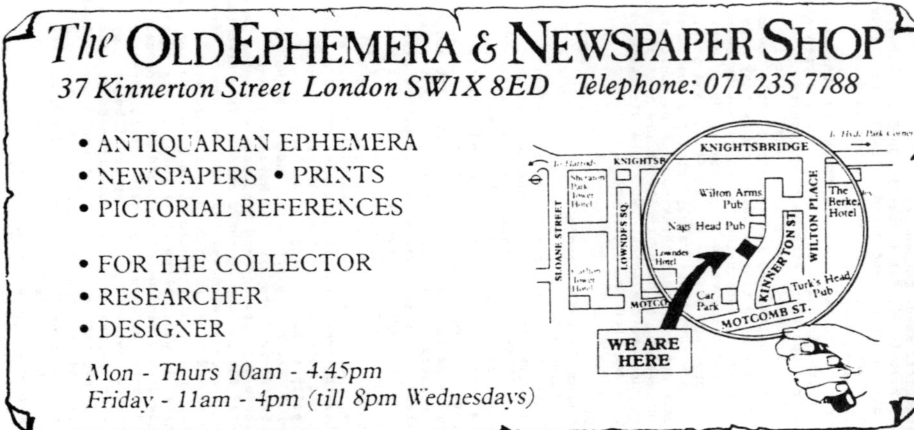
The OLD EPHEMERA & NEWSPAPER SHOP
37 Kinnerton Street London SW1X 8ED Telephone: 071 235 7788
• ANTIQUARIAN EPHEMERA
• NEWSPAPERS • PRINTS
• PICTORIAL REFERENCES
• FOR THE COLLECTOR
• RESEARCHER
• DESIGNER
Mon - Thurs 10am - 4.45pm
Friday - 11am - 4pm (till 8pm Wednesdays)
KNIGHTSBRIDGE
SLOANE STREET
LOWNDES SQ.
WILTON PLACE
KINNERTON ST
MOTCOMB ST.
Wilton Arms Pub
Nags Head Pub
Lowndes Hotel
Car Park
Turk's Head Pub
WE ARE HERE

GLOUCESTER ROAD BOOKSHOP **Gloucester Road**
123 Gloucester Road, London SW7
Mon-Fri, 8.30-10.30, Sat & Sun, 10.30-6.30. V.Rel
Lg R/C stk emphon Lit and Psued studies. The stk is in the process of taking over the whole shop and does not welcome interference from customers.

This shop is to be congratulated on its long and reliable opening hours. It nails the lie that if you open at particular hours there will be no customers. It is true that this is in a somewhat cosmopolitan area. (It is also to be congratulated on calling the shop by exactly the right name). A dealer has a hard time in this shop as they seem to have found some way of denaturing the books but by being open such long hours and being where it is, it is doing more than most shops to encourage people to look at it, and possibly buy books. I know that bksps mainly exist for the benefit of the bksp owner but you would think more shops would make some small concession, as here, to the people that they hope are going to purchase the books. TWC. Tube Gloucester Road, OOS turn right and shop is on corner.

RESPONSE **Earls Court**
300 Old Brompton Road, London SW5
Mon-Sat, 12.00-7.00 Unr
Small R stk, bl av cal, cnd and ab av prices. No T. It is the name that gives the game away, what normal bksp would call itself something so meaningless. It was clearly dreamt up by a committee of failed social workers, failed politicoes, failed advertising copywriters, failed librarians and would be Chinese Takeaway Owners. For this is a 'community' bookshop as is further shown by the fact that you will never see any members of the local 'community' in it. And who can blame them? The most obvious members of the Earls Court 'community' are able to provide their own lit which is original and of a much higher standard. They are the prostitutes. All over Earls Court you can see their tiny stickers, not a telephone box has missed their attention - which has the added benefit that most of the call boxes in Earls Court work, because the call girls make sure they do.

"Butterfly seeks mounting." "Warming Pam." "Miss Bendover." "Erections & Demolitions." "Bound to Please." and "Whoretensia." who lives in Hortensia Road.

All these enterprising and imaginative 'ladies' are prosecuted for putting up their cards. They used to display them in newsagents windows, then the newsagents were prosecuted and thus they had to seek other sites.

If 'Response' really wanted to do something for the local 'community' it would allow these young ladies to advertise in their now dreary window. They could not be prosecuted if they did charge because they would not be directly benefitting. But indirectly they would benefit by finding out of whom the real community of Earls Court consists, mainly of imaginative writers. Men would come (hopefully not literally) and read the adverts, they would also buy even Response duff books in an attempt to disguise their intentions. Alas, this is unlikely to happen, you could get more response in the place opposite a cemetary.

Tube Earls Court, OOS on Warwick Road exit turn left and first right. For the scenic route out on Earls Court Road, turn right and right at Brompton Road.

W. FOSTER Chiswick
183 Chiswick High Road, London W4
Mon-Sat, 10.30-5.30 (sometimes clsd Thurs and lunch)
Med size C/D stk ab av cal, cnd and prices. Please note new address, shop not yet open at time of writing. Tube Turnham Green, OOS turn left and right at Chiswick High Road.

FAIRCROSS BOOKS Chiswick
166 Thames Road, Strand On The Green, London W4
Open every day
Med size stk in Antiques shop, much better than av for an antique shop. R/C bks av cal, cnd and prices. TWC. Not strictly on Piccadilly Line but then it is not on any line despite being in London. It is a day out in London. Find North side of Kew Bridge and follow road that is alongside river east into central London shop is beyond railway bridge.

OSTERLEY BOOKSHOP Osterley
168a Thornbury Road, Osterley, London TW7
Mon-Sun, 10-5.30 Rel
Med size R/C stk, ab av cal, NSOC, av prices, bgns known. This shop is still a Drif Special despite all its attempts to become a Book & Magazine Collector Special (see dire tribe number). The owner has taken to a bizarre pricing system such as £4.63, which means that the book came in on the sixth of the third. The assistants all spend their time studying higher maths in an attempt to cope with this peculiarity. On a Sunday, which is the day I usually visit this place it attracts a curious collection of passers by, on their way to Osterley House. In theory I am in favour of these people but in practice I find them extremely objectionable. They do not move round the shop in any orderly fashion, nor do they know how to pull a book off a shelf (from the sides not from the top). They also eat, extremely loudly. They then are unable to find out how to pay, even though the directions are quite simple. Tube Osterley, OOS turn left and first right.

It could be that the reason I have gone off the above shop is that by the time I get to Osterley I tend to be in a bad mood. As the train for Heathrow stops at Acton Town alleged buskers get on and wait for the doors to close before they begin their dreadful renditions of sixties popsongs. They also do musical guides to those romantic stations between Acton and Heathrow. This is primarily for the benefit of the tourists who all seem to think this is extremely quaint. There is no escape for if you flee to another carriage they only follow you and so profitable has this enterprise become that there are now four or five groups who take over the whole train.

One Sunday one of them who could not dream up his own sixties pop songs asked if anybody had any requests. I saw my chance and said "Yes, my request is that you should stop playing." He did not feel disposed to accede to this request and accused me of being a fascist. I did not deny this charge but informed him, in the now silent carriage that his ignorance of music was only exceeded by his ignorance of politics. Had I been sticking to my alleged Fascist principles I would have kicked his teeth in and then asked him to stop playing. He then accused me of being a "Fucking pathetic fascist." He could have been right, but it was

pleasant to reflect on this in comparative silence all the way to Osterley.

This event did have a sequel a few months later. A television crew were making a film showing these musicians getting on the train and beginning to play before the train doors closed. I went up to the director and pointed out to him that there was a dreadful mistake in their film. He looked at me and told me not to interfere whilst something so important as filming was going on. He then carried on shooting the film. I then got in front of the camera, ever one for honesty in communication and pointed out his mistake. The idea that anybody should dare to interfere with the artistic licence of the BBC struck as definitely being the work of a fascist. When this film was shown I was reliably informed that I was depicted as a raving lunatic who was against culture. Damned right, but what I would like to know is when are the BBC going to pay me for using my performance?

THE VICTORIA LINE

FROM WOOD TO BRICK VIA THE ETHNIC

The following four shops are all in a single arcade (but are much larger than the average stalls. The best way to reach them is on the Victoria line tube and then take a BR train to Wood St OOS turn right under bridge and arcade is on left.

THE SPORTING BKSP ANTIQUE CITY MARKET **Walthamstow**
Unit 13, 98 Wood St, London E17
Mon-Sat, 9.30-5, clsd Thur.
Small spec stk of bks on sports, emphon cricket. TWC

PSYCHIC SENSE **Walthamstow**
Unit1, 98 Wood St, London E17
Mon-Sat, 9.30-5.30
Small spec in Occult and Esoteric, av cal, cnd and prices. TWC.

NORMAN LORD **Walthamstow**
Unit 3, 98 Wood St, London E17
Mon-Sat, 10-5, clsd Thurs
Med size R/C stk, emphon performing arts, av cal, cnd & prices.

RAYMOND PORT **Walthamstow**
Unit 4, 98 Wood St, London E17
Mon-Sat, 9.30-5
Med size R/C stk, av cal, cnd and prices.

THE ENFIELD BOOKSHOP **Enfield**
36 Gordon Road, Enfield, Middlesex
Tues-Sat, 10-5, clsd Wed
This is the ultimate Nearly bksp. It is nearly WAD. There is no sign on the fascia saying so but the owners call it The Gordon Road Bksp. A lot of people in Enfield nearly know where Gordon Road is, but not many people from the rest of London do. I am nearly sure they would get a lot more customers if they changed the name to The Enfield Bookshop. (And given the military overtones of this establishment I would also be keen on The Lee Enfield Bookshop).

The window is packed with books standing to attention like soldiers on parade. I felt like a Head of State giving them an inspection. Individually they were not much, but together they looked like a force to be reckoned with. As a mercenary dealer I would have much appreciated knowing how much each one cost and I am nearly certain a lot of other people would be nearly tempted if they knew how little it cost for this army.

Inside the troops are very neatly arranged so that you nearly do not want to take them off the shelves. A lot of the books in the Readers class nearly make it into the Collectors and a lot of the Collectors books nearly make it into the Dealers squad. These books compete for promotion and they nearly get it.

As with many military institutions there is nowhere near the amount of hostility you would expect. Nobody asks you what you want. Nobody tries to embarrass you into buying a book and nobody expects a courtesy purchase. I nearly got the feeling that there were bgns. BR: Enfield Town which is nearly on the Victoria Line (change at Seven Sisters). OOS turn left and right at main junction keep walking until you think you have nearly missed it. At the second parade of shops and The Wheatsheaf Pub turn left. The shop is nearly invisible until you are on top of it. It is nearly NAST butnearly impossible to find a bus. It is nrly on the way from Epping to Edgware. If London Transport would take up my

suggestion of building an M25 railway line joining up Epping, Enfield, Edgware, Stanmore and Yiewsley (which is nearly Heathrow) they could call it the EEESY line. Well it works...nearly.

PENDLEBURY'S **Stamford Hill**
Church House, Portland Road, Stamford Hill, London N16
Mon-Sat, 9.30-5, Sat -1, Rel
Med size spec in non-conformist theology; what a surprise!
I am not exactly certain what non-conformist theology isbut anyone who can open up a christian bksp in Stamford Hill certainly has to be a non-conformist. According tothe owner, none of the local Jewish population ever comes in his bksp; what a surprise.
Even the church had the decency to throw in the towel, but not this bugger. I would not be surprised to hear that he was contemplating other projects:
A Nudist bksp in Saville Row, perhaps? An Iraqi bksp in Aldershot possibly? A Cookery bksp in Ethiopia? A Paedophile bksp in Toytown? An SAS bksp in Dublin? A Back to Soweto bksp in Brixton?
If I was a Stamford Hill cowboy I would threaten him with the Wailing Wall, a brick at a time.
BR Stamford Hill, OOS turn left and first right and shop is behind Lending Library. Asking the way of men in long black coats is not recommended.

STOKE NEWINGTON

GREEN BADGE VALLEY

CIRCA **Stoke Newington**
144 Stoke Newington ChurchSt, London N16
Mon-Fri, 12.30-6.30, Sat 11.30-6
Small R stk, ab av cal, cnd, av prices. Stoke Newington readers are not like other readers. Their idea of light relief is Wittgenstein and Shulamith Firestone. The owner of this shop could write the definitive work on pseud pbk lit and most of the customers would buy it to make sure they were getting the right bks. BR Stoke Newington, OOS turn left and right past cemetary.

VORTEX **Stoke Newington**
139-141 Stoke Newington Church St, London N16
Mon-Fri, 11-6, Sat 10-6, Sun 12.30-6

A TRIBUTE TO THE EIGHTIES

This media sized radicalism shelved
With double volume fantasies,
All that is left over:
Anarch as in chaos,
Green as in naivety
Feminism as in dungarees,
Black studies as in depression.
New Age as in remainders,
Academic as in irrelevant.
Extremism as in overpricing.
Discount as in completely.

RC writes
I told him no good would come of employing that Iain Sinclair as a chauffeur; he would not go down a road unless it was called Albion.

HACKNEY

It is one of those ironies of fate that the one thing that could benefit Hackney is specifically forbidden by the local council: Hackney is a Nuclear Free Zone.

ARCADY **Hackney**
59 Wilton Way, Hackney, London E8
Thurs-Sat, 11-6, Sun 3-6
Med size R/C stk, keen on entertainment. Av cal, cnd and prices. P.poss. BR Hackney Central (change from Victoria line at Highbury and Islington), OOS turn right into Mare Street and second right into Wilton Way.

UPPER STREET BOOKSHOP **Islington**
182 Upper Street, London N1
Tues-Sat, 10-6
Med size R/C stk av cal, NSOC, emphon Gilbert & Sullivan and entertainment. Operatic prices. On the way to being a silver fish special. TWC. Tube Highbury & Islington, OOS turn right into Upper Street.

BRIXTON MARKET BOOKSHOP **Brixton**
Brixton Market, London SW2
Mon-Sat, 10-5
Small R stk, very low key but with definite potential to become a Drif Special. Not least because there is a veggie restaurant round the corner which is very good. Tube Brixton, OOS turn right and first right and first left into alleyway.

Brixton Stn is a clear example of success that London Transport is unable to cope with. According to LT too many people are using Brixton. At all times of the day let alone rush hour it is a struggle to get out of Brixton - I think it is easier to get out of the prison - once you have managed to get out what you see is that most of the same people you have just been battling with are now engaged in a fight to get on the buses to Streatham. There are indeed a lot of buses which stop at Brixton, they come from West Hampstead, Chalk Farm, Tufnell Park, Liverpool Street and Victoria. There are no buses that go from Brixton to Streatham direct. This not only inconveniences those people who are on long distance buses it makes for huge struggles at Brixton. The solution to this problem is simple, it is to extend the tube line to Streatham.

If you suggest this to London Transport there is a long silence, they will then tell you other people have suggested it. They will then say that there already are four British Rail stations in Streatham. If you endeavour they will tell you that because of the geology of South London it is impossible to build an underground, ommitting to point out that you are not asking for an underground but simply an extension of the tube line.

Building stations one at a time is not the cheapest method, however it is the most sensible. On the Victoria line trains stop at Blackhorse Road, but you never see anybody getting on or off there.

The way for LT to finance this would be to invent a new zone on the Travel Cards: Zone 7. There is no reason why tube stations should follow exact geographical demarcations. LT could charge £1 extra for the use of this line and still millions of people would use it rather than get off and fight their way on to the buses. Once the station at Streatham was opened it would then be possible to decide where it would go next either on through Norbury to Croydon, or off towards Crystal Palace. South London is devoid of tube lines because LT claims that there are enough railways but the problem with the railways is that they all terminate, just like LT when it hears a suggestion.

COLLECTED WORKS **Dulwich**
3 Melbourne Terrace, London SE22
Mon-Sat, 10-6, clsd Wed, Rel
Med size R/C stk, av cal, cnd and prices, emphon Mod Firsts (in South London?) But then the owner is a romantic whose current preoccupation is campaigning against BR's proposed route to the Channel Tunnel - BR should be thanked). BR West Dulwich, OOS turn right and right into side road. There is also a new bksp further along which cannot decide if it wants to do s/h bks or not.

CAMBERWELL BOOKSHOP **Camberwell**
28 Camberwell Grove, London SE5
Tue-Sat, 10-6
Med size spec in Art ref and design. NSOC, av cal and prices. BR Denmark Hill, OOS turn left and left at main junction turn right down pathway and shop is on this side of the road but best to walk from East Dulwich. Go up Dog Kennel Hill and continue into Grove Lane and as above.

KIRKDALE BOOKS **Sydenham**
272 Kirkdale, London SE26
Mon-Sat, 9.30-5.30, clsd Wed
Med sized R/C stk in new bksp indescribably boring. A John Major Special. Tube (see just thinking about it knocks you for six) it should be BR Penge East, OOS turn left in to Newlands Park and left at Sydenham Road. Sydenham is the closest station but it is imposs to get to. BR should be thanked for trying to make Sydenham look interesting. See also Hilyers Sydenham TIN.

THE MAGPIE SHOP **Beckenham**
54 High Street, Beckenham, Kent
Mon-Sat, 10-7 Rel

Med size R/C stk, in antique shop, but a lot better than av. Emphon ephemera. TWC. BR Beckenham Junction, OOS turn left and right into High Street. This shop is also open Sunday for the sale of ephemera, owing to the hypocritical British Sunday Trading laws it is not allowed to sell books.

THE BROMLEY BOOKSHOP **Bromley**
39-41 High Street, Bromley, Kent
Mon-Sat, 10-5
Med size R/C stk av cal, cnd and prices. Not exactly thrilling but an eminently sensible shop. BR: Bromley South, OOS turn left and entrance is about 100 yards on left at rear of alleyway.

VILLAGE BOOKS **Streatham**
17 Shrubbery Road, London SW16
Mon-Sat, 10.30-7, clsd Wed, Rel
New bksp with med sized s/h stk, av cal, cnd and prices. TWC. Shrubbery Road is alongside Streatham Police Station.

THE CENTRAL LINE

BROWSERS BOOKSHOP **Epping**
9 Station Road, Epping, Essex
Mon,Tue,Fri,Sat 10-5, Rel
Med size R/C stk, ab av cnd, av prices. TWC. P. poss. Tube: Epping,OOS ahead turn right. Shop is near T junction on left.

TERRY'S BOOKSHOP **Ilford**
26 Chapel Road, Ilford, Essex IG1
Mon-Sat, 10-4, Wed -2, Thurs clsd, Rel
Small/med size R stk with some C bks. NSOC. Av cal, cnd above av prices. It is the type of place where you would expect the books to be a lot cheaper. TWC. BR Ilford, change at Stratford, OOS turn right and follow road unto supermarket (a place where the British take their children to publically chastise them).

THE DARREN AND TRACY WASTES - K SCOTT Stratford
27 Romford Road, Stratford, London E15
Mon-Sat, 9-5.30, Rel
Med size R/C stk, av cal, cnd and prices. It was an int shop when it first opened but now it has contracted the summer sickness (see below) and looks terminal. Tube Stratford, fight your way out of Stratford Shopping Centre and turn left past the church, continue past traffic lights.

ASH RARE BOOKS **The City**
25 Royal Exchange, Threadneedle Street, London EC3
Mon-Fri, 10-5.30
Small C stk, ab av cal, cnd and prices. A bijou bksp. TWC. Tube Bank OOS and opp Bank of England. At the prices Mr Ash asks it helps if you have an account here.

See also Clarke Hall on Circle & District Line.

BLOOMSBURY

This group, like their namesakes, are very highly rated by each other.

See also Charing Cross Road on The Northern Line. From Tottenham Court Road go north and turn first right past the Dominion Cinema (I always wonder if this was the cinema Dylan Thomas wrote about when he said "And death shall have no dominion.")

FREW MACKENZIE — **Bloomsbury**
106 Gt. Russell St, London WC1
Mon-Fri, 10-6, Sat 10-2
Med size C/D stk, ab av cal, cnd and prices. Emphon Antqrn, Sets and Bindings. Run with missionary zeal by high priests of the bookfair religion.

MUSEUM BOOKSHOP — **Bloomsbury**
36 Gt. Russell St, London WC1
Mon-Fri, 10-5.30, Sat 11-5.30
Med size C spec shop emphon History and Archaeology. Ab av cal, cnd and prices. The bks obviously give off bad vibrations, the atmosphere is a cross between a High Court trail and a cemetary. TWC.

GREAT RUSSELL ST BOOKSHOP — **Bloomsbury**
44 Gt. Russell St, London WC1
Tues, Sat, 10.30-5.30, Sun, 12-3 Rel
Med size C/D stk, emphon Antqrn and Ill. Ab av cal, av cnd and prices. TWC.

FINE BOOKS ORIENTAL — **Bloomsbury**
46 Gt. Russell St, London WC1
Mon-Fri, 9.30-5.30, V.Rel
Med L spec in Middle East and Oriental, ab av cal, cnd, av prices. TWC.

ATLANTIS — **Bloomsbury**
48A Museum Street, London WC1
Mon-Fri 10-5.30, Sat 1-6 Rel
Med size spec in Esoteric and Occult. Av cal, cnd and prices. TWC.

BALLANTYNE AND DATE — **Bloomsbury**
38 Museum Street, London WC1
Mon-Sat, 10.30-6, Sun 12-6 V.Rel
Med size C stk, ab av cal, cnd, av prices (for Bloomsbury). Emphon Industrial History & Art and Design all aspects. WAD. From the C's point of view, Bloomsbury and Museum Street is a lot better area than the Charing Cross Road. Most of the Ds have a good idea of the subject they are dealing in and make considerable efforts to obtain books in that subject. In Charing Cross Road the Ds rely on position, whereas in Museum Street the Ds rely on the books. What the area does need is customers who are as good as the books.

LOUIS BONDY — **Bloomsbury**
16 Little Russell St, London WC1
Mon-Fri, 10.30-6.30, Sat 10.30-5.30

Small C/D stk, ab av cal, av cnd and prices. Emphon Antqrn, Caricature and Miniatures. T. Little Russell St is parallel to Gt Russel St, off Museum St.

SKOOB TWO Bloomsbury
19 Bury Place, Bloomsbury, London WC1
Mon-Sat, 10.30-6.30 Rel
Med/Lg R/C stk, emphon Occult and Acad/student. Ab av cal, cnd and prices. Discounts given to everybody. Bury Place is off Gt Russell St. Tube High Holborn, OOS ahead, left at Vernon Place and third right.

CHECK BOOKS Bloomsbury
31 Museum Street, London WC1
Mon-Sat, 10.30-6, Sun 12-6
Med/Lg C/D stk, ab av cal, cnd and prices. Emphon Travel and Art and 1st Eds. Bookfairy type stk but with much more imagination than most bookfairs can manage. This is an establishment that leads rather than follows. The same is true of the prices but I don't mind this. Shops like this one, and there are not enough of them, are entitled to charge what they do. They know who the customers are, they promote books which are a little bit out of the ordinary and they do not make customers embarrassed if they cannot afford the books. Once again, as in the case of the Edgware shop, this is not a lot to ask. This is undoubtedly the best Collectors shop in Great Britain.

BLOOMSBURY RARE BOOKS Bloomsbury
29 Museum Street, London WC1
Mon-Sat, 10.30-6, Sun 12-6 Rel
Med size C/D stk, emphon Antqrn, av cal, cnd and prices. KUTI. TWC.

VANBURGH RARE BOOKS Bloomsbury
40a Museum Street, London WC1
Mon-Sat, 10-5.30 Rel
Small C/D stk of Antqrn bks, ab av cal, cnd. I cannot say about the prices. It is so rare that you actually see so many antqrn bks in one place. Lots of shops in Britain call themselves antqrn Bookdealers, but this is the only shop that I know that actually has antqrn bks in any significant number. Also has bks on wine.

DAVID MAYOU Bloomsbury
2 Pied Bull Yard, Bury Place, London WC1
Mon-Sat, 10-6
Med size spec Mod 1st eds, Sets & Churchill. Gallery style shop. Ab av cal, cnd and prices. TWC. Pied Bull Yard is paved area off Bury Place. As Skoob 2.

CHARLES RUSSEL Bond Street
Grays Antiques Market, 58 Davies St, London W1
Mon-Fri, 10-5.45 Rel ***STOP PRESS: THIS SHOP NOW CLOSED***
Med size C/D stk, emphon Bindings, Sets and Plate bks, ab av cal, cnd and prices. TWC. Tube Bond St.

M & R GLENDALE Marylebone
9a New Cavendish Street, London W1

Mon-Fri, 10-6 Rel
Med size C/D stk emphon Juvenalia, entertainment and games. Ab av cal, cnd and prices. TWC. Tube Bond St, OOS cross to North side of Oxford St, and follow Marylebone Lane to Marylebone High St, continue and turn right at New Cavendish St entrance to shop is in Marylebone Street (Nast - about 1 mile).

HOSAIN'S **Marble Arch**
25 Connaught Street, London W2
This shop is the classic example of the s/h bksp which opens when it feels like opening, that sells bks to those people to whom it feels like selling and charges what it feels like charging. Hereinafter such shops will be called "Hosain Specials".

BAYSWATER BOOKS **Bayswater**
27A Craven Terrace, London W2
Mon-Sat, 11-7
Small R/C stk, av cal, cnd & prices. The most impressive thing about this shop is the owner, like Mr. Salteena he is partial to young ladies. With seemingly so little going for him he has them queueing up to be chatted up by him. In a business where attractive ladies are in short supply he has persuaded the customer to become substitutes, I am sure he could make more money teaching all the single males in book dealing howto do it. Similar shops, but none do it better, will be termed "Mr. Salteena Specials". Tube Lancaster Gate, OOS turn right and third left.

MUSIC AND VIDEO EXCHANGE **NottingHill Gate**
56 Notting Hill Gate, London W11
Mon-Sun, 10-8 Rel
Heavy Metal, heavy bks, heavy prices in a heavy atmosphere. Med size R/C stk, emphon some fast looking remainders. It is an odd shop, there is a large number of art reference bks butthere is nobody who knows about art. It is as if the bks were bought because they have expensive price tags. With its loud music and abrasive staff this place would be the ideal film set for a Jim Thompson novel. It has a hard edge which does not sit well with bks, at any moment you think one of the other customers is going to edge up to you and try to sell you a prohibited substance. Or even worse, try to buy one from you. There is a menace about this shop which many s/h bksp owners would love to be able to imitate. A lthrwr and Sado-Masochism Gazette Special. Tube Notting Hill Gate, OOS on toilets side - the toilets at Notting Hill are good preparation for this shop - and head towards Bayswater.

RC writes
Is "head" the right term, and how do you know about the Ladies toilets at Notting Hill anyway?

MELLOR AND BAXTER **NottingHill Gate**
121 Kensington Church St, London W8
Mon-Fri, 10-6.30, Sat 10-4 Rel
Med size C/D stk emphon antqrn lthrwr, and sets. Ab av cal, cnd and prices. TWC. Tube Notting Hill Gate, OOS head south.

THE PORTOBELLOW ROAD

ALL QUIET ON THE WEST TEN FRONT

The bookstalls in the Portobello Road open on a Saturday only. They mainly have bookfair type stock in shabbier surroundings. Contrary to popular opinion there are many bgns to be found but it does take some assiduous searching. The major problem is finding the stalls being given the number in the road does not help a lot as it is invariably obscured by other stalls. From Notting Hill Gate Tube follow the signs to the Portobello Road, ignore Burkes in Pembridge Road, the books are dreadful and not worth the effort of trying to extract them. At the junction of Portobello and Westbourne Grove turn left and there are about six bookstalls almost immediately to the left. There are then two stalls in the row opposite, one of which is upstairs, on the corner. Turn left into the Portobello and past the church hall on the right is a stall on the ground floor to the left, further along upstairs in the Dolphin arcade is another. There is also an ephemera shop on the right hand side.

If you continue walking through the fruit and veg market for about a mile you come to the cheap end of the Portobello Road (not the prices just the area) if you follow the market north and turn right into Golborne Road and continue towards the bridge you will be rewarded with the best Pattiserie in the whole area: The Lisboa, but be warned, it takes as long to get served as it does to savour the cakes.

A full list of the Portobello Road Bookstalls is given in the Town Index.

BERNARD SHAPERO **Holland Park**
80 Holland Park Avenue, London W11
Mon-Fri, 10-7, Sat -6, Rel
Lg C/D stk emphon Plate bks, Bindings and Sets. Despite the best efforts of the owner, bgns are known. Ab av cal, cnd and prices. TWC. Tube Holland Park, OOS, turn left.

THE DISTRICT LINE

DI STRICTLY KNOT TRUE

CLARKE HALL **The City**
7 Bride Court, Bride Lane, London EC4
Mon-Fri, 10.30-6.30
Med size R/C/D stk, av cal, ab av cnd, av prices. Emphon Mod 1sts Ill and Samuel Johnson. TWC. Tube Blackfriars, OOS towards Fleet Street and shop is on small alleyway near post box.

Change at Embankment for Charing Cross

THE KINGS ROAD

Children's books but no children, Art books but no art, Bindings bound to displease, Rare books but even rarer customers, General books due for a putsch, Blinding bargains for the not blind.

Despite the official opening hours, nothing in the Kings Road seems to start before midday. The only wayto doit is to walk from Sloane Square Tube towards Putney Bridge a distance of about four miles. Unless you like mystery tours do not take any of the buses, you will end up in such exotic parts of the civilisation as Battersea, Camden Town, Liverpool Street, and Stockwell, but not Putney Bridge.

BARBARA STONE **Kings Road**
Antiquarius, 135 Kings Road, London SW3
Mon-Sat, 10.30-5.30
Lg stall with Children bks and Ill, ab av cal, cnd and prices. TWC.

[Double check Trocchio now dead]

HARRINGTON BROTHERS **Kings Road**
The Chelsea Antiques Market, 253 Kings Road, London SW3
Mon-Sat, 10-6
The Harrington Brothers bill themselves as being Antqrn Booksellers and are proud members ofthe Antqrn Booksellers Assoc'n. What they are is sellers of tat and the ABA is a tatty organisation for allowing them in. In their window you will see large leather tomes that have been highly polished so that even more highly polished customers can have themselves photographed in front of them. Should you open these bks, and in the case of the Harrington's customers this is most unlikely, you will find that these are the rare coloured copies. And this is true; they were coloured by the Harringtons.

They also deal in Travel, Voyages and Maps. The rule is that it was a voyage as long as it had pictures. The value of the book is its break up price. The amount they ask is more than the total price as a collection of individual plates. There is nothing wrong with this but it is wrong that the Antqrn Booksellers Assoc'n should be endorsing it.

Currently starring in the window are a pair of Golf Pictures. To an untutored eye such as mine they looked as if they were circa 1890. I am interested in golf because it gives me a chance to wear my plus fours. I examined these pictures for about fifteen minutes and I must admit I had never seen anything like them. Eventually I summoned up the courage to go and ask how much theywere. The very polite young lady told me they were £125.00 each.

I blushed, thanked her and left. The moment she told me the price I knew I was a moron. £125 to the Harringtons is like tenpence to the rest of us. I went back and looked at the pictures again, how could I have been so stupid not to see that the paint was *too* new, in fact in some parts it did not even look as if it was dry. The golf ball would have been the size of a football if it had those proportions. The golf clubs were far too short, originally golf clubs were far

too long. And then most shameful of all, I suddenly realised that they were painted in what is known as the Venetian School. I have never been to Venice but I can say with some certainty that there were very few golf courses there in 1890.

The reason I had assumed that these things were worth looking at was because over the door it said "Antiquarian Books" and they displayed the sign of the Antiquarian Booksellers Association.

It is not the Harrington's fault, they do not know any better, and they have made considerable sums of money selling such rubbish. Indeed they now own the whole of the Chelsea Antiques Market. It is the fault of the ABA for allowing them to display their sign.

They should have politely told the Harringtons to go and join The Photographers Props Association, The Leatherware Guild, Libricides Anonymous, the Joe Orton Colouring Book Club.

The one organisation that would not have them is the W.C. Fields Appreciation Society, for the Harrington's motto is "Give every sucker an even break - of the book".

RC writes

Don't take any notice of that stupid bugger he is the only golf bookdealer who has never been on a golf course in his life. When he turned up in his plus four suit and offered to be the caddie of his one golf book customer, the man could not stop laughing. 200 miles we had driven and the bloke turned him down.

He was very keen on that suit, I think it was the most he had ever paid for one: £5. He bought it in the Red Cross shop around the corner from the Harrington's, that was what he was really doing looking in their window, trying to work out how he could batter the poor ladies in the charity shop down in price.

When he heard that this entire block was going to be pulled down he was overjoyed because he thought they would sell the suit for even less. Then much to his chagrin, a campaign was started to "save" this block from the Church Commissioners who owned it.

When his friend Mrs Wolfe (a friend is someone to whom he owes money or books) suggested at a meeting that what they should do is hold a prayer meeting for the Church Commissioners he was stuck. On the one hand he wanted them to pull the building down, but on the other hand he wanted to steal that line. He made the suggestion to the ladies in the Red Cross Charity shop and they thought it was so good they gave him the suit.

CHELSEA RARE BOOKS **Kings Road**
313 Kings Road, London SW3
Mon-Sat, 10-6
Med sized C/D stk, av cal, cnd and ab av prices. AWYW. WYLAH. Dry Ice Special.

20TH CENTURY BOX **Kings Road**
Kings Road, London SW3
Mon-Sat, 10-6
What you have to do with this shop is fill in your own address. It is a portable bksp. In less than a year it has

had three different locations. The price of the books changes almost as fast, upwards. The books themselves are not too bad, they're not too good either, but the whole thing looks so like a bookfair that it is distinctly offputting.

THORNTONS **Kings Road**
634 Kings Road, London SW6
Mon-Sat, 10-5.45 Rel
Med/Lg R/C/D stk, av cal, cnd and prices. Bgns known. This is the only place in the Kings Road that vaguely resembles a bksp. I am not overkeen on it myself but several other dealers are. Its a bit gloomy for me but some people are able to light up the place with their eyes when they see the prices. It is definitely WAD and it takes some time to do, and the stk changes fairly frequently, but I don't know...TWC. Tube Fulham Broadway, OOS straight ahead and left at bottom.
RC writes
What the miserable bugger means is that the girl whom he used to chat up into giving him 20% discounts has left.

THE CONSTANT READER **Fulham**
627 Fulham Road, London SW6
Mon-Sat, 10.30-6.30
Med/Lg R/C stk, strange cal, strange cnd, strange prices. This shop just keeps filling up with bks, of which I am in favour. Many of the bks I have never seen before which should make going into it int., but instead it is extremely irritating. The books are all of a type that librarians admire. In fact the more I think about it, the more they seem like those books that libraries are now so keen to sell off. It has always been my ambition to write an essay called 'why are librarians so dreary?' The books look like they were priced by a committee of librarians. Tube Fulham Broadway, OOS turn right and shop is at the bottom of North End Road.
RC writes
The reason the prop does not like the place is that he tried to do some middle eastern style haggling in here and came off so badly that he gave the guy more money than he was asking just to get out. Ever since then he has called him the Constant Bleeder.

By Putney Bridge tube station is a strange office which sells books. All the books would have been raving bestsellers fifty years ago, but now they look extremely tired. Even though it is a shop, and they do have books, it is not a bksp. I think it might be a memorial to J B Priestley.

Continue along the District line to Wimbledon for Niche (see the end of the Northern Line).

THE DARTFORD TO CHARING CROSS LINE

with deviations...

BLACKHEATH

NARCISSISM DIP

BOOKSHOP BLACKHEATH **Blackheath**
74 Tranquil Vale, Blackheath, London SE3
Mon-Sat, 9.30-5 Unr
Med/Lg R/C stk, av cal, cnd and prices. TWC. Making a bksp int is quite an easy task; Ittakes supreme skill to make it as boring as this one. Somebody had to carefully remove anything that might inspire interest even by accident. Instead of looking out over the village of Blackheath which is pleasant and int, it looks out over the heath which is flat, featureless and fouled, this has inspired the owner to make the bksp the same. BR: Blackheath, OOS turn left and keep to left until you come to the heath shop on the corner on right. Two doors down there is an Oxfam which has a large number of bks, but mainly the sort you would like to avoid.

STUDIO BOOKS **Blackheath**
2 Montpelier Vale, London SE3
Tues-Sat, 11-6
Med/Lg R/nearly C stk, av cal, cnd and prices. This is a good R shop but nobody in Blackheath appears to read, they seem to spend all their time looking at images of themselves and their village. It could be a good C shop if the owner did not think that all Cs were in his own image. BR Blackheath, OOS cross road (the most fun you are likely to have in Blackheath) turn left and right under arch and left to end of mews, shop is upstairs.

GREENWICH

STUDYING ITS NAVEL

SOUTH LONDON BOOK CENTRE **Greenwich**
18-19 Stockwell Street, Greenwich, London SE10
Wed, Thur, Sat & Sun, 9-5
Lg R/C stk, a mini bookfair. Even though there are lots of bks it is very hard to 'read' them as they are not in the same sections. The whole place has the same effect of The Readers Digest publishing Finnegans Wake. There is a definite gap in London for a large shop which just piles in the bks but has them sectioned as in Baggins in Rochester. The thing that is crucially wrong with Baggins is that it is in Rochester. BR Greenwich, OOS turn left and right at cinema. If coming from Dartford change at Charlton and return.

SPREAD EAGLE BOOKS **Greenwich**
8 Nevada Street, Greenwich, London SE10
Mon-Sun, 10.30-1 and 2.30-5
Med size R/C stk, int bks, unint prices. It looks like the set for a BBC version of Dickens. From South London Book Centre continue south and turnright just before theatre.

MARCET BOOKS **Greenwich**
4a Nelson Road, Greenwich, London SE10
Mon-Sun, 10.30-5.30
Med size R/C stk, av cal, cnd and prices. Bookfairy. Emphon maritime. TWC. BR Greenwich, OOS turn left, at church turn right against stream of one way traffic and left down alleyway.

ROGERS TURNER BOOKS **Greenwich**
27 Nelson Road, Greenwich, London SE10
Mon-Sat, 10-6
Med sized C/D spec shop, ab av cal, cnd and prices. Emphon Clocks, Science, German. TWC. Directions opp entrance to market.

MARITIME BOOKS **Greenwich**
23 Nelson Road, London SE10
Mon-Sat, 10-6, V.Rel
This is a spec shop par excellance. They sell new, s/h and antqrn maritime books all of an exceptionally high character. They know what they are doing and they do it extremely well. But what I would really like to tell you about, and unfortunately the swine swore me to secrecy, is that his ambition is to have a periscope in the basement so that he could inspect the customers as they came in and any that were prats, and spec shops attract quite a few, he would torpedo. It certainly would make going in bksps more int.

THE METROPOLITAN LINE

T H BARNARD **Uxbridge**
11 Windsor Street, Uxbridge UB8
Mon-Sat, 9-5, Wed -1, Rel
Med/Lg R/C stk av cal, cnd and prices. One of the few known examples of a bksp actually improving. They have refurbished the place and is more int. I do not think it is just the furnishing, definite bgns do now errupt. Tube Uxbridge, OOS ahead behind market building, if that is what it is. In Uxbridge the Town Hall looks like a car park. See also Eton.

THE HAYES BOOKSHOP **Uxbridge**
6 Glebe Avenue, Ickenham, Middlesex UB10
Mon-Sat, 9.30-5.30 (sometimes clsd Mondays) V.Rel
Med size R/C stk which usually repays studying despite the distraction of remainders. Very cheap but often the best bgns are in the more expensive bks. They also have the knack of producing bks that you do not see elsewhere. WAD. Etgow. Tube Ickenham, OOS turn left and shop is on left.

ETGOW, NETGOW & VETGOW

You lot all thought I had forgotten, but the truth is that this is the only bksp in London where they seem genuinely pleased to see potential customers, and me. I am not claiming that I am easy to get on with, in fact I would describe myself as netgow, on a good day.

In most of the shops I go into in London people start passing comments on my clothes, say that they thought I was dead because they have not seen me for a few months (this tends to be the bookfairies who automatically assume that if you are not seen at a bookfair you must be dead) or complain about my meanness.

If asked "How are You?" on a very good day it will be down and up (I have also noticed I only say this to people I like) on a good day I will respond with "terrible". And on a normal day you will be lucky to get a grunt. (There are three levels of grunts but it would take too long to explain).

The thing is I am a miserable bugger. I have always been a miserable bugger and I do not doubt that I always will, but what really irritates me is that people expect me to be otherwise.

I go in bookshops to look at books, if I wanted to talk to somebody I would ring the Samaritans. The only thing I am interested in hearing in bookshops is gossip and in my experience the only way to get gossip is not to ask for it. People in bookshops are always asking me for gossip and I never have a clue what to say.

Most bookdealers are there to say how much money they have made, or how much money they have lost. None of these things interest me at all. I am interested in The Economics of Rail Transport, Epistemology and Lady Body Builders, and that is just this week's obsession.

Most bookdealers have two topics of conversation: how much money they made/lost and what was on television last night. I have not any interest in either subject. My idea of a discussion is something that lasts four hours, and that is the outline. Most bookdealers, along with most of the British population can only concentrate on one subject for about twenty seconds. When I tell them this they accuse me of arrogance, damned right, and I feel I have a lot to be arrogant about.

One bookdealer did accuse me of being sententious. I was unable to say anything as I had no idea what it meant. When I got home and looked it up I discovered that it was a word with two meanings both of which applied to me. I was then puzzled as to whether he meant one or the other, or both. I hope it was both.

My definition of vetgow is what they do in this shop, they leave me alone.

GABRIEL'S **Willesden Junction**
47 Walm Lane, Willesden, London NW2
Mon-Sat, 10.30-6.30, Rel
Med size R shop, which has some very curious bks in it, and I am not referring to the pornographic ones. It is almost WAD just to see how different a bksp can be. Tube Willesden Green OOS turn right, shop is by station, given how industrious the owner is, I can see him buying the station. Do not confuse with Willesden Junction (a unique place no matter how often you go through it or stop at it, it is not possible to discover where it is).

STEPHEN FOSTER **Marylebone**
95 Bell Street, London NW1
Mon-Sat, 10.30-6, Rel

Med size R/C/D stk, av cal, cnd and prices. Almost unique in that it is a bksp without eccentricities, maybe he has not been doing it long enough. It is WAD for this alone. T. Tube Baker Street, OOS by Lost Property Exit, and straight ahead towards Marylebone Station where you can also alight. Turn right into Lisson Grove and left into Bell Street.

ARCHIVE BOOKSTORE **Marylebone**
63 Bell Street, London NW1
Mon-Sat, 10-6
Med sized R/C stk, emphon antqrn and music. NSOC. Some eccentric prices. It is poss that all the eccentricity that one would expect in Mr. Foster's shop has been drained into Mr. Meakers. T. Tube as Foster.

BIBLIOPOLA **Marylebone**
Alfie's Antique Market, 13-25 Church St, London NW8
Tues-Sat, 10-6
Med size spec antqrn, ills and children. Ab av cal, cnd and prices. This type of establishment is a severe puzzle to me. It is easy enough finding Church St but trying to find this place inside is a lot more diff. You then have to puzzle when it is open, for although the market may be open at the above times, the shop certainly is not. If and when you get in the bks have puzzling notations on them, not just the prices. Most of these inscriptions mean nothing to me, they refer to odd bibliographic details that are so obscure you wonder who has heard of them. I am now tortured by the idea that there are thousands of people going round bksps who not only know much more than I do, but are invisible. T & Disc. Continue north along Lisson Grove and left into Church Street.

THE SOUTH WEST FRONTIER

Most of the bookshops of South West London are extremely easy to get to, from Clapham Junction but attempting an organised tour is fraught with difficulties. Not least British Frail's fond belief that people only want to go in and out of London, and not around. At all costs avoid the buses, they have a will of their own; they are just waiting for it to go to probate.

THE DIVERSIONS OF PURLEY

(The above line is the soul reason I included the next shop)

PREDOMINANTLY PRINTED **Purley**
339 Brighton Road, Purley, Surrey
Mon-Sat, 10-5
Med size shp spec in Ephemera, some bks av cal, cnd and prices. TWC. BR Purley Oaks, OOS follow road around and turn right.

THE CROYDON BOOKSHOP **Carshalton**
304 Carshalton Road, Carshalton, Surrey
Mon-Sat, 10.30-5.30
Lg R/C stk av cal, cnd and prices. T. BR Sutton, OOS turn right and right at main road. Nast but do not attempt to get a bus.

THE WHITEHALL BOOKSHOP **Cheam**
45 The Broadway, Cheam, Surrey
Mon-Sat, 10-5, clsd Wed, Unr
Med size R/C stk, av cal, cnd and prices. BR Cheam, OOS on the other side turn right and cross crossroads, shop is on left. From Cheam take train south to Epsom, change and take another train north to Raynes Park, then another south to Norbiton or Thames Ditton. This is easier done than said.

De Tems ditto

ROBIN BOOKS **Thames Ditton**
6 High Street, Thames Ditton, Surrey
Mon-Sat, 10-5.30, clsd Wed
Med size R/C stk, nsoc, emphon Children's and Ill but does have other int bks, if only they would do something about the prices it would be on the way to being a Drif Special. AWYW and can be netgow. BR Thames Ditton, OOS turn right, and follow road into town.

ELIZABETH GANT **Thames Ditton**
52 High Street, Thames Ditton, Surrey
Mon-Sat, 10.30-5.30, Wed clsd. Rel
Med size R/C stk, emphon Childrens and Ill, ab av cal. Etgow. Directions as above.

BROWSERS **East Molesey**
74 Walton Road, East Molesey, Surrey
Tues-Sat, 10-5, clsd Wed
Small/med R stk with pretensions to being C. A Helen Hanff Special. BR Hampton Court, OOS cross road towards shops and follow main stream of traffic and bear right at roundabout past police station.

THE MOLE BOOKSHOP **East Molesey**
81 Walton Road, East Molesey, Surrey
Sats Rel - and some other days
Med size R/C stk, av cal, cnd and prices. Etgow. Keen on mountaineering. T. The one thing he does do exceptionally well is price the bks. Not the actual prices but the small stickers he puts inside the bks with the prices on them. This shows a respect for books lacking in most Dealers.

DERRICK NIGHTINGALE **Kingston u Thames**
32 Coombe Rd, Kingston upon Thames, Surrey
Mon-Sat, 9-5.30, Wed 1pm, Rel
Med size R/C/D stk, av cal, cnd and prices. Emphon 19th Century Lit. It is sad but true that thisis now the only serious s/h bksp in a huge arc from Richmond to Croydon. The only one left of a distinguished line. At first this closure

rate seems odd for such a middle class area, but when you consider that the PBFA's highest provincial membership is in Surrey all is explained. The bookfairies having depleted the stocks, now fish in richer seas.

HAMPTON STATION CHARITY BOOKSHOP **Hampton**
Hampton Station, Middlesex
Mon-Sun, 10-4
Small R stk, ab av for a charity shop. Mainly included and admired because it does it right, and it opens on a Sunday. I have no idea what this charity is for, nordo I care. They want my money and they sell books to get it. This place should act as a consultancy to other charities. I have often wondered why there is no out of town shopping mall entirely devoted to Charity Shops. It could be in a truly obscure location, which would mean that it would be extremely cheap, but the customers would have no problem finding it because even twenty five miles away, you would be able to hear the assistants bickering.

IAN SHERIDAN **Hampton**
34 Thames Street, Hampton, Middlesex
Mon-Sun, 10-7, Rel
Lg R/C stk. This is your chance to have a small part in a West End style production. This stage is set so that the owner can always star (previous commitments make it occasionally necessary to have an understudy but the aura lingers on). He certainly seems to be getting better scripts these days but no part work is considered too insignificant. Everything is taken in, the old, the neglected, even the unusable. The prices are from the pit to the gallery, but some confusion reigns over which is which. The intermission coffee is a lot better than served in most West End theatres as is the repartee. The encores can be a bit wearing. BR, OOS turn right and left at Percy Road into Thames St.

MARION PITMAN **Twickenham**
29 Hampton Road, Twickenham, Middlesex
This shop is both good and promising in that it has promised to close down for good. It is conveniently open only on Saturday afternoons: Thus it may be conveniently ignored the rest of the week. It is a shop for the mind and to be mined. It should be mined by those who mind about books. The owner is for animals and four animals: Squirrel, vixen, sloth and mammoth. The animals she and her stock are for is silverfish. BR Strawberry Hill, OOS into Wellesley Road and right into Walpole Road and left at Hampton Road.

ANTHONY HALL **Twickenham**
30 Staines Road, Twickenham, Middlesex
Mon-Fri, 9-5.30, clsd Wed at 1pm, Rel
Med size Spec with some Gen stk which is well worth looking at. Emphon Russia and Eastern Europe. From Hampton Road turn right into third cross street and right at Staines Road.

ALEC THORNE **Richmond**
9 Brewers Lane, Richmond upon Thames, Surrey
Mon-Sat, 9.30-5.30, clsd wed pm ***STOP PRESS: NOW CLOSED***
Small/med sized Junior HARRINGTON type stk.

BR & Tube Richmond, OOS turn left and cross road, follow round, third on right.

BALDUR BOOKSHOP **Richmond**
44 Hill Rise, Richmond, Surrey
Mon-Sat, 9.30-5.30, clsd Wed
Med size R/C stk av cal, cnd and prices. A Helen Hanff Special. BR Richmond, OOS and left past bridge up hill to left. There are also a small number of Children's bks in Richmond Traders at 32 Hill Rise.

W & A HOUBEN **Richmond**
2 Church Court, Richmond, Surrey
Mon-Sat, 10-6
New bksp with lg bsmt of s/h R/C bks, av cal, cnd and prices. TWC. BR Richmond, OOS turn left past where road divides.

LLOYDS **Kew**
9 Mortlake Terrace, Kew, Surrey
Mon-Sat, 10-5.30, Rel
Spec Gardening bksp with med size R/C stk, ab av cal, cnd and prices. TWC. Tube Kew Gardens, OOS straight ahead towards Kew Gardens and turn right at main road and right at traffic lights.

BOOKCELLAR **Earlsfield**
404 Garret Lane, Earlsfield, London SW18
Mon-Sat, 10-7
Med size R/C stk, slightly remaindery. Av cal, cnd and prices. BR Earlsfield, OOS turn left and shop is on right.

LISA MATHEWS **Earlsfield**
213 Garret Lane, Earlsfield, London SW18
Mon-Sat, 10.30-5.30
Med size R/C stk, av cal, NSOC, Hollywood prices. Emphon Detective fiction. T & Disc. You can spot it the moment you go through the door, the owner of this shop saw the film "The Big Sleep" and instantly wanted to be thelady in the bksp who let down her hair. I had not the heart to tell her that the big sleep is something most bookdealers do in their clothes. A Book & Magazine Collector Special.

IN A CLASS OF ITS OWN

THE FARRINGDON ROAD BOOKSTALL

Mon-Fri, 11-3, Sat 9.30.
Small, med and lg, battered, windswept, rained upon and frozen, varied but boring, different but mundane. High turnover but always replaced by similar items. This is just the customers but it is amazing how much they resemble the books. Tube Farringdon Road, OOS turn right and right.

ROUTE 12 O'CLOCK

NEWCASTLE

THE SCARFACED BEAU BRUMMEL

Newcastle is defined as anywhere covered by the £2.50 Metro Rover ticket which can be bought at the Central Station, but not elsewhere. The metro system is completely automatic but in an attempt to add some charm bands of roving inspectors have been instructed to appear as ferocious as possible. They all look like the baddies in Toytown.

Despite their closeness to the station it is not possible to get to all the shops in one day. *(RC: Not if you eat in every veggie restaurant in Newcastle it is not).* It is best to start at Steedman's which is the only shop to open at 9am. *(RC: Best not faced with a hangover).*

ROBERT A STEEDMAN **Newcastle**
8 Grey Street, Newcastle.
Mon-Sat, 9-5, Sat 12.30, V.Rel
Med size C/D stk, ab av cal, cnd and prices. AWYW, but so politely that it is almost a pleasure. The books at the front despite being their rejects can be extremely int. The ones at the back, behind the barrier, tend to be the main business. Solid Leather, Plate Bks and Local History. BR Central Station, OOS turn right and left at first main junction. Shop is disguised as a Building Society.

BEWICK BOOKS **Newcastle**
14 Clayton Road, Jesmond, Newcastle
Mon-Sat, 10.30-4, V.Rel
An antique shop with a BTA stk of s/h bks. Small (for a s/h bksp) but very well chosen, most antique Ds cannot stand bks mainly because they are so low priced, to them anything which is a hundred years old should be worth a fortune. Metro Jesmond, OOS double back parallel to rail line. (That swine RC always complains that I get streets the wrong way round, in Jesmond they have the station the wrong way round). Turn first left into Clayton Road.

BAY BOOKS **Newcastle**
10a Norman Road, Whitley Bay, Newcastle.
Mon, Thurs-Sat, 10.30-5
Small R stk primarily pbks, extremely good cnd. Some hardbacks, av cal and prices. TWC. P. poss. Metro Monkseaton, OOS, turn right into Norman Road and head for Whitley Bay.

OLIVERS BOOKSHOP **Newcastle**
48a Whitley Road, Whitley Bay, Newcastle
Mon-Sat, 11-5, clsd Wed
Med size R/C stk, nearly Ds. Takes a lot of perusing but can be worth it. P. poss. Metro Whitley Bay, OOS ahead and first right, nearly NAST.

AVENUE BOOKS **Newcastle**
Land of Green Ginger Front Street, Tynemouth.
Mon-Sat, 11-5, Rel

Med size R/C stk keen on Nat His and Ornithology. Av cal, cnd and prices. TWC. P. poss.

KEEL ROW BOOKS **Newcastle**
11 Fenwick Terrace, Preston Road, North Shields, Tyne & Wear
Mon & Fri, 10.30-5, Tue & Thur 2-6, Sat 10-5, Wed clsd.
Now close your eyes and I defy you to remember those hours. It took me ten minutes just to write them down. I think the 2 mornings off are the times he attends the local looney bin, and on the Wednesday he wallows in his collection of text books on advanced torture. Only a sadist would have such hours and only a masochist would go into this shop. From the outside it is very attractive but then so are Rottweilers. It is not until you are inside that you have doubts. After two hours looking into the jaws of his out and out dogs and being repulsed, I was terrified I had rabies. I certainly had not picked up anything else. I was dying to bite somebody and I was desperate for a drink. I looked at the owner but he seemed well chewed and his jokes were completely dry. I did not leave: I was put down. Metro North Shields, OOS, breathe in and smell all the charity shops, they may be poor, but you do stand a chance of the first bite, turn left and right at the top and left past the church, which has a notice advertising the local Samaritans. I suppose it is better than nothing but before I go in this shop again and indulge in a dogfight I shall be consulting a Spitfire Veteran.

In all honestly I must admit that I have met one person who thinks this shop is quite good: he wears a dog collar.

There is also a paperback shop in Cullercoats, by the Stn.

NORTH SHIELDS BOOKS **Newcastle**
7 Kirton Park Terrace, North Shields
Mon-Sat, 11-5.30, clsd Wed. Rel
Med size R/C stk needs some perusing. Very good cnd, av prices. Etgow. WAD. P. Poss. Does not conform to my belief that neat and tidy shops are always boring, after the last place it was a considerable relief. T & Disc. Continue past hospital - the services of which you may need if you frequent Keel Row.

The shop in South Shields is now closed. The two shops in Sunderland are for schizophrenics only.

DAVIS BOOKS **Newcastle**
140 Westgate Road, Newcastle
Mon-Sat, 10-5
New bksp with small/med remaindery stk. TWC. BR & Metro Central, OOS ahead, across into alleyway and turn left at second junction.

THE NEWCASTLE BOOKSHOP **Newcastle**
1 Side, Newcastle
Tue-Sat, 10-5, Rel
Med sized R/C/D stk, av cal, cnd and prices. Res stk of Applied Art & Design bks, ab av cal, cnd, av prices. WAD. Etgow. P. poss. BR Newcastle, OOS turn right and first right at junction, down towards river.

HENCOTES BOOKS AND ANTIQUES **Hexham**
8 Hencotes, Hexham, Northumberland
Mon - Sat, 9.30-4.30, Thur 3.00. V.Rel No lunch hour
Med size R/C stk, a Drif Special. BR Hexham, OOS turn left and right into town. Follow path into centre and shop is to right of Abbey. Keep to left of abbey and turn right at end of green. Nearest. Carlisle. Newcastle. Settle.

BLYTH

NOT "BLYTH IT WAS THAT DAWN TO BE ALIVE", BUT "HAIL TO THEE BLYTHE SPIRIT"

SKELTER **Blyth**

Tues,Thur,Fri 4.30-6, Sat 10-5
What outrageous act of normalcy could ever have possessed them to open on a Saturday, had it not been for that I would have given them the prize for the most original hours in Britain. True I would have liked them to stay open later in the evening but this is at least a step in the right direction. It is also true that I have not quite made it to this shop yet, but it is exactly the sort of place I like to worship, from afar. I have no idea what Blyth is like but I bet that there is a video shop there and I also bet that the video shop stays open until at least 8pm. Videos, for those of you who have not yet come across such strange things are those objects that you mistake for books in junk shops. The shops that hire them out do not need to post any times because the customers know that they will be open late at night.

BELFORD BOOKSHOP **Belford**
Market Place, Belford, Northumbria
Mon-Sat, 10-5, clsd Thur.
Med size R/C stk, av cal, cnd and prices. ETF. Nearest Scotland, Newcastle.

There is a small secondhand bookshop in Wooler but I have not got there, yet.

UNIVERSITY BOOKSHOP **Durham**
55/57 Saddler Street, Durham DH1 3ET
Mon-Sat, 9.30-5
New bksp with bta R/C stk, av cnd and prices. Acad/student orientated. BR Durham, OOS down into town turn left over bridge into market square and acute right up hill. There is a market stall which has a lg stk at home (Thur-Sat only and there is theological/general room in the market square, and that is it. Shotton' is almost solely prints.

VOKES & SON **Darlington**
14 Bondgate, Darlington
Mon-Sat, 9-5.30
Med size R/C/D stk slightly bookfairy, av cal, cnd and prices. T. P. poss. BR Darlington, OOS down drive turn left into town centre and right at T junction and first left. Nearest Durham, Stockton, Thirsk, Barnard Castle.

BARNARD GALLERY **Stockton**
No 3 Yard, Stockton, Cleveland
Tues-Sat, 10-4.30, Sat 5. clsd Thur
Small R/C stk, a Drif Special. Etgow. P. diff. BR Stockton, OOS into town right at T junction and left down alleyway by Market Hall and look for sign saying tourist information. Nearest Newcastle, Redcar, Stokesley, Darlington.

BRITISH FRAIL has the cheek to call Stockton Station: the heritage trail. It looks just like the station in Bolivia in the film Butch Cassidy and the Sundance Kid. It shows British Frails embarrassment at its heritage that it has allowed this station to become so neglected. It was here that railways were born and now like some incontinent relative it is being left to die. There is no need for British Frail to join the Heritage industry, all it needs is a little pride in its own history. If this were the first airport in the world, it would be a sacred shrine. Trains pass through it with the regularity of a constipated snail. British Frail sees it as a piece of youthful achne, a blackhead that is not discussed in polite company. They have cast it off like an old nappy.

The Engineers who created this work of genius, this straight line between two points deserve better that these spendthrift offspring. In their hearts they know they have wasted a great inheritance, that they have despoiled one of the greatest fortunes ever left in Britain. They cling to the money lenders terrified to throw off the cloak of indebtedness. Petrified to stand up and say it works, and we will make it profitable. Instead they talk of mealy mouthed profit centres, they mutter of retrenchment, and all the time they are taking money from local councils, from central government, from anybody who will give it to them at any price of self-abasement. Their only inventiveness is in finding new ways of sponging money.

To sit on Stockton station and wait two hours for a train is to see what a load of hypocrisy British Frail talks. If there had been management it would be possible to blame it. If there had been risks it would have been possible to criticise them. If there had been imagination it would have been possible to contemplate it.

THE GREAT AYTON BOOKSHOP **Great Ayton**
17 High Street, Great Ayton, North Yorkshire
Tues-Sat, 10-5.30, Wed 2. Sunday 2-5.30
Med size R/C stk av cal, cnd and prices. Not the world's most exciting but it is to be commended for opening on a Sunday. BR Great Ayton, ETF in centre of village. Nearest: Redcar, Scarborough, Helmsley, Stokesley.

THE STOKESLEY BOOKSHOP **Stokesley**
63 High Street, Stokesley, Cleveland
Mon-Sat, 10-5
Med size R/C stk keen on Mod 1sts, av cal, cnd and prices. TWC. P. poss. ETF in centre of town, BR Middlesbrough. V. NAST. Nearest Stockton, Great Ayton, Helmsley, Darlington.

REDCAR BOOKSHOP/...

REDCAR BOOKSHOP **Redcar**
39 Lord Street, Redcar, North Yorkshire
Tues-Sat, 10-5, clsd Thurs. Rel
Med size R stk, nrly a Drif Special, the prices bring it up to 49% but it needs that little bit more effort. Etgow. P. poss. BR Redcar, OOS towards clock towers and right into Lord Street. Nearest: Stockton, Saltburn, Stokesley.

If you come out of the above shop, turn left and left, there is another secondhand bookshop. There is no name on this street, there is no number on the door, there are no names or telephone numbers posted, there are no hours advertised for this is a designer bookshop. Painted black, and looking like something that would feature in Harper's Bazaar, it is indeed extremely attractive.

There is about this type of place an atmosphere that if you have to ask what hip means then you are not hip. Well bloody right, I am not hip. I am a lunatic who spends his life going round Britain, collecting secondhand books, but what am I supposed to do? Come back some other day? But what day, and how am I supposed to remember the name of the street and when? What do they expect me to do, move to Redcar? Why is it that the people who go in for designer products cannot come up with a simple handwritten notice, giving the name of the shop, the address, the telephone number, the opening hours, and a PS saying that they do not want me to call? Groucho Marx has a joke about not wanting to join any club that would have him as a member, but in the club of designer bookshops if you want to be a member then you are exactly the person they do not want.

SALTBURN BOOKSHOP **Saltburn**
3 Amber Street, Saltburn, Cleveland
Wed-Sat, 11-5, L 1-2, Rel
Med size R/nrly C stk. I had always remembered this place as being a Drif Special but it just did not seem to be making it this time round. Then I started asking for books and the place went up in my estimation, however I was not so successful that I could talk my way into the back room. T & Disc. BR Saltburn OOS on left hand side straight ahead and second left. Nearest Guisborough, Redcar, Scarborough.

HAMBLETON BOOKS **Thirsk**
43 Market Place, Thirsk, Yorkshire
Mon-Sat, 9.30-5, clsd Wed during winter
New bksp with lg rear stk of bks, av cal, cnd and prices. Keen on geology, res stk. BR: Thirsk, nearly NAST. OOS turn left towards town then ETF. Nearest: Durham, Helmsley, York, Boroughbridge.

BATES AND HINDMARCH **Boroughbridge**
Fishergate, Boroughbridge, North Yorks
Mon-Sat, 10.30-5
Small/med R/C stk which they price at ab D's prices. Emphon travel, especially India. ETF. BR: Thirsk, NAST (10 miles). Nearest: Thirsk, York, Harrogate, Ripon.

THE HARD CORPS

There has been a lot of chipping away at the granite face which the local leaflet does its best to disguise. It gives the impression there are dozens of shops, but in truth there are nine. It also leaves out one of the more interesting ones for having offended so many people, which is one of the problems with local leaflets; if they leave out shops you know about are they also leaving out shops you do not know about? It is sad, but there is no rehabilitation of offenders act for bookdealers.

SPELMAN'S **York**
70 Micklegate, York
Mon-Sat, 9-5.30, V.Rel
Lg R/C/D stk ab av cal, cnd and prices. Res stk of antqrn bks. The best thing about this shop is the opening hours especially the 9am part. The bks are almost solid roast beef, the sort you are supposed to have read, but never do. TWC. P. diff. BR: York, OOS turn left down drive and right through arch and left.

O'FLYNN ANTIQUARIAN BOOKS **York**
35 Micklegate, York
Mon-Sat, 9-6
Med/lg R/C stk. Emphon prints. NSOC. Adventurous prices. The only central shop in York which is int to look at. Merchant Navy School of Bookdealing Special. T & Disc. BR York OOS down hill into town and turn second to the right.

RC writes
The real reason the prop likes this shop so much, and the other dealers in York and elsewhere are so wary, has nothing to do with the stock, but is all to do with Mr. O'Flynn's sense of style. Whilst we were giving it the once over a rep from the local newspaper rang up trying to sell Mr. O'Flynn some advertising space. It took him a few minutes to remember but the same thing had happened the previous year, and when he did recollect the circumstances did he go into battle! He lambasted the newspaper for placing the ad poorly, he was appalled at the layout, he complained about a non-complimentary remark in the accompanying text, and he fulminated against newspapers in general. All this would have gone for nothing - what truly impressed the prop was that Mr. O'Flynn had not paid for the advert, and was telling the rep this. Not only had the rep walked into a man trap, he had not got a sniff of the bait. The idea that you could not only not pay the bills but hit your creditors over the head had not occurred to the prop before.

TAIKOO **York**
29 High Petergate, York
Mon-Fri, owner says BTR, but I have never seen a time when it was not attended.
Med size spec in Foreign Travel, very high cal, very good cnd, av prices, owner says. The bks are superlative, and this is just the ones on show (there are two res stks). What he should do is give lessons to all the other idiots who claim that they deal in travel and topography. WAD. P. diff

JACK DUNCAN'S York
36 Fossgate, York
Mon-Sat, 10-5.30, V.Rel
Lg C/D stk, a bookfairies idea of what a bksp should look like. This one consists of six sharing, and even though they do it better than one would expect, it has a curious leftover feel about it. Emphon Lit & Music. TWC. P.diff.

MINSTERGATES BOOKSHOP York
8 Minstergates, York
Mon-Sat, 10-5.30, Rel
Med size R/C stk, tourist orientated, emphon Folklore. Av cal, cnd and prices. TWC. P.diff.

A Bookstall has opened in Newark. NV.

BRIDGE BOOKSHOP Deeping St James
106 Church Street, Deeping Saint James, Peterborough
Mon-Sat, 10.30-5.30, Sun 2.30-5, clsd Thurs
Med size R/C stk, av cal, cnd and prices. TWC. Emphon local history. BR Peterborough (NAST 10 miles). ETF. Nearest Holbeach, Kings Lynn, Peterborough, Stamford.

ROBERT HUMM Stamford
Station House, Stamford, Lincolnshire
Mon-Sat, 9.30-5.30, V.Rel
Med size spec in Railway bks, new and s/h. Ab av cal, cnd, av prices. TWC. P.poss. BR: Stamford. Shop is on station. Nearest: Nottingham, Oakham, Peterborough, Wellingborough.

ST MARY'S BOOKS Stamford
9 St Mary's Hill, Stamford, Lincolnshire
Mon-Sun, 8.30-5.30 V.Rel
Small/med size R/C stk, nrly a Drif Special. Ave cal, cnd and prices. TWC. P.diff. BR: Stamford, OOS turn right at road and first left. Shop is at rear of newsagents over bridge.

CHEYNE LANE BOOKSHOP Stamford
Cheyne Lane, Stamford, Lincolnshire
Tues,Wed,Fri 10.30-4.30, Sat 10-2 & 2-4.30
Small R/C stk, bta. P.imposs. Continue into town turn right into Castle Street, Cheyne Lane is alleyway on left.

STANILAND BOOKSELLERS Stamford
4/5 Saint George's Street, Stamford, Lincolnshire
Mon-Sat, 10-5, V.Rel
Lg R/C/C stk, ab av cal, extremely good cnd. Av prices. TWC. P.diff. Despite the lg size of the stk there is no fiction and strangely this is reflected in the non fiction. There is no imagination in it either. It is as if the non fiction bks, having seen their relatives in fiction eliminated, are on their best behaviour for fear that the same fate may befall them. Continue up Cheyne Lane and turn right and right.

COUNTY BOOKSHOP Oakham
34 Northgate, Oakham, Rutland, Leicestershire
Mon-Sat, 10-5, Rel
Med/Lg R/C stk, slightly low key but does have some int bks

after you have waded through the crud. TWC. P.poss. Nearest as Stamford. BR: Oakham, OOS over bridge turn right out of exit and first left.

GOLDMARK BOOKS **Uppingham**
Orange Street, Uppingham, Rutland, Leics
Mon-Sat, 9-6, V.Rel
Med/Lg R/C stk, av cal, cnd and prices. A middling bksp in the middle of England where the owner speaks for England. TWC. P. poss. BR Oakham, NAST six miles. Nearest: Oakham, Peterborough, Wellingborough, Leicester.

THE RUTLAND BOOKSHOP **Uppingham**
13 High Street, Uppingham, Rutland, Leics
Tues-Sat, 11-1 and 2.15-5.30, clsd Thurs
Med size R/C stk, emphon Huntin' Shootin' and Fishin'. Despite which it is almost a Drif Special mainly because of the scatty lady who runs it. TWC. P.poss. From Goldmark's turn left and first right.

NOT JUST BOOKS **Uppingham**
Market Place (no No.) Uppingham, Rutland, Leics
Mon-Sat, 9.30-5.30
Med/Lg R/C stk nrly. It is not just prices as well. TWC. P.poss. From Rutland bksp go back down high street into Market Square and shop is above Midland Bank.

This route now leads on to Leicester

OLD SOKE BOOKS **Peterborough**
68 Burghley Road, Peterborough
Mon,Tues,Fri,Sat 10-5.30, Sat 5pm
Med/Lg R/C/D stk, av cal, NSOC, av prices. It would be WAD except that Peterborough is on all main routes. Vetgow. P.poss. BR Peterborough, OOS ahead, cross footbridge, turn left and right at shopping centre into Westgate St and left at Park Road which becomes Burghley Road. Nearest: Deepin St James, Ely, Bedford, Stamford.

T V COLES **Peterborough**
961 Lincoln Road, Peterborough
Mon-Sat, 10-5, clsed Wed. Rel
Med size R/C stk, av cal, cnd and prices. Keen on Military History. Slightly low key and an odd look about it. A Samuel Becket Drif Special. BR Petersborough, OOS onto main road and turn left and keep going, a military hike with Samuel Becket overtones. Nearest: Deeping St James, Ely, Hertford, Stamford.

THE FIRST GARDEN CITY
(a contest where coming second is preferable)

DAVID'S BOOKSHOP **Letchworth**
7 Eastcheap, Letchworth, Hertfordshire
Mon-Sat, 9-6 Rel.
New bksp with med size R/C stk av cal, cnd and prices. The most int thing about this shop is its smell. It is at the rear of a chemist and I would like to express my thanks to them because till I came in here I always thought that ladies

who smelt like this had not bathed. I thought that they had tried to disguise their reek by drowning it with cheap scent, I did not know you bought this smell retail. BR Letchworth, OOS to left and right into first shopping street. Nearest: Bedford, Sudbury, Hitchin, Aylesbury.

Hertford

THE OXFAM BOOKSHOP
9 Station Road, Hertford
Mon-Sat, 10.30-4.30, V.Rel
I never thought I would live to see the day when I would praise a charity bksp, butthis one has the supreme advantage over the official Hertford bksp in that it is open. No matter how bad a shop is, there is some hope when it is open. No matter how good a shop is, there is only irritation when it is clsd. The official shop in Hertford opens about as often as I praise charity bksps. BR Hertford, OOS turn right and continue. Nearest: Hitchin, Epping(London), Harpenden.

Hitchin

ERIC T MOORE
24 Bridge Street, Hitchin, Hertfordshire
Mon-Sat, 9.30-5.30, L 1-2.15, Wed 1, V.Rel
Med/Lg R/C stk, emphon Local History, solid roast beef, but there is also a room of res stk, which can be more int if you can gain entry. TWC. P.poss. BR Hitchin, OOS turn left into main road and continue to roundabout (1 mile) and turn right. Nearest: Letchworth, Hertford, Harpenden.

SCARBOROUGH, HULL, LINCOLN, KING'S LYNN, CAMBRIDGE, LONDON

SCARBOROUGH BOOKS — **Scarborough**
55 Castle Road, Scarborough, Yorks
Mon-Sun, 10-5.30 summer. Mon-Sat, 10-5 winter.
Med size R/C stk slightly remaindery, but possibly one of the best labelled shops of all time. Each section has a number and when somebody asks where a particular bk may be, the assistant simply tells them the number. Emphon Occult. TWC. P.poss. BR Scarborough, OOS slightly to right and ahead, right at Castle Road. Nearest: Saltburn, Bridlington, Helmsley.

There are also two antique shops with bks in Robin Hoods Bay.

PAST & PRESENTS — **Scarborough**
11a Ranshill Road, Scarborough
Mon-Sat, 11-5
Small R/C stk, low key in antique shop, av cnd and prices. BR Scarborough, OOS turn right and right, and over bridge and continue.

And as you come out of the station and go behind the Odeon Cinema there is an antique shop with bta bks, plus several junk shops.

J L BOOK EXCHANGE — **Bridlington**
72 Hildethorpe Road, Bridlington, Yorkshire
Mon-Sat, 8.30-8.30 summer. Mon-Sat 9-5.30 winter, Rel
Small R stk av cnd, cal and prices. TWC. KUTI. BR Bridlington, OOS turn to right tomain road and left about 100 yards. Nearest: Scarborough, Helmsley, Driffield.

THE DRIFFIELD BOOKSHOP — **Driffield**
21 Middle Street North, Driffield
Mon-Sat, 10-5.30, Thurs 6.30, Fri 10-8, V.Rel
Med size R/C/D stk, emphon on Mod 1sts and S/F. Ab av cal, cnd and prices. TWC. P.poss. BR Driffield, OOS turn right into town and continue to far side. Nearest: Bridlington, Helsey, Beverley.

The really int thing about the ab shop is that it opens late on Thurs and Fri. This makes it poss to visit all the shops on the Hull/Scarborough line in one day. Quite why more bksps do not open in the evening is hard to understand.

EASTGATE BOOKSHOP — **Beverley**
11 Eastgate, Beverley
Mon-Sat, 10-5, V.Rel
Med/lg R stk, av cal, cnd and prices. Also res stk of bks on Borneo. T. P.poss. BR Beverley, OOS take road at left of road ahead and first right. Nearest: Driffield, Cottingham, York.

ALEX ALEC SMITH — **Beverley**
31 Highgate, Beverley, Hull
Tues-Sat, 10-5, open Mon in summer
Med size R/C stk, ab av cal, cnd and prices. Bgns known. Emphon Lit. BR Beverley, OOS ahead and turn left and head for the Minster. Nearest: Driffield, Hull, York.

THE COTTINGHAM BOOKSHOP **Cottingham**
Cotta House, 169/171 Hallgate, Cottingham, Hull
Mon-Sat, 10-5, V.Rel
Med size R/C stk, ab av cal and cnd, av prices. A truly sensible shop. Small res stk. Etgow. TWC. BR Cottingham, OOS ahead turn right at Church Road and follow main road into town, shop is in arcade at far end on left. Nearest: Beverley, Hull, York.

From Hull to Scarborough is very easy to do by train and is possibly more lucrative than spending a day in York.

HULL

The British Remake of Dante's Inferno

KAYE BOOKS **Hull**
15-17 Hepworth Arcade, off Silver Street, Hull
Mon-Sat, 10-4.30, Thur 3
New bksp with small low key stk of R bks. I only included it in this section so that I could use that description of Hull.

HOW TO FIND A SECONDHAND BOOKSHOP

I had been told that there was a newly opened secondhand bookshop in Hull. Usually when I am given vague details I am extremely wary, several people enjoy sending me off on wild goose chases. To establish if there is any possibility of the rumour being true I ask them what other shops they know in the area, claiming complete ignorance myself. If they can get the ones I do know about right, then I am willing to give it a go.

Hull is a big place, but I had also been told that it was close to the University, unfortunately I had no idea where the University was. Education has never been one of my interests. At the railway station I got in a cab. This is not as extravagant as it may at first seem, taxi drivers are big readers and they often know where the local bookshops are, but the cab I got in had a driver who claimed there were no secondhand bookshops in Hull.

As I already knew of two this was not hopeful. I told him to drive me to the University. He went and asked his friend for directions.

On the way I kept my eyes peeled for health food shops, not out of hunger but there is not a secondhand bookshop in Britain that is not within walking distance of a health food shop.

The area around the University did not even have a grocery store, no wonder the students were so thin on the ground. I told the driver to go anywhere close that had a parade of shops, there was nowhere. I told him to take me back to the main shopping street and to stop outside the first charity shop he saw. The good news is that Hull has several charity shops but when I examined the books on the shelves they seemed to me to be the type that any local dealer would have snaffled immediately. They were extremely cheap and even if the dealer did not want them himself, he would have bought them to ensure that his potential customers did not get books more cheaply elsewhere.

I had to ask five ladies before I found one in the Blind charity shop who knew where the secondhand bookshop was. In my experience this is the thing that the ladies in charity shops love to tell, it makes them feel worthwhile, but I did notice that she had a curiously embarrassed look on her face. I gave the driver the address, and he looked at me and smiled. When we got to the place I saw why. It sold nothing but porn books. I am very much in favour of pornography, but I do not have to travel 200 miles to find it, there is more than enough in my local newsagent. Having worked in a pornographic bookstore I know that some of the staff can be highly literate people and when I enquired of the assistant he did indeed direct me to a bookshop. This turned out to be a religious one. (There are some very strange people who work in pornographic bookstores, but at least this was a step in the right direction).

By this time the taxi driver thought he was going to be able to retire and even I was wondering if I could afford the fare, but nonetheless I directed him to another shop that the religious bookstore owner had told me about.

This was not really a bookshop but a stationers, but whilst asking a customer, he told me that he had seen a secondhand bookshop on his way to school. I did not expect any interest in books from him; he was a schoolteacher. I got the address of the school and went in search of my cab driver. He remembered it well; he had been expelled from it. I asked him the most important question ... was there a health food shop handy? There was, we went.

I don't think I have ever found a bookshop in a more obscure place, even the taxi driver congratulated me as I parted with my last £20 note. BR Hull, OOS turn left, go all the way to the end of the road and turn left at the crossroads into a shopping street, turn right into next shopping street and third left towards a school.

CLEETHORPES

Where people who cannot afford Skegness go for their holidays

LAFAYETTE BOOKSELLERS Cleethorpes
6 High Street, Cleethorpes, Humberside
Tues-Sat, 10.30-4.30
Small R stk, av cal, cnd and prices. TWC. BR Cleethorpes, OOS turn right and left and first right. Nearest: Hull, Louth, Lincoln.

PIK A BOOK Cleethorpes
203 Grimsby Road, Cleethorpes, South Humberside
Mon-Sat, 10-5
Small R stk, primarily pbks. No T. From Lafayette continue west about one mile. There are also a couple of pbk shops in Grimsby.

JABBERWOCKY **Horncastle**
14 Saint Lawrence Street, Horncastle, Lincolnshire
Mon-Sat, 10-5
Med size R/C stk. Low key but not quite a Drif Special. Ave cnd, prices. TWC. P.poss. ETF or:

> Twas not brillig
> But the slythy cove did gyre and gimble in the way.
> All monies were the borrow groves
> And the home wrats out gave.

TIM SMITH'S BOOKS **Horncastle**
12 North Street, Horncastle, Lincolnshire
Mon-Sat, 10-5, clsd Wed. Rel
Med size R/C stk, a but unexciting, av cnd and prices. TWC. P.poss. BR Impossible. ETF. Nearest Louth, Boston, Lincoln.

LINCOLN

Religiously overlooked, but does offer a prayer of a chance

ELIZABETH NELSON **Lincoln**
Eastgate Antiques Centre, Eastgate, Lincoln.
Mon-Sat, 9.30-5, Rel.
Bta stall in antiques market, one of the few that succeeds in not being intimidating. Med size C bks, chosen with some care. Emphon collecting subjects. Ab av cnd, av prices. TWC. From Harlequin continue up hill past cathedral, turn right.

READERS REST **Lincoln**
13-14 Steep Hill, Lincoln
Mon-Sat, 9.30-5, often open on Sunday
Lg R stk confusingly mixed with new bks. It is extremely diff to peruse and the only reason for going in it is to rest from climbing the hill. TWC. BR Lincoln, OOS turn left and first right and head for the Cathedral. Nearest: Cleethorpes, Horncastle, Sleaford, Stamford.

HARLEQUIN GALLERY **Lincoln**
20-22 Steep Hill, Lincoln
Mon-Sat, 10.30-5, L 1-2.30 but often more extravagant on lunch
Med/lg C/D stk. Slightly roast beef with nouvelle cuisine trying to break through. Nrly WAD. TWC. as Readers Rest.

There are also some books in Frippery opp Harlequin and in the SPCK further up but neither counts as a proper s/h bksp.

ALAN REDMOND BOOKS **Billingborough**
25 High Street, Billingborough, Lincolnshire
Sat & Sun only. V.Rel - other times by easy appointment
Med size R/C stk, av cal, cnd and prices. Anoraksia Nervosa Special. Shop is in stables of private house. TWC. P.poss. BR Sleaford, NAST 5 miles. Nearest: Sleaford, Boston, Holbeach, Stamford.

WESTGATE BOOKSHOP **Sleaford**
45 Westgate, Sleaford, Lincolnshire
Mon-Sat, 10-5. Clsd Thurs, Rel
Med size R/C stk, a Drif Anoraksia Nervosa Special. The front of the shop is mainly pbks but there is a shed at the rear which responds to investigation but because of the cold the responses tend to diminish. The whole place is run as if they were rehearsing the pilot programme of a BBC comedy series about s/h bksps. Several people came in but mainly to audition. However I did like the joke: Have you any books of E.M. Forster? What did he write? Mainly paperbacks. BR Sleaford, OOS turn right and left and left at Market Square. Nearest: Boston, Horncastle, Peterborough.

There is also a print/bksp in Holbeach but NV.

PILGRIM BOOKS **Boston**
7 Red Lion Street, Boston, Lincolnshire
Wed 9-4 and Sat 9-5.
Med size R/C stk. Not quite a Drif Special as it is too neat but definitely WAD because of the prices. T. P.poss. BR Boston, OOS head for large church, turn left into Bank St and cut through Woolworths, shop to right. (Motorists should note that the right hand door is the only one wide enough.) Nearest: Horncastle, Holbeach, Sleaford.

BOOKWORM **King's Lynn**
15 Church Street, King's Lynn, Norfolk
Mon-Sat, 11-4
Med size R/C stk would be a drif special if it were not for the prices. P.poss. King's Lynn is to be congratulated on having more than adequate street maps, at the station and elsewhere. Nearest: Snettisham, Fakenham, Cambridge, Boston. **STOP PRESS: Shop has now moved to Tower Street. NFDA.**

THE DIAMOND BOOKSHOP **King's Lynn**
1 Diamond Terrace, King's Lynn, Norfolk
Sat 11-3 (which has a certain sense of style, but it is easy enough to ring up and ask to see the bks without obligation)
This must be the bksp with the shortest hours in Britain and despite being so thin she does not ever contemplate going to lunch. Med siz R/C stk, a Drif Special. Keen on music. T & Disc. P.poss. BR King's Lynn, OOS turn left and head west turn right at Saddlebed Road and shop is by Union Chapel (total about 2 miles but WAD).
RC writes
What a pervert he is, they only have to be female and over middle age and they can do nothing wrong. You look up the shop in Richmond and he nearly has hysterics because it only opens on a Saturday.

[There is a slight difference. This shop is admirably placed if you were coming from London or Leicester or Lincoln you will arrive in King's Lynn at around lunchtime. There is also a s/h shop, which is also WAD. Many of the other shops in this area only open on Saturday (Boston, Billingborough, Snettisham and Peterborough). But most crucially this shop is on a natural route. It is a crossing point for Norwich, the North Norfolk coast and for Cambridge.]

RC writes
Lying toad, why he really likes it is that you can get to King's Lynn on a network card

THE ELY BOOKSHOP **Ely**
11a St Mary's Street, Ely, Cambridgeshire
Mon-Sat, 10-3, clsd Tues, open long in summer.
Med size R/C stk, ab av cal & cnd, av prices. Slightly roast beef. T. P.poss. BR Ely, OOS head for cathedral and turn left opposite High Street. Nearest: Snettisham, Bury, Cambridge, Peterborough.

TORC BOOKS **Snettisham**
9 Hall Road, Snettisham, Norfolk
Sats 10-6 and allegedly Mon,Wed & Fri am
Med size R/C stk almost the epitome of a country town bksp. Av cal, cnd and prices. P.poss. BR King's Lynn (NAST 15 miles), ETF in downtown Snettisham (the bit by the bus stop). Nearest: Fakenham, Kings Lynn.

CAMBRIDGE

At the dawn of the Railway Era the local council decided to have as little to do with trains as was humanly possible. Permission was given for the railway station to be sited as far from the centre of Cambridge as was possible and yet still be called Cambridge.

Next the council set its mind to attempting to avoid the motor car, by prevaricating for as long as possible, but even it had to take notice some time and in 1960 motor cars were banned from the centre of Cambridge.

Now much to its horror Cambridge City Council have discovered that cycles can be a hazard and they are attempting to ban them.

Cambridge is renowned as a centre of advanced thinking.

G. DAVID **Cambridge**
3 Saint Edwards Passage, Cambridge
Mon-Sat, 9.30-5 Rel
Med size R/C/D stk, av cal & cnd, ab av prices. There is a second shop across the way which mainly stocks remainders and there is also a market stall in the nearby square. TWC. P.diff. BR Cambridge, OOS ahead turn right at main road and continue towards centre of town at square turn left and passage is ahead to the left. Nearest: Ely, Bury St Edmunds, Hertford, Bedford.

THE HAUNTED BOOKSHOP **Cambridge**
9 St. Edwards Passage, Cambridge
Mon-Sat, 9.30-5.30, L 1-2
Med size C/D stk, emphon childrens, ab av cal, cnd, av prices. Extremely knowledgable and helpful, directions as David's.

DEIGHTON BELL **Cambridge**
13 Trinity Street, Cambridge
Mon-Sat, 9.30-5.30, V.Rel

Med size C/D stk, emphon Lit, Bib and Antqrn. Ab av cal, cnd and prices. Very polite old style shop. TWC. From Haunted Bksp go back down passage turn left and Trinity St is off right hand corner of square.

QUINTO **Cambridge**
34 Trinity Street, Cambridge
Mon-Sat, 9-6, Rel
Med/lg R/C stk with pretentions to being D stk, ab av prices, av cal, cnd. Opp Deighton Bell.

GREEN STREET BOOKSHOP **Cambridge**
3 Green Street, Cambridge
Mon-Fri, 9.15-5. Sat 9.30-4.30. Rel
Med size C/D stk, very Acad, ab av cal, cnd and prices. Very helpful. T. Green St is at the side of Deighton Bell, their main shop round the corner now sells remainders only.

***THE UNMAUDLIN BOOKSOP** **Cambridge**
12a Magdalene Street, Cambridge
Mon-Sat, 10.30-6, Sun 2-5, Rel
Med size R/C stk, emphon fiction and politics. The only bksp in Cambridge that does not have a daunting atmosphere. T. P.diff. From Sidney Street continue north over bridge. SIOL.

THE OXFAM BOOKSHOP **Cambridge**
Sidney Street, Cambridge.
Mon-Sat, 10.30-4.30
Med size R/C stk bta charity shop, indeed this one is purpose built... by Galloway & Porter.

BURY BOOKSHOP **Bury St Edmunds**
28a Hatter Street, Bury St Edmunds, Suffolk
Mon-Sat, 9.30-5.30, Rel
New bksp with med size stk of R/C bks. Much bta for a new bksp. BR Bury St Edmunds, follow signs to town centre, turn left at south east corner of market square and first right. Nearest: Kings Lynn, Ipswich, Sudbury, Cambridge.

RC writes
I like that south east corner of Market Square. That creep gets lost every time he goes to Bury. Unless he gives the actual names of the streets never trust a word he says, mind you I would never trust a word he says anyway.

ROUTE 2 O'CLOCK

E A S T   A N G L I A

NORTH NORFOLK, NORWICH, IPSWICH, COLCHESTER

THE NORTH NORFOLK NORFIA

THE TIN DRUM BOOKSHOP **Fakenham**
32 Oak Street, Fakenham, Norfolk
Mon-Sat, 10-6, Wed 1
Lg R/C/D stk, a much more int than usual shop. NSOC and variable pricing, but this only adds to its charm. The owner is genuinely interested in trying to help you rather than just sell you a book. This is so rare in the s/h book business that it takes some getting used to, but you could spend a lot of time in this place just doing that. Res stk. P. poss. T & Disc. Vetgow. The disadvantage is that it is miles from anywhere. BR King's Lynn 20 miles. In Fakenham shop is to left of church going out of town. Nearest: Wells Next Sea, Holt, Wymondham, Kings Lynn.

There is a new bksp with some bks in Wells Road but seems to be subject to some disorder and there is also a record shop in Swaffham with some s/h bks. NV.

COOK **Wells Next Sea**
65 Straithe Street, Wells Next Sea, Norfolk
Mon-Sun, 10-5, less in winter
Small R/touristy shop av cal, cnd and prices. BR King's Lynn (NAST 25 miles, ETF at right angles to the mud front - it should be called Wells Next Mud. Nearest: Sheringham, Fakenham, King's Lynn.

SIMON GOUGH **Holt**
5 Fish Street Hill, Holt, Norfolk
Mon-Sat, 9.30-5.30
Med/lg C/D stk, emphon HSF. Av cal, ab av prices, solid roast beef come bookfairy. T & Disc. P.poss. Shop is in road one block beyond parking space. BR Sheringham, NAST 10 miles. Nearest: Sheringham, Norwich, Fakenham.

PETER'S BOOKSHOP **Sheringham**
19 St Peter's Road, Sheringham, Norfolk
Mon-Sun 10-6, summer. Winter clsd Sun,Mon,Wed
Lg R/C stk much bta tourist aimed shop which it appears to be from the hours. Almost a Drif Special. Av cnd and prices. BR Sheringham, OOS turn right and 2nd right. Nearest: Wells, Holt, Cromer.

BOOKWORMS **Cromer**
9 New Street, Cromer, Norfolk
Mon-Sat, 10-5, Sun 2-5, clsd Wed
Small/med sized R/C stk, bta cnd, av prices and cal. Well worth a look. BR Cromer, OOS left into town at main street, continue straight ahead and then turn left at end. Nearest: Sheringham, Norwich, Holt.

<u>NO WRICH, NO POOR</u>

Well worth a day now that it has the splendidly named Tombland Bookshop whose stock is definitely not for zombies. It makes you feel very much alive to see it. It is possible to get to all the shops in one day by train, but it is extremely difficult by car. Nearest: Cromer, Great Yarmouth, Wymondham, Holt.

THE TOMBLAND BOOKSHOP **Norwich**
8 Tombland, Norwich
Mon-Sat, 9.30-5, V.Rel
Med/lg R/C/D stk, ab av cal, av cnd, ab av prices but bgns known. The male half of the management does a splendid impression of Bertie Wooster which is a pose several successful book Ds in Britain attempt but none so successfully as him. WAD and definitely the best shop in East Anglia. BR Norwich, OOS turn right and left into town, keep to right hand side of road and turn left at first main junction, opp Anglia TV. Nearest Cromer, Gt Yarmouth, Beccles, Wymondham.

ST MICHAEL AT PLEA BOOKSHOP **Norwich**
Bank Plain, Norwich, Norfolk
Mon-Sat, 9.30-5
Med size R/C stk in an old church converted (if that is the right word) into an Antiques arcade. Bta for such and also non intimidating. TWC. P.diff. From Tombland go back, turn first right and look for church to left.

THE MOVIE SHOP **Norwich**
11 St Gregory's Alley, Norwich
Mon-Sat, 10-5
Small nrly spec shop of film memorabilia, but it does have some R/C/D bks, NSOC but more int that you might expect from the name. T & Disc. P.imposs. From St Michael at Plea continue east keeping to left and turn left into alleyway past church.

HENRY COLLINSON **Norwich**
Bagley's House, Bagley Court, Pottergate, Norwich
Mon-Sat, 8-5.30 (that is what it says here!)
Primarily a camera shop, the owner is distinctly unkeen that it should be known as a s/h bksp, and who can blame him but he will have to do a lot worse on the bookside not to attract attention. Med size R/C stk, ab av int, av prices and very pleasantly quirky. From Movie shop turn right and left.

SCIENTIFIC ANGLIAN **Norwich**
30 St Benedict St, Norwich
Times to suit owner
Med/lg R/C stk, NSOC, a silverfish special, av prices. From Movie shop turn left and left.

TRISTRAM AND JULIA HULL **Norwich**
72 St Benedict St, Norwich
Tues-Sat, 10-5.30, L 1-2, clsd Thurs
Med sized C/D stk, emphon Art and Design, especially printing. Ab av cal cnd and prices.

PETER CROWE **Norwich**
75 Upper St Giles Street, Norwich
Mon-Sat, 9.30-5.30
Lg R/C/D stk, ab av cal, cnd, av prices. Emphon roast beef and Local History, res stk next door (both shops are now combined). More promising than it looks. TWC. From Hull OOS turn left and cut through to next major street parallel and turn right towards church.

J R & H K ELLIS **Norwich**
53 St Giles Street, Norwich
Mon-Sat, 8-5.30
Med/lg R/C stk slightly remaindery but is to be congratulated on its early opening hours. They also manage a stall in the market which has the best informed pbk book D in Britain. From Crowe head back towards the centre of town.

THE IDEAL SECONDHAND BOOKSHOP **Ferrytown**
1 Station Street, Ferrytown
Mon-Fri, 6-9, Sat & Sun 10-5
Med size R/C stk, av prices, NSOC. Owner is deaf mute who cannot read or write, does not attend bookfairs, stays out of sight, does not offer cups of coffee and is not interested in tenth rate gossip about other bksp owners. No T. No p. poss. Shop is next door to veggie restaurant. Nearest: Grays, St Helens, Edgware, Morecambe.

A C & M THOMPSON **Wymondham**
1 Town Green, Wymondham, Norfolk
Mon-Sat, 10.15-5 Rel
Med size R/C stk very good cnd, av cal and prices. TWC. P.poss. BR Wymondham, ETF in centre of town. Nearest: Norwich, Beccles, Framlingham, Ely.

TURRET HOUSE BOOKS **Wymondham**
27 Middleton St, Wymondham, Norfolk
Mon-Sat, 9-6 Rel
Med size spec in History of Science and Microscope bks. Some general bks av cal, cnd & prices. Same road further along from Thompson's.

DAVID FERROW **Great Yarmouth**
77 Howard Street South, Great Yarmouth
Mon-Fri, 9.30-1, 2.30-5.30, Rel
Med/lg R/C/D stk, most of the Ds bks are kept in upstairs room by request. Solid roast beef. A lot goes in but not the same amount seems to emerge. Head of the Norfia. T. P.poss. BR Gt. Yarmouth, follow signs for town centre Car Park, shop opp. Nearest: Cromer, Lowestoft, Norwich.

<u>PROOF THAT THE LOWEST OFT PRODUCES THE BEST</u>

JOHN ROLPH **Lowestoft**
Manor House, Pakefield Street, Lowestoft
Tue-Sat, 11-1, 2.30-5, V.Rel
Med size R/C stk, av cnd, ab av cal, bl av prices. WAD not least for the atmosphere. This shop is the forebear of all Anoraksia Nervosa establishments, but Mr. Rolph with that touch of genius has installed several heaters and yet it is

still freezing. What keeps you warm is the books. They radiate the white heat of inspiration. This shop shows that books do not have to burn your fingers to fire the imagination. T. P. poss. BR Lowestoft, OOS turn right and right onto main London Road and walk for about 2 miles. Pakefield Street is the one with the petrol station on the corner and should not be confused with Pakefield Road. It took me 3 years to learn that. Nearest: Gt Yarmouth, Beccles, Westleton.

BESLEYS BOOKSHOP **Beccles**
4 Blyburgate, Beccles, Suffolk
Mon-Sat, 9.30-1, 2-5 Rel
Med size R/C/D slightly low key but decidedly int. WAD. This shop should be compulsory on the course in how to run a provincial bksp. It is when I see places like this, and there are nowhere near enough of them, hI know that all book Ds in Britain are just not trying hard enough. Each section in this shop has been chosen with care and attention. The bks are not all those dreadful tomes the bookfairies so love. There are bks from 50p to £50. There are bks that Rs want to read, indeed there is a notice on the door saying "Thick paperbacks wanted". The bks in the window make bks look int, most bksps make bks look like a form of punishment, which is a major achievement in itself. The owners can tell the diff between a R and a C. Thus they ask the former, but not the latter, if they need help. Even though many of the bks have come in over the counter they have been priced in such a way that they are likely to sell fast. It is staggering to think that so few of the s/h bksps can manage such a task. What this shop is doing is encouraging people to buy bks. What most shops do is discourage them. TWC. P.poss. BR Beccles, OOS straight ahead and third left, there is also a stall in the Waveney Antiques Market, but after this place nobody would bother. Nearest: Wymondham, Lowestoft, Framlingham, Bury St Edmunds.

PLEASURES **Southwold**
36 East Street, Southwold, Suffolk
Mon-Sat, 10-1 & 2.30-5, clsd Mon & Tues in winter. Rel
Med size R/C stk. Like the owner seems at first slightly boring but there are at times sparks of interest. Av cnd, ab av prices. TWC. P.poss. BR Haleston, NAST 7 miles. Nearest: Lowestoft, Westleton, Beccles.

CHAPEL BOOKS **Westleton**
Westleton, Suffolk
"usually open 7 days a week, afternoons (often 11-6 in summer) but always Sat & Sun 2-5 at least. BTR Westleton-616 to check)
And that gives the game away, you just know that this is not going to be any ordinary bksp. Those hours read like the announcements the vicar used to make before he got into boring you properly with the sermon. This establishment is the good book by other means. On the outside it claims to be a Primitive Methodist Chapel, on the inside...

I telephone and a voice tells me to come to the side door, how did he know I was trade? Maybe even god uses the tradesman's entrance in a Primitive Methodist Chapel. Maybe he is a spiritualist? At the side door there is a notice saying: Knock Loudly. Surely if he is a Spiritualist he should know when I have arrived. I knock, nothing happens, I knock again, nothing happens, I rattle the letterbox and still nothing happens. I remember the poem which begins: "Is there anybody there said the Traveller?" I can see carved into the wall a sign saying 'Primitive Methodist School'. Maybe they are only trainee Spiritualists. I look for something to hit the door with: a battering ram, bazooka, a thermic lance, but none of these are handy. I begin to have my doubts, this is no ordinary English village; it is nothing like Ambridge, they would have had all those things ready. Suddenly the door opens, and I realise I was thinking of the wrong poem. It should have been the next one down the page: The Rhyme of the Ancient Mariner. I will never make it as a spiritualist, and why don't they teach you useful poems at school.

He is dressed in a woolly hat, anorak and pyjamas, he seems surprised at my appearance, maybe I should not wear a coat in the country, but it is cold, especially here. He says that he thought I was not coming. He cannot be a spiritualist then, maybe he is a Hare Krishna, but then I remember I have not seen any Hare's for a long time. Maybe they made a takeover bid for the Primitive Methodists. He leads me in, I hope he is not leading me on. This is no ordinary chapel, it is crammed with books most of which do not appear to be unpacked yet. There are several other piles covered in rough clothes which I am instructed not to touch. Can these be dead Primitive Methodist? Losers in the takeover war? Or maybe they just died of the cold.

Surely these are not the books with which they taught young Primitive Methodists: advanced Calclous, maybe they are the books that Hare Krishna's read: Maybe there are spiritualists who come to this school.

On the walls there are pictures of babies, this must have been a school for very young Primitive Methodists. I can hear a child's voice, but I thought Hare Krishna's were celibate, maybe he is a failed Hare Krishna. I certainly know why the children did not get any older, they all froze to death. If Captain Oates had gone to a Primitive Methodist School he would still be alive today.

When he returned from something he made sure I did not see, I ask him about the Primitive Methodists, why did they need a chapel so large? He says they were mainly fishermen, and that they came from all over. They must have been some fishermen, the nearest coast is ten miles. Maybe this is where they learnt to freeze fish and went off and started the fish finger industry. Sure as hell mine were frozen. When you mention the books he changes, a warmth comes over him, perhaps it is his only source of heat. I ask how the books are priced and he says I can have anything I want for any amount I want.

A friend of mine used to work in an office in Oxford Street, on his way back from lunch a Hare Krishna would come up to him, and almost everybody else and hand him a record. The HK would then ask for a donation. My friend used to wait outside his office until a HK did this to him, he would take the record and then go inside and lock the door. The Hare Krishna's got a bit fed up with this and the head HK, if that

is the right term, went off and got a policeman. Together they went to my friend's office and the HK demanded his record back. "But you gave it to me!" said my friend. "And you are supposed to give a donation!" screamed the HK. My friend asked the policeman if a donation had to be given. The policeman wiped the smile off his face and said that he did not think so. My friend then put his newsly acquired record in the cupboard with his other sixteen HK records. When the devotee saw this he took a swipe at my friend. Which only goes to show that if you have a belief in religion you will be able to find a policeman when you need one.

Woolly hat returns and asks if I would like some coffee. I say yes, anything to keep warm, when he leaves I cannot concentrate on the books. Maybe the fishermen used to walk the ten miles from the coast in an effort to keep warm. Woolly hat returns, he has a jug of water, and a jar of coffee. Maybe this is the primitive method. "Ignore the prices!" he says. "Just pay what you feel." I feel nothing, but I am not as brave as my friend with the records. "Aren't you going to drink your coffee?" he asks. I wonder if he has put something in it. "I don't know how to make coffee," I said. He goes off again...I hope it is not on a quest to find a book on how to make coffee. I make a run for the door, it is barred. He comes back and says if you want me, you are supposed to bang this tin. What is he? Iron Man? And... "could you sign the book before you leave"? I look at it and can hardly see a name in it. If I put my name on that book did it mean that I would have to become a Hare Krishna/ Primitive Methodist for the next seven years. There is one good thing about the cold, it has killed off all the silverfish. When he returns I tell him I have signed, and before he can look I give him a £20 note, the books I have just grabbed come to £9. When he adds it up the total is £5.50. Maybe that is why they threw him out of the Hare Krishna's he was giving money to the people instead of asking for it. Or maybe it is the Primitive Methodist school of arithmetic. He looks at the money as if it was a strange apparition and tells me I will have to come again. I had not the courage to ask him the same thing.

YOXFORD BOOKSHOP **Yoxford**
High Street, Yoxford, Suffolk
Tends to be open mainly in the summer
Small R stk, T. P.poss. ETF on way into Yoxford. Another shop is rumoured to be opening in Yoxford in the summer of 1991. Nearest: Lowestoft, Westleton, Woodbridge, Framlingham.

TREWINS BOOKS **Aldebergh**
178B High Street, Aldebergh, Suffolk
Mon-Sat, 10.30-5, L 1-2
Small R/C stk in antique shop. Av cal, cnd and prices. T. P. poss. ETF in High Street. Nearest: Westleton, Framlingham.

MRS V. BELL **Framlingham**
19 Market Hill, Framlingham, Suffolk
Mon-Sat, 9.45-1 & 2-4.30, clsd Wed
Med size R stk, av cal, cnd & prices. TWC. P.poss. BR Woodbridge, NAST. ETF in Market Square. Nearest: Beccles, Westleton, Woodridge, Bury.

BLAKES BOOKS **Woodbridge**

88 The Thoroughfare, Woodbridge, Suffolk

Mon-SAt, 9.30-5, V.Rel

Med size R/C stk, more Ruth Rendell than Dorothy L Sayers, but definitely the sort of place the BBC would love for a rural detective. P.poss. BR Woodbridge, OOS turn slightly right and left down alleyway, and right. Nearest: Aldeburgh, Framlingham.

FELIXSTOWE

British Frail's fond belief that Ipswich and Felixstowe are not in the Southeast - whereas it does believe that King's Lynn and Exeter are - means that getting to Felixstowe by train is inordinately expensive for somewhere so close to London. However if you travel to Harwich, which is on the network Southeast, you are in for an extremely pleasant surprise. There is a ferry which goes to Felixstowe, it also does a tour of the harbour which must have been designed by the man who did the illustrations for The Boy's Own Paper. It would make the Wonder Book of Shipping look boring. Never was a harbour more industrious. There are huge car ferries bound for Hamburg, there are sutomatic Lighthouses, there are water police launches. There are tugs that look as if they are about to leap out. There are Cargo vessels from countries you never knew were by the sea. There are lifeboats ready to fall. A Pathe Newsreel would not have been able to do it justice. It made me want to join the merchant navy when I grow up. For a bookshop to compete against the full tour of the harbour it has to be good. Felixstowe succeeds admirably.

THE TREASURE CHEST **Felixstow**

70 Hamilton Road, Felixstowe, Suffolk

Mon-Sat 9-5.30, V.Rel

Lg R/C stk ab av cal, cnd, av prices. A very good general shop. WAD, res stk upstairs by request, although this may move to Castle Bkshp, Colchester, which is now owned by the same corporation. TWC. P.poss. BR Felixstowe, OOS turn right into turn and look for a trinket shop. The stamp shop on the seafront is a bit more reliable than it used to be but the bks are worse. Nearest: Woodbridge, also owned by above.

CLAUDE COX **Ipswich**

3 & 5 Silent Street, Ipswich

Mon-Sat, 10-5, clsd Wed, V.Rel

Med/lg R/C/D stk, ab av cal. Emphon Antqrn, printing, some abrasive pricing. WAD. T. Etgow. P.diff. They also have a stall in the market. BR Ipswich, OOS straight ahead, at black glass monolith turn right and follow signs for Felixstowe. Nearest: Woodbridge, Colchester, Sudbury.

VICTORIA BOOKS **Brightlingsea**

22 Victoria Place, Brightlingsea, Essex

Mon-Sat, 10.30-4.30, clsd Tues

Med size R/C stk with pretentions. Brightlingsea looks as if it is waiting for the BBC to turn up and film a boring seaside resort in Winter. BR Colchester, NAST 10 miles. Nearest: Colchester.

COLCHESTER

OK for a morning, best to park at foot of hill and walk. Nearest shops Sudbury, Ipswich, Brightlingsea, Coggeshall.

CASTLE BOOKSHOP **Colchester**
57 North Hill, Colchester, Essex
Mon-Sat, 9-5 Rel
Lg R/C/D stk, recently changed hands and well WAD. It used to seem larger under the previous owner. Locked room. TWC. Etgow. Well worth watching. BR Colchester, OOS turn right and continue straight along. Ignore all signs saying town centre.

GREYFRIARS BOOKS **Colchester**
92B East Hill, Colchester, Essex
Mon-Sat, 9.45-5.30, Rel
Med size R/C stk, spec in mining. T. From Castle bksp up hill turn left at main junction and continue until hill goes down.

ALPHABETS **Colchester**
13 Trinity Street, Colchester, Essex
Mon-Sat, 10-5, clsd Thur
Med size R/C stk KUTI, unbelievably dreary. Emphon Nat His. Accolades awarded to anyone who buys a book. TWC. From Greyfriars go back up hill turn left with one way traffic, turn right at bottom and right into pedestrian area, and Trinity Street is slightly to left.

SUFFOLK RARE BOOKS **Sudbury**
7 New Street, Sudbury, Suffolk
Tues,Thur,Fri & Sat, 10.30-4.30, Rel
Med size R/C/D stk. Res stk. Always keen to deal. T & Disc. P.poss. BR Sudbury (change at Mark's Tey) OOS head for church and turn left into North Street and left. Nearest: Lavenham, Hadleigh, Colchester, Clare.

THE BOOKEND **Brentwood**
38 Kings Road, Brentwood, Essex
Mon-Sat, 10-5.30, Thurs 1pm
Med size R/C stk, av cal, cnd and prices. Vetgow. BR Brentwood, OOS turn ahead and bear left at fork. Nearest: Saffron Walden, Maldon, Leigh on Sea, Grays

ALL BOOKS **Maldon**
2 Mill Road, Maldon, Essex
Mon-Sat, 10-5, clsd Wed, Sun 2-6, V.Rel
Med/lg R/C stk, suffers from the Summer Sickness. Emphon maritime. TWC. P.poss. BR Chelmsford & bus. NAST. ETF at the far end of town.

ELKIN MATTHEWS **Coggeshall**
16 Stoneham Street, Coggeshall, Essex
Mon-Fri, 9.30-1 & 2-4.30, Sat 10-1 & 2-6
Med size R/C/D stk emphon childrens and Ill. Can be very cheap in subject he is not keen on. T. ETF. Nearest Sudbury, Colchester, Maldon.

There is a second bksp in Coggeshall at 35 Stoneham Street but you have to ring the bell.

LEIGH GALLERY BOOKS **Leigh on Sea**
137 Leigh Road, Leigh on Sea, Essex
Tues-Sat, 10-4.45, clsd Wed, Rel
Med size R/C stk slightly low key but a very sensible shop. TWC. P.poss. BR Chalkwell (not Leigh on Sea), OOS turn left and right at Woodford Road and left. Nearest: Maldon, Southend, Grays.

BARRIE ELLEN **Westcliffe on Sea**
262 London Road, Westcliffe on Sea, Essex
Mon-Sat, 9.30-5 clsd Wed, Rel
Med size R/C stk, emphon Chess & Draughts. TWC. P.poss. From Leigh Gallery follow road east and continue along London Road, NAST. Nearest: Maldon, Leigh on Sea and Southend.

RC writes
You notice the bugger did not mention that he killed off this shop in the last edition.

ATTICUS BOOKS **Southend on Sea**
20 Alexandra Street, Southend on Sea, Essex
Sats only
Although owner claims more frequent hours he is wrong. Med size R/C stk, av cal, cnd and prices. Res stk, which you have to ask for very politely and reassure him that you are not a D. Sometimes it can be worth the effort. BR Southend Central, OOS into shopping precinct and 5th on right. Nearest: Maldon.

The one piece of good news is that Southend has lots of unrestructured charity shops.

GRAYS

Never was a place more aptly named, and most of the locals are unlikely to notice that it is mispelt. It is the sad victim of the chain store massacre and the bleeding burger joints suppurate everywhere, but as usual in the great British disaster, there is the Red Cross preparing a welcoming cup of tea, heavily disguised as:

BOB GILBERT (KENDON'S) **Grays**
10 London Road, Grays, Essex
Sats only 9.30-5 and some Thursdays. BTR
Med sized R/C Drif Special stk, despite the emphon Sporting and Local History bks - most of this locale looks like it was the sad loser in a very unsporting event - Despite all his denials the owner is Britain's best example of the Merchant Navy School of Bookdealing; Ready to set sail at a moment's notice, able to perform any task from swabbing the deck to steering the ship, weathers calms and storms with equal indifference, but above all, delivers the cargo. Outside it may be all grays, but this is the bksp as it should be, in black and white. BR Grays, OOS turn left into shopping precinct and left at the main road. Bksp is above antiques shop. Nearest: Brentwood, Leigh on Sea.

ROUTE 3.30

THE FOAM COUNTIES

FILLED WITH WETS WHO SUCK YOU DRY

All the secondhand bookshops in this section are easy to get to from London by car, but they do tend to be extremely difficult to park in. They are also very easy to get to by train. It is best to buy a network card (£12) which will entitle you to one third off the fares. British Frail's definition of the Southeast and mine are somewhat at variance. They claim that Exeter is in the Southeast but that Ipswich is not, however they radically change their minds when it comes to the Rover Ticket for this area. This particular rover ticket is more expensive than any of the others and of less use.

THE KENT COAST AND CANTERBURY

The trains are frequent but stop everywhere but by motor car you never seem to stop because the bookshops seem so infrequent.

THE GOLDEN HIND **Deal**
85 Beach Street, Deal, Kent
Mon-Sat, 10-5.30, Sun 2-5.30
Med size R/C stk, av cal, cnd, not av prices. Recently changed hands and has not had time to impose definite style yet. BR Deal, OOS to right and left to Sea front and left. Opp car park. Nearest: Sandwich, Folkestone, Wingham.

STRAND BOOKS Sandwich
21 Strand Street, Sandwich, Kent
Mon-Sat, 10-5.30, L 1-2.15, clsd Wed
Small R stk at C prices. TWC. P.diff. BR Sandwich, OOS turn left and right into unlikely looking street, over the embankment ahead, bear to left at fork in road. It sounds like you would need a tank but what this shop really needs is a bulldozer. Sandwich used to be an int place to buy bks in and this place is trading on that reputation. Nearest: Ramsgate, Folkestone, Wingham.

RAMSGATE

THREE MEN, NO BOAT, BUT LOTS OF DOGS

MICHAEL'S BOOKSHOP **Ramsgate**
72 Kings Street, Ramsgate, Kent
Mon-Sat, 9.30-5.30
A Remainder shop with a med sized stk of s/h R/C bks, more int than you would expect for a new bksp. TWC. OOS, turn right, continue along Wilfred Road, turn left and right King Street. I got these instructions from the cab driver who

gave them out as if it was secret information. It does not sound right to me, I think he must have been a double agent. All I can tell you is that Ramsgate is a very confusing place. The station is in a row of suburban houses, the streets have no names and the residents are thick, however it does have a phenomenal number of junk shops which can make getting lost worthwhile.

WINDMILL BARGAIN BOOKS **Ramsgate**
20 Grange Road, Ramsgate, Kent
Mon-Sat, 9-5.30, Rel
Small R shop a cross between a Samuel Beckett Special and a Drif Special, but does not quite make it to either. Directions as above.

There is also a bookstall in the Lido Market on Sat & Sun.

THE OLD RAMSGATE BOOKSHOP **Ramsgate**
1 Windmill Parade, Grange Road, Ramsgate
Mon-Sat, 10-5, clsd Thurs pm
Med/lg R stk. A sad collection of bks purchased from the previous owner, which accounts for the similar disposition of the current owner. TWC. P.poss. OOS straight ahead and bear right at hill, turn sharp right at bottom and follow until roundabout and right.

ALBION BOOKSHOP **Broadstairs**
29 Albion Street, Broadstairs, Kent
Mon-Sat, 9.30-5.30, L 1-2, Rel
Lg R/C stk bl av cal, av cnd and prices. TWC. The tiny battered black door like a street magicians silk top hat hides an entrancing masterpiece. Through it you enter an illusion, an apparition, a trompe de theatre. It seems like a palace of bks, a cathedral for Cs. Unsure where to begin you proceed through this Rheims with artifice, this magic lantern show without commentary searching for the right metaphor until you realise that it is an amateur theatrical.
These are the bks that appear in an advertising man's idea of a bksp, these are the tomes on either side of the french windows. These are the books against which city tycoons improve their image. The only magic is the source of the dull dust that has been dropped on them. BR Broadstairs, OOS turn right and left towards the seafront, at bottom turn left and right into alleyway. Nearest: Herne Bay, Ramsgate, Wingham.

PENDEES **Hernia Bay**
29 High Street, Herne Bay, Kent
Mon-Sat, 9-5, Thurs 9-1 but always seems to be open Thurs pm
Med size R/C stk, bl av cal, cnd - av prices. Nrly a Book and Magazine Collector Special. TWC and Disc. P.poss. BR Herne Bay, OOS turn right and follow road down and turn right.

BOOKS AND PIECES **Whitstable**
48 Oxford Road, Whitstable, Kent
Small/med sized R/nrly C stk, almost a Drif Special. TWC.

P.poss. I am not 100% certain about the name of this street as it is not signposted, nor am I certain about the number as this does not appear on the fascia. Nor am I certain about the hours as none are shown in the window. In pursuit of my ambition to become a top investigative journalist I asked the assistant if it was poss to have these details. She said "Whatever do you want to know that for, nobody else has ever asked?" And I was unable to think of any reply. However, I have now thought of one - if shops posted their name, address, telephone number and opening hours on the window where somebody as dim as me could copy them down it might help in my career as an investigative journalist and I would be able to give up compiling guides to s/h bksps that s/h bksp owners do not like. BR Whitstable, OOS over footbridge, turn right and continue to end of road and right under railway bridge. Shop is on left. There are a lg number of junk shops in Whitstable. Nearest: Faversham, Canterbury, Herne Bay.

***THE FAVERSHAM BOOKSHOP** **Faversham**
1a Gatefield Lane, Faversham, Kent
Mon-Sat, 10-1 & 2-5.30, clsd Thurs, no lunch Sat
Med size R/C stk, av cal, cnd and prices. Keen on Kipling. TWC. BR Faversham, OOS turn left and first right, shop is in alleyway just past Alexander Centre. Nearest: Whitstable, Chilham, Rochester.

BAGGINS BOOK BAZAAR **Rochester**
19 High Street, Rochester, Kent
Mon-Sun, 10-6 Rel
Very lg R/C stk. Bl av cal and cnd. Av prices. TWC. It is a dream; if you have been on a desert island. It is riveting; if you are demented. It is spellbinding; to the unsophisticated. It is nirvana; for the addicted C seeking a cure. For the D it is worth travelling miles for; to avoid. BR Strood, OOS follow road round to right and turn left under railway bridge and keep to right. Nearest: Faversham, Malling, Greenwich, London.

Dear Miss Manners,

I am a person with a 'past', I used to compile guides - just like Debretts but of the second hand book trade - but some unkind people accused me of being an impolite upstart and imposter. I was mortified by these entirely false allegations and vowed never to upset anybody ever again.

Then I met a new friend and she encouraged me to put pen to paper. I think she thought of it as a kind of therapy for me. I did not tell her all the dreadful things I had done, but I think she guessed and she volunteered to help me solve my problems.

When she attempted to place adverts in a trade journal, the editor/owner declined to accept on the grounds that I had previously offended his readers, but after much gentle persuasion by my friend, he agreed after what he called the necessary 'checks' or maybe he meant 'cheques'.

I was so embarrassed I did not know how to face my friend, but she made light of it by saying this was how business was conducted these days. /...

I tried to forget this dreadful insult by attending a well known book trade function in a West End Hotel where I chatted to a famous author, Mr. Iain Sinclair, and an internationally known book collector Mr. Donald Weekes. For me it was just like the old days, they were so kind and polite and I knew that they were trying hard not to mention my 'past'. But just as I thought I was taking the first step back into the only society which counts for me, the editor of the aforesaid journal came up to our gay little group and completely ignored me. He addressed all his remarks to Mr. Sinclair - a gentleman who has been kind enough to write flattering remarks about me in the past, when I most needed them. He asked Mr. Sinclair whether he had heard about my proposed guide of which he, the editor, claimed to be an ex-fan.

I was so embarrassed I slunk away to my suite and buried my head in tears. Dear Miss Manners, what should I have done?

Yours in desperation,
The Tsarina of all the Charing Cross Roads.

|Miss Manners replies:

What you need is something to occupy your time. Take up small tasks at first, such as compiling the guide. It should only take a fortnight or so. Include this experience and then send me a copy of the finished book for which I sent a cheque 3 years ago, and I can then use it as an example of how people should not behave.|

HEARTS OF OAK BOOKSHOP Rochester
63 High Street, Rochester, Kent
Mon-Sun, 10-6, Rel
Med/lg Spec in Military History, Maritime, Transport and Aviation. Bl av cal, cnd, av prices. It is just another department of Baggins; the shop should be called the Art of Hoax. TWC. Directions as above. P.poss.

ROUTE 4.30

WARNING!

Avoid coming back to London on the Dover/Folkestone line late in the evening unless you enjoy the company of the Great British Yobbo and Yobbette. They return from their daytrip to France - in reality a day trip to the duty free shop - with enough liquid refreshment to cover the English Channel should it run dry. They then proceed to sing songs they do not know, kiss people they do not know, and talk about things they do not know. The only thing they do want to know is everybody else. They are the reason that The Channel Tunnel is doomed to failure, for in their eyes it was specifically built for them to vomit into without missing.

What British Frail should do is dig the tunnel in the opposite direction into the British Countryside, then on their return trip these 'no knows' could be told that it was another duty free shop - then concrete should be poured on top of them. I for one would be happy to buy each of them a return ticket.

RC writes

There is nothing like a reformed alchie is there? That miserable bugger only gave up drink after he started a long weekend with £300 of somebody else's money to regain consciousness four days later, broke. What he objected to was that he was unable to witness wasting the money. As to objecting to the singing, what he really objected to was the fact that they started booing when he tried to sing the entire words of Rule Brittannia. He wanted to get up and walk away, but as none of them had spotted that he was wearing plus fours, he was too scared to do so - he sat on the train until everybody else had got off.

G & D J MARRIN **Folkestone**
149 Sandgate Road, Folkestone, Kent
Mon-Sat, 9.30-5.30, L 1-2.30. V.Rel
Med size R/C/D stk, av cal, cnd and prices. Emphon Local History and WWI (Res stk). I cannot work out if it is me getting older and more tolerant, or that I am looking for more ordinary books, or whether the shops that I used not to like have improved, or perhaps I am overjoyed that the other shop that used to be in this town has clsd down. But this place does definitely seem to have got a lot more int. BR Folkestone Central, OOS turn right and right under bridge. Ahead Cheriton Road, ahead Manor Road and right at Sandgate. P.poss. Nearest: Canterbury, Deal, Hythe.

THE OLD GALLERY BOOKSHOP **Hythe**
125 High Street, Hythe, Kent
Mon-Sat, 10-5
Med size R/C stk, keen on Local History, Military and Transport. Av cal, cnd and prices. WEABCOC. BR Sandling, OOS turn left. NAST for 2 miles, turn right at bottom of hill. Nearest: Canterbury, Folkestone, Rey.

THE FORGE BOOKSHOP **Chilham**
The Street, Chilham, Kent
Mon-Sat, 9.30-5.30, Rel
Small R/C stk, av cal, cnd and prices. Keen on Gardening and Cookery. TWC. P.poss. This is a very pleasant shop to be in, nobody jumps down your throat when you go through the door, nobody AWYW, nobody asks why you are buying a particular book, nor do you feel embarrassed if you leave without one. Clearly noother book D has explained to the owner that she has to do these things if she wants to become an established member of the British s/h booktrade. I think the only explanation can be that none of them talk to her because she is French. BR Chilham, OOS ahead turn left towards village and left at signpost. Nearest: Faversham, Canterbury, Folkestone, Tunbridge Wells.

PAUL HOLCOMBE **Canterbury**
5 North Lane, Canterbury, Kent
Mon 11-4, Tues clsd, Wed 10-4.30, Thurs clsd, Fri 10-5, Sat 10-5, Sun 12-4.
Lg R/C stk, av cal, cnd and prices, emphon Scientific,Technical and Industrial. As you will have guessed from the above opening times this is a diff shop. If you can manage to position yourself outside of it at the same

time as the owner you will be confronted with a small collection of notices as to who and who not is welcome in this establishment. By the time I had worked out whether I was allowed in or not, and summoned up the courage to see if the answer was right, the shop had clsd. This may not be a difficulty for most people as the shop is rumoured to be closing down anyway. BR Canterbury, OOS turn left at bottom of drive and left before Gate. This is from Canterbury West Stn.

DAVID MILES **Canterbury**
37 Northgate, Canterbury, Kent
Mon-Sat, 10-5, Rel
Lg C/D stk, ab av cal, cnd and prices. Emphon Childrens and Ill bks. It is when I see shops such as this that I know my irritation with the rest of the bksps of Britain is fully justified. I know that they are not trying. All the bks in this wonderful establishment are carefully chosen, those which do not fit in with the owner's interests have been priced to sell, thus there are many bgns for Ds and Cs. If you wanted a childrens or ill book this is the best bksp in Britain to come to. They may not necessarily have the book but they will know what you are talking about.

Shops such as this one show up how pathetic this island's other bksps are. It is sensibly sited, thus only those people who know about it are going to make their way there. Just looking in the window and into the shop tells you it is a C's bksp, and thus also attractive to Ds. The bks are sensibly laid out and easy to look at, my only criticism is that there are a trifle too many of them, but this is probably because I am not int in children's bks. This is also one of the few children's bksps where you feel that if a child did turn up they would not reach for the machine gun. This is possibly because the owner used to be a school teacher and knows how to deal with horrors. Indeed I remember him gently chastising me because I turned up late at a bookfair. The stk of this shop is bookfairy type, but the owner more than likely thinks of that as a compliment, and in this case he could be right because he clearly uses the bookfairs to buy bks rather than keep bks to sell them there. The real question with this bksp is are the customers good enough for it. WAD by Cs and Ds alike just to show them how it should be done. P.poss (well not really but worth trying) enter High St through the Gate, ignore the bkrm in the SPCK on the left and turn left at Cathedral Street.

BELL HARRY BOOKSHOP **Canterbury**
110 Northgate, Canterbury, Kent
Wed, Fri, Sat 10-5, sometimes lunch 1-2.15
Med size R/C stk av cal, cnd and prices, rumoured to be closing. Nearly opp Miles, see above.

THE CHAUCER BOOKSHOP **Canterbury**
6 Beer Cart Lane, Canterbury, Kent
Mon-Sat, 9.30-5.30, Rel
Med size R/C/D stk, av cal, cnd and prices. It is not bad but not goodeither. A Book Dealer Special. TWC. P.diff. From Miles go back to High St, turn left and right at Margaret St and right at end.

STEPHEN THOMPSON **Canterbury**
7 Longport, Canterbury, Kent
Mon-Sat, 10-5, L 1-2.15, clsd Thurs, Rel
Med size R/C stk, av cal, cnd and prices. Solid roast beef. TWC. Emphon local history.

LLOYD'S BOOKSHOP **Wingham**
27 High Street, Wingham, Kent
Mon-Sat 9.30-5, L 1-2.15, Rel
Med/lg R/C stk, av cal, cnd and prices but not quite as int as it used to be. T. P.poss. ETF. The High St is off to the side of the main road. Nearest: Herne Bay, Sandwich, Folkestone, Canterbury.

ROUTE 4.45

ANTHONY NEVILLE **Rye**
15 Market Street, Rye, E. Sussex
Mon-Sun, 10-5.30, clsd Tues
Med size C/D stk, ab av cal, cnd and prices. Solid roast beef, but can occasionally be quite int. TWC. Atmosphere like a fridge but is to be commended for opening on Sundays, if more shops of this type did so, I would not begrudge the time I have to waste going into them. There is also a junkshop with bks two doors down. BR Rye, OOS, weave way ahead to High St, turn left and right towards church, and left.

LANDGATE BOOKS **Rye**
Hilders Cliff (no No.), Rye, E. Sussex
Wed-Sat, 10-5 Unr
Med size R/C stk, av cal, cnd and prices. TWC. P.diff. BR Rye, OOS ahead weave way to High St and turn left, and continue along. There is also a bkstl in Rope Walk Market owned by the same person (to the left of the station) but both are rumoured to be closing. Nearest: Tunbridge Wells. Thats a load of rubbish Rye is near nowhere. It is between Hythe and Hastings.

There is also an antique shop with a bkrm in East Malling.

FOXED AND BOUND **West Malling**
8 West Street, West Malling, Kent
Tues-Sat, 10-5, Rel
Med size R/C stk, emphon Biography, Childrens and Folklore. Av cal, cnd, imaginative prices. TWC. P.poss.

The Naming of Parts: You are supposed to pronounce Malling as in mauling. As to the shop name I would not dare to imagine how it is pronounced. It is one of those strange names that is neither beautiful nor int, nor so unusual that you would always remember it, (unlike Treasure Island or Voltaire & Rousseau). Then there is the shop, the first time I went in I am sure the lady was calling me names under her breath because I was exceedingly wet and dripping water everywhere. The second time I went in she asked me for my name. In some ways this was a good sign as she had spotted that I was a dealer, but when I told her that there are several people who are not keen to hear my name spoken she was a trifle non-plussed. In her world everybody is introduced, even in Sainsbury's.

I was keen to be introduced to the books, for some of them are exceedingly int, but judging by the prices I wondered if they were really for sale. Certainly nobody I know would buy them at these prices, and then it occurred to me this is why she wanted me to be introduced.

This is not a real bksp. It is the image of a bksp in the BBC's idea of an English country village with its meaningless name that could not possibly give free publicity to any other bksp in the land. The owner is also the BBC's idea of what a bookdealer should look like and be like, having retired as a success from something else, unlike the reality where most bookdealers have retired as failures. The people who go into this shop are meant to stand by the door and say meaningful things just as they do in BBC plays, not grunt and say they cannot remember their names. You are not meant to buy the books they are there to be admired and thus it is extremely odd when nutters like me turn up, and you would be amazed how many there are in Kent - and attempt to buy the books. I have never seen anybody, other than in a BBC play, who wears a cocktail dress during the day. It must be really disappointing to her when I and the rest of the sweaty anorak brigade arrive. In her honour I have decided on a new acronym WEABCOC - Was Expecting A Better Class Of Customer. BR West Malling, OOS turn right and left at junction into village, turn left and right at end of fork. Nearest: Rochester, Canterbury, Tunbridge Wells, Westerham.
RC writes

You should see the dresses he wears in the afternoons!

ALAN TAYLOR SMITH BOOKS **Westerham**
4 The Grange, High Street, Westerham, Kent
Mon-Sat, 10-5
Antique shop with BTA R/C stk, ab av prices, but bgns known. Keen on Churchill (see statue of punk sprawled out on the village green). This gentleman does one thing a lot of other book Ds would do well to emulate, instead of asking what you want he says "If I can be of help please ask", which I thought was very polite. It managed to elicit a softer grunt from me. T & Disc. ETF in main street. Two of the other antique shops in this village have bkrms. Nearest: Bromley (see London), Tunbridge Wells, Haywards Heath, Reigate.

ROUTE 5 O'CLOCK

HASTINGS

No town in England has more secondhand bookshops than Hastings from the Creme de la Creme to la Grote de la Grote it spans the entire spectrum of book collecting. It is easy to get to by train, but can seem quite a way by car, unless you stop off at Tunbridge Wells. There are an incredible number of junk shops and I think it is the only town in Britain on which the charity shops have failed to make any impression. Just avoid it on a Wednesday.

HOWES BOOKSHOP **Hastings**
Trinity Hall, Braybrooke Terrace, Hastings, E. Sussex
Mon-Sat, 9.30-5, L 1-2, Sat am
V lg C/D stk ab av cal, cnd - at first seems ab av prices but this is not true. Emphon Antqrn, scholarly lit, and bib. It is more like a university library than a bksp and you do worry about your entry qualifications but this is a liberal arts college and there is no formal entry test. What you do need is stamina to withstand the course which demands a V high level of dedication to obtain any degree of satisfaction. The benefit of not dropping out can be high in the long term. WAD. TWC. P.poss (but V diff to find by car). BR Hastings, OOS and immediately to your right go down alley, turn right and left. Nearest: Tunbridge Wells, Rye, Eastbourne.

JOHN WILBRAHAM **Hastings**
18 George Street, Hastings, E. Sussex
Mon-Sat, 9.30-1 & 2-5.30, clsd Wed. V.Rel
Med size R/C/D stk, av cal, cnd and prices. Emphon antqrn. From outside it looks like a typical roast beef bksp but inside it is definitely nouvelle cuisine, despite going in for lthrwr and antqrn. T & Disc. P.diff. BR Hastings, OOS follow driveway down, turn left towards seafront and left until No Entry sign, and left.

HOW I ARRIVE AT A JUDGEMENT ON THE PRICES

The easiest way to upset a s/h bookdealer is to tell him or her that they are expensive. They always feel that their prices are reasonable and in fact they are correct, for the price of s/h bks relative to other items is extremely cheap.

The scale I use to describe the price range in bksps is known by double glazing salesmen as the "Churchill" test. The six volumes of The History of The Second World War is an extremely common book. If I saw it in a bksp at £10 I would describe that shop as being V cheap. If I saw it in another shop at £25 I would describe it as being average and if I saw it at £45 I would describe that shop as being expensive.

It is poss to charge much more for 1st editions, signed copies or those bound in Morocco, but if this is ignored and we think only about an ordinary copy in the first shop it is likely to sell within a week or so. In the second shop it may take a month, but in the third shop it may take a year. In some parts of the country Churchill is rated more highly (Westerham in Kent for example) and the shop that asks £45 may have to pay higher rents and rates, but this is of no concern to the person buying it. The scale is relative across the whole country.

If I was looking for a set of Churchill then I would try specialists first, more often than not they would have the book a lot cheaper than the average shop. For them a set of Churchill is of no interest unless it is a 1st ed., or signed or in a Morocco binding. They are often delighted to get rid of the ordinary set, however for a book such as Captain Broderick's Army in 1st ed. they may start at £1000. I do not know if this is cheap or expensive but a specialist dealer is much more likely to know how much he can ask. If I saw Captain Broderick's Army in a cheap shop at £45 I would buy it, but if I saw it in an expensive shop at £500 I would not be so sure because I would assume that they would know what they are doing. This is a dreadful mistake. You are far more likely to get bargains in expensive shops than in cheap ones. In cheap shops the books move fast. In expensive ones people do not go in them because they believe they are too pricey. It is an error to assume that expensive shops know what they are doing, quite often they know nothing because they have less experience of the books.

People who seldom go in bksps are often V impressed that the person behind the counter knows the prices of the bks, but the truth is that they do not know, they are only expressing an opinion which is exactly the thing that makes going round bksps interesting. There is no right price for a s/h book, there is only an average price. It is not my job to worry about how much the dealer paid for the book, or that he has high bills to pay, or that his premises are extremely elegant, or that the book is scarce in that area. I think all books are cheap, I also think all books are grossly undervalued but that does not mean that I buy them all. If I could buy them all I would more than likely give up.

Other directories (there are no other guide books - I am the only bugger thick enough to traipse round all the shops in Britain - the directories compile their misinformation by asking the dealers themselves). I will start again... Other directories use the system of giving the price range, at first this seems like a good idea, but in truth it tells you nothing. When it says that the upper limit is £200 does that mean they are never going to charge more than £200 for any book? When it says the lower limit is 50p how many books do they have at 50p?

When I go into a bksp the commodity of mine that the bksp is using is time and I want to know within five seconds how much the price level is, by choosing a book at random I can make a rough estimate.

In cheap shops all you have to do is look for the book you are interested in. In average priced shops you have to pull a lot more books off the shelves but you will be deterred more often. In expensive shops you should always look at the common things because they are often keen to get rid of them.

In shops where they have egregious prices, you have to look at everything because usually they have no idea what they are doing. This is why those shops are so irritating. And why they dislike dealers, because they pull lots of the books off of the shelf and put them back.

OLD HASTINGS BOOKSHOP **Hastings**
15 George Street, Old Hastings, E. Sussex
Mon-Sat, 10-4, Clsd Wed, Unr
Med size R/C stk, av cal, cnd and prices. Looks int from outside, which is quite often as close as you will get. BR etc as previous shop - Wilbraham.

TAMARISK **Hastings**
80 High Street, Hastings, E. Sussex
Mon-Fri, 10.30-5.30, L 1-2, Sat 10-5.30, Rel
Med size R/C stk emphon lit and music, av cal, cnd and prices. Rumoured to be undergoing a change. T. From Wilbraham continue to end of street and turn left.

BOOKMANS HALT **St Leonards**
127 Bohemia Road, St Leonards, E. Sussex
Mon-Sat, 10-1 & 2.30-5, clsd Wed. Rel
Med size R/C/D stk, low key. A Drif Special.

BEFORE AND AFTER - REALITY & IMAGE

If you stand on the west side of Bohemia Road in Saint Leonards, it is possible to see the two extremities of s/h bookdealing in one glance. Never have two shops that are so far apart been so close together. It is a picture that would drive television producers into ecstacy. It would be their idea of the balanced view. The colour supplements would bill it as before and after.

The bright newly opened shop on the left is called Helgato. I have no idea what this means, nor does anybody else that I have asked know. But it does have a wonderful cultivated classical ring to it. It is the type of word I feel I should know.

The dark dreary shop on the right is called Bookman's Halt. It is hard to decide which is more faded, its name, or the paintwork. But that name does tell you something; it says that this shop is from a different era.

There are no "Bookmen" any more. The last one died in captivity, his name was Frank Swinnerton. A bookman was somebody who not only read books, he wrote them, he thought about them, he enjoyed them, his life was books. In its own way the name Bookman's Halt is giving off a semiotic message.

If you cross-examine the owner he will tell you that he put those books in the window on purpose in order to deter people from asking him to take them out. If he had put interesting books in the window he would have to spend his entire life getting them out to show the potential customers. This is not a semiotic message at all: It is one-up-manship. He is so confident of selling his books that he feels he has not to add to their impressiveness. And he is right.

In Helgato the lighting is good, but unobtrusive. The books can all withstand careful contemplation. They are as bookdealers say, in good condition. But this is not the way things were when they were produced. These books have been protected as if they were some endangered species. Their covers are beautiful to look at, their pages even more glorious. These are books that care about their image and the people who will buy them are the image conscious. This is the '30s and '50s as we have been taught to remember it. Helgato is allegedly an antique shop but there were no antiques like this, then.

I am so old I can remember what shops looked like in the fifties, and it is not that carefully designed image conscious world that only existed in adverts. They looked like Bookmans Halt does now.

The books in Bookmans Halt have never been chosen by anyone, they have always been the rejected, they are the books that failed to get a review in the Saint Leonard's Gazette. Mr. Linklater's skill is in making people want these books and how he does it is by charging 1950's prices. Most of his books are less than when they came out new.

The books in Helgato have all been carefully chosen and are extremely interesting but even if I had the money to buy them I am not sure that I would want to. They are not books to be read, but books to be looked at. These are books for people who shop at Laura Ashley and have Sanderson Wallpaper. They are not books to tell you something, but books to tell your friends something about you.

Many of the books in Bookman's Halt you would have to justify to visitors. A book I bought in from here is called 'Scaffolding and How To Erect It'. When people see this book they always ask me if I used to work as a scaffolder, or whether I had to get it for somebody. The idea that I might be interested in scaffolding is not one that occurs to them. I have to buy several illustrated books for people but I have noticed that nobody ever asks me to justify them.

The difference in approach between the gentleman in Helgato and Mr. Linklater is also marked. The gentleman is keen to explain things to you without in any way trying to embarrass you into buying the books, but a certain level of knowledge is needed to discuss the books with him. It puzzles me where people get this knowledge. What have I been doing all my life that I do not know these things that seem so obvious to them? Maybe this knowledge comes free with the William Morris wallpaper and the Habitat furniture.

In Bookman's Halt you are lucky to get a grunt out of the owner, he lolls in his chair rather like that piece of pop art sculpture that was a model of Chairman Mao and armchair in one. If you ask him about the books he can usually manage to look determined but that is as far as it goes. Enthusiasm is not the name of the game.

It would not surprise me to hear that the gentleman in Helgato was a marketing executive, or that he had studied at The Harvard Business School. All his life he has been growing into the image of a modern bookdealer. He does not deal in secondhand books, he does not deal in antiquarian books, he deals in images.

Mr. Linklater is a secondhand bookseller, he is an antiquarian bookdealer, he provides a service that people without images want.

You leave Helgato with an image, from Bookman's Halt you take fond memories.

CAMILLA'S BOOKSHOP **Eastbourne**
57 Grove Road, Eastbourne, E.Sussex
Mon-Sat, 10-6 Rel

V lg R/C/D stk, bl av cal, cnd ab av prices. Beachy head for book Ds. The only good news is that you do not have to struggle to the top of the cliffs to commit suicide. In theory I am in favour of lg ramshackle shops such as this one, but in practice it is almost imposs to find anything. If you do come across a book you would like you would have to be fairly determined to buy it at the price marked and somehow after having spent so long looking for it you are reluctant to part with the money. A lg shop such as this only succeeds if it is cheap. This is not simply a question of me being a mean old bugger but a question of economics. To go through the bks carefully would take 3 to 4 hours. Unless your interest is stimulated every twenty minutes. The reward is not great enough. BR Eastbourne, OOS turn right and left, for Smith's continue along and turn left.

RAYMOND SMITH Eastbourne
30 South Street, Eastbourne, E Sussex
Mon-Sat, 9-5.30, clsd Wed. Rel
Med/lg R/C stk, ab av cal and cnd, av prices. A Bookdealer Special. TWC. P.poss. Rumoured to be up for sale.

HALLS BOOKSHOP Tunbridge Wells
20 Chapel Place, Tunbridge Wells, TN1 1YQ
Mon-Sat, 9.30-5, Rel
Med/lg R/C/D stk, V av cal, cnd and prices. It is almost exactly the way you would expect a bksp in Tunbridge Wells to look. From outside it is one of those pictures that appear in Country Life's Book of Britain circa 1930. Inside, it is how you would imagine a Gentlemans' Club. The decor is beautifully designed, but spartan. Portraits of forgotten ancestors line the wall complete with unpotted histories. The outside world is completely forgotten. Politics and Religion are infra dig. Roast beef only is served, nouvelle cuisine has yet to sully. There is even a club bore but then you notice something is wrongj; where are the sleepers? BR Tunbridge Wells, OOS turn right and straight ahead to paved zone.

LEWES

A SPLENDID MANTELL PIECE OVER THE GRATING

A G CUMMINGS Lewes
159 High Street (? - has recently crossed from other side of road), Lewes
Mon-Sat 10-5, L 1-2
Lg C/D stk, ab av cal, cnd and prices. Res Stk, WAD. One of the most admired booksellers in England. BR Lewes, OOS, turn right up hill and left at Main Street, SIOL.

FIFTEENTH CENTURY BOOKSHOP Lewes
99 High Street, Lewes
Mon-Sat, 10-5.30
Med size R/C stk, av cal and prices. NSOC. Slightly Book Dealerish. From Cummings OOSH, turn left, continue.

BOW WINDOWS **Lewes**

128 High Street, Lewes, E. Sussex

Mon-Sat, 9-5

Med size C/D stk, solid roast beef. A Bookdealer Special. Ab av cal, cnd and prices. TWC. P.poss. BR Lewes, OOS turn right into town and turn left at main street, shop is at far end of High Street.

THE BARN COLLECTORS MARKET **Seaford**

Church Lane, Seaford, E. Sussex

Tues, Thur, Sat 10-4.30

Lg R/C stk, a Drif Special. I had to go to this shop several times before I discovered that the bksp is upstairs - the bks downstairs are just the throw outs. My excuse is that it is a strange place. It is somewhere that Agatha Christie could have done a lot with (they certainly do a lot with Agatha Christie). There is a strange diluted menace that covers the place (maybe you can buy bottled menace and dilute to taste). Somehow, something is not quite right as if the owners had what Agatha thought of as 'pasts'. On their card it says the shop is open to 1600 hours. Maybe they were wrens or worked for BR. The layout of the place is rather like a school library, but unfortunately it does not have the only subject I was interested in at school. Oversize. All the bks are nearly's which made me think that there must be a locked room. When I went up to the counter, the lady was stamping bks just like a librarian. I asked her for specific bks and she kept saying no, but her lips did not move. I was half way down the stairs before I discovered there was a second lady behind the curtain doing the answering. BR Seaford, OOS turn right and right and shop is in alleyway behind church. Nearest: Lewes, Bexhill.

BRIGHTON

A WET DAY DREAM

Famed for its pregnant paws Brighton is the kitten of shy London bookdealers, especially those who cannot bear to be separated from the great furry womb. That usually inelastic band British Frail have stretched the umbilical cord, without knots it can be done in less than an hour (full marks). For booklets Brighton tends to be the first ten tative step. Should it end in tears, they can hastily return to the breast place there is. It is a good start for toddlers but for those who like to peddle there are better places to be an off spring.

Nearest: London, Eastbourne, Worthing

THE TRAFALGAR BOOKSHOP **Brighton**

44 Trafalgar Street, Brighton

Mon-Sat, 10-6, Sat 5, Rel

Med/lg R/C/D stk, av cal, cnd and prices. Emphon Sports espec horse racing. More a donkey derby than the Grand National. TWC. BR Brighton, OOS down steps to left and turn right.

DEJA VU/...

DEJA VU Brighton
21 Trafalgar Street, Brighton
Mon-Sat, 11-6
Med size spec in esoteric and occult. Netgow. Directions as above.

RC writes

Isn't he a vicious bugger, see that NETGOW, just ask yourself why it is there. How come a specialist shop is in the main section? It could have something to do with the fact that they got one over on the prop.

He had ordered a book from their catalogue, which he promptly sold for about four times the price. A few weeks later they sent him a reminder saying he had not coughed up. The prop just took this to be the early stages of negotiation. About a week later there was a message on the ansaphone, saying ring the above number.

This is an old ploy of debt collectors, often they say that they have an important message for you. The prop did nothing.

About a week later there was another message on the phone this time they were threatening to break both his arms and legs unless the money was forthcoming. I have not seen the prop look so happy in a long time.

He removed the cassette from the ansaphone and then, when he knew they would be out he rang up leaving a message saying he had an interesting recording of theirs, which he intended giving to the Brighton Police.

The next morning there was another message on the phone from them saying that he would need police protection unless he coughed up. This truly surprised the prop because he thought they were going to ring up and offer him money not to go near the police, and this now meant that he would have to carry out his threat. Solely so that it would impress the police he sent the DEJA VU a post dated cheque, that is post dated a month before it was actually written and he then rang up the Brighton Police.

The policeman on the other end of the line listened to the story and was V sympathetic, but when he heard that it was this mob from the occult bookshop he said "Well Sir, what jury is going to take them seriously" - however he did caution the prop for using obscene language.

He was so angry, not only did he think he was going to get some money out of them, he had also sent off the payment which he could not now revoke because the cheque was too old.

The diatribe he left on the answering machine would have made even the Brighton Police blanche, fortunately it did calm him down a bit.

He told me afterwards that what had really upset him was not having sent them the money or their threat to break both his arms and legs but they had not threatened to use their occult powers on him. They had not even said they would convert him into a frog.

COURTHOUSE BOOKSHOP Brighton
181 Edward Street, Brighton
Mon-Sat 10.30-4.30, Rel
181 Edward Street, Brighton
Mon-Sat, 10.30-4.30 Rel

Small/med size RC stk av cal, cnd and prices. A bit too tidy to be a Drif Special but close. From Trafalgar Street continue downhill, turn right towards the Pavilion, cross to left hand side and street is on left.

TALL STOREY'S **Brighton**
88 St James Street, Brighton
Mon-Sat, 10-6, longer during summer.
Med/Lg R/C stk, res stk D books, primarily Mod 1sts. This is a branch office of the indoor revolution. Black clothing is de rigeur. Earnestness is compulsory. A degree in left wing politics in a sin'e qua non. What is most int is how often the owners of these shops volunteer for the capitalist classes, see the Boutle & King Diretribe...
From Courthouse Books, St James St is next street parallel towards the sea.

COLIN PAGE **Brighton**
56 Duke Street, Brighton
Mon-Sat, 10-5.30
Med/lg C/D stk, ab av cal, cnd and prices, but bgns known. T & Disc. Res stk of Lthrwr Plate bks. Even the bks in the bsmt are better that most people have in their glass cases. From Tall Storey's continue back down towards Pavillion, cross straight ahead and Duke Street is to left.

There is also an antiques arcade, called Prinny's, closeby, but despite Mr. Page drawing me a map worthy of Mercator I was unable to find it. It is alleged to have several bookdealers in it. NV.

RC writes
If you did not go in every veggie restaurant on the way, you might be able to find time to find it.

HOLLEYMAN AND TREACHER **Brighton**
21a-22 Duke Street, Brighton
Mon-Sat, 9-5.30
Lg R/C/D stk, av cal, cnd and prices. Keen on music. This piece is from the classical repertoire. It is the Te Dium of bksps, a never ending fugue without rhapsody, crescendor or aria, above all there is no movement. It is just an endless strain. The only variation is provided by the conductor who appears to be keen on discord and it is he who chooses the staff. The only evidence of composition is decomposition. When you emerge it will be with glee or humming but I doubt if you will be in possession of a single tune.

N.F. BROOKES **Brighton**
12a Queens Road, Brighton
Mon-Sat, 9.30-5.30, Sun 11-1.30
Lg R/C stk, a Helen Hanff Special. It is hard to tell which are the remaindered bks and which are the s/h. Keen on foreign languages. TWC. P.diff. From Holleyman go to end of street, turn right and continue along towards station.

WORTHING

A GOOD PLACE TO CHECK OFF

Starring the Three Sisters in highlights from The Seagull and Uncle Vanya and the best bit of The Cherry Orchard.
P.poss. BR Best to get the fast train to Brighton & change.
Nearest: Horsham, Brighton, Arundel.

THE STEYNE BOOKSHOP **Worthing**
5 High Street, Worthing, W. Sussex
Mon-Sat, 10-5.30, Rel
Lg R/C/D stk, av cal, cnd and prices. After all the tedium the good news is that she has begun to wield the axe. BR Worthing OOS towards seafront, turn left at clock on stilts, and left at end of paved area.

KIM'S BOOKSHOP **Worthing**
33 West Buildings, Worthing, W. Sussex
Mon-Sat, 10-5.15, clsd Wed, Rel
Med/lg R/C stk, av cal, NSOC, av prices. Keen on Nat His - especially killing it - and orchids. TWC. From Steyne go back down paved street past the clock and West Bdgs is street on left.

BADGERS BOOKS **Worthing**
8-10 Gratwicke Road, Worthing, W. Sussex
Mon-Sat, 9.15-6 (really?)
Lg R/C stk, a trifle tedious but this is the country seen in four acts: The natural, the unnatural, the occult and the remainder. TWC. From clock tower continue westward in paved zone and turn right at end.

I was in Worthing with the alcoholic who claims to be my chauffeur, not from any qualms but from expediency I have an arrangement with him that I will pay for the first drink of the evening provided he does not drink during the day.

It was late in the afternoon when we arrived in Worthing and we were both tired and had had little success elsewhere. When we went into the bksp, the lady behind the counter started asking me what I was looking for. I rattled off the list of the most obscure bks that I desired and she kept saying no in more and more desperate tones, as if somehow I was making this list up just to annoy her.

I can never understand why bookdealers ask this question. If I tell them the bks I am genuinely looking for they say "No" as if it was absurd, if I say I am looking for a subject like golf, they say that everybody is looking for it implying that I should give up.

In desperation this lady turned to my chauffeur and asked him what he was looking for.

"The main thing I am looking for is the Off Licence."

She then proceeded to give him careful explicit instructions on how to find it. When he had left she looked at me as if to say why cannot you ask such reasonable questions.

By the time he returned I had indeed found out that she had nothing I wanted. When he came through the door he looked as if he had just been struck by a thunderbolt, at first I thought maybe the car had been stolen, or maybe he had been assaulted or perhaps he had some really bad news but it was worse than even I could imagine; the Off Licence was closed.

Without ceremony we departed, I was surprised that he had bothered to come back for me, but then I remembered that I would be paying. We left Worthing so fast that old age pensioners were knocked over by our gust. As we drove back towards London, even I was surprised at how few pubs there were on the road, on the way from Brighton there are pubs every ten yards, but on this road they were as common as interesting books in Worthing.

I did think of telling him that this part of Sussex was an experimental dry county, but he did not look quite in the mood to appreciate this. It was a good job I said nothing because he looked at me and said "If this is your idea of a practical joke I for one do not think it is funny".

By this time we had covered about fifteen miles in about five minutes, and I was eager to have him stop staring at me. I dared not attempt to get out of the car, as we were not close to a railway station. Now he was hunched over the wheel and not a word passed between us. All effort was concentrated on the search for a pub. Roundabouts came and went, the miles were eaten up, by this time both our throats were dry, if for different reasons.

I hoped it was not a mirage, but there on the horizon was a pub, well to be more accurate it was a hotel, but it had to have a bar. We drove straight across the roundabout, I don't think a patriot missile could have taken a more direct route. He was into the car park and out of the car before it had stopped. I had no idea what to do but just then a young man got in beside me and said "Can I park the car for you Sir?"

This was certainly not one of our normal haunts. Inside, the pile of the carpet was so deep it was obscuring my view of the bar. I had to ask another uniformed flunkey.

"The Cocktail Lounge is this way Sir."

By the time I got there I could see that one drink had already been downed (he was looking vaguely human again). As he saw me he turned to the lady behind the bar and said as if it was the first order "I will have a double whiskey and my friend here would like a tumbler of your finest orange juice". The drinks soon arrived and the lady turned tome and said that will be £8.80 Sir".

It was the only time I have ever seen him spill a drop. For £8.80 he could have bought one of our normal haunts. Not even he had the cheek to try and get another drink out of me, which was a good job as I had nowhere near enough money left. I had to give my last pound to the car jockey to get the car back.

ROUTE 6.30

LONDON - CHICHESTER

Its a long slow road a winding and by train it is even slower. Start at Victoria or follow the A29. The shops are all so sensible it makes you cry.

MARY HUBBARD **Emsworth**
10 South Street, Emsworth, Hampshire
Mon,Thur-Sat 10-5.30, V.Rel
Small R/C stk av cal, cnd and prices. Etgow. P.poss. BR Emsworth, OOS away from railway and follow signs for harbour. Nearest: Petersfield, Chichester, Havant.

Nearby there is a new bksp with some s/h bks. If I had just finished a course in positive thinking and was keen to win friends and influence people the only pleasant thing I could think of to say is that they are cheap.

ST PETERS BOOKSHOP Chichester
St Peters Church, West Street, Chichester
Tues-Sat, 10.30-5.30, L 1.30-2.30, Rel
Small/med size C/D stk, bookfairy av cal, cnd and prices. TWC. P.diff. From Chichester Bksp continue to cross and turn left.

I have just noticed that this address should be St Peters Arcade. There is of course a great deal of difference between a contemporary church and an arcade. To go into a church you have to pay whether you like it or not, in an arcade, you only have to pay if you find something you like.

CHICHESTER BOOKSHOP Chichester
39 Southgate, Chichester, W. Sussex
Mon-Sat, 9-5, they claim 5.30 but do tend to get restless about 5.
Lg R/C/D stk, av cal, cnd and prices. A solid roast beef establishment which serves up nouvelle cuisine without knowing it. There are res stks and also hidden stks, but alas of the most innocuous kind. If you can keep awake there are bgns to be had. TWC. P.diff. BR Chichester, OOS into town. Nearest: Petersfield, Arundel, Havant.

ARUNDEL BOOKSHOP **Arundel**
10 High Street, Arundel, W. Sussex
Mon-Sat, 9.15-5.15, L 1-2.15, summer Sun am, Rel
Lg R/C/D stk, av cal, cnd and prices. Emphon cookery and maritime. WAD. Apart from its closing for lunch I am V keen on this shop, mainly because other Ds are not. It is not far enough east for those Ds who like to go to Brighton and not far enough west for those Ds who go to Portsmouth. The trains are infrequent, there is a bypass and it is diff to P, but precisely because of these excuses it is worth going to and it is also worthwhile looking about for other shops in a similar situation. The one thing that puts me off this shop is the fact that too many Rs go in it. In theory I am V keen but when it comes to the practice, I tend to lose enthusiasm. It can be a trifle wearing listening to such wonderful remarks as "This must be a rare book, its purple." Now that I have persuaded several book Ds to stop talking to me, I am working on getting the public to do the same. What I need is something like the solution I saw in the Guardian: "Children shut up with rats." BR Arundel, OOS towards Castle and shop is on right. Nearest: Midhurst, Worthing, Chichester.

MURRAY & KENNET **Horsham**
102 Bishopric, Horsham, W. Sussex
Mon-Sat, 9-5.15, L 1.30-2.15, clsd Thur
Med/Lg R/C st, ab av cal and more int than most. Av prices. T. P.poss. Etgow. BR Horsham, OOS turn left and right at ring road and first right at signs for Billingshurst. Nearest: Dorking, Worthing, Godalming.

THE HORSHAM BOOKSHOP **Horsham**
4 Park Street, Horsham
Tues-Sat, 9.30-5.30, Rel
Med size R/C stk, av cal and cnd, ab av prices. Emphon cricket. TWC. AWYW. From Murray go back, cross main road into paved area, cross second junction and turn left.

REIGATE GALLERIES **Reigate**
45A Bell St, Reigate, Surrey
Mon-Sat, 9.30-5, Wed 1pm Rel
Med size R/C stk, Bookfairy, av cal, cnd and prices. BR Reigate, OOS turn right, continue to roundabout and then left under railway line and continue. Nearest: London Tunbridge Wells, Dorking, Horsham.

T S HILL BOOKS **Dorking**
122 South Street, Dorking, Surrey
Mon-Sat, 10-5, clsd Wed, Rel
Med size R/C stk, av cal, cnd and prices. TWC. P.diff. BR Dorking, OOS turn left and continue to T junction, turn right and keep left when road forks. Nearest: London Reigate, Horsham, Guildford.

ROUTE 6.45

THE ISLE OF WIGHT

IOW, PORTSMOUTH - GUILDFORD

You would have to be a complete fanatic to try to visit all the s/h bksps of the Isle of Wight in one day and I have done it.

I was aided by two things: firstly a lot of the shops were shut when they claimed to be open. Where bksps in the rest of Britain have notices on the door saying "Back in Five Minutes" - the most creative writing ever to appear in a s/h bksp - the shops in the Isle of Wight have a notice saying "Back in Five Months". It is just as reliable.

The second thing which helps considerably is the Bus service, which is wonderful. Mr Clive Linklater, the well known traveller of St Leonards claims this is untrue. He says that if you spend a week in the Isle of Wight you will soon be disabused of this notion. I would like to point out that you can tell from Mr. Linklater's joie de vivre, his uncare worn features, his eternal optimism and his insouciant presence that he has never tried using the London Bus service. On the day I went to the Isle of Wight I spent longer waiting for a bus to Waterloo Station than the entire time I spent waiting in the IOW. If you wish to spend a week in the IOW it is best to take a bike. The bksps could not be further apart if they tried and nor could they get more hills in between them.

It is best to start in Ryde and work your way anti clockwise round the island.

A one day bus rover ticket costs £3.90. The fare from Portsmouth is £5.50 return. You could almost buy the Isle of Wight for the price it costs to take a motor car there.

HERITAGE BOOKS Ryde, IOW
7 Cross Street, Ryde, Isle of Wight
Mon-Sat, 10-5, clsd Thurs, Rel
Med/lg R/C/D stk, av cal, cnd and prices. Looks like a nouvelle cuisine but it is in fact solid roast beef. Emphon Maritime. From Ryde Pier walk up hill and turn left at top. Nearest Newport, Cowes, Ventnor.

MR. MICAWBER Newport
61 Pyle Street, Newport, IOW
Mon-Sat, 10-5.30
New remainder bksp with small/med sized stk, av cal & cnd. I am always keen on this shop not so much because it is V good but because it is always open. It is sensibly sited and it is easy to do. TWC. From bus station continue along road, turn right and first left between two banks. Nearest: Cowes, Ryde, Ventnor, Freshwater.

*** THE NEVER OPEN BOOKSHOP** Cowes
65 High Street, Cowes, IOW
??
I have been to Cowes three times and not once have I ever found this shop open. I did get into it once by knocking up (I will rephrase that)...I got into it once by asking the lady in Julia Margaret Cameron shop who seems to have the key, but this time the lady had no idea what I was talking about. It is an int shop but what exactly is the point of having a bksp that is never open? A Helen Hanff Special. I am offering odds that it will appear in the Sunday Telegraph during Cowes Week.

This is the ultimate out to lunch bookshop

***THE OUT TO LUNCH BOOKSHOP** Yarmouth
High Street, no No. Yarmouth, IOW
Fri-Sat, 10-4, L 12.30-1.30, Sun 1-4
Can you believe it? Going to lunch when you are only open 14 hours a week.

To make a living out of s/h bks I need to get into seven bksps a day - on av. To get into seven bksps I have to plan to get into ten because of bad positioning. Shutting for lunch, half day closures, full day closures, death of aunts etc. I barely make a living. How does someone who opens 16hrs a week do it? And how can he afford to close for lunch? I am extremely keen on eating as the lady in the buffet at Newport Bus station will tell you - I think I am the only person who has ever been in that place more than once given how shocked the lady was to see me again - but if I started trying to include lunch hours in my timetable I would never get anywhere, let alone into seven bksps a day.

To plan a timetable that gets me to Yarmouth at 12 o'clock is asking me to give up doing the easiest shops first. This shop does not open until 10am. If I began in Yarmouth I would not hang around waiting for it, I would go to Freshwater where there is a much more int shop. In my experience the only people who can afford to go to lunch are publishers and journalists and they only do it because somebody else is paying.

THE GOLDEN HOURS BOOKSHOP **Freshwater**
School Green Road, Freshwater, Isle of Wight
Mon-Sat, 9-5, Rel
Med size R/C stk, a Drif Special. I have never seen anybody who could do more imaginative things with prices than this lady: Not only is she BSN she is PSN (Pricing sub normal). I think she must be a numeraphobe. That must be why it is called the Golden Hours Bksp: When are the golden hours? And there is no No in the street. The bks all have long explanations in front of that dreaded matter, the price, and when it comes to the price, I am sure she just uses figures that she has not used before. The price seems to bear no relation to anything computable. I once bought a book in here on "How to make curtains for Ocean Liners". I like to think of these type of bks as being drifiana but the price that was marked on it was about the same as it would cost for an ocean liner. We had a V int disc about this book but the noticeable thing was that at no time was she prepared to mention a figure. I left late in the afternoon understanding why it was called The Golden Hours Bksp. ETF in Freshwater as you go in from Newport.

L. J. SKLARROF **Totland**
Craiglee, The Broadway, Totland, Isle of Wight
Mon-Sat, 10-5, clsd Wed
Med size R/C/D stk, ab av cal, cnd and prices. Emphon Mod 1sts, Mervyn Peake and signed bks and letters. His own signature on the bks is also fairly impressive. The lady in Freshwater may not know what to do but this bloke knows down to the last £1 (there are no pennies on his prices). ETF

THE VENTNOR BOOKSHOP **Ventnor**
19 Pier Street, Ventnor, Isle of Wight
Mon-Sat, 10-5, clsd Wed & Thurs but varies the hours/days
Med/lg R/C/D stk, ab av cal, cnd and prices. The most int and worthwhile shop on the island and definitely WAD. It looks solid roast beef but there are lots of overlooked bgns. He looks extremely gloomy but he does not interfere unless you ask. Like me I think he is still trying to work out what happened to the warehouse full of bks that used to be out the back.

SANDOWN

Contrary to what other directories say - there is no s/h bksp in Sandown. There IS a garage whioch opens during the summer. It is hard to decide which is worse the bks or the smell. Well worth avoiding.

MOTHER GOOSE BOOKSHOP St Helens
Upper Green Road, St. Helens, Isle of Wight
Mon-Sat, 11.30-1 & 7.30-10
A med sized Drif Special, not least for the fact that it opens in the evening during the summer and it is easy to ring the lady if she is not there. And I wish more of you would do it because eV time I ring up she says "You are the man who rang last year." T & Disc. ETF in St Helens. By opening in the evening and being flexible this shop makes it poss to visit all the other shops in the Isle of Wight in one day. I wish I could convince more shops to do this.

RICHARD MARTIN Gosport
25 Stoke Road, Gosport, Hants
Tues-Sat, 10.15-1 & 2.15-5
Med size C spec shop emphon Maritime. Av cal, cnd and prices. T & Disc. P.poss. BR Portsmouth Harbour and then ferry to Gosport - from pierhead go straight ahead for about 1 mile to second parade of shops.

RC writes
You notice he does not dislike this bugger being in the middle of nowhere. This is because it gives him a chance to go on the ferry for free. You only have to pay if you are going back to Portsmouth. What he does is send me all the way round whilst he goes in the shops in Portsmouth.

PORTSMOUTH AND SOUTHSEA

THE SOUTH SEA BUBBLE

There are no s/h bksps in Portsmouth; they are all in Southsea, which believe it or not is the prosperous part of this island. If you saw the less endowed you too would become sympathetic to much maligned Adolph. He, when he tried to bomb it out of existence, did at least have a coordinated plan. The people that came after him had no idea what they were hoping to do. Completely fazed they built a motorway around the city. It is best to use this to get to Southsea, unless you are a masochist.

By train it is best to alight at Fratton for which you have to get on the slow train from Havant. The good news is that it is nrly worthwhile, not because of anything the town council has done but in spite of them. This is why the bksps are in Southsea; it has not been improved yet.

MILLERS BOOKS AND PRINTS Southsea
55 Fawcett Road, Southsea, Hampshire
Tues-Sat, 11-6, clsd Wed
Med size R/C stk, av cal, cnd and prices. AWYW but seldom has it. BR Fratton, OOS over bridge to left and straight ahead.

STAR BOOKSHOP Southsea
69 Fawcett Road, Southsea, Hampshire
Tues-Fri, 12-6.30, Sat 11-6, Rel
Med size R/C/D stk. This is by far the most int shop in

Southsea and well WAD. The opening hours are not because nothing happens in Portsmouth in the mornings, but because nothing happens there at all, and this shop is trying to do something about it.

ADELPHI BOOKS **Southsea**
1 Albert Road, Southsea, Hampshire
Tues-Fri, 11.30-4.30, Sat 10-5.30
Med size R/C stk, av cal, cnd and prices. A Bookdealer Special. From Star Bksp continue along Fawcett Road and turn right at main junction. Shop is opposite police station on left.

BOOK ACADEMY **Southsea**
13 Marmion Road, Southsea, Hampshire
Mon-Sat, 9-5, Rel
Med size R/C stk, av cal, cnd and prices. Excruciatingly boring. It suffers from arterial schlerosis, senile dementia and terminal lassitude. No wonder there is a res stk of religious bks. From Adelphi turn left into road behind police station and right at marmion (about half a mile).

BOOKENDS **Havant**
2 North Street, Havant, Hampshire
Mon-Sat, 9.30-5.30, Rel
Med size R/C stk, low key Book & Magazine Collector type, av cnd and prices. TWC. P.diff. BR Havant. OOS turn left and right and continue. Nearest: Petersfield, Chichester, Portsmouth, Southampton.

THE PETERSFIELD BOOKSHOP **Petersfield**
16a Chapel Street, Petersfield, Hampshire
Mon-Sat, 9-5.30
V Lg R/C/D stk, av cal, cnd and prices. Needs a lot of attention but can be rewarding. They also have a second smaller shop round the corner which seems to produce more bgns, maybe just because it is smaller. P.poss opp. BR Petersfield, OOS ahead, turn left at main junction for second shop continue along and turn right at T junction. Shop is on left. Nearest: Haslemere, Havant and Winchester.

JUST BOOKS **Haslemere**
2 Causewayside, High Street, Haslemere, Surrey
Mon-Sat, 9-5.15, Rel.
Not sure about that, I seem to remember it was clsd one afternoon. New bksp with med size R/C stk, dreary but good cnd. TWC. An Amateur Dramatic Society production of a Beckett Special. Waiting for Goodo. BR: Haslemere, OOS turn left follow road up to main junction and turn left. Nearest: Godalming, Hindhead, Petersfield, Reigate.

THE EUREKA BOOKSHOP **Godalming**
19a Church Street, Godalming, Surrey
Mon-Fri, 10.30-3, Wed 1pm, Sat 10.30-5
Small R/C stk, better than the house would lead you to believe. And certainly better than Godalming deserves. Av cal, cnd and prices. TWC. P.diff. BR: Godalming, OOS bear left towards church. Nearest: Guildford, Reigate, Haslemere, Farnham.

NSF BOOKS **Godalming**
9 Queen Street, Godalming, Surrey
Mon-Sat, 10-4, Rel
Med size R stk. A bta charity bksp. Heavy on the pbks but light on the prices. No T. P.poss. From Eureka continue to High Street, turn left and right.

GUILDFORD

There is no Guildford. I know there is a place called Guildford and I know that Guildford used to exist, but it does not exist any more. I know nobody else has said anything, but it is not there. You can deny the existence of God, you can express disbelief in the occult, you can say that you do not believe in charity but deny that Guildford exists and people just go quiet and then change the subject.

What used to happen when you went to Guildford was that you came out of the station, turned right, turned left over the bridge and went up the hill to Thorpe's. When I tried to do this at the beginning of the year I found myself cycling round a mini M25 unable to find a way off. As unlikely as it may seem I suspected Mr. Thorpe and Mr. Traylen were playing a practical joke on me. The only way to defeat them was to ignore them and so I cycled on to Haslemere.

The next time I went I used the Desert Storm plan. I pretended to be going to Reading and then I came back via Guildford. I watched carefully as the train pulled into the station, there was nobody around who could send secret messages to the cover up Guildford Committee or change the signs. All I could see was Car Parks.

Guildford is now a town dedicated to the greater glory of car parks. Ed Rouche and Christos would be proud of it. There are open plan car parks, multi storey car parks, short term car parks and feeder car parks. And there are lots of cars and occasionally you see some drivers but there is no Guildford that anybody can see.

Almost on tiptoe I got off the train, crept out of the station, turned right, turned left and walked straight into a car park. An alarm went off and a disembodied voice told me to produce my ticket and put it in the machine. There was nobody to ask, the machine just issued instructions. Years of scouting for the small gaps in life had accustomed me to finding the speedy way out, I spotted a sign saying 'Exit', I went through it and ended up back in the station.

The covert method was clearly not working, maybe Schwazcopf knew more about car parks than I did. I decided to change tactics, I would use the Sunday Times investigative journalist technique.

At 8.33 on a cold March morning I bought a day return ticket to Portsmouth Harbour, the station for the Isle of Wight. First class of course. I sat in the compartment, adjusted my trilby, my confidence and my cover story, and got to Guildford at 9.14. I stepped smartly off the train, a diesel of Queens class, walked to the station exit, looking neither left nor right and got into a cab and told the driver to take me to Thorpe's.

"I cannot do that gov, it is best to walk!"

For one second I let the front drop and then it dawned on me. Only a Sunday Times journalist would have seen Guildford Station as a triumph of modern architecture. To anybody sensible it was just a mass of scaffolding. There are no porters or ticket collectors anywhere. There are taxi drivers but they must work for the secret police; whoever heard of a taxi driver turning down a fare.

There is no Guildford, there has been some enormous accident, like Chernobyl, Five Mile Island or Bhopal and in the usual British method it is being covered up; with car parks.

Possibly a sub urban terrorist group such as the "Heritage Front" has removed the entire place to somewhere where it will be better appreciated. Any day now there will be a fifteen page memo in City Limits.

The other possibility is that everything has been sold off, that there is no Guildford left, that all those motor cars are just going there out of habit. Remembering the long lost days when nobody believed that the resources of Guildford would run out. Instead they just carried on selling it off - at Boot Fairs.

COBWEBS **Farnham**
29 The Woolmead, East Street, Farnham, Surrey
Mon-Sat, 10-5
Med/lg R/C/D stk av cal, cnd, exotic prices. (All the shops that I can ever remember in Farnham have always had this fond belief that their locals will pay more). This is a genuinely interesting shop which encouraged me to browse for far longer than normal despite there being no notices in the window.
It does everything I think a s/h bksp should not do, and yet it has more customers than I would have expected.

On the outside, it says 'Secondhand and Collectable Books'. I know what a s/h book is but what is a 'collectable book'? Surely all books must be collectable? It is no part of the job of bookdealers to tell the customers what to collect. If the owner thinks one book is more likely to be collected than another he should simply put the price up.

This shop has an enormous amount of window space but it is V diff to see most of the bks from the outside. By not putting bks in the window they are displaying that the shop is non threatening but it must be possible to do both.

Once inside I was somewhat deterred by the bizarre pricing, but remembered my rule, that if they charge too much it means they do not know what they are doing. This proved too much. It means that they do not know what they are doing. This proved correct, even if it took me an hour to prove it. But by letting me find a grossly underpriced book they managed to maintain my interest.

In the window of this shop there are notices about the dearth of browsers and this establishment is keen to encourage them.

In the days when there were browsers there were no notices trying to encourage them.

BYGONES **Farnham**
5a Castle Street, Farnham, Surrey
Tues-Sat, 10-5, Rel
Med size R/C/D stk. Slightly Bookfairy, roast beef, NSOC, but

V strong on prices. TWC. AWYW. BR Farnham OOS ahead towards church steeple and turn left and first right. Nearest: Farnborough, Godalming, Haslemere, New Arlesford.

ALTON SECONDHAND BOOKS Alton
11 Normandy Street, Alton, Hampshire
Mon-Sat, 9.30-5.30, Wed & Sat 5pm, Rel
Med size R/C stk, av cal, cnd and prices. A Drif Special despite the woman's own gush. TWC. P.poss. BR Alton, OOS ahead and turn right. Nearest: Farnham, Petersfield, Alresford.

ROUTE 7 O'CLOCK

SIDMOUTH - WINCHESTER

DORSET, SOMERSET AND UPSET

This is the forgotten part of England and I wish I could forget it too. It is extremely easy to get to by road and rail but extremely difficult to get round once you are there. The main route is the A303 which bypasses all the shops, the main rail route is the Salisbury/Exeter line which bypasses all the roads. If you attempt to get into 10 shops in a day you will be lucky if you manage five. I have tried doing it by motor car, by train and by bike and I have never once managed even that. If there was somewhere pleasant to stay I would try it for a week but there is nowhere attractive or central enough. It is twenty urbs and lots of urberts.

SIDMOUTH OLD BOOKS **Sidmouth**
12 Temple Street, Sidmouth, Devon
Mon-Sat, 10-5, clsd Thurs
Med size R/C stk, av cal, cnd and prices. Looks like it is about to close. ETF on the way into Sidmouth by police Station. Nearest: Honiton, Bridport, Exeter. BR: Honiton (NAST 10miles but efficient bus service links with trains).

PIC'S **Bridport**
11 South Street, Bridport, Dorset, DT6 3NR
Mon-Sat, 9-5, Thurs 1pm
Med size R/C stk, NSOC, av cal and prices. As you go through the door of this shop there is a smell and for a few brief fractions of a second you think it is the smell of a really good bksp, perhaps even a Drif Special, but on the last part of the sniff something astringent hits your nostrils. All this takes place in less than a half second, but all the time you spend in the shop you are haunted by this smell and how accurate a description it is of this shop. BR Weymouth, NAST 10miles. Nearest: Waytown, Weymouth, Sidmouth.

QUEST BOOKS **Weymouth**
13a Cove Street, Weymouth, Dorset
Mon-Sat, 10.30-5.30, L 1-2 Unr.
Small R stk almost a Drif Special. From Books Afloat, continue into town, turn right, go over bridge and keep to left.

BOOKS AFLOAT **Weymouth**
66 Park Street, Weymouth
tUES-sAT, 9.30-5.30, V.Rel
Med/lg R/C stk, ab av cal, cnd av prices. Spec in Maritime. Similar. T. P.diff. WAD.
This unique short term sample cruise has been carefully designed by an expert to fit the pockets of impecunious book collectors whilst maintaining all the luxuries and facilities for which ocean liners are justly famed.

Its berth has been especially chosen for convenience. It is a pebbles throw from the railway station, on the pierhead of a major road and within launching distance of the better sea lanes.

On board there is something to interest everybody. Those not of a nautical disposition are catered for on the port side. To starboard is the greatest attraction. This part of the deck is for those whose lungs and hearts expand at the whiff of sea air.

In the main it is pacific but it does not flee to harbour during violent storms. Every tide and cross current has been carefully coordinated. Waves of which others make mountains are expertly confronted. From the lowest depth to the highest sea spray, all are given equal space at the captain's table. This is the bksp of the seven c's: calm, collected, conscientious, careful, commendable, compulsive and cheap.

The captain offers his sincere thanks to the passengers for using "Books Afloat" and is confident that you will soon return for an even more memorable voyage.

SECOND READING BOOKSHOP Blandford Forum
7 Nightingale Court, East Street, Blandford Forum, Dorset
Mon-Sat, 9.30-5. Wed 1pm
Med size R/C stk, av cal, cnd and prices. Rumoured to be up for sale. BR Dorchester (NAST 20 miles). There are also 2 half shops in Blandford, see TIN. East Street is alongside church. Nearest: Shaftsbury, Southampton, Puddletown, Sherborne.

DORCHESTER

Currently no s/h bksps, but one rumoured

ANTIQUARIAN & SECONDHAND BOOKS Swanage
55 High Street, Swanage, Dorset
Mon-Sat, 10-5, Unr
Med/lg R/C stk, av cal cnd and prices. It looks beautiful, from the outside but inside is slightly disappointing. A Helen Hanff Special. TWC. P.diff. BR Wareham (NAST 10 miles). Nearest: Wareham, Bournemouth, Weymouth.

Bournemouth is an eminently sensible place, most of the shops stay open sensible hours and have sensible stocks. It is poss to walk it and the parking is relatively easy. By train it is best to alight at Pokesdown. Nearest: Weymouth, Lymington, Blandford Forum.

HOLDENHURST BOOKS Bournemouth
275 Holdenhurst Road, Bournemouth, Dorset
Mon-Sat, 10-5.30, clsd Wed, Rel
Med size R/C stk, av cal, cnd and prices. Emphon Motoring. BR Bournemouth, OOS on the other side turn right and left (North).

ASHLEY BOOKSHOP Bournemouth
30b Ashley Road, Boscombe, Bournemouth
Mon-Sat, 10-5.30

V Lg R/C stk, av cal, cnd and prices. Res Stk. BR Pokesdown, OOS turn right and turn right past paved area.

BEHOLD I COME QUICKLY

The above rubric is not the motto of the Premature Ejaculators Society but the legend which appears high on the wall in the disused church where the Ashley Bksp is situated. The Christian Church did not come quickly, it was twelve centuries before it began to flourish, for people who believe in the life everlasting this may indeed be a short time but for those of us who are more mortal it seems like the length of the average sermon.

The Christian Church and this bksp share a belief that if you have enough words you are bound to convert the unbelievers. Both believe in quantity rather than quality; anything rather than nothing; persistance rather than perspecacity; tenacity rather than temptation.

The originators and current custodians of that rubric display a total lack of comprehension of most people's desires. Most people are not interested in coming quickly.

YESTERDAY'S BOOKS **Bournemouth**
65-67 Bennet Road, Bournemouth, Dorset
Mon-Sat, 9.30-5.30, Rel
Med size R/C/D stk, av cal, cnd and prices. Res stk of Africana. Diff to find but worth the effort. From Ashley Bksp proceed North, turn left at main junction and continue to footbridge, cross, turn right and left and first left.

H & S ROWAN **Bournemouth**
459 Christchurch Road, Boscombe, Bournemouth
Mon-Sat, 9-6, Rel
Med/lg R/C/D stk, av cal, cnd and prices. I always find this shop dreary and unint. but several other book Ds claim I do not know what I am talking about. BR: Pokesdow, OOS continue westward.

SIDNEY WRIGHT **Bournemouth**
12&13 Royal Arcade, Bournemouth, Dorset
Mon-Sat, 9-5.30
New bksp with lg R/C stk. A Helen Hanff Special. Av cal, cnd and prices. TWC. Shop is in arcade of Christchurch Road near the Ashley Bksp.

BOOKS AND MAPS **Bournemouth**
122 Tuckton Road, Southbourne, Bournemouth
Mon-Sat, 9.30-5.30
Med size R/C/D stk, av cal, cnd, imaginative prices. This shop is the cheer leader for Bournemouth, but the members of the main team are extremely reluctant to have anything to do with such high pressure promotion. The owner is rather like one of those warm-up men that they have on television programmes before the real show begins. His contribution often seems funnier than the whole of the star performance. He makes the entire show seem better than it really is, but afterwards you do wonder what it was you found so enter-

taining. Some of his best jokes are the prices, however like all great comedians he does adapt his act to suit the audience. AND, like all warm-up men he dreams of being a star in his own right and is hoping to open in Bournemouth. Already you can hear the shuffling of feet round Winton. As an old stager myself I advised him the best poss name for a shop is the name of the area in which it is situated, however in his case, I feel a small degree of egotism would not only be beneficial but positively help him get recognised. He should call it THE BORN MOUTH BOOKSHOP

BOOKS AND THINGS **New Milton**
99 Old Milton Road, New Milton, Hampshire
Mon-Sat, 9.30-5.30, Wed 1pm, Unr
BILL GRIM'S PROGRESS. This bksp is an allegory: for the owner it is a bad dream for the rest of us it is a good nightmare. This Christian who is always weeping and wondering how to prevent the destruction of himself has closed his ears to the entreaties of the Worldly Wise that he should leave. He has hidden himself behind the wicket gate which gets bigger and bigger (sorry wrong dream) and now dreams of the celestial city (Bournemouth) but he knows that there he shall encounter Simple, Sloth and Presumption (Readers, Collectors and Dealers). His wife, Discretion, Piety, Prudence and Charity has built him the house beautiful and shown him the delectable mountains of books, but for him it will be the valley of humiliation if he sells them. At Vanity Fair he refuses to buy anything, this is how he has come to the hill of Lucre (that and his wife's earnings as a dinner lady). He is not fool enough to touch the free silver mine which is his stock. He will keep to the narrow path (if he can find it between the books) There is a key called promise but it has been lost.

They don't call me Mr. Great Heart for nothing; there will now be a collection.

BEAGLE BOOKS **Sway**
1 Middle Road, Sway, Hampshire
Mon-Fri, 10-4, clsd Wed, Sat 9-1
This is the bksp as pleasant occupation and good for the image. The concept of selling books plays little part.

In theory Sway is easy to get to by road and rail, but in practice what is more likely to happen is that you will go to Lymington which has two shops that open sensible hours, have no lunch and are much more likely to produce books. I have set off three times to get to Sway and have not made it once. I can see that they might be keen not to have me in their shop but I am fairly confident that being where they are deters many other customers as well.

There will now be a guest appearance by Mr T C late of Southampton who wishes to remain anonymous, on the grounds that I could say something which would get him into trouble. He writes, and I stress that his remarks have not been censored in any way and further have been given his usual full consideration: "Bookfairy".

HUGHES & SMEETH **Lymington**
9 Gosport Street, Lymington, Hampshire
Mon-Sat, 9.30-5, Rel

Small med size R/C stk, ab av cal, cnd av prices. Emphon Maritime, TWC. P.diff. BR Lymington Town, OOS ahead and turn left shop is by junction. Nearest: Sway Milton and Freshwater IOW.

TRIANGLE BOOKS **Lymington**
70 High Street, Lymington, Hampshire
Mon-Sat, 10-5, Rel
Med size R/C stk, larger than av bkstl in much more pleasant than av antiques market. Slightly bookfairy. T. P.poss. From Hughes & Smeeth go straight up hill and shop is opposite Town Hall.

CHANGE AT BROCKENHURST FOR LYMINGTON AND SWAY

NORTHAM BOOKS **Southampton**
30 Northam Road, Southampton
Wed-Sat, 10-6
Med size R/C stk, nrly a Drif Special (all they have to do is lower the prices). TWC and disc. From Gilberts go back to Main Street, turn left and right and straight ahead at roundabout.

H.M. GILBERT **Southampton**
2 Portland Street, Southampton
Mon-Sat, 8.30-5 Rel
Lg R/C stk, av cal, cnd and prices. The one admirable feature of the RSPCA is that it does put down dogs. I would admire the ABA if they put down bksps that are filled with dogs. TWC. BR: Southampton, OOS on ocean liner side up hill past the civic centre which looks like a warning to shipping and turn right at main shopping street and right again at Portland Street. Nearest: Salisbury, Winchester, Gosport, Lymington.

WINCHESTER

DESERVES A SAWN OFF RIFLE

PETER M DALY **Winchester**
10a Jewry Street, Winchester
Wed,Fri,Sat 10-5, Sat L 1-2? Rel
Small med sized stk, C/D, av cal, cnd and prices. Bookfairy. Emphon Nat His, Mountaineering. T. Etgow. P.diff. BR Winchester, OOS to bottom of road turn right and follow road into town. Shop is at rear of antiques arcade.

H M GILBERT **Winchester**
19 The Square, Winchester
Mon-Sat, 9-5.30, Rel
New bksp with med sized R/C stk, av cal, cnd and prices. The owners of this establishment are so keen on dogs they have bought the kennel on the opp side of the square to house their pups. After sniffing round here for 30 minutes, not getting one bite in and being shushed for barking I felt too much like a muzzled bitch to leg over to the other place.

The SPCK around the corner to the left has some s/h bks. From the Oxfam go back to Green Street, turn left, right at the bottom and left past the statue.

E. S. WICKS **Farnborough**

48 Peabody Road, Farnborough
Mon-Sat, 9-5, Fri & Sat 5.30
Recently changed hands and address in street. Med/lg R/C stk, av cal, cnd, bl av prices. It is an odd place. BR Farnborough Main, OOS into main road, turn right and continue for one mile - turn left at green and second left. Camp Hill Station but there are few trains. The other establishment in Farnborough is seldom open - see TIN. Nearest: Henley, Farnham, New Alresford.

BLACKLOCKS **Englefield Green**

8 Victoria Street, Englefield Green, Surrey
Mon-Sat, 9-5, Rel
Small R/C stk, av cal, cnd and prices. Keen on Military. Also has some stk at The Bookshop, Station Approach, Virginia Water. I had avoided going to this place for years mainly because it seemed to be in the middle of nowhere. It was not on a route to anywhere and it sounded as if it was going to be just another village bksp that somebody had opened instead of retiring. That the opp was true I did not discover until I actually went there. If a monomaniac such as me is deterred then I think I am justified in thinking that many other people were likewise deterred. What shops like this should do is call themselves by the name of the most prominent town. It does not matter whether it is true or not the crucial part is to get the customers coming. The name if should be called is the Egham Bksp. If the Greek who lives down the road can call himself the Duke of Edinburgh, there is absolutely no reason why a bksp that is two miles from Egham Station cannot have a fantasy name.

ROUTE 8 O'CLOCK

PENZANCE - EXETER - SALISBURY

PENZANCE RARE BOOKS **Penzance**
43 Causewayhead, Penzance, Cornwall
Mon-Sat, 9-5.30, Rel
Med/lg R/C/D stk which, with a little more effort, would truly become WAD. This shop does have int bks, it just needs slightly more of them to make it worthwhile driving all the way. By car, Penzance is always further than you think. By train it is a wonderfully long journey. There is never a time when I go through Paddington Station late at night, that I do not want to get on the train for Penzance. When a gentleman in London told me that there were six bksps in Penzance I could not resist the temptation. I left at midnight and arrived at 9am (it is some journey by train too). But the best I could come up with was 2½ shops. There is this one, which also has a pbk shop across the street, there is Argante, there is an antique shop with bks, there is the Occult shop in Quayside which has a V small amount of s/h and there is about to be opened in New Street, another shop in the chain owned by the people in Camborne. But bksps as I define them there are only 2½. With the improvement in Falmouth it is nearly worth a trip, but a little more is required to make it definitely worthwhile. BR Penzance, OOS turn right and right and left into Market Jew Street, turn right past Market Building. P.diff. OWOWS. POCS.
RC Writes
The real reason he always wants to go to Penzance is that he has four different liaisons with Indian ladies in Southall, none of whom know about the other. You get to Southall from Paddington.

ARGANTE **Penzance**
1 Princes Street, Penzance, Cornwall

Small/med size R/C stk, nrly a Drif Special. Just because of the name - Argante was the Spear Carrier for King Arthur, but it clearly did not leave a lot of time for reading books - T. Etgow. P.diff. From Penzance Rare Books go back down hill and straight across road and first left.

THE MIRROR AND THE LAMP **St Ives**
1 Saint Andrews Street, St Ives, Cornwall
Tues, Wed, Fri & Sat 1-6
Small stk of poetry and art, also sells pictures. I only went to St Ives because I had read in the Sunday Telegraph that there was a splendid s/h bksp there. Instead all I found was this place, which is open, if that is the right term, 20 hours a week. Less than 20 hours and I do not classify it as a bksp, but what really irritated me was that you cannot see into the shop. I know from asking other people that it deals in art and poetry and the truth is that when I get into these type of shops, I have no idea who they are for, it certainly is not for the likes of me. Most of the people in St Ives are working class tourists, what is the point of nrly opening a shop that caters to half a dozen

pseuds. It is not for want of trying, or rather not for want of somebody wanting to teach me. For years, my chauffeur was Mr Iain Sinclair, ye poete, and despite several long lessons I was never able to understand how you learnt about poetry bks of which there were only ten copies. Not the main advantage of this shop is that it is easy to miss it. I could even get to admire it, if they closed down.

STRAND BOOKS **Padstow**
4 The Strand, Padstow, Cornwall
Mon-Sat, 9-5, Wed 1pm, much more during summer
Med size R/C stk, a silverfish special with shark prices. ETF. Nearest: St Columb Major.

FALMOUTH

NO VOLUME CONTROL

I did not know that the reason that it is called Falmouth is that every year they have a contest to see who can make the most noise unaided. The seagulls take some beating, but the tourists do win by force of numbers, especially when they go inside anywhere. There is now more opportunity for them espec in the bksps, which have tripled. They have practice sessions in the charity shops which have also tripled. Artificial aids such as motor cars are felt to be unsporting so no allowance is made for them. Nearest: Truro, Penzance.

BROWSERS BOOKSHOP **Falmouth**
13 St George's Arcade, Falmouth, Cornwall
Mon-Sun, 10-6, Rel
Med/lg R/C nrly Ds stk, genuinely int bks which you do not see elsewhere. WAD. Av cal and prices. Bgns known. TWC. P.diff. Owows. Pocs. BR Falmouth Town (the Dell - no idea) OOS turn left and left into shopping street and follow through past bend. Shop is in arcade on left. Nearest: Truro, Penzance.

BOOKMARK **Falmouth**
94 High Street, Falmouth, Cornwall
Mon-Sat, 10-5, Rel
Med/nrly lg R/C stk, keen on Lit and Stiener. Has voice like a junior foghorn. T. Res stk. Etgow. P.diff. From Browsers turn left out of arcade and continue up hill, shop is on right.

TONY POWELL **Falmouth**
2 Old Brewery Yard, High Street, Falmouth, Cornwall
Mon-Sat, 10-4
Small/med size R/C stk, a Book & Magazine Collector Special, av cal, cnd, adventurous pricing. Major contestant in fog horn contest. TWC. P.diff. From Bookmark continue up hill to Antiques Centre on left.

JUST BOOKS **Truro**
9 Pindar Mews, Truro, Cornwall
Mon-Sat, 10-5, clsd Thurs
Med sized R/C stk, av cal, cnd unjust prices. TWC. There is also a charity bksp by the Marks & Spencer round the corner.

BR Truro, OOS turn left and follow round into town centre, bear left into Victoria Road. Turn left when you see the Marks & Spencers and shop is in newish alleyway to the left. (This is the abbreviated route). Nearest: Padstow, Fowey, Falmouth, Penzance.

COLLECTORS CORNER **St Columb Major**
7 Bank Street, St Columb Major, Cornwall
Mon-Sat, 10-5, Rel
Med size R/C stk, slightly Book & Magazine Collector Special but can be worth a look, in a car. BR St Columb Road (NAST 3 miles) into town straight ahead and then left, shop is immediately on right. Nearest: Padstow, Fowey, Truro.

BOOK ENDS **Fowey**
4 South Street, Fowey, Cornwall
Mon-Sat, 9.30-6
Med size R/C stk, av cal, cnd and prices. Keen on Local His and Nautical. ETF. Nearest: Padstow, Looe, Truro, NV.

THE OLD HALL BOOKSHOP **Looe**
Shutta Road, East Looe, Cornwall
Mon-Sat, 10-5.30, less in winter
Med size R/C/D stk, well nrly D and nearly WAD. T. Etgow. P.diff. BR Looe, OOS turn right and continue to Barclays Bank - where all the boats are moored - and turn sharp left up hill. Nearest: Launceston, Plymouth, Fowey.

PLYMOUTH

THE CONCRETE BUNGLE

THE BARBICAN BOOKSHOP **Plymouth**
46 Southside Street, Plymouth, Devon
Mon-Sat, 10.30-5.30
Med size R/C stk, a Helen Hanff Special. The owner of this shop is possessed of a rare talent. He can spot the world's most boring bks and sell them. This does tell a little about Plymouth which is poss the most boring city in Britain. As you walk from the station you become almost comatose with its dreariness. I bet the market for sleeping pills in Plymouth is non existent. Almost every shop and building you pass is a 'centre' of some kind. This deadening effect has occurred in other places, but only in Plymouth do they seem to have eliminated the only shopfronts which are int in most towns - those of undertakers. In Plymouth it would be called a dead centre. BR Plymouth, OOS ahead and follow signs from station to city centre, keep going until you see signs for the Hoe and then turn left and right into an unsuspecting dreary looking street. Nearest: Ashburton, Kingsbridge, East Looe.

There is also a pbk stall with some hardbacks in the Pannier Market opp.

CORNERSTONE BOOKS **Plymouth**
New Street Antiques Centre, The Barbican, Plymouth
Mon-Sat, 10-5
Med size R/C stk which is a bit too high in cal to be a Drif Special but only needs a little adjustment. (*RC: What he*

means is that he is too tight to pay this guy's prices). Almost WAD. This establishment is a prize example of life's unfairness - just in case you need a handy example that it - it is full of int bks but cannot display them properly because of lack of space - it is slightly bigger than a coffin - but the prat round the corner in Barbican Books has more space than he has air between his ears. He is about as suited to being a s/h book D as the Queen is to being a cleaning lady and yet both are dumpy. When I write my manual on suicide I shall be sending him a free copy. From Barbican continue south and turn right and right, slightly back on yourself, do not confuse this with the first bkstl you see in Southside.

ROOM AT THE TOP **Kingsbridge**
The Shambles, Market Arcade, Fore Street, Kingsbridge, Devon
Mon-Sat, 9-5, Thurs & Sat 12. Rel
Med size R/C/nrly D stk. There are some V smooth bks in this shop. I think she spends most of her time sandpapering them with her tongue. TWC. P.diff. BR Totnes (NAST 15miles) ETF by church on hill. Nearest: Plymouth, Totnes, Brixham.

I say "Easy To Find" and given some of the s/h bksps I have had to find it definitely is but when I went into a local charity shop and started giving a fellow bksp crawler the third degree about any other local shops, he had not heard of this one. He had been on holiday in Kingsbridge for a week and had not yet stumbled across it, and yet he knew of three shops in Leek - his hometown - whereas I thought there were only two. The Kingsbridge shop was losing this man's custom by not making itself more prominent. To not get this man's custom was a serious failing on the part of this shop. It is true that it is on the local leaflet but most ordinary customers do not travel, and this gentleman was unaware of it.

For me the Kingsbridge shop had been a distinct pleasure. I had caught the seven o'clock ferry from Kingswear to Dartmouth, the proper ferry had broken down and had been replaced by a rowing boat that was almost shorter than my bike. I had then cycled over the Slapton Sands, which is not near Slapton and has no sand, and overcome some of the steepest hills in Britain to arrive in Kingsbridge at nine o'clock just as the shop opened. I could see that the lady was distinctly nervous of this sweaty behemoth skinhead who spent only £2.95 but if you don't want to have me as a customer you have to attract ordinary people. I can put up with the hopeless B&Bs that do not serve breakfast until 9, I can put up with risking life and limb and bike on the ocean wave, I can put up with a rehearsal for the tour de France, but theonly thing I cannot stand is to see a shop filled with ordinary customers.

THE BOOK WARREN **Brixham**
9a Bolton Street, Brixham, Devon
Mon-Sat, 10-4.30, clsd Wed in winter
Small/med size R/C stk, which has a certain sense of style and can produce some int bks. TWC. P.diff. BR Paignton (NAST 5 miles). Follow signs for Brixham and turn right immediately at crossroads, by town hall, shop is next to betting office on right. Nearest: Goodrington, Kingsbridge, Totnes.

BIDDY'S BOOKSHOP **Goodrington**
99 Dartmouth Road, Goodrington, Paignton, Devon
Mon-Sun, 10-4.30, much more in summer. Rel
This is definitely a Drif Special, not least because it was open on a Sunday night after I had been to St Ives to visit the bksp there and had been secretly hoping that it would be open on a Sunday, only to discover that it opens for twenty hours a week, that it was not poss to see the bks through the window and that the only good thing about St Ives is the view as you leave the station. Shops such as the one in St Ives are always claiming that they would open if there were customers but this is an out and out lie. The shop in Goodrington had customers on a Sunday night at 9pm. It beats me who the people in St Ives think they are going to sell to. This shop knows that it is selling to the people who cannot afford to go to Costa Del Sol for their holidays and it has the bks which are appropriate to their lack of income, and mine. BR Paignton, OOS follow signs for Brixham and bksp is almost opp swimming pool. Ignore the Steam Railway and its stations for the price of a ticket you could expect to buy a locomotive. Nearest: Totnes, Paignton, Brixham.

THE POCKET BOOKSHOP **Paignton**
159 Winner Street, Paignton, Devon
Mon-Sat, 10.30-6, in summer, Rel
This seaside, seed sized shop cedes no side, indeed it seethes on all sides in, the deed seems to soon done. Done you wish he would seize the shells of other shops, but memory shows what shells some shops are. This one has the shell to its ear and the sound is the sighs of satisfaction. BR Paignton, the scenic route, OOS turn left and right into alleyway, follow round cross main road, ahead turn right past church and left, shop is ahead. Nearest: Totnes, Newton Abbot, Goodrington.

LINDY'S **Newton Abbot**
58 Queen Street, Newton Abbot, Devon
Mon-Sat, 9.30-5, Thurs 1
Lg R/C stk, emphon ephemera, ab av cal, cnd, av prices. Res stk of theology. This is the only religious bksp I have seen where the owner is actually keen on the stuff. WAD. BR Newton Abbot, OOS ahead into town and shop is in main street on left, upstairs. Nearest: Teignmouth, Paignton, Ashburton, Bovey Tracey.

TOTNES

THE NIKED LUNCH

PEDLARS PACK **Totnes**
4 The Palins, Totnes, Devon
Mon-Sat, 9-5
Med/lg C/D stk, bookfairy but well worth a look. BR Totnes, OOS, turn left and follow signs into Town Centre, shop is at bottom of hill before bridge. Nearest: Ashburton, Paignton, Kingsbridge, Plymouth.

COLLARDS **Totnes**
4 Castle Street, Totnes, Devon
Mon-Sat, 10-5, BTR Jan-March
Med/lg R/C stk, emphon Detective fiction, av cal, cnd and prices. T. P.diff. Continue up Fore Street and turn right. Further up the hill is a new children's bksp with a small stk of similar s/h.

THE BOOKWORM **Teignmouth**
26 Regent Street, Teignmouth, Devon
Mon-Sat, 10.30-6.30, more in summer. Rel
Med size R/C stk, low key, low cnd, av prices. TWC. P.diff. Nearest: Dawlish, Newton Abbot, Exeter.

THE OLD BOOKSHOP **Dawlish**
Strand Hill, Dawlish
Mon-Sat, 10-5, Suns in summer
Med size R/C stk, slightly gliterace. Av cal, cnd and prices. TWC. P.diff. BR Dawlish, OOS turn left and right at bottom and follow road round to left and then come back on yourself. Nearest: Exeter, Teignmouth, Newton Abbot.

EXETER

Exeter is the main inspiration for my belief that cathedral cities are a dead loss, for books. P.diff. OWOWS. POCS. Nearest: Tiverton, Honiton, Dawlish, Ashburton.

EXETER RARE BOOKS **Exeter**
12a Guildhall Shopping Centre, Exeter, Devon
Mon-Sat, 10-5, L 1-2.30
Med size C/D stk, a narcoleptics dream. I am committing suicide soon and I would not look at bks so depressing, and yet here are people allegedly in favour of living and all they do is collect bks that would bore you to death. TWC. BR Exeter Central, OOS turn left and shop is in a major candidate for the world's most ugly shopping mall contest.

DICKEN'S CENTENARY BOOK CASE **Exeter**
City Arcade, Fore Street, Exeter
Mon-Sat, 10-5
Med size R/C stk, av cal, cnd and prices. TWC. P.diff. (Ignore the previous entry you will never find your way out of that shopping centre. This guide only has to tell you how to get to a place, and boy am I glad that I don't have to work out how to get out) and continue along across roads and into arcade on left.

G.M. WOODHEAD **Honiton**
53 High Street, Honiton, Devon
Mon-Sat, 10-5, L 1-2.15
Lg R stk in antiques shop. An almost worth avoiding Silverfish Special. Like the catholics it promises heaven and also like them nobody has ever come back with definite proof. TWC. P.poss. It is at the other end of town to Brockwell.

BROCKWELL BOOKS/...

BROCKWELL BOOKS **Honiton**
174 High Street, Honiton, Devon
Mon-Sat, 10-5.30, V.Rel
Lg R/C stk ab av cal, cnd, av prices. Etgow. Slightly Literace. BR Honiton, OOS turn left and left under bridge and left at High Street. Shop is at end of town on left. There are also two bta bkstls in Antiques markets which you pass on the way. Nearest: Chard, Crewkerne, Sidmouth, Exeter.

CHARD BOOKSHOP **Chard**
2 Pig Lane, Holyrood Street, Chard, Somerset
Tues-Sat, 9.30-5, Rel
Med/Sm R/C stk, av cal, cnd and prices. Keen on Asia, bookfairy. T. Etgow. P.poss. Pig Lane is an alleyway off Holyrood Street which is off the main drag. BR Crewkerne (NAST 10 miles) Nearest: Taunton, Crewkerne, Axminster, Honiton.

HARE & HOUNDS BOOKS **Waytown**
Hare & Hounds Pub, Waytown, Dorset
This place sounds like a practical joke but I assure you it does exist. I am not sure of the opening hours, you will have to speak to my chauffeur about that *(RC: that alkie knows better than anybody what pub opening hours are.)* The bks are in the upstairs rooms of a public house, and a V public house it is. The evening I went there I was dressed in my plus fours suit. There was no lighting in the bkrms and to find out the price of the bks I had to go into what I am informed is called ye saloon bar, my presence caused muchmerriment to the local populace. This was odd as most of them looked as if they had failed to make it into a Thomas Hardy novel because of old age. The bks were genuinely int for R/C and Ds but there was a very self conscious atmosphere about everybody. I think if I went again I would go during non opening hours. Waytown is on the road from Crewkerne to Bridport and it is almost the only building on that road. Nearest: Crewkerne, Bridport, Axminster.

COACH HOUSE BOOKS Crewkerne
1 North Street, Crewkerne, Somerset
Mon-Sat, 10-6, Rel
Small C spec Military shop av cal, cnd and prices. Is to be congratulated on the hours and that he keeps to them. TWC. P.poss. From last shop turn right out of precinct and keep ahead.

There is also a junk shop called Oscars but it is only good if you like dogs.

***THE d CONSTRUCTED BOOKSHOP** **Crewkerne**
17 Falkland Square, Crewkerne, Somerset
Tues-Sat, 9.45-5.15. V.Rel
Med size R/C stk, a Drif Special. If I lived in Crewkerne this shop would be my natural haunt, almost all the bks are extremely int and wayward, as are the prices, but you can feel the mood of definite hope the moment you walk through the door. For the ordinary R this must indeed be an attractive shop not least because it is in a shopping precinct. It has none of that, you must be an intellectual

or a C to come in here, type of atmosphere. You can see the owner imprisoned at the rear of the shop and there are lots of cubby holes if you don't like being watched. There are bks all over the floor which is always an inspiring sight. I often wonder if you just had a bksp which only had boxes of bks whether it would not be more profitable than putting in shelves. The bks have been chosen with some sense of understanding and not so that they will impress Bookfairies, but what I like most is that most other Ds do not like it. BR Crewkerne, OOS ahead into town and shop is in precinct on right. Nearest: Chard, Sherborne, Wayport, Honiton.

CHAPTER HOUSE BOOKSHOP AND GALLERY **Sherborne**
Trendle Street (no No.) Sherborne
Mon-Sat, 10-5.30, L 1-2
You could almost deduce everything there is to know about this bksp from the above details. Byits name you can tell it is prolix. The absence of number tells you it has no idea where it is, or where it is going. By opening hours you can tell that it is straightlaced and out to lunch.

It is a lg/med R/C stk for people with largely med minds. The cnd of the stk is largely med and the prices are med/lg. Its idea of an eccentric is a large medium. BR Sherborne, which at least is small and beautiful, OOS towards the lg med church and turn left. See also TIN. Nearest: Frome, Shaftesbury, Weymouth, Crewkerne.

THE BOOK IN HAND **Shaftsbury**
17 Bell Street, Shaftsbury, Dorset
Mon-Sat, 10-4.30, L 1-2 (different in Winter) clsd Wed
Med size R/C stk, which always manages to be extremely int. They generally have a type of book that you do not see elsewhere. It is the way I imagine shops were before the 2nd World War. It is WAD just to see something so different. BR Gillingham (NAST 5 miles). Shop is opp main car park and post modernist supermarket. That what it is this bksp is a premodernist bksp. There are hardly any bks that were published yesterday. They do not have a telephone. The prices are value rather than what can be achieved. Even the train that goes through Gillingham looks as if it was made pre-war, it is going to be replaced by a more modern unit officially known as a networker and known to train spotters as a not worker - cycling from the station to Shaftsbury is like being in some pre war film. There is no multi lane highway, only a curved behedged emptiness.

BROWSERS **Shaftsbury**
Long Cross, Shaftsbury, Dorset
Mon-Sat, 10-5.30, Unr
I have only ever tried to get into this shop once and it was clsd on a Sat afternoon. To have contracted the dorset disease within weeks of opening is surely not a good sign.

To get to this place I asked the lady in Book in Hand, who very kindly told me to go out of the door, past the famous car park but keep to the right at the telephone box on the opp side, turn right and then bear slightly left. When I got to the end of the road before it turned right I was to turn towards the left down the hill, by this time I was completely confused even though I did not say a word. She continued giving me directions which were by now meaningless. Without wishing to be rude to this lady *(RC: Always duck when he says that)* she was just confusing the matter, and confirming my belief that asking people the way is a mistake, unless you understand the scale.

In the country people regard extremely short distances as being important. The telephone box she was talking about was less than fifty yards from the shop, the way she described it to me I had assumed that it was about half an hour away. The correct directions from this shop are OOSH, turn left and right and left down hill and continue, not that I am suggesting you should do it as the blasted place was closed. In London if you asked somebody the way to Shepherds Bush they would tell you to go to the Bayswater Road and continue, a distance of about three miles. For those people who come to London from the country it must be equally confusing. This is one of the reasons it is imperative to have a London Street atlas. Even with the directions I give you are going to get lost unless you have an atlas. When Londoners describe where somewhere is, they omit all but the most obvious features.

At Euston, a Scottish gentleman once asked me how to get to Glasgow, I told him to go OOS and turn left and continue for 400 miles, it was not until I got to Kings Cross that it occurred to me that he might have been looking for that station. The most crucial thing to ask people when you ask directions is the scale. This is why it is best to ask people such as road sweepers, dustmen, postmen, and traffic wardens; they walk everywhere.

D M BEACH Salisbury
52 High Street, Salisbury
Mon-Sat, 9-5.30, Rel
Med/lg R/C stk. This is the only beach in the world that is not worth combing. The tide of fashion is unknown to it, the waves of time have not been able to affect its featureless shore. Its shell is extremely attractive, but inside dwell spineless creatures whose decaying bodies have become entangled in nylon lines. The castaways have no exciting tales to relate, no great sea epics, no thrilling adventures. They are numb and numberless. The only example of vegetation is the owner with his palms outstretched. He is hoping to sell this sad story for an epic sum.

BIDEFORD - TAUNTON - BRISTOL - BATH- NEWBURY - LONDON

SCUDDERS EMPORIUM **Bideford**
11 Bridge Street, Bideford, North Devon
Mon-Sat, 9.30-5.30
Antique shop with bta R/C bks, av cnd and prices. BR Barnstaple (NAST 10 miles). In Bideford go over bridge and straight up hill and shop is on right. There are also other antique shops with bks. Nearest: Barnstaple, South Molton.

TARKA BOOKS **Barnstaple**
121 Boutport Street, Barnstaple, Devon
Tues-Sat, 10-5
Med size R/C stk, av cal, cnd and prices. BR: Barnstaple, OOS turn right into town (or rather ahead, follow ring road round to left and Boutport Street is on left about ½ mile. Nearest: Ilfracombe, South Molton, Bideford.

There is also a bta bkstl in Barnstaple Market.

ALCOMBE BOOKS **Minehead**
26 Alcombe Road, Minehead, Somerset
Mon-Sat, 10-5
Med size R/C stk av cal, cnd, and prices. Follow signs for Alcombe. Nearest: Barnstaple, Dulverton, Weston Super Mare.

ROTHWELL AND DUNWORTH **Dulverton**
2 Bridge Street, Dulverton, Somerset
Mon-Sat, 10-5, L 1-2, EC Thurs, less in Winter, BTR
Med size R/C/D stk, emphon HSF. Av cal, cnd and prices.

In Nether Stowey there is a stamp shop which has a bta stk of bks.

ROTHWELL AND DUNWORTH **Taunton**
14 Paul Street, Taunton
Mon-Sat, 11-5.15, Sat 9.30-1
Med size R/C stk, av cal, cnd and prices, emphon cricket.

STAPLEGROVE BOOKS **Taunton**
19 Staplegrove Road, Taunton, Somerset TA1 3PF
Mon-Sat 10-5
Med size R/C stk, av cal, cnd and prices. OOS, turn right towards town and left into Staplegrove. Nearest: Weston, Lanport, Chard, Tiverton.

SIMONS BOOKS **Somerton**
Broad Street, Somerton
Tues-Sat, 10-5.30, Rel
Med/nrly lg R/C stk, ab av cal, cnd, av prices. T. P.poss. BR: Castle Cary (NAST) ETF in centre of village, which it has now been established that Just William was brought up here. Nearest: Glastonbury, Castle Cary, Crewkerne, Longport.

HADDONS BOOKSHOP **Glastonbury**
30 Benedict Street, Glastonbury, Somerset
Mon-Sat, 9-5.30
I am not sure about those times, med size R/C stk, av cal,

cnd and prices. TWC. P.poss. BR Castle Cary (NAST 10 miles) ETF, look for signs saying car park and cut through alleyway. Nearest: Wells, Castle Cary, Sherborne, Somerton.

COURTYARD BOOKS **Wells**
Old Palace Yard, Priory Road, Wells, Somerset
Mon-Sat, 10-5.30
Med/lgish R/C stk, NSOC, but some int bks, ab av prices. BR Bath, NAST 15 miles. Shop is near Bus station. Nearest: Bath, Frome, Glastonbury, Weston Supermare.

STERLING BOOKS **Weston Super Mare**
43a Locking Road, Weston Super Mare, Avon.
Mon-Sat, 9-6, L 1-2, clsd Thur
Lg R/C/D stk, slightly roast beef, av cnd, ab av prices. BR Weston Super Mare, OOS ahead over bridge and turn right out of town, SIOL. Nearest: Clevedon, Wells, Minehead.

MANNA BOOKS **Weston Super Mare**
30 Orchard Street, Weston Super Mare, Avon
Mon-Sat, 10-5, clsd Wed
Med size R/C stk, emphon New Age and esoteric. Av cal, cnd and prices. From Sterling Bks turn right OOSH, into town and Orchard Street, is third or fourth on right.

SEVERN BOOKS **Weston Super Mare**
48 Severn Road, Weston Super Mare, Avon
Mon-Sat, 10-5, Sun in summer
Med size R/C stk, B&MC Specialish. Av Cal, cnd and prices. TWC. P.poss. BR Weston, OOS turn left, go all the way to the end of the road and turn left and then continue for three blocks and SIOL.

BRISTOL

THE SECRET SEVEN

BRISTOL BOOKS **Bristol**
5 North Street, Bedminster, Bristol
Mon-Sat, 10-6
Small/med sized R/C stk emphon pbks, av cal, cnd and prices. BR: Bristol Temple Meads, OOS ahead turn right, first left and left towards Bedminster. Walk through shopping street turn right and left.

BRISTOL BOOKS **Bristol**
180 Cheltenham Road, Bristol
Mon-Sat, 10-6
Med size R/C stk, emphon pbks, low key, av cnd and prices. TWC. P.poss. BR Bristol Temple Meads, OOS ahead and follow signs for City Centre and then A38 for Gloucester, NAST but it is easy to get bus to City Centre.

COTHAM HILL BOOKSHOPS **Bristol**
29a Cotham Hill, Bristol
Mon-Sat, 9.30-5.30, Rel

Med/lg R/C/D stk, emphon Art despite being a bit of a bookfairy this is the best shop in Bristol and well WAD. P.poss. From Wise Owl, turn left out of shop, turn right into Saint Michael's Hill (about 100 yards), continue up hill keep to left and turn left beyond roundabout.

THE WISE OWL BOOKSHOP **Bristol**
26 Upper Maudlin Street, Bristol
Mon-Sat, 10.30-5.30, Rel
Med/lg R/C stk, emphon Occult and Music. Av cal, cnd and prices. It took me years to find out there was a bsmt. TWC. From Bristol Bks go back towards City Centre and turn right at signs to cycleway towards Broadmead and Hospital.

PATTERSON AND LIDDLE **Bristol**
2c Chandos Road, Redland, Bristol
Mon-Sat, 10-6
Med size R/C/D stk, very bookfairy, emphon Railways. Av cnd and prices. T. P.poss. From Cotham Hill, turn left out of door, turn first right and continue to T junction, turn right and first right over railway bridge.

JOHN ROBERTS **Bristol**
43 Triangle West Clifton, Bristol
Mon-Sat 9-5
Med size R/C stk, av cal, cnd and prices. Not ETF but it does have a lot of very cheap bks, also res stk, av cnd and prices. TWC. P.diff. From Patterson & Liddle return to Cotham Hill, turn right and left into Whiteladies Road, and right at bottom of road.

See also UTA's Books in TIN.

GEORGE'S BOOKSHOP **Bristol**
52 Park Street, Bristol
Mon-Sat, 9-5.30, Rel
Med/lg C/D stk, ab av cal, cnd and prices. Emphon Bib and Classics. Solid roast beef but extremely good cnd. TWC. From Roberts turn right OOSH and right down hill.

BAILEY'S BOOKSHOP **Chipping Sodbury**
15 Horse Street, Chipping Sodbury
Mon-Sat, 10-5, clsd Wed
Med size R/C stk, av cal, cnd and prices. TWC. P.poss. BR Bath (NAST 10 miles). Nearest: Gloucester, Cirencester, Bath, Bristol.

BATH

WHERE THE FAMOUS FIVE RETIRED TO

ASPIDISTRA **Bath**
46 St James Place, Parade, Bath
Mon-Sat, 10.30-5.30
Med size R/C stk, av cal, NSOC, but can be more worthwhile than you would at first imagine. BR Bath, OOS turn left, turn right past bus station then left.

DERENK AND GLENDA WALLIS Bath
6 Chapel Row, Bath
Mon-Sat, 10-5
Med/lg R/C/D stk, ab av cal, cnd and prices, emphon childrens and ill. But nonetheless V int, despite its lg size it does not become boring which is something I wish they would franchise to other bksps. TWC. From Aspidistra continue north along Monmouth St and 5th right.

BANKES BOOKS Bath
5 St Margarets Buildings, Bath, Avon
Mon-Sat, 10-5
Med/lg R/C/D stk, ab av cal, cnd and prices. Despite the owner's intentions, this is a genuinely int bksp. All the bks have a second thing going for them. They are not just bindings, or ill bks or Travel, there is too much inspiration behind them to be that, and the owner does not have enough experience of the dreary world of bookfairs to know the difference.

It was his intention to attract what used to be known as the carriage trade and up market tourists, but the mistake he has made is to assume that these people can read. What they are mainly looking for are bks as souvenirs, bks to be photographed against, and bks with pictures. For them content does not bring contentment. There is no reason why he should not attempt to sell bks to these people but at the moment he attracts too many of the sweaty anorak brigade, and they deter the tourists. Drif's patent lesson in how to attract up market tourists:

1. The bks in the window should be few, but int. Too many bks put tourists off. They should be open at the most attractive illustration, and small handwritten note (to add the human touch) should say underneath what type of illustration it is, by whom, when it was done and how much the book is. Most up market tourists will then come in and ask for the £75 book, and the sweaty anorak brigade will march off in a huff.

2. The shop should not be too well lit, which this one gets right, there is nothing tourists love more than the idea that they are going into a quaint old bksp that has been there for years (this one has been there two years - but that is exactly the point - this is also good for deterring the sweaty anoraks, who like to be able to examine bks in microscopic detail, maybe you could have a light switch which reacted to the SA brigade, it went off when it saw their nylon.

3. Almost more important than the bks is the carpet, nothing works as well as intimidation by carpet. When people talk of up market hotels, they always mention the carpet, nothing looks as out of place as trainers on carpet. It is a strange paradox that the most expensive carpet will last longer than the cheapest one, but low rent bksps always go for the cheap carpet.

That's it, nothing else is necessary, if the prices don't get rid of the sweaty anoraks then the carpet will.

Send off £50 now for next lesson: How to intimidate a stuck up, up market bksp whilst wearing trainers, beige trousers and anorak. Actual examples given, using Bayntuns as test bed.

Another mini bookfair has just opened on the far corner of St Margarets Buildings, shared by bookfairies at rest.

CAMDEN BOOKS **Bath**
146 Walcot Street, Bath
Fri, Sat, Mon and some other days
Med/lg C/D stk, emphon art and architecture. If you think the ones downstairs are expensive you should see the ones upstairs!

BATH BOOK EXCHANGE **Bath**
35 Broad Street, Bath
Mon-Sat, 9-12.30 & 1-5
Med size R stk, with pretensions to being a C shop. (This is Timmy the Dogs)

D'ARCY BOOKS **Devizes**
The Chequers, High Street, Devizes, Wilts
Mon-Sat, 10.30-5.30
Med/lg R/C stk ab av cal, cnd, av prices. It is certainly one of the most beautiful bksps in the country and is now one of the more int ones. It not only looks the way the editors of colour supplements imagine bksps should look, it also has all the nooks they can imagine. WAD. P.poss. BR Swindon (NAST 15 miles). Find central carpark, walk down alleyway near Tesco's and ahead and left. Nearest: Bath, Marlborough, Salisbury, Bradford on Avon.

THE ANTIQUE & BOOK COLLECTOR **Marlborough**
Katherine House, The Parade, Marlborough, Wilts
Mon-Sat, 9.45-5.30, Rel
Med/lg C/D stk, bookfairy. Indeed it is like a mini bookfair in itself. There are sections on Travel & Exploration. Mod 1sts, Railways and Ill. WAD. P.poss. BR Swindon, Newbury, Devizes, Bath.

VICTORIA BOOKSHOP **Swindon**
30 Wood Street, Swindon, Wilts
Mon-Sat 9-5.30
Med/lg R/C stk. People who seldom go in s/h bksps are usually very much against the idea of burning bks, but I think if they went in this place they would very much change their minds. It would be truly pleasurable to see this place go up in flames. The bks are so dry that just one spark would enlighten the whole place. OOS (Swindon) ahead, turn left at bus station, turn right at signs for old town & continue.

INVICTA BOOKSHOP **Newbury**
8 Cromwell Place, Newbury, Berks
Mon-Sat, 10.30-5, Rel
Med/lg R/C stk, av cal, cnd and prices. Emphon cookery. A more than averagely int shop almost WAD. P.diff. BR Newbury, OOS towards bridge, turn left and follow into main street,

shop is in alleyway almost opp Marks & Spencer. Nearest: Oxford, Reading, Winchester, Marlborough.

ETON ANTIQUE BOOKSHOP **Eton**
88 High Street, Eton, Berkshire
Mon-Sat, 10-5.30, Sun 12-6
Med size C/D stk, av cal, cnd, ab av prices. Tourist orientated (the locals think a book is something you appear in or get given for free), but well WAD. P.poss. BR Windsor (there are two stations) follow signs for Eton, over the bridge. Nearest: Penn, Uxbridge, Farnborough, Reading.

ROUTE 9.30

THE MALVERN HILLS, THE COTSWOLDS, THE OXFORD ILLS & THE PIEBOLDS

CHAPTERS **Hereford**
17 Union Street, Hereford
Mon-Sat 9-5, Sat 9.15-5
Med size R/C stk, seems much bta for a charity shop, but then I have only seen it from the outside. BR Hereford, OOS turn left and head for cathedral and you pass it.

PIERPOINT GALLERY **Hereford**
10 Church Street, Hereford
Mon-Sat, 9.15-5.30
Med size R/C stk, av cal, cnd and prices currently up for sale. From Chapters, OOS, turn left into alleyway opposite Market Hall.

THE HEREFORD BOOKSHOP **Hereford**
24 Church Street, Hereford
Mon-Sat, 9.15-5.30
New bksp with upstairs room of roast beef, av cal, cnd and prices. Directions as Pierpoint.

BATSTONE BOOKS **Malmesbury**
12 Gloucester Street, Malmesbury, Wilts
Tues-Sat, 10-5, L 1-2
Med/small R/C stk, emphon Occult and esoteric. Ab av cal, cnd, av prices. BR Swindon (NAST 12 miles) ETF. Nearest: Cirencester, Swindon, Marlborough, Bath.

ROSS OLD BOOK AND PRINT SHOP **Ross on Wye**
51-52 The High Street, Ross on Wye
Mon-Sat, 10-5
Med/nrly lg R/C/D stk, av cal, cnd and prices. Looks like a solid roast beef shop from the outside, but inside it is definitely nouvelle cuisine. WAD. P.poss. ETF in High Street. BR Hereford, (NAST 12 miles). Nearest: Hereford, Newent, Chepstow, Monmouth.

COBWEBS **Newent**
8/10 Church Street, Newent
Mon-Sat, 9-5, L 1-2, clsd Wed

Med/lg R/C stk, bl av cal, NSOC, av prices. A Readers Digest special. There are also bks in the bsmt. ETF on the road in from Gloucester, part of antiques market. Nearest: Ledbury, Gloucester, Ross.

KEITH SMITH BOOKS **Ledbury**
78B The Home End, Ledbury, Herefordshire
Tues-Sat, 10-5
Small/med sized R/C stk, bookfairy, av cal, cnd and prices. BR Ledbury, OOS ahead into town and shop is on right. Se you can tell that I do genuinely go round these places, if you looked on a map that direction would read OOS, turn left but because of the way the station exit is laid out, its ahead. I shall use this as proof when people say I never actually go round these shops.

RC Writes
What people say is that you do not go round these bksps with your eyes open, and that your motto is better Strafe than sorry.

PRIORY BOOKS **Malvern**
Church Walk (no No.), Malvern
Tues-Sat, 10-5, L 12.45-2
Med size R/C stk, V good cnd, av cal and prices. Literace. BR Worcester, oh that's wrong. Malvern is so boring that I have complete amnesia when I write about it, I have tried to get this entry right seven times, find your own bloody way, only bores go there.

RC writes
See I told you, he is an ex-alkie, its all that water that upsets him.

THE MALVERN BOOKSHOP **Malvern**
7 Abbery Road, Malvern
Mon-Sat, 9.15-5, clsd Wed
Med size R/C stk, av cal, cnd and prices. The triumph of mediocrity, it is not that there is anything wrong with the bks, there is just nothing right with them. Us cranks, or rather this crank, can get extremely fed up with such worthy tomes, I go in for fruit and wholemeal roughage, this smooth refined diet is perfect for smooth refined people, but it is not for us roughs. TWC. From Priory go up hill and turn left and left.

HOLBOURNE BOOKS **Worcester**
67 Upper Tything, Worcester
Mon-Sat, 10-5, no times posted on the grounds that the owner sometimes engages in other activities of an unspecified nature*
Where it is not poss to keep to set hours, it is better to post this piece of info rather than leave the customers in ignorance. Having said that, I have never seen a time when this shop was actually clsd during the day. If only those shops which post hours were as Rel my life would be a great deal easier (aren't I good at being pompous?)
Med/lg R/C/D stk, av cal, cnd and prices. Emphon Nat His. It takes a while to wade through it all but I always get to

the bank in the end. BR Worcester, Foregate Street, OOS turn right and continue past grammar school. Nearest: Birmingham, Stratford, Malvern, Leominster.

RC writes

The man is an ecologist, the prop looks on the countryside as the bit they have not filled in yet.

IAN K. PUGH **Pershore**

40 Bridge Street, Pershore, Worcestershire

Mon-Sat, 10-5, clsd Thur, Rel

Med/nrly lg R/C/D stk, av cal, cnd, ab av prices. Res stk for the chosen few. A shop so normal it upsets me. BR Pershore, OOS turn left into town (NASTish 1 mile). Nearest: Worcester, Evesham, Tewkesbury, Great Malvern.

There is also a R/C stk in the picture framers opp, which is worth a look.

BOOKWORMS **Evesham**

81 Port Street, Evesham, Worcestershire

Tues-Sat, 9.30-5, Rel

Med size R/C stk, NSOC. Av prices. BR Evesham, cannot remember where the station is but to get to this shop you follow the signs for Broadway. Nearest: Worcester, Broadway, Cheltenham, Pershore

STRATFORD TREVERS **Broadway**

45 High Street, Broadway, Worcestershire

Mon-Sat, 9.30-5.30, L 1-2.15, Sun 2.15-5.30, Rel

Med/lg Helen Hanff Special. This is the bksp as Broadway musical complete with scalpers prices. They also get the Oscar for longest running book (at least four years to my certain knowledge). The chorus looks a bit tired too. Nearest: Stratford, Moreton, Stow, Evesham.

They do not have anything as low life as a railway, you either arrive in a limousine or not at all.

WAYFARERS BOOKS **Tewkesbury**

19 Church Street, Tewkesbury, Glos

Mon-Sat, 10-5, V.Rel

Med size R/C stk, av cal, cnd and prices. BR Cheltenham (NAST 10miles) ETF by cathedral. Nearest: Malvern, Pershore, Gloucester, Newent.

DOUBLE GLOUCESTER

Just by looking at Gloucester you can tell that the residents are thick. The old town had an internal organisation which was poss to easily comprehend, but now it looks as if it bought its town centre s/h from Birmingham. If you ask one of the subnorms who inhabit the place they will tell you the bksp is just round the corner: it was; two miles away. I asked another and she pointed to somewhere that could have stretched from Mongolia to Hawai. In the end I had to bribe an urchin to take me there. He thought Gloucester was a great place. Presumably because he could supplement his pocket money by showing lost visitors the way round

QUAYSIDE BOOKSHOP **Gloucester**
2 Severn Road, Gloucester
Everyday 10-5.30
Med/lg R/C stk, ab av cal, cnd and prices. Much more int than usual and almost WAD. TWC. P.poss. BR Gloucester, OOS turn right onto ring road, left into Northgate (not signposted, street to left of cathedral?) Continue past crossroads, look for lg buildings signed Antiques Centre, shop is behind. Nearest: Cheltenham, Burford, Stroud, Newent.

Bang next door, or rather very quietly next door, is a junk shop (sorry Antique shop) with bks. I had asked in the previous shop if there was any other bksp in Gloucester. I clearly did not make my question simple enough for the denizens of Gloucester, because the owner assured me that there was none. It was only when I saw an urchin (of which Gloucester seems to possess a super abundance) carrying out a book, that I wandered into the place. True it is not a bksp, but it does have some extremely int bks. Most antique shops go wildly wrong when it comes to bks, but whoever selected and priced these had taste and discrimination. It was clear that someone with an interest in bks was behind the place. It emerged that the owner used to have a s/h bksp. It would almost have been poss to deduce this from the stk. What these bks showed is that it is the person behind the bks rather than the bks, which is the most important factor.

Quite why the other gentleman did not wish to tell me about this place is hard to understand. Two bksps next to one another are not in competition. The only competition is in the buying and in most cases people do not bring in int bks. In a town like Gloucester it makes sense for the bksps to be close together. The locals are sothick that they have to be told everything twice.

ALAN HANCOX **Cheltenham**
101 The Promenade, Cheltenham, Glos
Mon-Sat, 9.45-4.45, L 1-2.15, Rel, clsd Wed pm
Med/lg R/C stk, keen on Lit and Art. It is like going to a concert in a library. TWC. P.poss. BR Cheltenham, OOS turn right and follow signs for town centre and bus station. Nearest: Tewkesbury, Stow on the Wold, Cirencester, Gloucester.

MICHAEL RAYNER **Cheltenham**
11 St Lukes Road, Cheltenham, Glos
Thurs-Sat, 10-6
Small/med size, R/C stk, bookfairy, ab av cal, cnd and prices. T. P.poss. From Station turn right into Lansdowne Rd and continue along Montpelier Terrace, turn left at Eagle Star Building Society and first right.

There is also a bkstl in the indoor Antiques Market in Suffolk Road.

HEYNES BOOKSHOP/...

HEYNES BOOKSHOP **Cheltenham**
49 Clarence Street, Cheltenham, Glos
Mon-Sat, 10-5
Med size R/C stk, NSOC, av cal, ab av prices. T & Disc. P.diff. Those of you who have never ready Billy Liar, The Good Soldier Scweik, Felix Crull or Oblomov can save yourselves the trouble by ringing the number in the window which says that the shop is for sale.

IMPRINT **Stroud**
31 High Street, Stroud, Glos
Mon-Sat, 10-5.30, Rel
Med size R/C stk with immensely attractive style. The other place in Stroud is not exactly ugly, but this one is beautiful. The window has been done with care. The inside has a lovely atmosphere, which it has taken a while to establish and the bks are int. It is no accident that it leans towards entertainment; it looks like something out of a film: The Bookman of Alcatraz, The Hound of Music! I Was A Fugitive From a Chain Store! Singing In The Main! and Some Set Boulevard. BR Stroud, OOS ahead, turn right and left past tower and right at top.

ALAN AND JOAN TUCKER **Stroud**
Station Road (no No.), Stroud, Glos
Mon-Sat, 10-5, L 12.30-1.30, clsd Thur
New bksp with a lot bta R/C stk, av cnd and prices. TWC. P.poss. BR Stroud, OOS, SIOL upstairs of new bksp. Nearest: Cheltenham, Cirencester, Nailsworth, Gloucester.

VALENTINE'S BOOKS **Nailsworth**
Day's Mill, Old Market, Nailsworth, Glos
Mon-Sat, 9-5.30, L 1-2
Med sized R/C nrly D stk, av cal, cnd and prices, keen on Lit and John Clare. Bookfairy. BR Stroud (NAST 5 miles) ETF by bus station. Nearest: Stroud, Cirencester, Malmsbury, Chipping Sodbury.

THOMPSON'S BOOKSHOP **Cirencester**
Dunstall House, Park Street, Cirencester, Glos
Tues-Sat, 10-5
Med/lg R/C & spec stk for Architecture bks, ab av cal, cnd and prices. Owner does impressions of Bertie Wooster, unasked. ETF in centre of town. Nearest: Cheltenham, Burford, Swindon, Stroud.

FOUR SHIRE BOOKS **Morton in Marsh**
17 High Street, Morton in Marsh, Glos
Mon-Sat, 11-5
Med size R/C stk, which claims to specialize in needlework. But this is exactly the type of shop that is a total waste of time. If you are genuinely int in needlework coming here is only likely to deter you. Not enough sowing and too much Lese majeste, and I will be darned if I am going there again. BR Morton in Marsh, OOS turn right into town and left at High Street SIOL beyond Market hall. Nearest: Stratford, Brackley, Burford, Broadway.

They also have a sampler in Stow on the Wold

BOOKBOX **Stow on the Wold**

Chantry House, Sheep Street, Stow on the Wold
Mon-Sat, 10-5, clsd Wed. BTR in Winter
Med/lg C/D stk, av cal, cnd and prices. Emphon Country pursuits. T. P.poss. BR Moreton (NAST 7 miles) ETF just keep walking you will find it. Nearest: Moreton, Woodstock, Burford, Cheltenham. See TIN (2 other shops).

THE AFTERNOON BOOKSHOP **Woodstock**

21 Oxford Street, Woodstock, Oxon
Almost as good as calling a shop by the name of the area in which it is located is calling it by the hours when it is open. But then this shop is more than just a friendly fascia. In Oxford you need a certain degree of confidence to go into the bksps, another degree to understand the stk, and you feel as though you will get the third if you leave empty handed, whereas this shop is a joy without qualification.

The bus from Oxford stops right outside the door, the window is immensely attractive. You are in before you have noticed it. The bks are clearly aimed at Cs without being acad. The prices are clearly marked but above all leaving empty handed is not a trauma. From now on the only time I shall spend in Oxford will be mourning.

THE WOODSTOCK BOOKSHOP **Woodstock**

3 Market Place, Woodstock, Oxon
Mon-Sat, 10-5, L 1-2, Rel
Med size C/D stk, spec in out of print Oxford University press bks. Ab av cal cnd and av prices. You would have thought that one of the shops in Oxford would have gone in for this subject but they were more than likely put off by the fact that people might be interested, or perhaps they had not got round to doing anything about it yet, if that is the case this shop has pulled off an OP OUP coup. BR Oxford (NAST five miles but buses are good). Nearest: Brackley, Aylesbury, Oxford, Burford.

OXFORD

After a day in the Oxford s/h bksps you feel as if you should be awarded a first class honours degree, but as in real life only the already rich are likely to come away with any glittering prizes. There are fifteen different colleges purveying exactly the same fare. Entry qualifications are high, and you are expected to have a grounding in all the subjects, no matter how arcane but nobody tells you what the whole thing is for. It certainly is not pleasure.

THE O LEVEL BOOKSHOP **Oxford**

Oxford Antiques Centre, 27 Park End Street, Oxford
Tues-Sat, 10.30-5.30 Rel
Med size R/C stk av cal, cnd and prices. Suitable for those attending sixth form college. It is a good introduction to Oxford but like most introductions you have to have studied all the text to understand it. BR Oxford, OOS on the other side and turn left into town.

WATERFIELDS Oxford
36 Park Street, Oxford
Mon-Sat, 9.30-5.30
Very large Swats stk, every A level subject there is, and if you do not study it carefully enough they look as if they might give you a detention. This is the shop the other Oxford Booksellers expect you to have gone to first. TWC. P.diff. Directions as above.

OXFORD ANTIQUE TRADING COMPANY Oxford
Unit 30, 40/41 Park End Street, Oxford
Stall in Antiques Market, NV.

THE LITTLE BOOKSHOP Oxford
Lane 2, covered Market, High Street, Oxford
Mon-Sat, 10-5.30
Small R stk, av cal, cnd, ab av prices. The only part of the Oxford Disease that this shop seems to have contracted is the pricing. If you want to drop out of the course early, this is the place to do it. TWC. From Waterfields continue into town through the paved shopping street to the high street, and market is on left.

THE CLASSICS BOOKSHOP Oxford
3 Turl Street, Oxford
Mon-Sat, 10-5.30
Med size spec, ab av cal, av cnd and classic Oxford prices. When it says Classics Bksp you must understand that this is a trick question. It does not mean that this looks like a classic bksp or that they treat you in the classic bksp manner - a mixture of disdain and despair, what it does mean is that they specialise in those classic Oxford subjects: dead languages, dead history and dead boring. This is indeed the classic response from most customers, but unless you can convince the owners of this establishment that you find the subject rivetting then you are not going to go far with the other shops. From The Little Bookshop, turn left out of the market and first left.

NINER & HILL Oxford
43 High Street, Oxford
Mon-Sat, 10-5.30
Med size C/D stk, ab av, cal, cnd and prices. For post graduates only.

TITLES Oxford
15 Turl Street, Oxford
Mon-Sat, 9.30-5.30
Med size C/D stk, high table with a good cellar. Tough entry requirements as above.

BLACKWELL'S Oxford
48-51 Broad Street, Oxford
Mon-Sat, 9-5
V lg Acad C stk, ab av cal, cnd and prices. This is the Oxford Centre for Advanced Studies, you keep advancing into different rooms and get nowhere. Each department now has its own s/h section in an effort to deter Ds from buying the stk. From Artemis go back over Magdalene Bridge, turn first right and first left and left at end by Bodlein.

THORNTONS Oxford
11 Broad Street, Oxford
Mon-Sat, 9.30-5.30, Rel
Lg Acad C ab av cal, cnd and prices. Spec in foreign languages, espec English. This is the compulsory year abroad to round off your education. Out of Blackwell's turn right.

OXFAM BOOKSHOP Oxford
56 Saint Giles, Oxford
Mon-Sat, 10-5
Med sized R/C stk, bta charity shop. From Thorntons OOS turn left and right at end of street.

TOBY ENGLISH Wallingford
Lamb Arcade, Wallingford, Oxon
Mon-Sat, 10-4.30
Med/lg R/C/D stk, more int than av, and more int prices too. Keen on SF & Fantasy. Etgow. P.poss. BR Cholsey, OOS on north side and keep walking (NAST 4 miles). Shop is in Antiques Market at crossroads, but do not be deterred by this it is more of a proper shop than those with more regular premises. Nearest: Oxford, Henley, Reading, Swinton. Some review copies in the new bksp in Wallingford. ETF.

THE ATTIC Henley on Thames
4 Station Road, Henley on Thames
Mon-Sat, 9.30-6, Sun 11-5
Med size R/C stk, literace. Av cal, cnd and prices. BR Henley, OOS turn left. Nearest: Wallingford, Penn, Windsor, Reading.

RICHARD WAY Henley on Thames
54 Friday Street, Henley on Thames
Mon-Sat, 10-5.30
Med size R/C/D stk, emphon rowing ave, cal cnd and prices. T. P.poss.

RC writes
Isn't he a miserable git, no extolling the virtues of the bike, no mention of the number of times he has walked off with bgns from this bksp, no mention of the last time he was in here. This might not be unconnected with the fact, a) that he did not get anywhere, and b) when he was praising a catalogue of Vicars clothing that he had just bought she asked him if he enjoyed living vicariously.
Notice he also forgot to give the directions, when you go over the bridge from Reading, turn left and first right.

THE COTTAGE BOOKSHOP Penn
Elm Road (no No.), Penn, Bucks
Mon-Sat, 10-5, L 1-2.15
V Lg R stk, bl av cal, av cnd, low prices. T. P. poss. BR Beaconsfield, OOS on Model Village side and turn left. Follow signs for Penn, which start well but soon disappear. Do not turn off road just keep going for four miles. At Penn Pond turn right and come back on yourself. Nearest: Aylesbury, Uxbridge, Windsor, Henley.

PENN

MY TEAR, THEN THE SWORD

Bulwer Lytton is credited with writing the worst opening sentence in the English language. The Penn Bookshop has a wonderful opening but thereafter it carries on with Bulwer Lytton's great work. What he did with words, this shop does with bks. His most common book - I counted fourteen copies in this shop - is the Caxton's. If you have not read it do not worry, a visit to this shop will give you a good idea of the plot. It is about a middle class family and you could not get more middle class than Penn. I was stopped by the police for walking to this shop. If you want to go through the Buckinghamshire countryside, you must have a Range Rover, or a BMW or at least a VW. You are also allowed to jog, or ride a mountain bike, but walking is not something people do in Penn, or Buckinghamshire. The hero of the Caxton's is writing a "History of Human Error". Almost every book in this shop would have been a candidate. They were either mistakes when they were written, or when they were published or when they were bought. They are doubly mistaken the second time round. The bk gets published with help from his son Pisistratus (I wish I could have made that up - who says BL was a bad novelist). In my experience the low life dealers who frequent this shop do not have names quite as good, but its not for want of trying. Most of them are subsidised, either by the Social Security or by their parents. Seeing all these bks and realising that somebody has wasted their life writing them, brings tears to your eyes. That people are in the business of preserving them makes you want to weep. If you do find an int book you will want to bawl.

It attracts Readers and Raiders, the former seethe and scythe, the latter buy and bye. The moment the owner sees a book he is sighing the prices, the only thing that stops him is the size, but were he to bite the bullet and bullet the blight then it could be a great novel two storey.

THE BOOKSHOP SQUARE EDGE **Aylesbury**
38 Kingsbury, Aylesbury, Buckinghamshire.
Mon-Sat, 10.30-5.30, Rel
Med size R/C stk, more int than av, av cnd and prices. Keen on New Zealand and Katherine Mansfield. TWC. P.diff. BR Aylesbury, OOS ahead to Friars Shopping Centre. Continue past Market Square and then through to second square. Nearest: Newport Pagnell, St Albans, Penn, Oxford.

ROUTE 10.30

SOUTHPORT-LIVERPOOL-WOLVERHAMPTON-BIRMINGHAM-COVENTRY STRATFORD-BRACKLEY

SOUTHPORT

The elevated status of the s/h bksps of Southport is not dependant on the fact that they are all on the first floor but upon their superior selection to the Hoi Polloi of Liverpool.

C K BROADHURST **Southport**
5-7 Market Street, Southport, Merseyside
Mon-Sat, 9-5.30, Tues 1pm (Is that last part right? I have never noticed that before but then I only ever go to this place at 9am in the morning that way I am guaranteed a wonderful start to a new day)
Lg R/C/D stk, above figuratively and literally a new bksp, also above most of the s/h bksps of Britain, Res stk, emphon bindings, Topog and Mod Lit. In fact all solid roast beef subjects but prepared in such an attractive way that they are tempting to a vegetarian. WAD. TWC. P.poss. BR Southport (British Frail's idea of an appropriate building for the glory that is Southport is a high tech pig sty) OOS turn left and right and immediately left and right. Nearest: Preston, Ormskirk, Liverpool.

BRYAN KERNAGHAN **Southport**
53-55 Wayfarers Arcade, Lord Street, Southport
Mon-Sat, 10-5
Med size R/C/D stk, ab av cal, cnd and prices. WAD. Bookfairy. T. P.diff. From Broadhurst OOS turn right and left and cross road and shop is upstairs in arcade on left.
RC writes
That moron has left out Rosemary Books!

ANTHONY PARKINSON Southport
359 Lord Street, Southport
Mon-Sun, 10.30-5
Med size R/C stk, slight emphon technical, also slight emphasis to being a Drif Special because it opens on a Sunday. From Wayfarers Arcade turn left and shop is well signposted upstairs on left.

LIVERPOOL

GUNS AND CULTURE

It is best to buy the local one day rover ticket which can cover the area from Southport to Birkenhead, but it does have some bizarre restriction about when you can use it and these are heavily enforced by pairs of pairs of ticket inspectors, who feel so insecure that they have a police escort riding shotgun. The bksps with one noticeable exception have improved immensely. The pairs of pairs are just the ticket, but the first shop deserves to be bilked. A shotgun is too cultured for it.

HAZLEDENE BOOKSHOP Liverpool
61 Renshaw Street, Liverpool
Mon-Sat, 11-5, Unr
Med size C/D stk of Mod 1st editions and Lit. Ab av cal, cnd and prices.

OUT OF PRINT Liverpool
97 Renshaw Street, Liverpool
Mon-Sat, 10-5
Med size R/C stk, ab av cal, cnd and service, acts as almoner to those who have had the misfortune to go into the Hazledene bksp.

HENRY BOHN Liverpool
32 Berry Street, Liverpool
Mon-Sat, 10-6
Med size R/C stk, slightly dowergetic with Mayfair Mercenary prices, but does make the occasional slip up and is then worthwhile. From Out Of Print turn left and continue. SIOR.

REID OF LIVERPOOL Liverpool
105 Mount Pleasant, Liverpool
Mon-Sat, 10.30-6
Med/lg R/C/D stk, an extremely int shop and well WAD. From Bohn go back towards the derelict church and turn right up hill and right. On the way you pass a pbk shop called Atticus.

BOOK ENDS West Kirby
4 Hilbre Road, West Kirby, Wirral
Mon-Sat, 10-4, L 1-2.
Med size R/C stk slightly low key but nrly a Drif Special. BR West Kirby, OOS turn slightly right, turn left and left into another parade of shops and left at Hilbre Road which looks residential, and go all the way to the end.

MERE BOOKS **Ormskirk**
48 Southport Road, Ormskirk, Lancs
Mon-Fri, 9.30-5.30
Med size R/C stk, almost a Drif Special. The bks are not up to my level but the prices definitely are. You have to ask to see the bks, but it is no hassle. BR Ormskirk, OOS, turn right and continue until you come to the House of Hammer Church and turn right, shop is in office on right. Nearest: Preston, Southport, Liverpool.

I have also heard of a bkrm in Skelmersdale, which sounds unlikely but I am assured it is true. NV.

CASTLE BOOK CENTRE **Northwich**
85 Chester Road, Northwich, Cheshire
Mon-Sat, 10-5.30, Wed 4.30
Med size R/C stk, nrly a Drif Special and nearly a silverfish special. Av cal, cnd and prices. BR Greenbank, OOS turn right towards town. Nearest: Liverpool, Altrincham, Crewe, Chester

GUILDMASTER BOOKS **Nantwich**
81 Welsh Row, Nantwich, Cheshire
Open every day 10-dusk (what sensible opening hours)
Med size R/C stk, some new bks, av cal, cnd and prices. A redundancy bookseler, great on the stories of what he has got but not keen to part with it. However the town is almost WAD because it has not been improved. BR Nantwich, OOS turn right towards town and follow Ring road round to left, coast river, turn left over bridge...
RC: what did you think we were going to do, swim?...
Nearest: Crewe, Stoke on Trent, Whitchurch, Holt.

ANTIQUARIAN BOOK CENTRE **Stoke on Trent**
30-32 Hope Street, Hanley, Stoke on Trent
Mon-Sat, 10.30-5.30
Med size R/C stk, av cal, cnd and prices. Keen on the technical. I keep trying to think of a word to describe shops such as this one, the books have a slightly tired look, but they do wake you up, but there is a level of alertness above which they do not rise and this is matched by the price. They have from the outside that grainy weather beaten look. The only term I can think of is Stokers Bksp. BR Stoke on Trent, OOS turn left and continue into town (1 mile) and follow road round to left and shopping centre, and Hope Street is second right. Nearest: Leek, Derby, Stafford, Crewe.

ROBERT A PICKEN **Stafford**
11 Goal Road, Stafford
Mon-Sat, 10-5, clsd Wed
Small/med sized R/C stk, av cal, cnd and prices. BR Stafford, OOS ahead turn left and follow sign for Stone, if this fails breathe in and smell the unique smell of a British Prison, and head in that direction. Nearest: Stoke on Trent, Burton on Trent, Wolverhampton, Shrewsbury.

BIRMINGHAM AND THE WEST MIDLANDS

The good news is that they are going to pull the centre of Birmingham down; the bad news is that they are going to rebuild it. Having eliminated all the s/h bksps from the centre of town, they are determined that they will never get a second chance. Like the flower that grows straight up through tarmac, on Oldbury station some shops have managed to survive. They look a little battered but they have defied the odds. Those furthest from the centre have done best. This means that you have to buy One Day Rover ticket (which costs £5 but can be used as far as Worcester, Lichfield, Coventry and Shrewsbury). P.Poss outside most of the shops, but you risk being an object of extreme interest from the locals, who regard stopping as worse than autocide.

BOOKSTACK **Wolverhampton**
53 Bath Road, Wolverhampton
Mon-Sat, 10-4 + on alternate days (don't ask!)
Med/lg R/C stk, bl av cal, cnd, av prices. On the way to being a Silverfish Special. TWC. From Berry Street, OOS turn left and right and left to ring road, turn right onto it (you have even less chance of surviving if you use the pedestrian underpass, and turn first left and left. Shop is in private house on right.

BERRY STREET BOOKSHOP **Wolverhampton**
35 Berry Street, Wolverhampton
Mon-Fri, 10-5
Med size R/C stk, low key, av cal cnd and prices. T. P.poss. BR Wolverhampton, OOS ahead into turn turn left at Princess Street, third block on left. Nearest: Stafford, Lichfield, Halesowen, Shrewsbury.

SIMMONS BOOKSHOP **Wednesbury**
37 Lower High Street, Wednesbury
Mon-Sat, 9-5.30, clsd Thur (7.30 Fri evenings)
You would not believe how kind and tolerant keeping a shop open until 7.30 makes me.
Lg R/C stk, almost a Drif Special, presumably if I can have a separate division of Irish Drif Specials, I can also have one for the West Midlands, an area which has suffered from Council Terrorism for the last thirty years, rather than the independent kind. There is a res stk of R fiction. Etgow. P.poss. BR Wolverhampton + bus (NAST 5 miles and Birmingham buses are not user friendly, they mainly see their job as being obstacles to try and slow down the motorists, however it is worth making the effort to detour to this shop espec on a Friday evening when all the locals are preparing to get tanked up.

STAFFS BOOKSHOP **Lichfield**
4 & 6 Dam Street, Lichfield, Staffs
Mon-Sat, 9.30-5.30. V.Rel
Lg R/C/D stk, ab av cal, cnd and prices. Emphon Childrens and Ill. This is the Provincial bksp par excellance. This shop is indeed a rare bksp, in fact it is almost unique. It is when I see such shops that I know my rage against the

incompetents, the ex polytechnic lecturers, the Bookfairies and the redundancy booksellers is not only justified, it is not strong enough. Were it not such a hopeless task I would recommend that the owner give lessons in how to run a provincial bksp. Methusalah might stand a better chance.

This shop is excellently sited. Lichfield is a town on the crossroads to many others. The railway service whilst not great, is good. The town itself is attractive to many other groups of people besides book Cs. The opening hours are what you would expect a provincial bksp to be, without the aid of a computer it is poss to work out when this shop is likely to be open.

All this is before you have gone through the door and once you have seen the bks in the window you would have to be a West Midlander not to go through the door.

Inside it is midway between a museum and a private collection. There are bks in glass cases that show off how little imagination museums and libraries have. There are bks on the shelves that would give most childrens book Ds hysterics because they are not in as new cnd, but what is a book for if it is not to be read? "To Sell" say the bookfairies, as loudly as they know how in an attempt to convince themselves that this is what happens at bookfairs.

The bks in this shop are not those orphans you see on the front pages of newspapers, nor are they those well scrubbed never snotty nosed little horrors you see presenting flowers to celebrities. These are children as they are, sometimes fun, sometimes sad, sometimes irritating. Some have high IQs others are not so bright, but above all, somebody somewhere wants them. BR Lichfield, OOS head for Cathedral and shop is beyond to left. Nearest: Burton upon Trent, Polesworth, Marston Green, Wolverhampton.

G & J CHESTERS Polesworth
19 Bridge Street, Polesworth, Staffs
Mon-Sat, 9.30-5.30, Wed 9.30-9. Rel
I think this shop and its opening hours were the only time I ever came close to impressing the Tank Commander (see Scotland). Not only did I remember that it was open on a Wednesday eve, I was able to find it first time round - Birmingham. The Tank Commander had by now got used to the idea that I have to surround a town at least twice before I have some vague idea where I am. It has a lg C/D stk, emphon British Topog and Acad. Ab av cal, cnd and prices. TWC. P.poss. ETF above parade of shops to the left fork as you come from Tamworth. Hang on is that the right way round. Nearest: Burton on Trent, Leicester, Coventry, Wednesdbury.

NORTHFIELD BOOKSHOP AND FURNISHINGS Northfield
51-53 Church Road, Northfield, West Midlands
Mon-Sat, 9.30-4.30, Wed *1pm
Lg R/C stk, a cross between a Silverfish Special and a Drif Special, but does look like it is well worth a look. BR I dunno which station, but I do know that Northfield is the wrong one.

MAXWELL'S BOOKS Acocks Green
22 Shaftmoor Lane, Acocks Green, West Midlands
Mon-Sat, 10- Rel

Med size R/C stk, a Stokers bksp. Av cal, cnd and prices. TWC. P.poss. BR Spring Road (not Acocks Grn unless you like walking) OOS ahead and right. Nearest: Selly Oak, Marston Green, Northfield.

STEPHEN WYCHERLEY Selly Oak
508 Bristol Road, Selly Oak, Birmingham
Mon-Sat, 10-5.30
This is the s/h bksp as parody, an imitation of immorality. From the outside it looks like a Samuel Beckett Special, as in the opening of Murphy large parts are roped off, but then it veers to Orwells, Keep The Aspidistra Flying, however there is not a lot of resemblance between Selly Oak and Hampstead, least of all in the customers most of whom are gormless and aghast. BR Selly Oak, OOS turn left down to main road and turn right towards centre of Birmingham.

BIRMINGHAM BOOKSHOP Selly Oak
567 Bristol Road, Birmingham
Mon-Sat, 10-5
Med/lg R/C stk, av cal, NSOC, av prices. A Stokers Special. Directions as above.

BLITZGEIST Birmingham
189 High Street, Harbourne, Birmingham
Mon-Sat, 10-7
High pressure literace, the video book, heavy metal music and light fantasy. All gloss, no mat, the red carpet treatment for all, nothing stops his brain sells. From Birmingham Bksp continue south, turn right at Harbourne Lane which becomes Lordswood Road and right, at High Street.

BEECH BOOKS Rowley Regis
288 Oldbury Road, Rowley Regis, W Midlands
Mon-Sat, 11-3, Fr & Sat -5pm
Med size R/C bks slightly low key - a Drif Special. Av cnd and prices. TWC. P.poss. BR Rowley Regis, OOS turn right and left towards town.

CLENT BOOKS Halesowen
52a Summerhill, Halesowen, W Midlands
Mon-Fri, 11-5.30? check that.
Med size R/C stk, av cal, cnd and prices. Bookfairy but slightly more int than most. BR (NAST 5 miles) from bus station turn left towards Safeway supermarket and Summerhill is directly opp.

TAPLINS BOOKSHOP Marston Green
62 Station Road, Marston Green, West Midlands
Mon-Sat, 11-5, Rel
Med/lg R/C stk, av cal, cnd and prices. That's in comparison to Birmingham. It is very int. BR Marston Green, OOS on car park side and turn right beyond car park, past florist. Nearest: Polesworth, Coventry, Northfield, Acocks Green

GOSFORD BOOKS Coventry
116 Gosford Street, Coventry, W Midlands
Mon-Fri, 10-5.30, Sat 5pm
Med size R/C stk, keen on Philosophy. Tries hard to be

irascible but fails miserably. T & Disc. P.diff. BR Coventry, OOS ahead into town centre, turn right at statue of Lady Godiva which is covered up and continue. Nearest: Marston Green, Hinckley, Northampton and Warwick.

ARMSTRONGS BOOKS AND COLLECTIBLES **Coventry**
163 Sovereign Road, Earlston, Coventry
Mon-Sat, 10-1.30 and 2.30-6
Keen on the liquid lunch. Med size R/C stk B&MC Special, av cal, cnd and prices. KUTI, but fails miserably. Out of Gosford, turn left, back to the covered up Lady Godiva and attempt to go straight ahead until you come to the row of plastic tudor buildings. Close your eyes and head for the Ring Road which you go under and towards an infant school. Heading for railway viadcut keep to left and go under tunnel and then straight ahead. This is known as the scenic route, I would not recommend the unscenic route. Essentially what you must do on this route is keep straight ahead, easier than it sounds but NAST.

DUNCAN ALSOP **Warwick**
26 Smith Street, Warwick
Mon-Sat, 9.30-5.30
Med/lg R/C/nrly D stk, keen on Local History. Res stk at rear, slightly roast beef. ETF in centre of town but imposs to get to from Warwick Station. Nearest: Birmingham, Coventry, Northampton and Hereford.

ROBERT VAUGHAN **Stratford on Avon**
20 Chapel Street, Stratford on Avon, Warwicks
Mon-Sat, 9-5.30
Med/lg C/D stk, solid roast beef. Emphon the local arab. Ab av cal, cnd and prices. TWC. P.poss. Nearest: Warwick, Brackley, Worcester, Broadway.

THE OLD HALL BOOKSHOP **Brackley**
32 Market Place, Brackley
Mon-Sat, 9.30-5.30, L 1-2
Lg R/C stk, ab av cal, cnd and prices. Not only is this shop WAD, it is poss to detour to it. On the day I went to it my intention was to end up in Worcester. At 4.15 I had finished looking at the shops in Stratford. It would have been poss to get to Worcester but it would only have been possible to do one of the shops as they all close at 5pm. Rather than be frustrated by not being able to get into 2 of them, I decided to go to Brackley which opens to 5.30. Had Brackley clsd at 5 we would not have bothered to take the risk. As it was, we got there just before 5, and were out a few minutes later, but there was no feeling that we were being rushed.

Almost everything in this shop is done for the benefit of the customers. They do close for lunch, but I am prepared to overlook that. In the hallway there are exceedingly cheap Rs bks which must encourage the beginners of Brackley. It is a general shop with a bias towards Mod Lit. Without being obsessive, the bks are all in good cnd. It seems to be that those that are not, are the ones that end up on the cheap shelves. All the sections are carefully labelled and it is extremely easy to follow the layout.

ROUTE 11 O'CLOCK

CARLISLE - CUMBRIA - PRESTON - MANCHESTER

CARLISLE

A day which begins with that full English breakfast that is Carlisle Station, could only ever be described as a roaring success. Nothing that life or book collecting could throw at you could in any way erase the glory of that experience. Bankruptcy, castration, suicide, or even discovering that your favourite bksp had closed down and that the owner had run away to join the bookfairies, all these will appear as mere trivialities once you have seen the wonder and magic of England's most spectacular station.

The outside is a piece of deception worthy of the Roman Catholic Church. But why arrive in such a pedestrian manner when you could come complete with a train. As in a cathedral your eyes will lift to the roof and you will forever be grateful to the hoopla stand owners of the world for making such a crowning achievement poss. Hadrian would have loved such walls as these, even the toughest Scotsman would have died of embarrassment had he tried to climb them in a kilt. The floor floors you. Only a magic performance could take place on such a stage. And indeed this is what happens for every night trains arrive and depart which are unknown to the timetablers of British Rail, they stop for less than five seconds and then disappear. If you ask about them you are told they do not exist. Determined to prove I was not dreaming I once got on one of these trains in the belief that it must go either to Glasgow or Edinburgh. It did neither, it went to Inverness. Trains arrive and are sawn in half without a word. I was once on such a train, I went on to Glasgow - my bike went on to Stranraer. Trains depart from this station and arrive in London 2½ hours later, I once got on such a train, the passengers were all from the local Womens' Institute on their way to the Chelsea Flower Show. It is the only time in my life that I have ever felt conspicuously underdressed. The places to which British Frail does admit that trains go would make a truly collectable poster: Aspatria, the Greek Dancer, the compere without compare, Blair Atholl, that well known troop Galashiels, just before the intermission, Haltwhistle and the stars of the show brought up on British Frail's one successful line of poetry renowned from Carlisle to Leeds Lazonby and Kirkoswald.

Odd props appear: an eighteen foot long single oar on its way from Oxford to Belfast. A tandem tricycle. A five hundred foot length of brass chain and that most rare item, neat and tidy train spotters. As a rule Train Spotters are the only group of people who dress worse than book dealers, but not in Carlisle.

For this is a real station, not a mock airport,. there is no concourse, there are platforms, trains arrive and leave in a natural direction. It is easy to find things out, everything works properly from the floor sweeper to the station master, unlike Newcastle which was designed by somebody with a visual stutter, the things on this station all appear to be in the right place.

So rare is Carlisle station that after you have left you wonder if it is not itself just an illusion and if it is not it is certainly performance art.

THE BOOK CASE **Carlisle**
17 Castle Street, Carlisle, Cumbria
Mon-Sat, 10-5
Med/lg R/C stk, excruciatingly boring. BR Carlisle, OOS turn left into main shopping street and continue through to Castle.

CUMBRIA

A HOST OF GOLDEN ANORAKS

I stole that line from Robin Dennys of Any Amount of Books in the Charing Cross Road. I offered him money for it but the miserable bastard would not sell. I am too dim to make up my own lines but I am bright enough to spot a perfect one when I see it, and am quite happy to buy any that are on offer, failing that I liberate them.

For the purposes of this guide Cumbria is defined as anywhere west of the line Carlisle-Lancaster. The popular image is that it is crowded in summer and desolate in winter. Neither of these views matches the reality. It is true that the police close off parts of Cumbria by blocking the motorway exits but if you cycle from Whitehaven to Penrith you are unlikely to see another person, except a caged one. In coaches and cars they crane their eyes at the sight of a human being.

ST ANDREWS BOOKSHOP **Penrith**
St Andrews's Walk,(no No.) Penrith, Cumbria
Mon-Sat, 9-5, Wed 1pm. V.Rel
New bksp with med/small stk of C bks, keen on Nat His and ornithology. Av cnd, slightly over av prices. TWC. WAD. P.diff. BR Penrith, OOS turn left down drive and right into town (ignore signs which say Town Centre which are for motorists - the people who are always going the wrong way in life. Continue to clock tower and passage is beyond. Nearest: Carlisle, Alston, Carnforth, Keswick.

LANCASTER

BOMBER

ATTICUS **Lancaster**
26 King Street, Lancaster
Mon-Sat, 10.30-5.30
Small/med R/c stk, student/acad orientated, also has crime fiction. T. P.diff. BR lancaster OOS turn right up drive and left and right at main junction, SIOR. Nearest: Carnforth, Giggleswick, Preston, Morecambe.

There is also a pbk junky bksp further down on the A6.

MCCORMACKS **Lancaster**
6&6a Rosemary Lane, Lancaster
Mon-Sat 10-5, clsd Wed, Rel
Med/lg C/D stk ab av cal, cnd and prices. TWC. From Atticus turn left OOS and follow one way system round to second car park, shop adjacent, do not bother unless you have a chauffeur.

THIS GUIDE NOW GOES ON AN ANTI CLOCKWISE TOUR OF CUMBRIA, APART FROM A FEW PRAISEWORTHY EXCEPTIONS, CUMBRIA ON A SUNDAY IS A CEMETERY WITH LIGHTS.

THE CARNFORTH BOOKSHOP **Carnforth**
38-42 Market Street, Carnforth, Lancs
Mon-Sat, 9.30-5.30, V.Rel
Very lg R/C stk, av cnd, cal and prices. Lg? It is bloody enormously dispiriting. R/C? You would need a collection of Rs to successfully peruse all the titles. T and very helpful. P.poss. BR Carnforth - the station where they made Brief Encounters, they were certainly not thinking of this shop. OOS turn left and right into town. Nearest: Penrith, Lancaster, Morecambe

PETER BAIN SMITH **Cartmel**
Bank Court, Cartmel, Cumbria
Everyday 11-6, clsd Mon & Tue in Winter, Rel
Med/lg R/C stk, av cal, bl av cnd, ab av prices, butcan be WAD espec on a Sunday. Also has room of childrens bks. TWC. P. diff. BR Cark & Cartmel, OOS up track, turn right into village and first right past pub (not towards Holkham Hall as the signs seem to indicate also ignore the signs in Cartmel which is NAST - 2 miles.

THE OLD STORY TELLERS BOOKSHOP **Ulverston**
11 Fountain Street, Ulverston, Cumbria
Tues-Sat, 10-5.30, clsd Wed, Rel
Med size R/C stk, emphon local history, av cal, cnd and prices. Etgow. P. diff. BR Ulverston. OOS turn left and left over bridge continue through town and turn right past Heritage Centre where they sell bks on Saturday. There are also some bks further along Fountain Street in Oddfellows Hall. Nearest: Gosforth, Cartmel, Barrow in Furness.

I shall never forget Ulverston; it was the place at which I learnt the right length to wear my kilt. Eight kilted bagpipers got off the train and I began studying their knees, they seemed a trifle put out by this but I felt that it was important to hold my own consumer survey regardless of the consumers. After much research I had established that the right official lengthfor a kilt is the mid knee, however, my in-depth surveys of Scottish men's knees had led me to believe that the normal length was just above the knee.

When I enquired of the Bagpipers they all said it should be just above the knee. The reason for this is that they have no wish to be confused with Englishmen who always wear their kilts just below the knee. I have thus been saved from committing an even worse faux pas than wearing brown brogues with my kilt. It should of course be black. Why I shall never forget Ulverston is that the train left without me.

MOSTLY BOOKS **Barrow in Furness**
247 Rawlinson Street, Barrow in Furness, Cumbria
Tues-Sat, 11-5, clsd Thurs, Rel
Med size R/C/D stk, emphon Technical aspects of handicrafts i.e. Spon's Workshop Receipts type of book almost becoming a spec shop. Ab av cal, cnd, av prices. Etgow. P.poss. BR Barrow, OOS turn left down drive and straight across crossroads, SIOL. Nearest: Gosforth, Ulverston.

ARCHIE MILES **Gosforth**
Beck Place (no No.), Gosforth, Cumbria
Tues-Sat, 10-6, Sun 2-6, Rel
Med size C/D stk, ab av cal, cnd and prices. T. P.poss. BR Seascale (NAST 2 miles) ETF in village. Nearest: Whitehaven, Ambleside, Ulverston.

MICHAEL MOON **Whitehaven**
41-43 Roper Street, Whitehaven, Cumbria
Mon-Sat, 9.30-5
Very lg R/C/D stk, WAD. Takes some ploughing to and through, but can be a good harvest. T. P.poss. BR Whitehaven. Nearest: Carlisle, Cockermouth, Gosforth.

WINKWORTH'S Cockermouth
102 Main Street, Cockermouth, Cumbria
Mon-Sat, 9.30-5, Rel
New bksp with bta med size R/C stk, keen on Lake District. Also has some slightly different to normal bks. TWC. P.poss. BR Whitehaven (NAST 15 miles) but has good bus service unlike Caldbeck. Nearest: Carlisle, Penrith, Keswick, Whitehaven.

APPLEBY'S BOOKS **Keswick**
5 St John's Street, Keswick, Cumbria
Mon-Sat, 10-5, Suns during summer (summer in Cumbria is defined as less than three inches of rain per hour).
Med size R/C/D stk, av cal, cnd and prices. Ds stk is in office. Emphon cricket. Etgow. P.diff. Street is opp main entrance to the tourist centre, the place where all the people who come in coaches ask how long it is before the next bus back to Leeds. Nearest: Cockermouth, Penrith, Ambleside, Whitehaven.

BOOK COTTAGE Braithwaite
Braithwaite, Keswick, Cumbria
Mainly open during summer season See above for details. BTR
Med size R stk which would be a Silverfish Special but the Silverfish have had the sense to leave because it is so cold. FARTS. TWC. P.poss. ETF alongside cafe. Braithwaite is small village 2 miles north of Keswick.

THE LITTLE BOOKSHOP **Ambleside**
1 Cheapside, Ambleside, Cumbria
Mon-Sat, 9-5, clsd Thurs
This is the most inappropriately named shop in Britain. It should be called the Medium Bookshop, for although it is small in size the stk is med sized, the bks are of med cal and the prices are med. The only thing unmed about it, is its location, which I could not begin to describe. TWC. P.poss. Nearest: Keswick, Kendal, Cartmel, Gosford.

KIRKLAND BOOKS **Kendal**
68 Kirkland, Kendal, Cumbria
Mon-Sat, 10-5, clsd Thurs
Med sized R/C stk, av cal, cnd and prices. Recently changed hands and tends to be a bit neat and tidy, but maybe they will learn. BR Kendal, OOS turn left down drive and right into Wildman Street. Follow all the way to main street and turn left and then follow round curve. Nearest Penrith, Sedbergh, Carnforth, Ambleside.

PRESTON

The citizens of northern cities all vye for the title Gritty Northerners. They mainly perform this self allotted task by sneering at anything which smacks of the smarmy south, but not in Preston where they feel that all outsiders are from the south. The only good news is that there is a Road Improvement Scheme, with luck it will manage to obliterate the hole of Preston.

THE BOOKHOUSE **Preston**
63-65 Fylde Road, Preston, Lancs
Mon-Sat, 10-5.30, Rel
Med size R/C stk, student/acad orientated, av cal, cnd and prices. Does produce the occasional int bk, TWC. P.poss. BR Preston, OOS up drive, turn right and left with flow of one way traffic and follow signs for Blackpool for about half a mile. Nearest: Preston, Oswaldwystle, Leyland, Blackpool.

HALEWOOD & SONS **Preston**
68 & 37 Friargate, Preston, Lancs
Mon-Sat, 9.15-5.30, Rel
Lg C/D stk, ab av cal, cnd and prices. Res stk by request. This shop is not dissimilar to a newspaper empire. Each part is seemingly independent but each supports the other. Like newspapers they can be fawning, smug, aggressive and bombastic, all on the same day. The owner has the same attitude to women as The Sun, except that he has been at it sixty years longer. His clone-like offspring have the resources of The Sunday Times, except that they manage to exhibit even more hypocrisy. There is the same admiration for titles as at The Times, except that their's are even more down at heel. They change face as often as Today Newspaper, but for them the Sky is only the limit when it comes to the prices.

Above the fascia of this establishment there used to be a sign which read: 'Temple of the Muses'. I for one would be prepared to contribute to the erection of a replacement sign with slightly adjusted wording: 'Temple of The Abuses'.

From Bookhouse go back to the roundabout and take left hand for towards the town centre, SIOR. Preston is currently the victim of a road improvement scheme, it genuinely could be described as an improvement if it demolished these premises.

BOOKS FOR EVERY ONE **Preston**
13 Lowthian Street, Preston, Lancs
Mon-Sat, 10-5, Rel

Small R stk, keen on childrens and pbks. The previous owners have now gone into the video business. From Halewood, cross through shopping centre and find signposts on opp side of the road.

CHEVET BOOKS **Blackpool**
157 Dickson Road, Blackpool
Mon-Sat, 9.30-7, Sun in summer
Med size R/C stk slightly low key, nrly a Drif Special. T & Disc. BR Blackpool, OOS towards right hand side of station and turn right, SIOR.

There is also a pbk shop towards the left of the station by the market.

GREAT GRANDFATHERS **Leyland**
82 Towngate, Leyland, Lancs
Tues-Sat, 9.30-5.30, clsd Wed, Rel
Med/lg R/C/D stk, ab av cal, cnd, av prices. Keen on Nat Hist. Forget the twee name, this is definitely WAD, there is a res stk, but he is not keen to show it. Etgow. P.poss. BR Leyland, OOS turn left down bridge and follow road round to left, at roundabout turn right into shopping street and follow road round to left, about a mile from the station. Nearest: Preston, Oswaldwistle, Wigan, Ormskirk.

THE BOOKHOUSE **Wigan**
8 The Wiend, Wigan, Lancs
Mon-Sat, 10.30-5.30
Med size R/C stk, av cal, cnd and prices. Lightly student remainder orientated. BR Wigan (both) OOS turn away from bridge towards town centre and turn right into alleyway opp mock tudor building (not the only thing that gets mocked in Wigan). Nearest: Leyland, Prestwich (Manchester), Northwich, Ormskirk.

MANCHESTER

Manchester longs to be known as the second city of England and it certainly deserves the title. It is the epitome of all that is second rate. You have to second guess the names of the streets, the motorists will not give you a second chance to cross the roads, even the new buildings look as if they are seconds, hardly anything is worth a second look. It is certainly not the sort of place where you would dream of having a second home. The Mancunian's idea of aspiration is a tent with a second storey. They do not give a second thought to a s/h bksp. The chances of finding an int s/h bk are as great as that of the second coming. The one piece of good news is that you can ignore it without a second thought.
PEOPLE OF MANCHESTER: We demand a second opinion.
Me: You are extremely ugly.

About the only bgn in Manchester is the £2 rover ticket which will get you to most of the shops listed in this section, but because of the way the rail lines are laid out it will take at least two full days to visit all the shops. This part of the guide is laid out clockwise.

LITTLE HOLCOMBE BOOKS **Ramsbottom**
52 Bridge Street, Ramsbottom, Gtr Manchester
Mon-Sat, 9.30-5, Wed 1pm, Rel
Med size R/C stk emphon childrens and ill. Etgow. P.poss. BR Bury (NAST 5 miles). Nearest: Haslingden, Rochdale, Prestwich, Wigan.

BROWSERS **Prestwich**
14 Warwick Street, Prestwich, Gtr Manchester
Mon-Sat, 10-5, clsd Wed
Med size R/C stk, av cal, cnd and prices. BR Prestwich, OOS turn right and right and left. Nearest: Ramsbottom

FENNEL BOOKS **Manchester**
23 Fennel Street, Manchester
Mon-Sat, 10-5.30, Rel
Med/lg R/C stk, the most int shop in Manchester. There is an originality about the choice of the bks which far surpasses that of all the other Manchester bksps. There is no need to detour to it, it is directly opp Victoria Station, OOS ahead and across to building which looks like a railway station. There are other bkstls in the Corn Exchange above but in comparison to this one above they are a total waste of time. They make the B&MC look erudite. There is also a bksp a few doors along where all the publications are shrink wrapped in cellophane. Quite why they feel the customers should want to indulge in safe sex with bks is not something I am keen to find out.

PARAMOUNT BOOK EXCHANGE **Manchester**
Withy Grove (no No.), Manchester
Mon-Sun, 9-7
Lg R nearly C stk emphon pbks. It is harder to decide which is louder the covers of the bks or the pop music. BR Victoria, Manchester, OOS to left turn right onto main road and second left.

GIBBS BOOKSHOP **Manchester**
10 Charlotte Street, Manchester
Mon-Sat, 9.30-5
Med/lg C/D stk, emphon student/acad and remainders. Some Ds bks. BR Manchester, Piccadilly, OOS ahead turn left at Portland Street (the bus station) and third right at Charlotte St, shop is in basement.

MCGILLS BOOKSHOP **Manchester**
184 Oxford Road, Chorlton on Medlock, Manchester
Mon-Sat, 10.30-5.30
Med size R/C stk, slightly down at heel, keen on Student/Acad type bks. BR Manchester, Oxford Road, OOS down to Oxford Road and turn left.

GEORGE KELSALL **Littleborough**
22 Church Street, Littleborough, Manchester
Mon-Sat, 9.30-5.30, clsd Tues
New & s/h bksp with med size R/C/D stk, I am not overkeen but a lot of people in the Manchester area rate it. TWC. BR Littleborough, OOS ahead and left, Nearest: Todmorden, Huddersfield, Uppermill, Ramsbottom.

BRIAN BARLOW Manchester
52 Beech Road, Chorlton Cum Hardy, Manchester
Mon-Sat, 10-5.30, EC Wed.
Med size low key R/C stk, emphon Penguins. P.poss. BR Stretford, OOS turn left into Edge Lane which becomes High Lane turn right into Moor Road and first right into Beech Road (NAST).

THE CREME DE LA CREME BOOKSHOP Hale
64a Park Road, Hale, Manchester
Tues,Thur,Fri & Sat, 10-6, Rel
Small C/D stk, ab av cal, cnd and prices. Emphon Travel and Bookfairy subjects. Etgow. P.poss. (Like most bookfairies he has trouble conceiving of a world without cars). BR Hale, OOS into main shopping street, ahead until you come to a pub called the Bleeding Wolf turn left and follow road round to left.

ABACUS BOOKS Altrincham
24 Regent Road, Altrincham, Manchester
Mon-Sat, 10-5
New bksp with med size R/C stk where it is imposs to tell which are which. What this place needs is some Jewish Lightning. BR Altrincham, OOS turn left onto main road and right towards carpark.

GRENVILLE STREET BOOKSHOP Stockport
105 Grenville Street, Edgeley, Manchester
Tues-Sat, 10-6
Med/lg R/C/D stk, emphon Travel. It is the most Victorian bksp in Britain and it requires a slightly Victorian dedication to work through all the stk. There is a strong class divide between those bks which the owner feels have breeding (the Travel) and those which were not produced in such fortunate circumstances. There is a single mindedness the like of which made Victorian Britain so great. BR Stockport, OOS on ticket barrier side and double back on yourself, down tunnel towards what looks like a coal mine, turn left, turn right into paved zone and turn right at church at end, approx 1 mile. That small piece of information took me 5 years to find out.

THE HEATON'S BOOKSHOP Stockport
13 School Lane, Heaton Chapel, Manchester
Mon-Sat, 10.30-4.30
This shop conclusively demonstrates that you can only find out about a bksp by visiting it. The bks are the ultimate Drif Special upper class. Unfortunately it looks like it is going to close down. BR Heaton Chapel, OOS turn left, cross river of death if poss and continue. SIOR.

MOORLAND BOOKS Upper Mill
Alexander Craft Centre, Upper Mill, Oldham
Wed & Fri 11-4, Sat & Sun 11-5
Med size R/C stk, bta cal, bta cnd, av prices. Slightly Literace and touristy orientated but almost WAD on a Sunday. I had never got to this place before and had assumed that it was imposs because BR said it was. BR Greenfield, (but alas there is no service on a Sunday), OOS up hill and continue towards Upper Mill, approx 1 mile.

ROMILLEY LITTLE BOOKSHOP **Romilley**
1 Hill Street, Romilley, Cheshire
BTR 061 4274853
Small R/C stk, av cal, cnd and prices. Recommended that you take your own ladder. BR Romilley, OOS turn left into village, ETF.

THE HIGH STREET BOOKSHOP **Newmills**
6 High Street, Newmills, Stockport
Mon-Sat, 10-4.30 and sometimes clsd Wed
Med size primarily a pbk shop but does have some hardbacks at curious prices which make them int. BR Newmills, OOS up path and ahead and turn left at shopping street and SIOR.

THE MARPLE BRIDGE BOOKSHOP **Marple Bridge**
42 Town Street, Marple Bridge, Manchester
Mon-Sat, 10-5, Sun 2-5, clsd Wed
Med size R/C stk, ab av cal, cnd and prices. Emphon fiction. Literace. Bookfairy. Etgow. P.poss. BR Marple, OOS up path and turn left and right and left towards shops.

ROUTE 11.30

HARROGATE-LEEDS-HALIFAX-SHEFFIELD-LEICESTER

RIPON BOOKSHOP **Harrogate**
6 Station Bridge, Harrogate
Mon-Sat, 10-5 Unr
Med size R/C stk, roast beef. Emphon Yorkshire. TWC. P.diff. BR Harrogate, OOS turn left and left. Nearest: York, Leeds, Ripon.

THE HARROGATE BOOKSHOP **Harrogate**
29 Cheltenham Crescent, Harrogate
Mon-Sat, 10-5.30, Rel
Med/lg R/C/D stk, solid roast beef but with juniper sauce, emphon music. WAD. Vetgow and very helpful. BR Harrogate, OOS, turn right and second left and follow road round.

J E COURTNEY **Harrogate**
5 Mount Parade, Harrogate
Tues-Sat, 10-5.30
Small C spec stk, emphon Maritime. Av cal, ab av cnd, av prices. TWC. P.poss. From Harrogate Bksp go back towards station and turn second left.

BOOKSTOP BOOKSHOP **Harrogate**
11 Mayfield Grove, Harrogate
Mon-Sat, 10-5.30, Wed 1pm
Med size R/C stk, slightly Lit. Keen on pbks, but worth a look. P.poss. From Courtneys OOSH, continue into Franklin Road & right at Strawberry Dale Terrace, shop is on corner.

CHILTON BOOKS **Skipton**
49 Belmont Bridge, Skipton
Mon-Sat, 10-5, clsd Tues
Med size R/C stk, av cal, cnd and prices. Currently up for sale. BR Skipton, OOS turn right. Nearest: Settle, Harrogate, Saltaire, Preston.

THE BOX OF DELIGHTS **Skipton**
25 Otley Street, Skipton
Mon-Sat, 11-5.30, clsd Tues & Thur
Med size C/D stk, ab av cal, emphon Ill & childrens. More than av imagination shown in stk, and sometimes prices. WAD. P.poss. From above continue into town, turn left and Otley Street is halfway along.

I appear to have missed a third shop in Skipton of which I am totally ignorant.

LEEDS

KINDLY LIGHTS

Not quite as good as Sheffield, but very good from the transport point of view, despite all attempts by the management to make it the worst mainline station in Britain*.

P.poss. OWOWS. POCS. Nearest: Harrogate, Hull, Wakefield, Bradford. Leeds is notable for being in the Metro area, which has the cheapest one day ticket in Great Britain (£1.90). This ticket covers all the shops listed in this section other than if denoted.

MR MILES **Leeds**
12 Great George Street, Leeds
Mon-Sat, 9-5.30
V lge R/C/D stk, acad roast beef, but can be well worth a look. BR Leeds, OOS ahead, cross main road and continue to Headrow, turn right at town hall and Mr Miles is behind.

ST MICHAELS BOOKSHOP **Leeds**
69 St Michael's Lane, Headingly, Leeds
Mon-Sat, 10.30-5.45
Med size R/C stk, emphon on Cricket, but bta Spec general stk. Etgow. P.poss. From Allerton turn left along Headingly Lane and third left at St Michael's Lane, shop is opp Cricket ground.

ALMAR BOOKS **Leeds**
10 Commercial Road, Kirkstall, Leeds
Mon-Sat, 10.15-5
Med size R/C stk, about to change hands, and rumoured to become a remainder shop. From St Michaels Lane continue past cricket ground, turn right into Kirkstall Hill, left into Kirkstall Lane and turn left into Kirkstall Road. You can get a bus which goes to this bksp. The bus stop is known as the Barcelona stop. The bksp is known as the homage to Catatonia.

BOOKSIDE **Leeds**
Midland Back Passage, Midland Road, Leeds
Mon-Sat, 10-6
Med/lg R/C student pbk orientated, the hardbacks are silver fish orientated. This shop is well sign posted if you approach it from Allerton. Do not attempt to find it from St Michaels.

ALLERTON BOOKS **Leeds**
11a Headingly Lane, Hyde Park, Leeds
Mon-Sat, 9.30-5.30
Med size R/C/nrly D stk, slightly student orientated, Etgow. P.poss. From Miles OOSH, right and right keeping twin peaked building to left, continue straight ahead for 1½ miles, SIOL. (It is not worth trying to get a train to Headingly).

BRADFORD

A short walk in the Hindu Crush

***THE SILVERFISH SPECIAL BOOKSHOP** **Bradford**
Southgate (no No.), Bradford
Phone number obscured by plastic flowers. Small/med size R/C stk, a bit grotty to be a Drif Special, but it is definitely a Silverfish Special. BR Bradford Interchange, OOS down

drive, and straight ahead into Bridge St which becomes Sunbridge and turn left past Sunwins. Nearest: Saltaire, Halifax.

THE BODHRAN **Saltaire**
9 Victoria Road, Saltaire, Bradford
Mon-Sat, 10-5
Med size R/C - Listener's shop. Ab av cal, cnd and prices. Emphon Celtic Music (to which a vast number of things seem to be indirectly related).

FALCON BOOKS **Saltaire**
13/13a Victoria Road, Saltaire, Bradford
Mon-Sun, 2-5
Med size R/C stk, keen on Crime Fiction and Lit. Av cal, cnd and prices. Directions as above, further down. A Bodhran is an Irish musical instrument. After listening to it and having to contort myself to look at some of the bks, this bod ran as well. BR: Saltaire, OOS turn left up path and right at top.

BOWDON BOOKS **Oswaldwistle**
300 Accrington Road, Oswaldwistle, Lancs
Tues-Sat, 10-5.30, Sat 4pm, Rel
Med size C/D stk, ab av cal, cnd, av prices. Emphon Textiles & needlework. WAD. T. P.poss. BR Oswaldwistle and church, OOS turn left and follow for ½ mile.

Ossy (as these of us who have been there call it) looks like Londonderry, only in Ossy there has never been any bombing. It was designed to look like that. It is hard to imagine why anyone should live in Ossy by choice, but the owner of this shop claims to like it, this causes a slight problem as their choice of bks is extremely good. I had been expecting something on the level of a Londonderry shop, where, what I call a Silverfish Special counts as a C/D shop.

It may well be that my belief that the location of a bksp is 51% of its success is wrong, for from the outside Oswaldwistle has very little going for it. Maybe bksps should open up in such depressing places, but it is hard to think of anywhere quite as bad. Nearest: Kirkby, Lonsdale, Todmorden, Haslingden, Preston.

THE COLLECTOR **Halifax**
30 The Collonade, Piece Hall, West Yorks
Mon-Sat, 10-5.30, clsd Thur
Med size Spec in Military History. Av cal, cnd and prices. BR Halifax, OOS and ahead and right into Piece Hall, the beautiful building on the right.

WEST RIDING BOOKS AND PICTURES **Halifax**
12 Piece Hall, Halifax
Fri-Sun 11-5
Med size R/C stk, av cal, cnd and prices.

Dr A.B.N. Ormal of the Halifax Institute of Cognitive Studies (HICS) a psychiatrist writes:

On June 26, the patient, a deranged skinhead was brought into my clinic by the police. He claimed to be Raymond Drif Field Carver. He gave his profession as compiling guides to s/h bksps (the primary reason the police referred him to me). He was muttering to himself such statements as "When will it ever end, I've been compiling this guide now for six months, and I went into the bksp at the corner of the Piece Hall, which was enormous, and filled with bks that would drive the brightest mad, and then the owner said that I had no idea what a bksp was like, that I could not tell the difference between a R bksp and a C shop or a D shop and that I was incapable of coherent thought."

When questioned, the patient, was muttering to himself that he had failed to get to such places as Hebden Bridge, Todmorden, Haworth and Colne. It is clear that nobody sane would want to go to these places, I have had him certified. I also decline to treat him as a patient on the grounds that he might give me nightmares.

ROBLYN'S **Huddersfield**
18 Westgate, Huddersfield
Mon-Sat, 9.30-5
Med size R/C stk, emphon pbks, but it does hardbacks better than most of that ilk. TWC. P.diff. Nearest: Halifax, Wakefield, Holmfirth, Littleborough.

Shop in Lockwood seldom open.

DAISY LANE BOOKS **Holmfirth**
Towngate, Holmfirth, W. Yorks
Mon-Sun, 9-5.30, Rel
Med/lg R/C stk with a slightly antqrn look. Etgow. Av cnd and prices. TWC. P.diff. BR Huddersfield, Metro ticket, NAST 5 miles. ETF by bus station. Nearest: Huddersfield, Wakefield, Sheffield, Rochdale.

TOLL HOUSE BOOKS **Holmfirth**
32/34 Huddersfield Road, Holmfirth
Mon-Sat, 9.30-5
Med/lg new & s/h bks. Ab av cal, slightly literace bks. If I was a better writer I could describe how two such similar shops as these look so different. TWC. ETF.

LEO BOOKS **Wakefield**
4 Vicarage Street South, Wakefield
Mon-Sat, 10-5, Sat 4.30, Rel
Med size R/C stk, NSOC, V int stk, low prices. A Drif cum Silverfish Special, a classic of the Merchant Navy School of Bookdealing, TWC. P.diff. BR Wakefield, Westgate, OOS ahead to church, turn left, past it and first right down hill and left 100 yards ahead. Nearest: Leeds, Doncaster, Sheffield, Huddersfield.

THE SEVEN SAM AWRY

SHEFFIELD

GRUEL BRITTANNIA

It is a bit like the last night at the proms, you have to endure a lot of crud and aggravation before you get to the rousing parts. Cage composed the railway station, Stockhausen arranged the ring road of Wagnerian proportions and the pedestrian is ignored. But the verses of the bksps just force you to join in to make a grand finale.

ALAN HILL **Sheffield**
Glossop Road (no No.), Sheffield
Mon-Sat, 10-5.30, Rel
Med, nrly lg R/C/D stk. A bit Bookfairyish but well worth a look. Bgns known. TWC. P. diff. BR Sheffield, OOS turn left onto the ring road and follow signs for Glossop, at Glossop Road approx 1½ miles. This is definitely not the scenic route but it is the most efficient and leads easily to the other shops.

THE BOOK AND ART SHOP **Sheffield**
204 West Street, Sheffield
Mon-Sat, 10-5.30, Rel
Med size R/C/D stk, NSOC, but does come up with some int bks. Av prices. T. From Alan Hill OOSH, turn right into town, SIOL.

RARE & RACY **Sheffield**
164-166 Devonshire St, Sheffield
Mon-Sat, 10-6, V.Rel
Med/lg R/C/D stk. Ab av cal, cnd and prices. Has become distinctly bookfairyish and the music is as deafening as ever. From the outside it is almost a Helen Hanff Special, but inside it is a Fiona Pitt Kethley/Melody Maker Special, all racy promises, but little action. I could put up with it sounding like a nightclub if the buggers would open even later (in Sheffield 6 counts as late).

BIFF BOOKS & RECORDS **Sheffield**
11 Commonside, Walkley, Sheffield
Tues-Sat, 11-5.30, Sat 10, some Mon pms
Med size R/C stk, student/pseud orientated, heavy on the pbks. Etgow. P.diff. Continue on Ring Road and turn left at signs for Walkley.

TILLEY'S VINTAGE MAGAZINE SHOP **Sheffield**
281 Shoreham Road, Sheffield
Tues, Fri & Sat
Primarily post war magazines and comics.

BOOK HOUSE **Sheffield**
456-458 Glossop Road, Sheffield
Mon-Sat, 10-6
Small R/C stk, a Samuel Becket Special, never have so few bks managed to take up so large a space. TWC. P.poss. From Alan Hill turn left and continue up Glossop Road for 1 mile.

Y.S.F. **Sheffield**
Sharrowvale Road (no No.), Sheffield
Mon-Sat, ??
Recently moved and not yet open, suffice it to say that YSF stands for Yorkshire Secondhand Facts - it is well known that facts are different in Yorkshire. TWC. From Book House turn left and first right down hill. Turn right at bottom following edge of park, ahead right at junction and left and back on yourself at junction road into Sharrowvale.

THE PORTER BOOKSHOP **Sheffield**
227 Sharrowvale Road, Sheffield
Mon-Sat, 11-5.30
Med size R/C stk, av cal, cnd, not exactly my taste, but I still found it int. The other shops in Sheffield are all slightly deranged, whereas this one is extremely well arranged. It is odd that I should be attached to it. As YSF.

R.F. BARRET **Matlock**
The Courtyard, Dale Road, Matlock
Mon-Sat, 9.30-5, Rel
Med size R/C stk, ab av cal, cnd, av prices. BR Matlock, OOS ahead and to right. SIOR in precinct. Nearest: Chesterfield, Sutton in Ashfield, Leek and Bakewell

JARVIS BOOKS **Matlock**
57 Smedley Street East, Matlock
Mon-Sat, 9.30-5.30
Med size R/C stk, emphon Mountaineering. Now with new added bsmt mainly of fiction. BR Matlock, OOS turn left over bridge and straight up hill ahead. When you have walked up Everest, turn right.

SCARTHIN BOOKS **Cromford**
The Promenade, (no No.), Scarthin, Cromford
Mon-Sat, 10-6, L 1.30-2.30, sometimes open Sun
Lg R/C stk, av cal, cnd and prices. BR Cromford, OOS, down path and into town on right and shop is by pond, also on right. Nearest: Matlock, Derby, Nottingham and Bakewell.

LAURA'S BOOKSHOP **Derby**
58 Osmaston Road, Derby
Tues-Sat, 10.15-5.30, clsd Thur, Rel
Med/lg R/C/D stk, much improved. WAD. P.poss at rear. BR Derby OOS ahead and turn right at main road, turn left at roundabout and first right. Nearest: Matlock, Sutton in Ashfield, Burton upon Trent.

There are also shops in Chesterfield, Bakewell, Sutton in Ashfield and Mansfield, but NV.

NOTTINGHAM

JERMY & WESTERMAN about to close, but will be taken over by Geoff Blore who has the other shop in Mansfield Road. See TIN.

FOREST BOOKS **Leicester**
41-42 Silver Arcade, Silver Street, Leicester
Mon-Sat, 9.30-5
Med size lgish R/C stk, a Drif Special, best if you take your own lighting. P.diff. BR Leicester, OOS turn right and continue ahead into town centre and turn left at Pub. Silver Arcade is building on left, shop is on second floor.

THE BLACK CAT BOOKSHOP **Leicester**
37-38 Silver Arcade, Silver Street, Leicester
Mon-Sat, 9.30-5
Med size R/C stk, av cal, cnd and prices. As above

MAYNARD & BRADLEY **Leicester**
1 Royal Arcade, Silver Street, Leicester
Mon-Sat, 9.30-5.30
Med size C/D stk. Bookfairies, emphon on Local History but can be well worth a look. From Royal Arcade OOSH turn left and shop is in arcade on right.

LENTONS is excluded. Also **MCCORMACKS** which mainly deals in SF and pbks - see TIN.

CLARENDON BOOKS **Leicester**
144 Park Road, Leicester
Tues-Sat, 10-5, Sun pm in summer
Med size R/C stk, a Drif Special which is to be commended for opening on Sunday as do the shops in Cromford and Matlock. BR Leicester OOS turn left, go past roundabout, second right.

PARK BOOK SHOP **Wellingborough**
12 Park Road, Wellingborough, Hants
Mon-Sat, 10-5
Med size R/C stk, av cal, cnd and prices. BR Wellingborough, OOS into town and Park St is directly of one way system. Nearest: Leicester, Peterborough, Bedford and Northampton.

WOOTON BILLINGHAM **Northampton**
79 St Giles St, Northampton
Mon-Sat, 10-5
Med size R/C stk, av cal, cnd and prices but very unexciting. BR Northampton OOS turn left into town and follow straight through for 1 mile, not poss in motor car. Nearest: Wellingborough, Bedford, Newport Pagnell, Stratford u Avon.

OCCULTIQUE **Northampton**
73 Kettering Road, Northampton
Mon-Sat, 10-5
Sm spec stk of occult bks with some general stk and worth a look. From Wooton Billingham OOSH turn left and left and right at paved zone and then follow signs from Wellingborough. SIOL on Kettering Road.

ABINGTON BOOKSHOP **Northampton**
327 Wellingborough Road, Northampton
Mon-Sat, 10-5, Thurs 4pm
Med size R/C stk, av cal, cnd and prices. From Occultique go back to one way system and turn left and follow signs for Wellingborough.

WAILS FROM THE BORE DERS

This tour begins in that well known hospice for bks, Hay on Wye. It then continues the journey through time down the borders and along the coasts of Wales.

I have attempted it in a motor car and ended up in a mountainous rage. I have tried it on a bicycle and became a slag heap. I attempted it in a train and ended up with tunnel vision, and by bus I was left behind. There is but one consolation - it is better than a wake in Eire.

HAY RICK

I used to be in favour of burning bks, but now I have seen the error of my ways and have moved on to being in favour of burning bksps.

I have sought help from the criminal classes, and my solicitor says I should not be so eager to spread my inflamatory ideas. Apparently there was a famous legal case where a young man attempted to burn a hay rick. He set about the task without matches, or fuel and in a rainstorm. These slight handicaps notwithstanding he was arrested and charged with attempted arson - found guilty he was sentenced to death. Things are completely different now; you get life.

The main problem with burning bks is that it is so difficult to do properly; inordinate amounts of fuel and effort are needed to obtain a successful conflagration, but the one consolation is that even a failed attempt, and until now all attempts have been failures, will attract the oxygen of publicity. This is why it is imperative to invite journalists to any proposed book-burning. Only they can produce enough hot air at the right place.

The ill fed masses and their feeders, the literary lunchers, are appalled at the notion of burning bks, for them it is akin to burning the main course. That many bks are bad, wrong, deceitful, harmful, obsolete, but above all contaminants, is not something to which we should object. For they believe that all issues deserve to be discussed, by the right people, and preferably over lunch. For these people the crucial thing is to eat in the right place.

The library at Alexandria was burnt to a cinder in 391 thus ensuring its place in the history of the lost treasures of civilisation and as a spark which was to ignite research into book-burning. Alas, the bks were not bks as we know them; they were rolls of papyrus, but at least the heat was in the right place.

It was Savanrola who made the great leap forward in the art of burning bks. He was burnt at the stake clutching a bible to his chest. Despite massive efforts by onlookers, this bible was successfully destroyed. This proves that Savanrola's heart was in the right place.

It was the Nazis who gave book-burning such a bad name, and deservedly so; they were so bad at doing it. They used vast amounts of fossil fuels with little success. They had forgotten the lesson of Savanrola; a successful burning needs a human element. Despite this incompetence t heir name is synonomous with book-burning because they did it with a *flare* for publicity. They invited journalists, literary figures and film crews, above all they had enough spirit to have a go. Even if it was not enough for the bks to burn this proves that their hearth was in the right place.

It is the progressive fantasy that even if a way is found to successfully burn books there will always be one hero who will save literature. Ray Bradbury in his novel 'Fahrenheit 451' was the mightiest espouser of this wet liberal notion. But would Mr. Bradbury be such a welcome hero to those green liberals today? The limited edition of his most famous book was bound in asbestos. I can see that this would become a burning issue, knowing these people well, I can foretell that there would be a split, but you would only be able to hear them if you were in the right place.

Either Hay is in the wrong place or the customers are. The closest towns are all 20miles away and they can only summon up one real s/h bksp between them. Any customer for Hay has to get there first. Town Planners know that people will drive for twenty minutes - that it is not the distance but the ease of getting there that is the most important factor.

There are superguns who explode out of London claiming that they can reach Hay in under three hours, and sometimes they are right. But invariably they arrive as a shell.

There are trains to Hereford, I will not say the service is irregular, but it was the last time I used a steam train. I expected to see a hansom cab at the station.

There are indeed cabs at Hereford who are keen to take you to Hay. It is such a good job that the cabbies will wait until you have finished looking at the bks there, even if it means staying overnight.

There is a bus service from Hereford. It is the number one. It is called that because there is only one bus on it.

I have cycled from Hereford to Hay, or rather I should say I have pushed my bike from Hereford to Hay, the road was so bad that my inner tube exploded. I pushed on, literally, remembering the bike shop in Hay only to discover that it is now a bksp.

I have tried hitchhiking. I think I had more luck on the road from Kabul to Kaluk. At least in Afghanistan people did not swear at me for being a hippie, when they possibly had more cause.

I have walked from Hereford to Hay, not voluntarily. I missed the last bus at 5.50pm and I did not relish waiting 40 hours for the next one. I walked ten miles that evening, and ten miles the next morning before it dawned on me that I would have to get back. Even I could tell that a forty mile hike to buy three bks could not be described as a success.

Hay is the grand folly of one man: Mr. Richard Booth. After having failed as a bookdealer in England he moved to Wales on the ground that the properties were cheaper there and it was cheaper. That there were no customers was irrelevant, nobody ever bought his bks anyway. He then conceived the idea that if there were other bookdealers in Hay he might become famous for being first. It is hard to decide who showed the least foresight, Mr. Booth, or those other bookdealers who came after him. There are not enough centres of population within 50miles of Hay to make the place viable. Mr. Booth attempted to solve this problem by persuading the other dealers in the town to buy his bks, but not even they are that stupid.

The lack of natural catchment area caused another problem; there was nobody to buy bks from. This was why in the '60s and '70s expeditions led by Mr. Booth, scoured the country desperate to buy bks... When the bksp owners saw what the dealers of Hay bought, they could see little point in going there. Another small problem occurred - well Mr. Booth saw it as a small problem - people kept asking to be paid for the bks they had sold. Soon Mr. Booth took on the mantle of The Bankrupt Bookseller. The history of Hay is the history of bad debts. The one volume of which Mr. Booth could make a roaring success is entitled "How Not To Pay Your Bills and Survive" by the late '70s there was scarcely a bookdealer in Britain who would take one of Mr. Booth's cheques and thiswas why he started ranging round Europe, America and Australia, but first he sent out the expeditionary force of the publicity battalions.

Mr. Booth's ability to persuade bookdealers to part with bks for free has only ever been outmatched by his ability to persuade the media to give him publicity for free. Amid much attention he declared himself King of Hay. He then started selling bks by weight, next he began selling bks for burning.

What did not get so much publicity was the finance that was forthcoming from the Welsh Tourist office, the absolving of rate payments and the deluge of unpaid bills.

Mr. Booth's publicity stunts had attracted the attention of Leon Morelli, a man skilled in the art of book keeping. He had trained as an accountant and had worked for the post office. During one of the great strikes of the '70s he had begun his own postal service for bookdealers. Having made a considerable success of this, and only seeing the bks which sold he moved into the business of buying bksps. He did not know of the skill and experience of the average s/h bookseller. It was his fond belief that if they could do it - so could he. He bought several old established bksps in London and the Provinces, never for one moment questioning why they were all suddenly up for sale; At one stage he owned 7 shops, and when the bks did not sell in one premises he would remove them and try to sell them elsewhere. The same thing that happened at bookfairs occurred to Mr. Morelli's bks, they began to disintegrate. Neither Mr. Morelli nor his minions understood about condition. Mr. Morelli then discovered, or was that the aim all the time? That the sites of his shops were worth more than the bks. He is now credited with closing down more s/h bksps than any other person in Britain. Mr. Morelli has tried hard to take on Mr. Booth's mantle, but he just does not understand about Public Relations. He promised the locals he would get rid of the hippies, a good move but not one that was likely to work. He attempted to topple Mr. Booth from his Kingdom but failed to see that that was only ensuring that Mr. Booth became even stronger.

Mr. Booth looks like everybody's idea of a s/h bookdealer. He is shambling, unkempt, quixotic and bungling and thus perfect for television which is only able to deal in preconceived images.

Mr. Morelli wears suits, has slicked down hair and looks as if the only book he ever reads is the Annual Report. He looks like a book keeper should.

One of Mr. Booth's more original ideas - the definition of the word original is anything that attracts publicity - was to start offering bks for burning. This was bound to upset the shibboleths of middle class journalists and television folk and Mr. Booth knew this.

These expense accounters had been trained to see the book as a sacred object. There were articles in the press, and then on radio, and then on television, for most TV journalists do not believe in the truth of anything until they read about it, and they all came, with their drivers, and hangers on, and stayed at Mr. Morelli's hotel. (There was to be no walking from Hereford for the expense accounters).

Such is the media fascination with Hay and s/h bks that another group of individuals saw that it was not necessary to move dusty, broken down, unsaleable bks around the country when you could get the similar looking authors far cheaper. My ignorance of literature is such that I have no idea what goes on at a Literary Festival, but I do know, oh how I know, that they generate endless reams of publicity.

As far as I can work out a literary festival is somewhere where writers whom you thought were long dead try to prove that they are very much alive by drinking as much free alcohol as poss. They then write about how much alcohol other writers consumed correct the impression that they consumed too much. Thereafter they attempt to review the bks of people who only ever appear at Literary Festivals in an attempt to prove that they were completely sober when they met them.

Mr. Booth chagrin'd at the thought of not having come up with a literary festival himself, then started campaigning against it, which gave the literary festivaleers even more to write about. This is known as inspiration.

They have a little difficulty with the meaning of words in Hay on Wye. They describe it as being "via Hereford" which is only 20miles away. Mr. Booth describes his establishment as being the biggest bksp in the world, he obviously missed his vocation, he should have been an estate agent. Most people describe bksps by the number of bks.

Mr. Minet's emporium in Rochester may be physically smaller but there are definitely more bks in it.

There are establishments which call themselves: The Poetry Bookshop, The Childrens' Bookshop, The American Indian Bookshop, if you are looking for bks in these subjects these establishments are all well worth avoiding. Their definition of their chosen subject is amazingly limited. Hay on Wye describes itself as being the town of bks, this is about the only claim which is true. It is filled with Readers Diegests, The incomplete Works of the Idle, false account books, and spineless polemics.

RC writes

Does this mean you don't like the place?

I cannot bring myself to write individual despatches of the bksps in Hay on Wye, it would be akin to commenting on a single squadron after the last great battle has been lost. If you look carefully, you can spot the Field Marshall claiming it was a great victory and there are badly injured Generals, ready to fight yet again. There are convalescing Colonels and quavering Captains, willing to lead if instructed, but mainly there are just ordinary soldiers waiting patiently to be taken off the battlefield. There are so many it is hard to tell them apart, only their injuries differentiate them. Many are close to death and do not know it, others are severely injured and putting on a brave face. The vast majority have superficial wounds and are laughing with relief, but it is no joke. This time round they are alive but what of the future? They have only their memories. These footsoldiers stood on the sidelines at the great battle of Sothebys. They withstood the boot camp of the Farringdon Road. They have long service medals from bookfairs. They were devorated in forgotten fields. They were temporarily promoted to catalogues, but returned to base when they failed the ultimate test. And now they wait to be disbanded in an obscure Welsh Depot, the better to enrich their mercenary masters.

If you are a Reader it is too much, if you are a Collector is is too little, if you are a Dealer it is too mediocre.

There is a solution; Burn it all - the bks - the bksps - the owners - the literary festivaleers - the journalists - the acres of publicity - the tourists - just burn them all. It will work. Bks burn with enough hot air and fossil fools. It would make the burning at Alexandria look like childs play; It would make Savanrola look like a beginner. Instead of having to rely on a sporadic outburst, TV journalists could help plan the burnings. It could go on for weeks, nobody else would be hurt, there is nobody else around for miles.

I don't doubt that phoenix-like Mr. Booth would survive the blaze and he would garner all the publicity, nor do I doubt that the asbestos skinned Mr. Morelli would emerge richer than ever, for what flame could be greater, than their burning ambitions.

It is clear that Mr. Booth and Mr. Morelli should go into partnership. They could open up one enormous shop. Mr. Morelli could provide the building and Mr. Booth the hot air. A sort of hotel, where other dealers would send all their bks on holiday. Instead of having 18 establishments with the same stock, Mr. Morelli would have to learn to be ruthless and allow only one of each book on the shelves. Thus it would not be poss to go to Hay and see the umpteenth copy of the Scallop Book, or The Art of Needlework.

If the things I have suggested were to happen then I would be content to walk twenty miles for there would be no match for the Hay Rick.

H M LOCKYER **Abergevenny**

Monk Street (no NO.), Abergevenny

Mon-Sat, 9.30-5.30, Rel

Lg/med R/C stk, almost solid roast beef, but after the nouvelle cuisine of Hay, it is a joy to behold. Served in the old fashioned way, it has a distinctly rural taste to it. WAD. P.diff. ETF on one way system opp church. BR Abergevenny OOS turn left into town and right at beginning of paved street. Nearest: Hay, Monmouth, Cardiff, Carmarthen.

The above shop is omitted from the list of Welsh book Ds. It may well be true that they are too mean to pay the cost but its exclusion makes you wonder what other bksps have been left out. What local leaflets should do is include these bksps and just point out that they did not pay.

BRIAN STEVENS **Monmouth**
1 Church Street, Monmouth, Wales
Mon-Sat, 10-5, L 1-2, clsd Thurs, Rel
Med size R/C stk, av cal, cnd and prices. The Welsh Te Dium. BR Abergevenny (NAST 10miles) ETF. Nearest: Hereford, Ross on Wye (England), Chepstow, Abergevenny.

BRIDGEND BOOK BARN **Bridgend**
Unit 3 Stormy Down Ind Est, Stormy Down, Bridgend, Wales
Mon-Sun, 10-5.30
Med size R/C stk, emphon S/F pbks and Welsh. Av cal, cnd and prices. T. P.poss. Nearest: Brecon, Cardiff, Swansea. NV.

CAPITAL BOOKSHOP **Cardiff**
27 Morgan Arcade, Cardiff, CF1 2AF
Mon-Sat, 10-5.30, Rel
Med/lg R/C stk, ab av cal, cnd, av prices, keen on Welsh History. TWC. P.poss. BR Cardiff, OOS turn right and left into shopping st and right into arcade, about a ¼ mile along.

ROATH BOOKS **Cardiff**
188 City Road, Cardiff
Mon-Sat, 10.30-5.30
Small/med size R/C stk, A B&MC Special, but unlike them does not know what he is doing. Ave cal, cnd and prices. T. Etgow. P.poss. From Capital turn back into Queen Street, and head west and turn left opp the Royal Infirmary.

ALBANY BOOKS **Cardiff**
206 City Road, Cardiff
Tues-Sat, 10-5.30
Med/lg R/C/D stk, emphon Gliterace, av cal, cnd, ab av prices. TWC. P.poss. From Roath continue north.

DYLAN'S BOOKSTORE **Swansea**
Salubrious Passage, Swansea
Mon-Sat, 10-5 (owner claims -ish but in comparison to most bksps in Wales and England this is being extremely hard on himself).
Med/Lg R/C/D stk, ab av cal, cnd and prices. This shop's stk is made up of equal amounts of imagination and push. As much imagination goes into selecting the bks as pricing them and as much push goes into finding them as selling them. T. P.poss. BR Swansea, OOS ahead into High Street and turn right about 250 yards. Nearest: Cardiff, Carmarthen.

THE OLD BOOK MART **Swansea**
37 St Helens Road, Swansea
Mon-Sat, 10-5
Med size R/C stk, remaindery keen on Occult, av cal, cnd and prices. T. From Dylans go back towards station turn left into The Kingsway and continue. NV. I have decidedly gone off Occult bksps.

RC writes
What about Ralph the Book, the one next to the pub?

It was so dead the last time I went in there that I couldn't face it again - I've lost my interest in mortuaries.

CARMARTHEN BOOKS **Carmarthen**
1 St Mary Street, Carmarthen, Dyfed
Mon-Sat, 10-5, clsd Thurs
Med/lg R/C stk, av cal, cnd and prices, keen on Ill and Welsh. BR Carmarthen, OOS into town, turn right into town centre and find Guildhall Square. Nearest: Lampeter, Swansea.

CORRAN BOOKS **Laugharne**
King Street (no No.), Laugharne, Dyfed
Mon-Sat, 11-5, Sun 2-5 in summer
V lg R/C stk, emphon Lit, espec Welsh. Anoraksia Nervosa. ETF in main street. TWC. P.poss. BR Carmarthen (NAST 10 miles). Nearest: Lampeter, Carmarthen.

CARNINGLI CENTRE **Newport**
East Street, Newport, Dyfed
Mon-Sat, 9.30-5.30, clsd Wed 1pm
Med size R stk, av cal, ab av cnd, av prices. Mainly aimed at tourists. ETF in main street. BR Fishguard (NAST 10 miles). Nearest: Aberystwyth, Lampeter, Laugharne.

DYFI VALLEY BOOKSHOP **Machynlleth**
6 Doll Street, Machynlleth, Powys, Wales
Mon-Sat, 10-6, L 12.30-1.30, clsd Thurs
Med size R/C stk, av cal, cnd and prices. ETF. NV. Nearest: Llanrwyst, Llandloes, Lampeter.

WEST WALES BOOKS **Lampeter**
Railway Hotel, Tregaron, Lampeter
Mon-Sat, 10-6
Med size R/C stk, new and s/h, av cal, cnd and prices. BR Aberystwyth, NAST 20 miles. NV. ETF. Nearest: Machynlleth, Llandoes, Newport.

YSTWYTH BOOKS **Aberystwyth**
7 Princess Street, Aberystwyth, Dyfed
Mon-Sat, 9.30-5, clsd Wed winter
Med size R/C stk, Acad student orientated, ab av cal, cnd, av prices. Also does new bks, s/h are upstairs. ETF. Nearest: Machynleth, Kington, Newport.

THE BALCONY BOOKSHOP **Caernarfon**
The Old Market Hall, Palace Street, Caernarfon, Gwynned
Mon-Sat, 10.30-5, Winter 11-4.45, clsd Thurs
Small/med sized R/C stk, av cal, cnd and prices. TWC. P.diff. BR Bangor (NAST 10 miles) ETF by Castle. Nearest: Bangor, Bethesda, Llanrwyst, Machynllyth.

A E MORRIS **Bethesda**
40 High Street, Bethesda, Gwynned
Mon-Sat, 9.30-5.30
Med size C/D stk, ab av cal, cnd and prices. Emphon Bindings

and Plate bks and Childrens and Ill. T & Disc. P.poss. BR Bangor (NAST 7 miles), ETF. Nearest: Bangor, Caernarfon, Llanrwyst, Conway.

RC *You are not going to leave it just like that are you?*
d Why not?
RC *Even the West Midlands Serious Crime Squad could come up with a statement with more truth in it than that.*
d If I tell the truth, I will be accused of being anti semitic, two faced and dealing in stereotypes.
RC *I think calling him a Jewish lightning conductor and homunculous might just fit in there.*
d I'm trying to become more diplomatic in my old age.
RC *That was why you asked him about the law of Return was it?*
d I am puzzled by why he chose Bethesda.
RC *So you are genuinely going to say nothing? I don't believe it, I never thought I would live to see the day you would pull your punches, whatever next? I know, you could start telling people about the twenty years you spent in the loony bin.*
d It was not twenty years and it was not a loony bin.
RC *There is no need to get touchie, we shall be back in the cradle of Western civilisation soon.*
d Why? Are we going back to London?
RC *Well seeing that you have given up writing, what's the point of trekking round all these shops and anyway I will be able to dine out on this story for about the next 3 months.*
d Listen! How can I say that going into his shop is like thinking you were invited to a BAR MITZVAH and finding out that they were selling Time Shares in Tel Aviv. That he charges slightly less than General Schwarkscopf, or that given the choice between dealing with him or dealing with a bath full of leeches you would choose the leeches on the grounds that when they had got your blood they would let you go.
RC *But I thought you said you liked him.*
d That is the problem - I do.

BANGOR BOOKS **Bangor**
122 High Street, Bangor, Gwynned
Mon-Sat, 9.30-5, clsd Wed in winter
Med size R/C stk, bta, av cal and prices. TWC. P.diff. BR Bangor, OOS turn right into town at major junction, continue and then turn left. Nearest: Holyhead, Conway, Bethesda, Caernarfon.

ANGLESEY BOOKS **Holyhead**
1 Thomas Street, Holyhead, Anglesey, Gwynned
Mon-Sat, 10-4.30, Tues 1pm. V.rel
Med size R/C stk, ab av cal, cnd, av prices. Bgns known. Into doing the business. Emphon Mountaineering, Etgow, WAD, P.poss. BR Holyhead, OOS turn right into town and left at Coop. Nearest: Dublin, Bangor.

***THE CONWAY BOOKSHOP** **Conway**
21 High Street, Conway, Gwynned
Mon-Sat, 10-6, Sun 11-2, less in winter

Med size R/C stk which tries hard to be a tourist shop but fortunately fails. TWC. P.diff. BR Conway, ETF. Nearest: Llandudno, Colwyn Bay, Llanrwyst, Bethesda.

DAVID HUGHES **Llandudno**
21 Madoc Street, Llandudno, Gwynned
Mon-Sat, 10.30-5, L 1-2.30, clsd Wed
This is the ultimate Out to Lunch Bksp, Welsh division. There has never been a time when he has not announced that it is lunch time as I walked into the shop. Most bksp crawlers are going to start the day from somewhere around Chester and more than likely Colwyn Bay. It is almost inevitable that they are going to arrive here at lunchtime. Like the author of 'Finnegan's Wake', this shop expects you to spend your life waiting on him. The bks are arranged (if that is the word) in no particular order. Thus it takes much longer than an ordinary shop. A person who is interested in a single subject has to wade his way through every book on the many shelves, which is great for the owner, but rather time consuming for the rest of us. Like the greatest bores, it has words which are of some interest, it is the length of time in getting to them which is the killer.

PALACE BOOKS **Llandudno**
33 Madoc Street, Llandudno, Gwynedd
Mon-Sun 9.30-5.30
Remainder shop with small s/h stk, av cal, cnd and prices. For the last year or so a virulent strain of the Summer sickness has been affecting the North Wales coast. Under the direction of Palace Bks, which used to be an int shop in Caernarfon, a new breed of Remainder/ S/h bksps sprung up all along the North Welsh coast. The bks stocked in these places claim to be remainders, but are in fact publishers overstocks supplied by the eponymous discoverer of the plague. At one stage there were eight of these establishments claiming to be s/h shops but now it appears that only this one is left.

RHOS POINT BOOKS **Rhos on Sea**
85 The Promenade, Rhos on Sea, Clwyd
Summer every day 9.30-5.30, winter Tue-Sat 10-5, Wed 1pm
Small/med sized R/C stk, espec int to those with narrow shoulders, but broad minds. WAD. P.diff. BR Colwyn Bay (NAST 4 miles) ETF. Nearest: Colwyn Bay, Llanrwyst, Llandudno.

In North Wales the buses have been privatised, which means there are currently lots of them, but it is diff to work out which ones are going where. It is best to buy the £3.50 rover ticket (not the £4.50 - don't ask).

BAY BOOKSHOP **Colwyn Bay**
14 Seaview Road, Colwyn Bay, Clwyd
Mon-Sat, 9.30-4.30, clsd Wed pm in winter
Med/lg R/C stk, av cal, cnd and prices. Recently changed ownership and seems to be changing style. TWC. P.poss. BR Colwyn Bay, OOS turn to left and follow round. Nearest: Chester, Llanrwyst, Rhos Point

COLWYN BOOKS **Colwyn Bay**
66 Abergale Road, Colwyn Bay, Clwyd
Opening hours currently read like bathnight schedule at St

Trinians, basically Mon-Sat.
It is run with a slightly school-masterish/vicar type of enthusiasm and with constant mutterings about how he must tidy up. The bks are slightly school libraryish but it did have my favourite subject from school days: Oversize. From Bay Books, OOSH turn right and right up to main shopping street and left.

PROSPECT BOOKS AND PRINTS **Llanrwyst**
18 Denbigh Street, Llanrwyst, Gwynned
Mon-Sat, 9-5
Med size C/D stk, emphon HSF, ab av cal, cnd and prices. TWC. P.poss. BR Conway (NAST 10miles). NV. Nearest: Conway, Ruthin, Llandloes, Bangor.

There is also a s/h bkstl in Mold Market with a res stk at home. NV.

STOTHERT ANTIQUARIAN BOOKS **Chester**
4 St Nicholas Street, Chester
Mon-Sat, 9.30-5.30, L 1-2
Med size R/C stk, av cal, cnd slightly roast beef. TWC. P.poss. BR Chester, OOS turn right and left and right onto ring road, then turn left and SIOL. Nearest: Liverpool, Nantwich, Wrexham, Colwyn Bay.

There is also a bta bkstl in the market nrly opp by the world's most hideous hotel.

CASTLE BOOKSHOP **Holt**
Castle Street, Holt, Clwyd
Mon-Sat, 10-6
Med size R/C nrly D stk, emphon Art & Architecture. Ab av cal, cnd, av prices. TWC. P.poss. BR Wrexham (NAST 5 miles). Nearest: Chester, Nantwich, Whitchurch, Wrexham.

GLYN'S BOOKS **Wrexham**
1 Overton Arcade, Wrexham, Clwyd
Mon-Sat, 10-5
Small/med size R/C stk, emphon Mod 1sts, there is also a res stk of more Dealerish bks nearby. ETF on High Street which gets round the confusion that there are two stations in Wrexham. Nearest: Chester, Holt, Shrewsbury, Machynlleth.

CANDLE LANE BOOKS **Shrewsbury**
28 Princess Street, Shrewsbury
Mon-Sat, 9.30-5, Rel
Lg R/C/D stk almost solid roast beef but definite bgns known. BR Shrewsbury, OOS turn left into town and follow through for half mile until you get to Market Street turn left and continue past tourism office. Nearest: Wrexham,Wolverhampton.

QUARRY BOOKS **Shrewsbury**
24 Claremont Hill, Shrewsbury
Mon-Sat, 9.30-5.30, Rel
Med/lg R/C stk, in comparison to the other shop in Shrewsbury this is definitely nouvelle cuisine, but that only tells you about the other shop. Av cal, cnd and adventurous prices, butsome int bks. From Candle Lane Bks, OOSH turn left, left at main tree, right at main junction and second left.

MAINLY BOOKS **Leominster**
7 School Lane, Leominster, Herefords
Mon-Sat, 9.30-6
Med size R/C stk, slightly low key but does look as if it should have bgns in it, but I have yet to find one. BR Leominster, OOS turn left into town, left at main junction and right at sign for tourist office. Nearest: Ludlow, Worcester, Hereford, Kington.

Around the corner there is a stamp shop which also has mainly R's bks.

D G & A S EVANS **Brecon**
7 The Street, Brecon, Powys
Mon-Sat, 9-5, clsd 1pm Wed
New bksp with R/C stk slightly low key, but not as tedium inducing as Hay on Wye. The point about Brecon is that you have to go there. There is a 20minute respite between this shop and the next closest one, and in this time you are able to recharge your batteries, rekindle your enthusiasm, and dare I even suggest it, look round the town at things other than bks, which in the case of Brecon can be very pleasant. BR Even more NAST than Hay on Wye. Climeri. 20 miles and no buses. Nearest: Llandloes, Hay, Abergevenny, Lampeter.

RC writes
What's happened to Talgarth you gross incompetent!

BELFAST

For those of us used to the never ending war of attrition that is laughingly known as life in London it is a much looked forward to pleasure to enjoy rest and recreation in Belfast. In this armistice zone it is poss to walk the streets and not be terrorised by beggars.

Here it is poss to cross the road without threats of intimidation, or actual maiming by the self appointed men of violence; motorists.

In London nothing makes you feel as insecure as the security men.

In Belfast only serious incidents are treated seriously. The most diff thing for a war refugee to come to terms with, is that the shops in Belfast do not automatically treat you as if you were an enemy of the status quo. It comes as a dreadful shock to get home at night and not feel bombed out. The one slight disadvantage is that the bksps open late and close early - were some of the shops in London to do this they might be spared a blasting from me - but they have not heard of 'Lunch'. This is despite the presence of many pleasant cafes, which in London would cost you an arm and a leg.

MEWS ANTIQUES **Belfast**
260 Antrim Road, Belfast
Mon-Sat, 10-5, Rel
Primarily an antique shop selling fireplaces, but within there is a great room in which burns a collection of bks that will warm you heart and will not burn your fingers. NIR (Northern Ireland Railway) York Road (the terminal for Larne), OOS ahead and right into Queen Street, left into Limstone Road and right into Antrim Road, SIOL.

***THE KNOWS HORRENDA BOOKSHOP** **Belfast**
23 Lower North Street, Belfast
No times posted but 6 days a week
Med size R/C stk, emphon pbks and horror novels in very good cnd. However the owner almost has the word on his lips begin asking for collectable titles, and claims that business is so bad that he is thinking of closing down, but I doubt it. Around here the motto is "Knows Horrenda". From Mews Antiques go back down Antrim Road into town (A6) turn left into Peter Hill, where the Westlink crosses and continue into Lower North Street.

ARCADE BOOKS **Belfast**
10-12 Gresham Street, Belfast
Mon-Sat, 10-5
Med size R/C stk, an Irish driff special. Etgow. From North Street double back and turn second left into Gresham Street.

VOLUME ONE **Belfast**
Unit 10 The Arcade, Belfast
Mon-Sat, 10-5
Med size R/C stk, an Irish Drif Special, emphon pbks. All the time he was earholding me I kept trying to work out whether Volume One was at the bottom of the scale, or at the

top. I was too scared to risk asking him to change it either way. From Arcade bks turn left and left into arcade.

***THE NO NO. BOOKSHOP** Belfast
No number in Union Street, which does not appear on the detailed map issued by the Belfast Tourist Centre, no times posted on door, no phone number, no way of seeing what stock it has through the window. There is no way I am going to tell you how I know, but the bks are definite no hopers. No T. and no directions.

ROMA RYAN Belfast
73 Dublin Road, Belfast
Mon-Sat, 11-5.30
Med size R/C stk, ab av cal, cnd, av prices, emphon Irish. Etgow. T. From Royal Avenue locate the town hall that looks like it was bought cheaply after the end of the Habsburg Empire on far side, turn left into Bedford Avenue and continue into Dublin Road, SIOR.

PROSPECT HOUSE BOOKS Belfast
93 Dublin Road, Belfast
Mon-Sat, 11-5, Sat 4.45
Med/lg C/D stk, ab av cal, cnd and prices. Emphon Irish. WAD. P.poss. This is by far the best s/h and antqrn bksp in N. Ireland (all of which are superior to anything in Eire), and it is almost worth the fare from England (£24) because of this place the other shops become worthwhile. The bks are extremely well chosen not even the slight hint of bookfairyishness can distract from their excellence or charm. There is an originality about them which is seen all too rarely, as Roma Ryan.

BOOKFINDERS Belfast
47 University Road, Belfast
Mon-Sat, 11-5.30
Med size R/C stk, student/acad orientated, av cal, cnd and prices. TWC. P.poss. From Prospect House continue straight ahead.

LEAVES BOOKSHOP Belfast
84a Stranmillis Road, Belfast
Mon-Fri, 10.45-4, Sat 10-5
Med size R/C stk, slightly student/acad, but of a type that I see around, but am unable to think of a fitting description. Emphon R.D. Laing and his philosophy, that is not the bks that's the owner who is a complete course in the subject. From Bookfinders continue along University Road and bear left by Botanic Gardens. There are also some student/acad Irish bks in the University Bksp which you pass on the way to this one, but not enough to get an education. Leaves Bksp is upstairs by the bustop.

WELL READ Belfast
171 Ormeau Road, Belfast
Mon-Sat, 1-6 which counts as late night in Belfast
Med size R stk, av cal, bl av cnd, av prices. When I first saw this shop I thought that "Well Read" was a really good name for a bksp, then when I went in I saw that it was an apt

description of most of the bks, but there was one group of bks that was almost untouched: The Complete Works of Lenin, and then it dawned on me that this shop was even better named than I had previously thought. From Leaves, OOS turn right back down Stranmillis Road, and right onto Embankment and across to the road where all the traffic hurtles at 5pm (I told you six was late in Belfast) and then turn left, shops is opp Post Office (I bet they find that truly inspiring).

There is also a charity bksp in Rugby Road behind Well Read, it is also well behind Well Read in quality.

WORLD OF BOOKS Belfast
329 Woodstock Road, Belfast
Mon-Sat, 10-5
Med size R/C stk, av cal, cnd and prices. Conforms to the rule that any shop called World of Books is bound to be dreary. Emphon remainders and theology. From Well Read OOSH, turn left and keep walking, turn right towards Central Station then continue over bridge and turn right with signs for Woodstock Road. This shop also has branches in Holywell and Newtownards but as I felt it had already damaged enough of my few remaining brain cells I was not keen to give it a second chance. See TIN.

THE OTHER BOOKSHOP Bangor
4 Dufferin Avenue, Bangor
Mon-Sat, 10-5
Med size R/C stk, emphon pbks remaindery but does have other int bks. NIR Bangor, OOS turn left.

***ALMOST IDENTICAL TO THE OTHER BOOKSHOP** Bangor
30 Dufferin Ave, Bangor
Mon-Sat, 10-5
As above.

***THE IRISH DRIF SPECIAL** Coleraine
Mac's Market, Railway Place, Coleraine
Mon-Sat, 10.30-4.30
Med size R stk, av cal, NSOC, av prices. The ultimate Irish Drif Special. The difference between an Irish Drif Special and an English one is nothing to do with the fact that the bks are a lot more low key, or that the shops tend to be Samuel Beckett Specials, or that they are filled with Silverfish. It has to do with the undoubted fact that the owners of these shops are always able to persuade me to buy these bks. NIR Coleraine, OOS and second left. There is also a War on Want with a significant number of bks but with no significant titles.

THE COLERAINE BOOKSHOP Coleraine
5 Stone Row, Coleraine
Mon-Sat, 10-5, clsd Thurs, Rel
Med size R/C/D stk, av cal, cnd and prices. Emphon Irish. NIR Coleraine, OOS turn left into town.

/...

During the summer there is a permanent mini bookfair in Port Rush, there is also a bookshop in Port Stewart but NV and NFDA.

BOOK BARGAINS **Londonderry**
47 Spenser Road, Londonderry
Mon-Sat, 10-5, L 1-2
Med size R/C stk, emphon pbks and literace. Ave cal, cnd and prices. NIR Londonderry, OOS turn left and right and right towards radio mast which is atop one of the most blatant examples of police brutality to be seen in Northern Ireland.

***THE ECAWKI BOOKSHOP** **Londonderry**
Carlisle Road (no No.), Londonderry
Mon-Sat, 10-5, clsd Tues (and when out buying)
Which judging by the stk does not seem to be too often. Small/med size R stk, a Drif Special, Irish Division. This shop is a classic example of the type common in Eire - the other type is the egregiously overpriced literace - which is slightly strange. I may have this wrong but I think this shop is a protestant establishment - only in Northern Ireland do such things matter - how you tell is by the new postcards which are all of the Royal Family. In Northern Ireland people are always trying to guess which side you are on being English does not count as being neutral, if anything it is worse than being on the wrong side. In Eire there are even more subtle ways of telling whether you are of the right disposition or not. An English voice is distinctly unwelcome - the Northern Irish find this hard to believe but we minority groups have ways of detecting such things. I lived in Southall for three years before the man in the newsagent said hello to me. What I am trying to tell you is that Eire is a dead loss. NIR Londonderry, OOS turn right and right over bridge and second right up hill.

THE END OF CIVILISATION AS WE KNOW IT

If you think this bksp is bad you should see the ones in Eire

SCOTLAND

THE ARTIC - U - LATE CIRCLE

The number of s/h bksps in Scotland has severely declined, other than in Edinburgh. But this has resulted in a vast improvement, other than in Edinburgh. The shops have an individuality of stock which is refreshing, other than in Edinburgh. All of them have large stks of Scottish bks, other than in Edinburgh, where they only specialise in Edinburgh. Most of the shops are open Mon-Sat, 10-5 and close for lunch, other than in Edinburgh, where they only open after lunch. It has always been a puzzle to me what Edinburgh Booksellers do in the morning. Admittedly I have never been asked, but I certainly would not be keen to indulge in the other, with any of them.

WHY I NO LONGER TRAVEL IN MOTOR CARS

OR

TANKS FOR THE MEMORY

Although I profess to be an ardent cyclist, for years it was my very secret dream to own a pre-war Rolls Royce which would be driven by a grey suited, peaked capped paragon who would not only deliver me in complete silence to the doorstep of every s/h bksp in Britain but would be able to find veggie restaurants of sufficient calibre for my demanding tastes. And, furthermore, would be able to obtain a hotel room which I considered pleasant. So far I have achieved a substantial part of this dream. I have the grey suit and the peaked cap. All I need now is the car and chauffeur.

Several people do indeed offer themselves as chauffeur in the mistaken belief that I know the fastest way to all the best shops, that I know all the one way streets, and that I know where to park. They also assume that I know all the opening hours off by heart and that I know all the shops with res stks. It is touching to see that there is still some sense of fantasy left in the world. If I knew just one of all these things I would not be writing guide books for a living. The one major advantage of this mistaken belief on the part of the applicants is that they usually applied for the job by taking me out to dinner. And this is how I can afford to eat in my favourite restaurant.

As I told the current applicant for position of chauffeur, although I did not tell him that was what I wanted him to be, this esteemed establishment was the only restaurant I had ever discovered that served swedes. I could see that the candidate was keen to leave, he was an Israeli. His trepidation had a distinct advantage, he was being brief and generous. He was offering to drive me round every shop in Scotland, or any that I chose to go to. I grunted disapproval of this notion, mainly because the swedes had not been cooked with enough salt, a common failing in veggie restaurants. Whilst the waiter attempted to rectify this disaster, I informed him, the waiter that is, that I also loved Brussel Sprouts. My host then offered to pay all my food bills. He clearly thought that I was going to come cheaply.

"I must tell you", I said, "that my favourite meal consists of Jersey potatoes, Brussel sprouts and swedes".

"That sounds a trifle racialist and cannibalistic", he said.

The waiter returned with both the swedes and the brussel sprouds, I was mollified. He asked me to accept his humble apologies. I did so. My host thought I was talking to him.

"There is also a small problem of finance!" I said, wondering what I could successfully order for dessert.

"You mean you have no money?" he said

I was not certain if I liked his wit, but he had indeed understood my problem.

"Don't worry", he said, "I will finance the entire venture".

I carefully established exactly what he meant. He was going to pay for this meal, he was going to pay for all my meals in Scotland, he was going to pay for the hotels, and he was going to pay all the motoring costs.

I said nothing, my thoughts were fully occupied with the brussel sprouts, they were a little too salty, a common problem in veggie restaurants. He took my silence to mean that I was about to turn him down and said ...

"I will even finance the buying of all your books!"

There was nothing for it, I would have to stop and consider, why do people always interrupt when I have important things to decide. I chose the banana fritter for dessert, and then turned my attention to him.

Even I, in my pre-occupied state, could see that it was a step towards achieving my secret ambtion. I looked at him, carefully sizing him up, the grey suit was going to fit perfectly but I was not so sure about the peaked cap.

I could see that it was not going to be easy travelling, he was a former Israeli Tank Commander, and thus getting him to wear a uniform could present a slight problem. I decided on the diplomatic approach. I wore my four piece (with cap) Donegal tweed, plus four suit. Its bottle green beautifully set off by yellow and orange flecks and contrasting even more beautifully with my yellow Argyll socks, however this turned out to be a slight sartorial error.

I had not realised that the Tank Commander did not go in for punctuality, thus it was that I had to wait for two hours outside Aylesbury Railway Station, withstanding ribald remarks. The local school children had spotted that I was wearing black brogues, this was a dreadful faux pas on my part, and I wondered if I should call the whole thing off. (For the benefit of those bookdealers who are reading this piece, I should point out that black brogues should only be worn with a kilt).

That is why we only reached Carlisle by 9pm. I just had to return for the brown pair.

Unbeknownst to me I had been deputised to find the hotels. The land ladies of Carlisle have the same sense of humour as the youth of Aylesbury, but one of them did have more charity.

She emerged from her abode shaking an umbrella with which she attempted to give me a pair of pierced ears, after she had established that I had not in any way damaged her lance she demanded to know what I was doing standing on her doorstep. I told her that I was seeking a room.

"Well why don't you rent one instead of squatting on my steps?" she asked.

I told her I was indeed keen to do this if she had one to let. I then remembered to say there were two of us. She looked at me as if I was demented, and she had not even seen the socks yet.

"Well I do not allow that sort of thing in my house, it will have to be two rooms or nothing."

I handed over the money before she could change her mind.

"Would you like to come to church with me?" she asked.

"I think my friend would love to go with you first thing in the morning", I said, "But I have to be away at seven".

"That is perfect, there is a service at six" she said, walking off in the direction of the largest church I had ever seen.

Then I remembered she had not given me any keys. I was terrified of having to explain this to the Tank Commander, and leant against the door to work out what I should do. As I did so it opened and I fell on the mat. I told the Tank Commander that we would be leaving at six to get an early start.

All I can say about the surroundings is I am glad I was asleep some of the time. The bed had seen service as a contour map of the Highlands. I did not have sweet dreams, instead I imagined there was a constant banging on the door and that I was being dragged off to pray to men who dressed strangely, but I awoke suddenly when the door opened. I thought it was the Tank Commander's idea of a joke and that we were going to make an early start. If was 3.15am. It was the landlady. I wondered if she had deduced that we were not Christians and come to turf us out. I tried to remember the appropriate parable for these occasions.

"I have had it on my conscience all night", she said.

That was it, I knew it, she was a Wee Free.

"I could not let you two gentlemen leave without breakfast for which you have paid, so I have decided to return the money that breakfast would have cost". And with that she put a fiver in my hand.

My only previous experience with ladies and financial transactions late at night in hotels, had been in the other direction, and I was unable to work outhow to deal with this situation, however I had three hours to think about it, as I could not then get back to sleep.

We left at six, the pair of us in like mood. She had also woken up the Tank Commander and given him a fiver. I felt that this was an auspicious start, but the Tank Commander was less complimentary.

We arrived at John Smith's shop at nine, the Tank Commander was very impressed, but not as much as I was. I had been aiming for Cooper Hay and had not expected to get this close. For me Glasgow is always a city of utter confusion. I usually find the bksps by closing my eyes and praying.

We ascended the steps, the Tank Commander presented his credentials to the lady behind the desk, who was extremely polite. I had not the courage to tell him she was the cleaning woman. I was desperate to talk to her myself, cleaners always know where everything is. As the TC perused the shelves, I asked her sotto voce where Cooper Hay's establishment was.

Seeing that I was not good with English she drew me a map, and then explained it to me: "Go out of the shop, turn left, and right and it is at an acute angle". I thanked her.

I then searched in vain for a dictionary which would explain to me what an acute angle is. In Scotland, it is impossible to get a job as a cleaner unless you have a degree in mathematics.

My major objective in seeking out Cooper was to get him to tell me about all the newly opened bksps near Voltaire & Rousseau. I knew the TC would find the stock in Cooper Hay so rivetting that he would not hear our conversation.

"I don't know why you are asking me?" said Cooper in his loudest voice, "you know where they all are".

The TC was laden down when we left the shop, he wanted to get a cab back to the car. I was keen as well, I could have got the driver to take us to V&R.

I remember that dreadful trek well, it was at least half a mile back to the car. What impressed me most is how much invective the TC got in such a short space of time. From then on I vowed that we would only go to towns with one bookshop and one street. I did not tell the TC this and told him to follow the signs for Stirling, much to my amazement we ended up outside one ofthe newly opened shops.

"Stop!" I screamed.

"I thought you said we were going to Stirling?"

"I meant after we had finished here".

He looked at me as if I were a traitor in the ranks, but fortunately the shop was more attractive, and even I knew howto get to the three shops round the corner.

I declined to go into V&R on the grounds that the last time I had been there they had beaten up a child. I find it always spoils my concentration, or so I told the TC. The truth was that I wanted to concentrate on the map and see if I could remember where Stirling was.

I had just enough time; he was in V&R for three hours. When the TC emerged he was raving about how good it was.

"Why didn't we go in there first?"

"Er, it did not open until 10am", I liked.

"That is funny, I could swear the owner told me it opened at 9, let me have a look at your guide book?"

"I have forgotten to bring it with me", I said. "After all, why do you need the guide book if you have the compiler?"

As we drove away the proprietor of V&R brought out a child and proceeded to belt the living daylights out of it. The TC saidit was just a cultural difference and I was being absurdly sensitive.

"What did you say about that shop?" said the TC.

"I said it was vastly over-rated and left a nasty taste in the mouth".

"That's typical of you, making irrelevant comments, that was the finest shop in Glasgow."

FN (In Britain, the reason people have children is that if they had dogs they would be arrested for cruelty).

"We have only been in three so far!"
"And whose fault is that?"
"Stirling is the other way." I said.
"Why didn't you say before?"
"I did not want to spoil your flow."
"Now I will have to drive even faster to make up for lost time."
"How much lost time is 250 yards?"
"Don't be facetious or make strange faces", he said.
"You spent three hours in that shop!"
"The best choices are made early".
It was while I was making a strange face and trying to think up a facetious remark that I spotted another shop.
"SSSTOPPPP!"
"If you object to my remarks I suggest you change your life's objectives, after all you are not doing very well with them so far, are you?"
"Never mind the objectives, we have just gone past a bksp".
He certainly did not learn his U turns from Mrs Thatcher, but I did wonder if I was going to be held responsible for the pavement being 10ft wide. On the long trek into the shop, a Glaswegian wino asked me if I had any spare change. I told him "Yes, thank you", and walked into the bksp to the accompaniment of some spectacular invective. The shop was so bad that I almost repeated it to the owner.
When we emerged, another wino made his way toward me. I used my new found powers of adjectival description on him.
The TC wanted to know why the winos and beggars were always attracted to me. I did not tell him the truth that they were able to spot a kindred spirit at a hundred yards, instead I said that it was because I was so well dressed that they automatically assumed that I was the one with all the money.
"Well the next one that comes up to you, you tell him that you are just a bankrupt, that I am the one with all the money, I am the one paying for the hotels, the motor car, the food and the books."
It seemed to me that now was a good time to present him with the grey suit, but before I could get it out of the box, we were hurtling down the motorway.
He treated all other motorists as if they were hostile. But he was determined not to take any prisoners. Those that did not get out of our way received a volley of abuse that would have shocked a Glaswegian wino.
One potential VC had the temerity to decrease his speed to 90 - it was a built up zone - the Tank Commander beeped his horn and leant out of the car as we overtook and screamed, "My man is going to take your number and report you".
Fortunately this police car had more important business. When I told the TC who had been driving that car he just said "Wimps".
"In future take down the number of any car that does not drive properly."
"How would they know our number?" I said
"I told you to stop being facetious."
"You have to be joking."
"Just do as I tell you, I will show you how to get this problem sorted out."
"I can't find a pen."
"Memorise them."

Things were not turning out quite the way I had expected.

"What are you going to do with these numbers?"

"When I get back to a sensible country I will get my ambassador to write to them."

I wondered if I had got it wrong again, maybe he worked for Colonel Qadaffi

I knew that the shop in Stirling was close to the Castle. My mistake was to assume that the Castle Carpark was close to the bksp. All the way to the shop I had visions of being confronted by the UN secretary, calling on behalf of the TC.

Fortunately the TC liked the Stirling Bksp, this gave me a chance to work out where the second shop in Stirling was. When I returned the TC and Mr. McCuthcheon were in heated debate over a bibliography of Heiroglyphic bibles. The TC asked me if I had ever seen it before, when I said yes, he used that as proof that it had to be a common book. Mr. McCuthcheon said I could have just been lucky. I did not like the way this conversation was going.

I told the TC that we would have to leave for Edinburgh soon if we wanted to get a hotel. The truth is that the hotels in Edinburgh are appalling, but the veggies are wonderful.

Not even I could miss when we pulled up in front of a row of twenty hotels. Inside the place looked vaguely familiar. Then I remembered I had vowed never to come to it again. "I have been in this B&B before" I said.

The owner looked at me as if I was something that had stalked in off the street accidentally.

"This is NOT a Bed and Breakfast, this is a hotel!"

I think it means they can charge more.

We ate in Henderson's, I chomped at the plateful and he champed at the bit. One of the great unsung joys of raw carrots is that nobody can disturb you whilst you are eating them, or so I thought. He started passing me notes.

"This is a list of things I want you to do tonight", he said, addressing me as if I was in London. I think it was his belief that carrots improve your sight by making your hearing worse.

Alone in the hotel room I remembered his instructions. "Work out exactly where we are going tomorrow, ring the dealers and have an exact itinerary. We cannot afford to waste time again."

I lay down on the bed and wondered what I should do, before I knew there was a terrible banging on the door, I was having another nightmare. The banging got louder, more incessant, the door attempted to come into the room of its own volition. I pulled the covers over my head. I head heard about AIDS and Edinburgh but nobody could be this desperate for a sleeping partner.

The TC suddenly burst into the room and I knew it was not a nightmare. It was worse.

"That swine in Voltaire & Rousseau has sold me a duff book: The map at the back has been photocopied."

"Oh dear!", I said. "Well don't worry we can take it back on the way home."

Sunday morning found us... no that is not quite right, I will start again. Sunday morning lost us in St. Andrew's. I will start that again as well, it lost me. Previously I had only ever cycled to St. Andrews and getting my bearings at

60mph in the Market Street is not something at which I would claim any skill. Before the Tank Commander could train his gums on me I directed him to Newport on Tay, and then, accidentally, spotted the house I wanted. I knew it would be a long trek back but the thing about torture is that after a while you become immune to it. Twelve paces would soon be over I told myself.

We did not need to ring the bell, the Tank Commander's fury brought the owner to the door. He was wearing pyjamas.

"Is he ill?" whispered the TC.

"He soon will be", I said.

Whilst the TC double checked for photocopied maps, I chatted to the owner. He told me that another shop was just about to open in St Andrews and that they were putting bks on the shelves at this very moment. Even I could tell he was being diplomatic, espec when he offered to drive us there because the TC said it was a long walk back to our car.

"It will hinder our tight schedule", said the TC.

"It will have no effect on our schedule", I said.

We got to the shop, or rather we nearly got to the shop. I think we were at least three paces past it, I had not the heart to tell the TC that I had been trying for the place 100 yards back.

When the owners of the shop were safely between me and the TC I began to make jokes, or as the TC would say, 'facetious remarks and faces'. The TC did not take kindly to this.

"I have walked across deserts, I have fought my way out of battles, but what I will not put up with is gross incompetence." This was said in a voice so loud that it frightened the only other customer away.

"Is there any chance of our getting into the other bksp?" I asked the owner of this one.

"I doubt it," she said, "that was the owner who just left".

The TC had pulled out of the shop, got into the car and headed the other shopkeeper off before he got to the end of the street. Maybe I was wrong, maybe there was an advantage in being able to drive like that.

By the time I reached the shop the owner was visibly quaking. I could see that I had been going about this incorrectly. From now on I would let the TC be the Hard Man and I would be the soft.

"Are there any other shops open on a Sunday morning?"

"Well, I am not really open," he said looking at the TC.

"What I meant was are there any other shops that would open for us?"

I remembered this technique from the film The Battle of Algiers, if the little fish gives you a bigger fish, you let the little fish go.

And Mair Wilkes is certainly a bigger fish. Such a pity about Newport on Tay. It has only one street, and there is only one bksp in that street. We went up and down that street so often that I began to know what a pinball felt like. Luckily for me we nearly got nudged by the car coming the other way and the TC was forced to slow down to sixty, then I spotted Mr. Wilkes who had come out to see the biggest traffic jam in Newport on Tay's history.

I am extremely grateful to Mr. Mair and Mr. Wilkes for showing me that it was not poss to hold a reasonable conversation with the TC. They are respectively experts in

Scottish History and Psychology, two subjects almost invented to deal with people like the TC, but even their erudition and loquaciousness were unable to stem his flow. He was the sort of person who would take up the contrary point of view just for the hell of it. When Mr. Wilkes attempted to defend the Arts Council the Tank Commander launched into him like Macbeth after his assertion training course. I sided with Mr. Wilkes, even though I cannot stand Arts Councils either. I sought solace in a book called 'Human Beings Under Extreme Circumstances', but I decided against it, the TC was not a human being. He bought a boxful of bks which were to go on his shelves marked 'Peaceful Living'. I could see that we were not going to get on. I am good at summing up situations quickly.

"Where are we going now?" said the TC as we headed for Aberdeen.

Where indeed I thought. "I think we had better have a rediscussion of the terms of our agreement!" I said.

"There is no need for any rediscussion, your job is to find the shops, mine is to get you there. And in truth he was an extremely good driver, he never got tired, he never complained of how far the next shop was, he never wasted time discussing unrelated issues, and he would drive all the hours that I told him to. And he was driving me round the bend.

We got to Aberdeen about four in the afternoon, and I was forced to break the news to him. There were no more bksps to be got into that day. He was beside himself with anger. I just wished that he was not beside me. He then proceeded to catalogue my faults, I was fascinated. I would not have missed it for the world. There were faults I never knew I had, there were faults I did not even know the meaning of - well do you know what sententious means, it was wonderful, it lasted about an hour, and that was just a brief outline. It has always been my opinion that what people say is irrelevant, it is how long it goes on for that counts. But despite this last temptation I had resolved not to travel with him any more. Always one for the direct approach I said to him; "There are a couple of minor points that I think it might be worthwhile our discussing".

"Let's do it now."

"No, I would like to discuss it over dinner."

"There you are prevaricating again."

"What do you mean, I have got to eat, haven't I?"

We found a hotel, or rather the TC found a place that said carpark, and I noticed that it said hotel afterwards. I longed for a bath, I wanted it to be a good clean fight.

The hotel was beautiful, all the rooms were soundproof, it had signs saying 'Do Not Disturb', it had rushing water in the bath which made it almost imposs for me to hear the banging on the door, and when the bathroom door closed I could not hear it at all. I soaped and planned tactics. I would offer him a deal, he would carry on paying all the bills and we would do it my way. This seemed like a reasonable compromise to me.

When I emerged some two hours later the TC was furiously pacing the hallway like an expectant father.

"What have you been doing in there? I was just about to ring the fire brigade."

"I have faults that not even you have seen."

We walked out into the carpark, by now I knew it was hopeless to try and get him to walk. Aberdeen at 70mph does not last long. But I was determined to let nothing upset me.

"I suppose you want to go to a rabbit food restaurant?" he said.

"I am happy to eat anywhere", I said. In truth I knew there were no veggie restaurants open on a Sunday evening. Eventually we found a restaurant or rather we found a sign which said 'Car Park/Food'. I imagined that this would be some sort of picnic for motorists, but it turned out to be a very up market Italian restaurant.

Inside, it was more like a nightclub for American Oil Executives. But suddenly, I became very keen on the place, I could see that the executives were worried that the North Sea might not have enough resources to pay the bill. When the waiter brought the menu, I was even more overjoyed, I was going to have to order main dishes of meat to get the side dishes of vegetables for free. None cost less than £10, it was sheer poetry. The waiter and I were great friends within seconds. I was contemplating the look on the Tank Commander's face when he saw the bill, and the waiter was contemplating the tip.

"Look just cut the divine comedy, when are we going to have one of these famous discussions of yours?"

"When I have finished the meal," I said.

"See. I guessed you were not seriously interested in books. If you were really keen you would want to get this problem sorted out now."

I can speak on personal experience of this matter, if you are hit on the head with a baseball bat, it does not hurt - at first. It is only when you wake up in hospital three days later that you begin to feel the pain.

I am not trying to boast when I say that I think I have been in more s/h bksps than anyone else in Britain. There are people who have been going in bksps longer than me but I do not think there is anybody who has been in as many varied s/h bksps as I have. The main reason I go in bksps is to buy bks to read. This will come as a dreadful shock to most bookdealers, who regard that occupation as something best left to time wasters. I do not know how many bks I have read, but suffice it to say that it takes being hit round the head with a baseball bat to deter me.

And the location of a baseball bat was a subject I was heavily interested in at that moment, but I was not as skilled in the ways of warfare as the TC. Having hurt me with a southpaw, he followed through with a right jab. He turned to the waiter and said, "Just bring the rabbit food. He claims to be a vegetarian, its a passing fad of his.

Gentle reader, I have been a vegetarian for 25 years, I don't know how long it is before something stops being a passing fad, but I have a vague suspicion that 25 years must be nearly close. I am not trying to persuade you to become a vegetarian although I would like there to be more vegetarians so that there were more vegetarian restaurants. But the next time somebody tries to tell you that vegetarians are calm, kind, gentle, loving people, do not believe them. I was not only contemplating gutting the bastard, I intended to remove his insides while he was still alive. I was then going to force him down his throat, and to further make my point, I was going to eat him.

As I said earlier being hit round the head with a baseball bat was something that I have experienced. But until that evening I have never been hit on both sides of the head at the same time. I was unconscious, even to the catalogue of minor misdemeanours that the TC delivered for the next two hours. I know it must have been 2 hours because the staff were packing away the tables before I regained consciousness.

With much effort I emerged in a state of shock but still sane enough to hold a reasonable conversation.

"Listen Shithead, we either do it my way or not at all," I said.

"You don't have the money to make it home."

"I have put up with you for two days, I have got you into five bksps in Scotland on a Sunday, I will get you into every shop in Scotland in the next week. There is not anything I cannot do if I put my mind to it. Getting back to London without you, is something I look forward to."

"And where are we going tomorrow?"

"Winram's."

"Well why don't we go and check it out now, so that you will know the way."

I will always remember that restaurant, especially the kindness of the waiters, and the way they clapped when we left.

I think we drove down every street in Aberdeen. I claimed Amnesia, but there comes a time after travelling at 90mph when you are bound to see a street you have not previously encountered. Fortunately for me, the Tank Commander did not notice that Winram's bksp was at the back of the restaurant we had been in.

As I sat in the passenger seat trying to work out how to get back to London with no money, I heard a familiar refrain. The Tank Commander cursing me.

"You moron, you incompetent, you buffoon, you numbskull, you half wit, you cannot even get bksp hours correct."

"Listen you prick, drive me back to the station now."

"Would you two gentlemen mind restraining your language."

The pair of us turned round in horror, it was Ma Winram. I must give the bastard his due, he poured out more oil than Kuwait. He then told her that I had spent the evening telling him how wonderful her shop was and that was the reason we were outside at 10pm on a Sunday evening, and how eager he was to inspect it, how he would look on it as a personal favour, if he could view it, how as a fellow member of the ABA he was charmed to meet her. She succumbed, and we were in.

We co-operated on being as charming as poss, the TC even went to the extreme length of buying some of her bks, although I did see him check for photocopies.

We exited at 11 and I crowed about the wonders of serendipity.

"Oh yes, but you have missed your train."

When some time later I returned to Aberdeen to research this guide, I discovered that the natives of the town regard walking in the same light as the TC. Winrams was even more pleasant than I remembered it, and so too were the customers. When I am trying to find out about bksps, I prefer to ask other customers rather than the owners of bksps who seldom have time to travel. A customer in Mrs Winram's told me about another shop in Aberdeen, he did not know where it was but he knew that it existed. This shop is The Rosemount Bksp. It only took me an hour to find it, the difficulty was not in finding the shop but in finding sensible people such as traffic wardens, postmen, roadsweepers, they were all extremely helpful, but they did not know where it was. One suggested that I try the library. In my experience this is a mistake. I did however find an Oxfam Charity Bksp which nobody told me about. The bks were dreadful but that is not the point, by looking for one thing, I found another. And whilst in the Oxfam I asked the customers if they knew where The Rosemount Bksp was, none did, they had heard that there was a bksp in the area, but they treated it as if it were in some far off land. By the time I did find it, I was beginning to think that maybe the TC was right, I was an incompetent.

I tried my usual approach on the owner and asked him if there were any other shops. He told me about Winram's, and he also told me about the Oxfam. I decided to enquire further and he said that there was another shop on the dark side of town, but that I would have to be desperate. When I told him I would happily walk to it if he gave me directions, he looked at me as if I was going off on the last great trek. It was about as far as from Piccadilly to Oxford Circus.

When I did find it, I discovered that it had been there for at least three years, the Rosemount Bookshop had just moved, but it too had been in Aberdeen when I had visited it with the TC, but because of the other small problems I had, I had been unable to find out about them.

For the motorist life is a silent movie, that is why they hate to stall, it is part of the living theatre. To them a pedestrian is somebody who only has a walk-on part in life, in training for when they have reel power. The drama cycle is seen as an outmoded form pushed by cranks. They know they are car strated but still they try to perform, ever dreaming of coming faster. Car-cooned against reality they see everything in black and white. Car-petted they see all others as having reached rock bottom. It is seen as a Car-dinal sin to leave the car, worse it is a car-tastrophe.

For these farts there is only one car-minative; the open road, all else is seen as an obstruction, piles to be endured. Their dream is the permanent motion. These arseholes see themselves as the van of destiny, but that rotting smell is a car-case.

Like all addicts they publicly fantasise about stopping, but secretly they will not unless their next fix is within sight. Car parks anonymous but we want a private place, what is life without rush. For them it has to be door to door delivery. They swear they are going to give it up someday, but not just yet, they vow that they will return, but this is like the promise of all addicts - 'if only we could stop!' they say, and before they know it, they are past it.

The one thing the TC did show me, but did not tell me is how hopeless motor cars are for visiting the bksps of Britain. Don't worry I am not going to try and deter you, there is no way of curing addicts. It is abstinence or nothing. In a motor car the primary consideration is the parking. If the average motorist thinks he cannot park outside the shop he is less inclined to attempt to go into that shop. A shop has to be good enough to make the effort of parking worthwhile. These shops are literally few and far between, that is why motorists think you have to have a motor car. But in truth you can never know what book a bksp is going to have. If you could, all you would have to do is ring them up.

When you are in a motor car there is always the temptation to drive on when you see the sign - 'Back in Ten Minutes' - vowing to return later, but you never do.

For bookdealers, like other people motor cars are primarily status symbols. The logic is the bigger and better the motor car, the bigger and better the dealer is, which ignores a quiet truth, that the better a dealer is, the less books they buy, and therefore the less need for a huge great safe to put it in.

If you arrive at a bksp on foot, and it is shut, (this may come as a surprise to motorists but this is quite a common state of affairs) you are much more likely to put some effort into getting into that shop, or finding some way of rebuking the owner. (My own method is to leave small notes through the door).

The TC was also in favour of ringing up a shop and telling them you are coming. I have no wish to appear pompous about this, but I can think of several shops that would take evasive action if they knew I was coming, and that is putting it at its mildest. The other problem with ringing up a shop is that you then commit yourself to going to it. I have started the day heading for Penzance, and ended up in Penrith. I feel that if I had told some of the shops in Cornwall that I was coming they would be even more angry with me than they already are. Yet another problem with ringing a shop is that it gives them time to get out the bks they would like to sell you, rather than the ones you would like to buy. It takes courage enough to get out of most bksps without making a courtesy purchase, getting out of one where I had made an appointment is not something that I could contemplate. From my point of view the clincher about not ringing bksps is that they do not have any opportunity to make the coffee. After having endured rain, mud, tarmac, grit, the freezing cold, the boiling hot, the tepid and the featureless, all of which I have seen described as coffee, I prefer to go without.

In a motor car there is no method of learning the way to the shop. The one way streets of Britain change more often than the bksps. In a motor car you are travelling too fast to be able to perceive semiotic signals, such as health food shops, s/h shops and even street names. Nor is it poss to travel slowly. When you walk, you automatically learn such things.

What really upset the TC about my inability to get the car parked outside the door, was not that I was incapable of doing it, but that I showed no willingness to learn. He would have gladly spent his life showing me the great parking spaces of the world. He knew of carparks that others had only fantasised about. From him Heaven was a carpark, Hell was no carpark and purgatory was having me looking for the carpark.

I must apologise if on previous occasions I have misled

some of my readers. When I say parking poss - it means somewhere just below purgatory.

My only defence is that I have had a very sheltered upbringing - my parents could not afford a nanny and there was no door to door delivery, when I was seven, my elder sister was given a pedal car, I think that was maybe when my hatred of cars began. I pushed her over a cliff.

The approved school which I attended regarded P. as something we were not supposed to do. In Broadmoor dodgems meant avoiding the strait jacket. It was not until I ran away with the TC that I had to guess it had other meanings.

The TC was also in favour of announcing himself when he went into a bksp whereas I favour saying nothing. Neither of these tactics is wholly right or wholly wrong. In some shops opening conversation with the owner can indeed produce unexpected results. This is one of the reasons I do not like doing it. As dealers and collectors we are involved in a big game. We are Big Game hunters. There are two ways of catching game, you can either storm it or creep up on it, but once you have stormed it you must be prepared to carry on the fight, whereas if you creep up on them you can also creep away and return another day when events are more in your favour.

Because of the Tank Commander's undoubted charm I was able to get into many places that I had not previously been, but now because of the TC there are many places where I am known, and I would prefer not to be.

What I did like about the TC was that he had some great opinions, according to him there is no proof that smoking is bad for you, needless to say he was a smoker and when I pointed out that his smoking made my clothes smell, his reply "But it does not cause a permanent injury." He said it as if he wished it would.

It was also his opinion that my lack of interest in s/h bks was amply demonstrated by my abysmal ignorance of the sex lives of other book dealers. What upset him was not that I did not know who was sleeping with whom, but that I showed absolutely no enthusiasm for finding out. According to him had I been a serious book dealer I would have been cognisant of all the facts. I am not trying to claim that my own sex life is so interesting that I do not have to take any interest in anybody else's, in fact at times I wonder if I do have a sex ife at all, but I do think I would have to be a lot more desperate than I am to take an interest in the sex lives of others, espec book dealers. If it is nothing to do with me, what has it got to do with me? Nor do I understand what it has to do with bks, but the TC maintained that this only showed how little I knew.

Another of my fantasies has to do with those strange, sometimes violent altercations which motorists regard as vital to life. I have yet to see two pedestrians threatening to castrate one another because one of them did not move off fast enough at the lights.

I was once involved in one of these pieces of living drama at the junction of Shaftesbury Avenue and Charing Cross Road. The driver of a truck strongly objected to my turning right by overtaking him, as is normal in those situations. I informed him that he was a member of the opposite sex. Unfortunately the lights changed faster than I expected and he delivered his reply in person over the handlebars. I must say I was truly impressed. He should have been starring in Shaftesbury Avenue, not driving down it. His invective was so good I wanted to record it, but no sooner had he finished one completely apposite description of me, than he had moved on to the next. Even I was putout when the motorists behind him started beeping their horns. They tried to tell him what they thought of him, but it only showed up their total lack of style.

As he roared off I tried to tell him that when I became rich I wanted to hire him for use in exactly the same situation. So the next time a motorist had the temerity to describe me as being a member of the opposite sex, I would turn to my head of invective and get him to respond on my behalf.

The Tank Commander was ideal for this job, the only trouble was having to put up with him the rest of the time, but I had thought of a solution to this. At the rear of the Roller I would have another small trailer and when he had finished shouting and screaming on my behalf, all I would have to do is pat him on the shoulder and return him to it. It could be called a hoarse box.

His attempts to drive me round the bend encouraged me to attempt to drive him into the ground. One day we were in Fort William, it was my turn to choose the restaurant. Without his noticing I had spotted that the local veggie was the equivalent of a grease cafe - these places are known to veggies as The Salad of the Bad Cafes. I told him that I thought there was another bksp in Oban, just down the road, but that it would be a bit of a risk as it only opened in the summer. In fact I was fully aware that it was closed. By the time we got close to Oban I remembered that there was a shop in Glasgow that opened on a Tuesday evening until 9pm. (It opened most evenings until nine) but I thought it would sound better that way. I also told him that this would give him an opportunity to return his book to Voltaire & Rousseau. How was I to know that Voltaire & Rousseau closed at 6pm and that the other shop had closed down. I told him there was nothing else for us to do but go to Edinburgh. And thus it was that I was able to get into my favourite vegetarian restaurant (Scottish Division).

When the waiter came I simply asked for all the specials, the waiter then turned to the TC and asked him what he would like.

"What do you recommend for a meat eater?" he said.

"I recommend you try the restaurant across the road, Sir."

It was well worth travelling 200 miles for.

Another advantage I discovered of travelling round with the TC was that I could use him as a bodyguard. We had walked into one shop and were no sooner through the door than the owner took a flying leap at me, it was just before he got his fingers round my neck that I suddenly remembered that I had upset him on some previous occasion. The TC had to get between us and tell the irrate shopkeeper that his was a wonderful shop that I thought we could not avoid even if there had been some slight disagreement on a previous occasion. I think it was the TC spending £200 that got me out in one piece. Boy was I glad we had not phoned him, there would more than likely have been a contingent of the local hooligans to deal with.

Thereafter the TC made me give him a brief synopsis of my relations with the next shop. Thus it was that I had to tell him that I might be classified as slightly lower than persona non grata in one Edinburgh shop. This was a slight exaggeration on my part: I would have put it closer to being an enemy of the state.

I waited outside while the TC went in. I practiced my car karate and changed into my bovver boots and then followed him. As I went through the door it looked like a trailer for Brief Encounter. She was all but smiling and he was laughing at what she thought were jokes. They didn't even see me coming, despite my kicking the glass case as I went by. For twenty minutes they were at it, the pair of them, oozing enough charm to make Barbara Cartland cringe. If it had been any closer to closing time I'm sure they would have eloped to Gretna. I clicked my heels and my toes and regretted not having brought a stink bomb. If she wasn't doing it on purpose, he certainly was. I stormed out as quietly as poss, muttering under my breath. "You may have changed, but I certainly haven't".

By the time the Tank Commander returned I was contemplating pushing the car into her basement. I was surprised to see there was no lipstick on his collar.

"You see", he said, "all you have to do is be polite and you'll get everything you want".

(There are some things I don't want).

All the time I was with the TC I was trying to find ways to irritate him as much as he irritated me, just nothing seemed to work. I did manage to make him lose his temper but it would only last for a few seconds. Speaking as somebody who has held some good grudges for at least thirty years, I found this even more annoying. Such is my collection of grudges that I had to institute a rule that I will not air them publicly if they are older than one year. However, in the case of the TC I am prepared to make this exception.

It was quite by accident that I discovered how to irritate him, I look upon it as one of the great days of my life. It confirmed my belief that the best things happen accidentally.

We were in the Inverness Bksp and the TC had of course struck up a conversation. The owner of the shop, out of politeness was driven to ask me how the trip was going. I made a few non-commital remarks, then I told him we had seen a bibliography of hieroglyphic Bibles in Stirling, but that it had seemed a bit expensive. Out of the corner of my eye I had seen the TC beginning to jump up and down. I took this as a signal that he wanted to leave. I was nearly right, what he wanted to do was strangle me.

"That is typical of you, we will have to get back to Stirling before that swine buys that bibliography!"

"That seems a bit unlikely."

"You are always prepared to spoil other people's deals."

"What, you think he is on the phone now ringing Stirling and is about to sell that bibliography for thousands?"

"I don't doubt it."

I had discovered the way to get him to stop talking at me, all I had to do was upset him over a deal. The silence between Inverness and Stirling was spectacular, the enmity breathtaking, the snowcaps of hatred were truly memorable, the valleys of gloom on his part, amazing to behold. Then we had a scene which spoiled the scenery.

It happened when he asked me how far it was to Stirling? I told him we were about half way there.

"When I ask where we are, I want an exact geographical location."

"Pull over, and I will give you an exact geographical location," I said. He pulled over, I got out of the car, picked up my bags and started trying to hitch a lift. It is not until you get out of a motor car that you realise how empty Scotland is. The TC was fuming, espec as I had remembered to put the atlas in my bag.

"Alright, get back in the car, we will have to get back to Stirling before five."

The thought of being stuck out in the Scottish Highlands all night was too much even for me, and I got back in the car. It was an icy silence, all the way to Stirling. I consoled myself with the dream that the man in Inverness had rung Stirling and bought the book. Unfortunately for me, it had not happened. The blasted thing was still there, but at least it meant we could get back to Edinburgh and eat at my favourite restaurant again. I could not have organised it better.

And so it went on, like hunch catastrophe and the pun dance yid. We would arrive in frontier towns ready to take on all comers, armed with cash and audacity, we would outgun the locals. We came away financially richer, but that was it.

Not once did we do anything that was nothing to do with bks, not once did we meet anybody who was not a book person, indeed the TC was unable to believe that there were such people and he claimed that it showed my desire to live in a fantasy world, that I thought there were.

We were in yet another forgotten service station when to raise the intellectual tone I started playing peek a boo with a five year old girl. Much to his horror the TC got involved. When we left, and I had said goodbye to the child, the TC turned to me and asked, "what kind of bks does she buy?" For her sake, I hope she never does.

The final rift came on a gloriously sunny summer afternoon which made even Edinburgh seem warm, with my usual total incompetence I had managed to get the car parked at least 8 feet beyond the door of the shop. By now the TC suspected I was doing it on purpose. He just could not believe that anybody could be so stupid unintentionally, but he had given up with passing judgment, the trouble with swear words is that there are so few of them.

The long trek to the bksp was made even more memorable by the total absence of a grunt on his part. Once inside, we pretended not to know one another, nor did he introduce himself, Heaven knows what multi-million pound deal I could have spoiled, and he was determined not to give me another chance. All was ruined when I had to ask him to pay for a book I wished to purchase, whilst he wrote the cheque, somewhat reluctantly I felt, I clutched the tome which was going to make the entire trip worthwhile. The shop keeper asked if I would like a bag. I was loathe to part with the book but saw another opportunity.

"Yes, please, it will need protection if it snows before we get back to the car."

What a fool I was, he had not finished writing the cheque.

His inhibition about using the same invective twice completely deserted him. He catalogued my faults with an erudition that did him proud. I did think he had missed one, but it turned out that what I was hearing was by way of being a general outline. As I listened to this litany, my belief that I am a total failure began to desert me. For him I was a heroic failure. I was the disaster to end disasters. Inured to such loquatiousness I looked out of the window and wondered how I could get him to write that cheque. It was the toughest decision I had faced so far. Should I tell him we were getting a parking ticket or should I wait and hope that he would calm down and continue his great writing career.

The only thing that kept him from strangling me was that he had done quite well at buying books. So much so, that he announced he was going to do the American Bookfair with this, his British stock and to aid the romance he was going to tell his potential customers that I had been his guide round Britain. Needless to say I was not best pleased to hear of this development, but then suddenly I saw an opportunity.

"If you are going to do a British stand at the Bookfair", I said, "you would look a lot more appropriate if you wore an English suit. I have just the thing for you."

That very evening we drove back to London from Edinburgh. Conversation, if it can be called that, was re-opened to discuss the fastest way of getting into London. Of all the topics in the world guaranteed to cause enmity, this is it. I jumped in feet first. He wanted me to tell him when we got to the M25, I thought we had left it a bit late, we were somewhere near Carlisle, and it was while we were rowing that I noticed we had overshot the Great Ringway. To my joy he announced that he had an appointment that evening, which I had now ensured he was going to miss. As usual, vanity got the better of me, and I asked him where he had to be.

"Old Oak Common at 8pm."

I told him to follow my instruction and we would be there at 7.

"I have no faith in your instructions or judgment."

"Which way were you thinking of going?"

"Everybody knows that when you come off the motorway you drive down the Edgware Road and turn right at Harrow Road. Even a moron knows that."

By now I was used to giving the directions. I had virtually become like a robot. At the end of the motorway I got him to his destination in under ten minutes. Mainly because he slowed down when we were in London, but he was still not impressed. Instead, he blamed me because we had arrived too early, far too early, and the person he wanted to see had not got home yet.

I told him to drive me to Paddington Station, it was not until we were inside it, that he realised I had got him there. He had never come into Paddington the back way before. The train I wanted was right next to the driveway, I used my last ounce of skill and got the car right next to the guard stand, and with much enthusiasm, I closed the train doors on him and motor cars for ever.

I would not like the TC to feel that I dislike him. It was not until I met him I had no idea what a life of bliss I led. For weeks afterwards I was walking on air, it was just heaven to be alive.

I am not attempting to claim that all motorists are like the Tank Commander, on the contrary, in my experience he was unique. He was possessed of all the faults that other motorists only fantasise about. He would have killed anything that got in
his way, and I would have urged him on, that is why I no longer travel in motor cars.

I was reminded of the Tank Commander when I was in a s/h clothes shop in Penzance - he was absolutely right I am not the least bit interested in s/h bks - and there I bought the complete livery of an engine driver. I have a new dream now I want my own private steam train, with sleeping car, bath carriage and library attached. For me the permanent way will have new meaning. I shall be able to start and stop where I please, oh and a veggie dining car, how could I forget something like that. And I suppose I shall have to have a carriage for the servants. I shall go to sleep in Fort William and wake in London, spend the day in Charing Cross and then be off again to Perth. I am further ahead with this ambition than I am with the one to have a pre world Rolls Royce, I not only have the uniform, I have become a train squatter.

This tour was conducted in a carefree car free manner in July 1991 and it almost completely expunged the horrors I endured with the TC.

The optimum ticket is a four day flexi rover which cost £48 but can be used for long enough to visit all the shops of mainland, Scotland. To get to the Island bksps you would need more than a month of Sundays. Driving, even without a lunatic it is always further than you think. Scottish s/h bksps tend to be more reliable about their hours, but they are much less flexible than their English counterparts about staying open after hours. When it says 5.30 on the door they close at 5.30 and they expect you to return tomorrow.

THE INVERNESS BOOKSHOP **Inverness**
10 Bank Street, Inverness
Mon-Sat, 10-5.30
This bksp is at the pinnacle of the s/h bookselling in Scotland, and it is way above the snowline of England's peaks. The foothills of the Scottish lowlands which lead to it are as training grounds. For the walker it has gentle slopes, for the climber it has severe tests, for the mountaineer it has unchallenged peaks. Its reflection is the river which it overlooks, it is never the same flow twice. Over its rocks may come sand and silt, but an experienced prospector knows that that is where you find gold. There is no facet that it does not present. Its troughs and morains only show up its best face. There are occasional avalanches when hidden resources are revealed but these come as a surprise even to the frequent climber.

It exacts a hard price from the unprepared, even the experienced can expect to pay in blood and for some it is a killer. It is not the height of a mountain which causes injury but the carelessness of the climber.

English tourists often complain of a cold wind, but world travellers rarely experience it. The locals are used to the climate. As you rise it does get chillier and there is a reserve which can cause frostbite.
But no wind effects its calm, no storm changes its face, it seems to have been there forever and yet it is always new.

This shop is indeed the summit of s/h bookdealing. BR Inverness, OOS turn right and left alongside market, down to river and turn left.

HIGHLAND ANTIQUES **Inverness**
15 Tomnahurich Street, Inverness
Mon-Sat, 10-5, clsd Wed
Antique shop with bta R/C stk, emphon HSF. Ab av cal, cnd and prices. TWC. P.poss. From Inverness bksp cross bridge and straight ahead.

There is also a branch in Nairn but this is NV.

There is also a s/h bksp in the market opposite Inverness Railway station, but as this market is locked at 5.30 and your exceedingly humble investigator did not find out about it till 5.31 (upon being evicted for overstaying my welcome at the Inverness bksp) I was not able to find out much about it. Had this been a sensible shop, i.e. one that was on a street where you could look in I could have doorstepped it.

Doorstepping consists of arriving at a shut bksp - the normal state of affairs - trying the door three times, banging on the window, trying the side door, standing on the bike and knocking on the upper windows and then trying to draw attention to yourself.

You can do this by sitting on the doorstep, sooner or later someone will come and tell you the bksp is clsd, from this person you attempt to find out when it will be open again.

The day I went to Inverness I began life - or my imitation of it - in Fort William some sixty miles away. Because it is now imposs to take a bike on Scottish trains I was unable to cycle. I attempted to hitch hike but after having walked 10 miles to Speen Bridge and seeing the train pull in I changed my mind. It is indeed a very pleasant trip to Glasgow, but I had already done it. From the City of Culture, I proceeded to Stirling, Bridge of Allen, Perth and Dunkeld. To get to Inverness in time I had to skip Blair Atholl. It is true that there is a bus from Fort William but having spent £48 on a rail ticket, I was too mean to spend a fiver on a bus.

My point is that to discover any details of the shop in Inverness Market I would have had to stay in Inverness overnight. By having a bksp in a market or shopping precinct you are cutting yourself off from the greatest potential group of customers - passers by. By not opening after six, you are cutting yourself off from another large group of customers: those who have jobs. If the Co-op in Inverness can stay open until eight, the newsagent opens until nine and the video shop unti later, why can't the bksp?

A day spent in Aberdeen and St Andrews is far more likely to produce int bks than one spent in Edinburgh. Aberdeen is very easy to get to and it is extremely easy to park. Nearest Inverness, Montrose, Blair Atholl, POCS. OWOWS.

***OXFAMS WORST BOOKSHOP** **Aberdeen**
27 Rosemount Viaduct, Aberdeen
Mon-Sat, 10-4.30, Wed 10-12
Med size R stk, bad even for a charity shop, included only as a reference point. You can hear the dogs barking from the railway station. BR Aberdeen, OOS with platforms on left hand side, up steps turn left and right into Bridge Street* cross Union Street and continue towards library and viaduct, SIOL, that was the easy bit.

*If you are not in Bridge Street at this stage, all is lost, it is better to try for St Andrews, under no circumstances ask an Aberdonian the way. When they hear you have walked the 200 yards from the station they will think you are a relative of Marco Polo and will start shouting at you.

ROSEMOUNT BOOKSHOP **Aberdeen**
3 Gilgomston Steps, Aberdeen
Mon-Sat, 10.30-5.30, L 1-2, V.Rel
Med size R/C stk, keen on Lit, ab av cal, cnd, av prices. TWC. P.poss. From Oxfam OOSH turn left, follow main road round to left turn right into Gilgamaston Park which becomes Raeburn Place and left. (essentially behind the library).

G R WINRAM/...

G R WINRAM **Aberdeen**
90 Leadside Road, Aberdeen
Mon-Sat, 10-5.30, L 1-2, clsd Wed, V.Rel
Med size R/C stk, av cal, cnd and prices. This bksp is the provincial bksp of my dreams, it has bks that I never see elsewhere. It has bks that are int, it has bks that you can afford to buy. It is uncontaminated by the monomania of bookfairies, there is no pathetic obsession with cnd. From the outside it looks like a Helen Hanff Special but inside it is a true story. It is a bksp of charm and allurement, but above all it has bks that can be read and profited from. The Scottish equivalent of Vetgow. From Oxfam, OOSH turn left and follow Rosemount viaduct through to Esslemount and turn left into Leadside Road.

RC writes
What a toad, have you noticed how he is always keenest on the middle aged females. Why he really likes this shop is that she is the only Scottish bookseller who managed to get the TC to shut up, with a single look she did it. He has been practising that look ever since. He's doing ok with the dresses, but the rest of it seems to have eluded him.

THE OLD CLOCK REPAIR SERVICE **Aberdeen**
197 King Street, Aberdeen
Mon-Sat, 10-5
Be sure to clock that name. This is indeed a shop to watch. To see its second hand you will have to do what the owner never does, polish its face, then open its long case to examine the intricate works, once in perfect order, but now in need of repair. What sort of movement is it that produces that tick? Is it biological or mechanical? Every second a book is borne, downwards, only to be saved yet another time by the minute hand of the time defying superman housed in the tiny capsule at the rear, unexpectedly powered by quarts, he rings out the alarm repeatedly. Our determination is approved thrice every quarter. Is this a wind up? Only for Aberdonians is this place a chimera for those of us used to the 24 hour clock it is a *daze* work. From Oxfam OOSH turn right, turn left at Union Street, and continue for about two thirds of a mile and left into King Street. Shop is almost opposite its exact counterpart - Safeway. This is not strictly accurate but itis a better time than most Aberdonians will give you.

THE MONTROSE BOOKSHOP **Montrose**
91 Murray Street, Montrose
Tues-Sat, 10-4, clsd Wed
Med size R/C stk, av cal, cnd and prices. Almost a Drif Special, needs more low key bks. BR Montrose, OOS ahead up steps (which I am told in Scotland is called a wynd, but that could be a wynd up) and turn left into High Street and continue. Nearest: Aberdeen, Dunkeld, St Andrews.

MAIR WILKES **Newport on Tay**
3 St Mary's Lane, Newport on Tay, Fife
Sats 9.30-5.30 or by appointment but there seldom seems to be a time when they are not there during the week and unlike most places where you have to make an appointment there is

none of that claustrophobic feeling that you have to buy a bk to get out.
Lg C/D stk, ab av cal, cnd and prices. Emphon Psychology, Scottish History, but with many other much more int bks. What am I talking about, I like Psychology bks. WAD. P.poss. BR Dundee (NAST 2 miles on other side of river). Nearest: Montrose, St Andrews, Perth.

RC writes

The real reason he likes this shop is that it showed him that there was no way of winning against the TC. It was from them that he bought a book called The White Flag Principle, How to Lose Wars and Why. It was only a hundred pages or so, but by the time the TC had stopped haranguing them he had learnt all its major lessons.

There is also a small shop in Newburgh open on summer weekends only.

ST ANDREWS

A TRUE BLUE CROSS SECTION

There are six places to buy books in St Andrews, together with a large number of charity shops, but this Hay on Wye of the North is a genuinely pleasant place to be. It does not suffer from monoculture, indeed there are many other interesting things to do. Its only disadvantage is that it is NAST (Leuchars 5 miles), but it is on the way to many sensible places such as Aberdeen, Stirling and Edinburgh. P.poss.

QUARTOS **St Andrews**
8 Golf Place, St. Andrews, Fife
Mon-Sat, 9.30-5.30, L 1-2.15
Med size R/C stk, av cal, cnd and prices. Poss infection of the Summer sickness at the front. NTWMES but can be quite pleasant. TWC. P.poss. As you go into town from Leuchars Golf Place, SIOL.

BILLSONS OF ST ANDREWS **St Andrews**
15 Greyfriars Gardens, St Andrews, Fife
Thurs-Sun, 2.30-5
Primarily a print shop but has small high cal stk of Scottish bks. Ab av cal, cnd and prices. From Quarto, OOSH turn right and left and third right.

There is also a regular s/h bkstl in the market, on the way to Bouquiniste.

BOUQUINISTE **St Andrews**
31 Market Street, St Andrews, Fife
Mon-Sat, 10-5, clsd Thurs in winter

Med size R/C stk, almost a Drif Special, but has too much on Scotland for me. From Billson's continue, left at Market St, and follow through until you think you have gone too far.

A & T MCILREAVY **St Andrews**
57 South Street, St Andrews, Fife
Mon-Sat, 10-5, Rel
Lg C/D stk, ab av cal, cnd and prices. Emphon Lit and Scottish. WAD. P. poss. From Bouquiniste turn right, left and left (is that right? well its that street anyway).

BOOK O BOOKS **St Andrews**
South Street (no No.) St Andrews, Fife
Mon-Sun, 9-9
This is certainly true of the summer but I wouldn't bank on it in the winter. A med size R/C stk, a definite Drif Special. I am not sure but there are lots of nrly's in Scotland - and is also int how many apostrophe's there are in St. Andrew's. My atlas gives it as: St Andrews, but that cannot be right, it would have to be Saint Andrews. P.poss. From McIlreavy, turn right and look for Vine Leaf restaurant by Post Office. Shop is at rear.

BOOK ENDS **Kirkcaldy**
I am not sure if have got that name right, by the time I had got back to the railway station and started writing this entry I had totally forgotten the name of this shop, and this was the only name that came to what for want of a better word, I will call my mind. This is why bksps should try to have appropriate or int names such as Voltaire & Rousseau (its a wonderful name, such a pity about the shop, but at least I do remember it)
449 High Street, Kirkcaldy, Scotland
And don't for one moment think that this shop is going to be easy to find. I had been to Kirkcaldy on another occassion and left not knowing it had a High Street. I also met a bookdealer in Kirkcaldy who did not know that this shop existed.
Tues-Sat, 10-5
Med size R/C stk, ab av cal, cnd and prices. She is extremely enthusiastic but not about showing the res stk. She also appears to be the only person in Kirkcaldy who is not affected by amnesia, once you tell her you are looking for a particular book she shows every book that could possibly be related to it. Maybe she is effected by Kirkcaldy, she appears to have no sense of time. TWC. P.poss. BR Kirkcaldy, OOS through the '60s inspired station (BR has forgotten that the better a building looks on the drawing board the worse it is in real life) through the gardens to the Adam Smith Theatre - that cannot be right, what did Adam Smith have to do with the theatre?) turn left into St Brycedale Ave (I must have been taking drugs that afternoon, who the hell was St Brycedale, he certainly is not in Julian's dictionary) maybe he was the patron saint of Amnesia, continue for five minutes and turn right into a one way street with no name - se it is not only me that forgets things, go down hill - its the story of my life - turn right at the bottom and left towards a building that looks like a sanitorium for the demented and is most welcoming.

The good news is that it can be done in one day, the bad news is that you feel obliged to do it. I think that Glasgow and the rest of Scotland are much more rewarding. In Edinburgh the bks have a tired look to them, as if they had been in some never ending bookfair which had not the strength to break up. Because of the lethargy of the shops on the north side it is best to start at James Thin, which is to be congratulated on its spectacular opening hours. The other thing you have to remember in Edinburgh is that they have Bank holidays that don't exist anywhere else. As far as I am concerned they could have one permanent Bank Holiday. I am not exactly certain why I loathe Edinburgh so, for I have bought some int bks there and it has eight veggie restaurants and there are lots of old style charity shops, and it is easy to walk to all the bksps.

RC writes

Why he dislikes it is that they all started laughing at him when he had his kilt on, the wrong way round.

JAMES THIN **Edinburgh**
53-59 South Bridge, Edinburgh
Mon-Sun, 9-10,. V.Rel
Lg new bksp with med size R/C stk slightly low key student orientated but there is a res stk of Ds bks by appointment. For me this is not only a shop from which the sun shines, it should be knighted, it makes most of the other bksps in Edinburgh seem dowergetic. If only they would keep their premises open as long as their mouths. BR Edinburgh/ Waverley, hard to describe but ETF.

GT BOOKS **Edinburgh**
8 Drummond Street, Edinburgh
Mon-Sat, 10-5.30
Med size R/C stk emphon remainders. The Merchant Navy School of bookdealing. WAD for the repartee, if not the bks. I have no proof but I would bet that the GT stands for Gin & Tonic rather than Grande Tourer. From James Thin, turn left OOSH and first left.

BOOKFARE **Edinburgh**
8 Victoria Street, Edinburgh
Mon-Sat, 10.30-5.30
Med size R/C stk, av cal, cnd and prices. Almost as bookfairy as its name implies, nor worth waiting for if you finish in Thin's or GT quickly. From GT go back to South Bridge turn left and right and right and follow round to left.

There are currently two bkstls in 'Byzantium' in Victoria Street but the turnover appears to be fairly fast.

PETER BELL **Edinburgh**
68 Westport, Edinburgh
Mon-Sat, 10.30-5.30
This shop is worth waiting for, it is medium sized C/D stk, ab av cal, cnd and prices. Emphon Lit, History and Womens' Biography. WAD. From Bookfare continue down Victoria St and turn right into Grassmarket which leads to Westport.

ARMCHAIR BOOKS **Edinburgh**
72 Westport, Edinburgh
Mon-Sat, 10.30-6
Med size R/C stk, av cal, cnd and prices. Not so much Habitat as Waring & Gillow. TWC.

GRANT & SHAW **See TIN**

WESTPORT BOOKS **Edinbugh**
151 Westport, Edinburgh
Mon-Fri, 10-5.30, Sat 11-5
Med size R/C stk, a Helen Hanff special. The film version with musical accompaniment. Av cal, cnd and prices.

OLD GRINDLES **Edinburgh**
Spittal Street (no No.), Edinburgh
Mon-Sun, 9-9
Med/lg R/C/D stk, ab av cal, cnd, av prices. Emphon Lit. It certainly has to be the most int shop in Edinburgh, but unfortunately that does not mean much. It is certainly well worth going to, but the stk could do with as much imagination as the owner's apparel. No T. From Westport continue up hill and ahead, turn right with stream of traffic and shop is on corner of Bread Street and Spittal Street.

CASTLE BOOKS **Edinburgh**
204 Canongate, Edinburgh
Mon-Sat, 11-5, open Sunday in summer
Well I am glad to see that some notice is taken of the customers. If this shop would bother to open at 9am it would clearly be the first one to go to in Edinburgh, as it is you have to double back, there is no other way. When a bksp opens officially at 11.30 they always look surprised when somebody such as myself stands outside the door waiting forit to open, but I was outside this shop at 11 and 23 people tried to get in. It is not worth it once you do get in but that is not the point. Med size R/C stk, av cal cnd and prices. From Thin's go back towards Princes Street and turn right.

ANDREW PRINGLE **Edinburgh**
7 Dundas Street, Edinburgh
Mon-Fri, 9.30-5.30, L 12.30-1.30, Sat 10-1
Not strictly a bksp as you have to ring a bell and go upstairs, but it has such an int stk that it is worthile overcoming these handicaps. The bks are primarily literature and travel, selected with an independence of mind that is refreshing to see, however there is a slight blight of bookfairyishness. If he would give up doing them I would be prepared to ring his bell even louder and he could ascend to even greater heights.

I always remember Hanover Street as the one near the Scott Memorial where I get lost, it leads into Dundas Street before you know it.

DUNDAS BOOKSHOP **Edinburgh**
23a Dundas Street, Edinburgh
Tues-Sat, 12-5.30
Med size R/C stk, av cal, cnd and prices. T.

BROUGHTON BOOKS **Edinburgh**
2a Broughton Place, Edinburgh
Tues-Fri, 12-6, Sat 12.30-5.30
Med size R/C stk, av cal, cnd and prices, has a curious school dinners feel about it. From Dundas Bks turn right and right to Nest St parallel, turn right and right.

MCNAUGHTONS **Edinburgh**
3a Haddington Place, Edinburgh
Tues-Sat, 9.30-5.30
Med/lg C/D stk, ab av cal, cnd and prices but with more variety than most of the other Edinburgh shops can manage.

In Perth I discovered a Fish & Chip shop that had a menu that was almost as long as my wait for a train to Inverness. Experienced as I am at extracting vegan meals from fish and chip shops, I am always loathe to enter until I am sure that it is poss for me not to come away with an empty stomach. The reason for my trepidation is my abhorence of chips. The large number of items on this menu made it extremely diff for me to read. Years of eating carrots has done nothing for my eyesight. I was heartened to see several other buffers entering the premises. I followed in their train expecting them to give me enough time to come to a major decision.

I was hardly through the door when I was asked what I wanted. This seemed grossly unfair but nobody else seemed about to complain.

"I am just thinking", I said.

"The Philosophical away Oer the other side of the town".

"I am attempting to read your elaborate menu", I said.

"If ye cannae read ye shoudne be in here, yer holdin all the other folks up."

And he was right, by now there were four other people behind me.

"Serve them first", I said magnanimously or so I thought.

Almost in unison they issued a strange mantra which despite my years studying eastern religions I was unable to comprehend.

"Effs upper pleas"

On whose behalf they were pleading I was unable to tell. The Lord High Chancellor of this court of common please again turned his attention to me. At the risk of causing hilarity among the plea bargainers of Perth, I told his honour that I would like one of every vegetarian item on the menu.

"We dannae serve vegetarian hagis!" he said.

"I think I shall be able to survive that deprivation" I replied.

Having established what it was I wanted he announced that it would be £3.65. The sight of my money seemed to reassure him that I was serious. He then proceeded to prepare a meal the like of which I have never encountered in a fish and chip shop before. It consisted of Baked apple (as everybody knows it is always best to eat fruit as the first course of a meal). The main course consisted of battered mushrooms together with onion rings and mushy peas, plus pickled cucumbers, followed by Banana Fritter.

Whilst these delicasies were being prepared I studied the menu in an attempt to work out what it was the other customers were asking for. I could see nothing even vaguely similar but then in the Deaths column I saw an item which had me even more confused. It said "Mock chops". I could not resist asking what this was.

"I took you to be a veggie - that's sausage".

The above fish and chip shop in Perth and the further above bksp in Edinburgh have much in common, but I feel that the bksp just has the edge. It serves mock roast beef.

LATTO BOOKS **Musselburgh**
3 Eakside East, Musselburgh
Mon-Sat, 9-5, Wed 1
Med/lg R/C stk, ab av cal, cnd and prices. TWC. P.poss. Musselburgh is 8 miles from the centre of Edinburgh. SIOL as you go into town. There is no railway.

There are also rumours of shops in Kelso and in Biggar, NFDA.

GLASGOW

THE BAND OF HOPE

The number of s/h bksps has gone down but this has brought about a vast improvement in the quality, however despite the small number it takes at least a day to visit them all.

When I came out of the Central Station I had no idea how to get to Cooper Hay's shop. It would have driven the TC mad, and this cheered me up considerably. I looked left and I looked right, right seemed to be prosperous for bksps even one of Cooper's cal, I turned left for all of 25 yards, I then had to make the same decision again. I chose the right way, literally and walked for two blocks, instinctively I knew it was on the left, I turned and found myself in a square that I had never seen before, but it did look like the right sort of area, I tried the next block back. That did not work. So I tried the next block forward. That did not work either. But then I saw a sign that said Bath Street, I was in the right street, but going the wrong way, then I doubled back and found the shop, a little further away than I had expected. What I am trying to tell you is it is poss to find bksps by instinct.

They are usually in secondary shopping streets. They are usually near Health Food stores, they are usually near other s/h shops. Cooper Hay's has none of these features but I found it.

COOPER HAY **Glasgow**
203 Bath Street, Glasgow
Mon-Fri, 10-5, Sat 10-1
Med/lg C/D stk ab av cal, cnd av prices. This is one of the few C/D shops that it is a genuine pleasure to be in, the bks are outstandingly well chosen, both in cnd and content, and even if you cannot afford it there is always something of int. WAD. BR Glasgow Central, OOS by main gates turn left and right and third left. Nearest: Stirling, Edinburgh, Carlisle.

CALEDONIA BOOKS Glasgow
483 Great Western Road, Kelvin Bridge, Glasgow
Mon-Sat, 10.30-6
Lg R/C stk, ab av cal, cnd, av prices, takes some time to browse through because of the curious customers, there is a res stk in the bsmt and a threat of cheaper bks round the corner. What the Glasgow shops have that the Edinburgh ones don't is style. Plus they also have customers. In Edinburgh they only have tourists. When I go in a bksp I ignore all the sections and start at the top left hand corner and work my way round clockwise, twice. If there is somebody at the stack where I wish to look I stand directly behind them, and when they say "Am I in your way?" I say "No, no, no, it is perfectly alright", and they always move, you don't need to touch them, you don't even need to get close to them, all you need to do is look straight through them. It works every time - except in this shop. This is the only place I have been into where that system failed. I am not sure whether I admire it or not, but it is a unique shop. From Cooper Hay, turn left OOSH, right over bridge underpass, left at St George's Cross and continue (follow signs for Dumbarton) about 1½ miles.

There is also a bkstl in the Byres Road, but NV.

GILMOREHILL BOOKS Glasgow
43 Bank Street, Glasgow
Mon-Sat, 11-6
Med size R/C stk, slightly remaindery, av cal, cnd and prices. TWC. P poss. From Caledonian Bksp turn left and left.

VOLTAIRE & ROUSSEAU Glasgow
12 Otago Lane, Glasgow
Mon-Sat, 11-6.30
Small/med (now much reduced since recent fire - I have an alibi). It is a great name, pity about the shop, R/C stk, NSOC, av prices. From Gilmorehill turn left and left and right and left.

ADAM BOOKS Glasgow
13 Battlefield Avenue, Glasgow
Mon-Sat, 10.30-5.30
Newly opened R/C stk (ex John Smiths and a bit lifeless at the moment but looks as if it could improve). BR Mount Florida, OOS on south side along path, turn right and first left.

WORDSWORTH & CO Glasgow
4 Johnston Street, Paisley, Glasgow
Mon-Sat, 10.15-5.30
Med size R/C stk, a Drif Special (which is the other thing Edinburgh lacks). TWC. P.poss. BR Paisley, Gilmour Street. OOS from forecourt, turn right towards town hall into St Mirren St and fourth left.

WESTWORDS Greenock
14 Newton Street, Greenock, Glasgow
Mon-Sat, 9.30-5.30
Med size R/C stk slightly low key, Drif Special. BR Greenock West, OOS turn right.

MCCLAREN BOOKS **Helensburgh**
91 West Clyde Street, Helensburgh
Mon-Sat, 9.30-5.30, L 1-2, clsd Wed, Rel
Med/lg Spec shop of Maritime stk, ab av cal, av prices. Also has good general stk. WAD. This is some detour, given how efficiently this shop is run and given their interest in the Maritime, I always expect them to have organised a ferry service from Greenock which is 5 miles away by boat, but 40 by train. It would certainly save a lot of time and I always like going by ferry to a bksp.

CORN EXCHANGE BOOKSHOP **Stirling**
53 King Street, Stirling
Mon-Fri, 10-3, Sat 10-5, L 1-2
Med size R/C stk, almost a Drif Special, not least because you have to go through a new man's clothes shop to get to the books. Quite often when I go in bksps the owners give me a run down of my clothes - as if somehow I did not know what I was wearing - and they also run them down - usually on the grounds that they are s/h - quite why people who spend their lives dealing in s/h bks should find s/h clothes so reprehensible is hard for me to understand. Until I went into this shop, I thought that most bookdealers got their clothes from some sort of cooperative run by the PBFA to maintain the image of bookdealers. It was extremely easy to organise because there was only one size, no discernable style and no clash of colour because everything was grey. I did not realise you could buy clothes this awful new. BR Stirling, OOS ahead to third block parallel and slightly left.

THE STIRLING BOOKSHOP **Stirling**
30 Spittal Street, Stirling
Mon-Sat, 10-5
Lg R/C/D stk, ab av cal, cnd, av prices. Bgns known, usually manages to come up with some truly int bks. Emphon Scottish, TWC. P.poss. From Corn Exchange go up hill towards castle.

BRIDGE OF ALLEN BOOKS **Bridge of Allen**
2 Henderson Street, Bridge of Allen, Stirlingshire
Mon-Sat, 9.30-5.30, occasional Suns
Med size C/D stk, emphon Acad and Scottish, ab ave cal, cnd and prices. The league of Scottish Lady Bookdealers has clearly been laying on the Non Assertion Courses and this one has graduated top of the class. The owner of this shop is extremely keen on books in good cnd, but I maintain that this is just a Ds fetish. Cs are asked more for bks in good cnd, and this is in some way meant to make the bks better, and the Cs now subscribe to this philosophy in imitation of the dealers. The previous day I was in Wordsworth, definitely not a Cs shop but it was packed with people who simply wanted to read bks. They were buying them for content. I bump intoless and less people in Cs shops - this one was an exception simply because there are less and less bks in good cnd. Most Rs are happy with any copy. Cs seek out better copies after they have any copy (other than those trained by Ds of course). Ds seek out mint copies as a way of not having to buy bks. I maintain that there are only two cnd's of books: With Cover; good, Without cover; bad.

BR Bridge of Allen, OOS up steps and turn right into town. Nearest: Perth, St Andrews, Stirling, Helensburgh.

British Frail has given up with timetables at Bridge of Allen but the frequency of the trains makes up for it. That should be Scotrail which appears to be far more efficient than BR, not least of its advantages is that it runs night trains.

PERTH

FOR THE PETHVERTED WITH A GRANNY NOT

PERTH BOOKS Perth
3a Abbot Street, Perth
Mon-Sat, 10-5, clsd Wed, clsd Sat 1 in winter
Small med size R/C stk, ab av cal, cnd, av prices. Also does new bks. A strangely quiet shop, I always feel he talks softly and carries a big stick. BR Perth, OOS turn right under bridge, right over bridge and ahead past the fish and chip shop that sells mock chops (sausages). Nearest Dunkeld, St Andrews, Stirling, Edinburgh

DUNKELD ANTIQUES Dunkeld
Tay Terrace (no No.) Dunkeld, Perthshire
Mon-Sat, 10-5.30, Sun 12-5.30 (but usually plus in my experience)
A much bta antique shop with bks, med/lg stk, ab av, cal, cnd and prices. TWC. Disc. BR Dunkeld & Birnham (rings a bell eh?), OOS turn left and right over bridge.

BLAIR ATHOLL BROWSE Blair Atholl
by Blair Atholl Station, Perthshire
Mon-Sun, 12-8
Med sized R/C stk, WAD, av cal, cnd and prices. Unlike the moron in Inverness this shop does everything correctly. Firstly it is in a sensible place. Blair Atholl attracts people all the year round. It is on a main road between Inverness and Stirling, it is on the rail line (it is almost right on the rail line). No changes are necessary. You can see what sort of bks it has from the outside, thus anybody can walk by at any time they choose. In Blair Atholl people walk around the railway station looking at it as if it was some derelict Abbey, which it nrly is. It not only has magnificent opening hours, it has them clearly posted, but best of all it is poss to see exactly what type of stk it has from the outside.

I wrote the whole of the above before I had set a foot in this shop, but because it was so attractive I vowed to retùrn, despite it causing considerable delay to my schedule. This is exactly the business that bksps should be in. Who ever wanted to return to a bookfair?

I don't doubt that it takes considerable effort to achieve the above, but I also do not doubt that unless the bksps of Britain make the effort they too will be out of print.

When I actually did get into this shop the prices were a

little surprising but the point is that they did get me back. BR Blair Atholl, what do you mean directions? What sort of morons are you? Alright, alright, OOS turn right for three feet, ahead nine feet and left 24feet (approx)

THE IDEAL SECONDHAND BOOKSHOP **Ferrytown**
1 Station Street, Ferrytown
Mon-Fri, 6-9, Sat & Sun 10-5
Med size R/C stk, av prices, NSOC. Owner is deaf mute who cannot read or write, does not attend bookfairs, stays out of sight, does not offer cups of coffee and is not interested in tenth rate gossip about other bksp owners. No T. No p. poss. Shop is next door to veggie restaurant. Nearest: Grays, St Helens, Edgware, Morecambe.

This brain terminates here, its not much but it is the best I can boo. If you have any complaints don't tell me, I already have more than I can handle. It took me nine months to write this guide, when it should have only taken three. One day I will get it write.

T O W N   I N D E X

This section contains brief details of every secondhand bookshop in Britain known to me. Wales, Northern Ireland and Scotland are included in this single alphabetical index, but London is treated separately. I define London as being anywhere within the M25 Motorway. Those of you who hold the quaint belief that Uxbridge is in Middlesex or Epping in Essex will be reminded at the appropriate place.

ABERDEEN

ROSEMOUNT BOOKSHOP, 3 Gilgamaston Steps, Aberdeen. 0224 639355. Mon-Sat, 10-5.30, L 1-2. Med size R/C stk av cal cnd and prices. Emphon lit.

G.R. WINRAM, 90 Leaside Road, Aberdeen, Scotland AB2 4TU. 0224 630673. Mon-Sat, 10-5.30, L 1-2. Clsd Wed. Med size R/C stk av cal cnd and prices. WAD.

OXFAM'S WORST BOOKSHOP*, 27 Rosemount Viaduct, Aberdeen, Scotland 0224 642490. Mon-Sat, 10-4.30, Wed, 10-12. Med size R stk low key av prices.

THE OLD CLOCK REPAIR SERVICE, 197 King Street, Aberdeen, Scotland 0224 627695. Mon-Sat, 10-5. Med size R/C stk NSOC, ab av prices, but int.

ABERGAVENNY

H.M. LOCKYER, Monk Street, Abergavenny, Wales NP7 5NF. 0873 5825. Mon-Sat, 9.30-5.30. Lg/med size R/C stk. Emphon Rural subjects. TWC.

ABERYSTWYTH

YSTWYTH BOOKS, 7 Princess Street, Aberystwyth, Dyfed, Wales. SY25 1DX. 0970 617511. Mon-Sat, 9.30-5. Clsd Wed winter. Med size R/C stk ab av cal cnd. Av prices. Emphon acad.

ACOCKS GREEN

MAXWELLS BOOKSHOP, 22 Shaftmoor Lane, Acocks Green, West Midlands B27 7RS. 021 7068379. Mon-Sat, 10.30-4.45. Med size R/C stk av cal cnd and prices keen on technical subjects

ALDEBERGH

TREWINS BOOKS, 178B, High Street, Aldebergh, Suffolk IP15 5AN. 098 684649. Mon-Sat, 10-1 and 2-5. Wed clsd. Small R/C stk av cal cnd prices. T.

ALSTON, CUMBRIA

There is an antique shop which is allegedly a Drif Special but I have no been to it.

ALTON

ALTON SECONDHAND BOOKS, 11 Normandy Street, Alton, Hampshire GU34 1DD. Mon-Sat, 9.30-5.30, Wed & Sat, 5. Med size R/C stk av cal cnd and prices.

ALTRINCHAM, MANCHESTER

ABACUS BOOKS, 34 Regent Road, Altrincham, Cheshire. 061 8285106. Mon-Sat,10-5, Wed, 4. It is imposs to decide if this is a new bksp with s/h bks or a s/h bksp with new bks. No differentiation is made by the management whose eyes light up every time a sale is made. As this is almost the only source of light it is best to take your own torch. I am decidedly keen to take a torch to it. NIMS on the grounds that it encourages my incendrism.

AMBLESIDE

THE LITTLE BOOKSHOP, 1 Cheapside, Ambleside, Cumbria LA12 0AR. 05394 32094. Mon-Sat, 9-5. Clsd Thurs. Med size R/C stk av cal cnd and prices.

ARUNDEL

THE ARUNDEL BOOKSHOP, 10 High Street, Arundel, West Sussex. BN18 9AB. 0903 882680. Mon-Sat, 9.15-5.15, L 1-2.15. Some Sun ams. Lg R/C/D stk av cal cnd and prices

ASHBOURNE, DERBYSHIRE

Antique shop with bks NV

ASHBURTON, DEVON

THE DARTMOOR BOOKSHOP, 2 Kingsbridge Lane, Ashburton, Devon. 0364 53356. Mon-Sat, 9.30-5.30. Med size R/C/D stk ab av cal cnd and prices. Emphon Local History. NIMS. GIOPIC. (Gross incompetence on part of compiler).

ASHBURTON RARE BOOKS, 20 West Street, Ashburton, Devon. 0364 53341. Mon-Sat, 11-5. Slightly longer in summer. Med size C/D stk av cal cnd and prices. NIMS. GIOPIC.

ASHBY DE LA ZOUCHE, LEICESTERSHIRE

Rumour of bksp but NV despite the fact that I would love to just because of the name, but it is a damned diff place to get to.

AXMINSTER

THE OLD CURIOSITY SHOP, 7 South Street, Axminster EX13 5AD. 0297 33010. Mon-Sat, 8.30-5.30, Wed 1. Small R stk in rear of curio shop av cal cnd and prices. NIMS to small and low key but worth looking at if you are in that area early enough.

AYLESBURY

THE BOOKSHOP SQUARE EDGE, 38 Kingsbury, Aylesbury, Buckinghamshire HP20 2JE. 0296 89480. Mon-Sat, 10.30-5.30. Med size R/C stk av cal cnd and prices. TWC.

PETER EATON'S, The Lilies, Weedon, Aylesbury, Bucks. HP22 4AS. 0296 641393. Mon-Sat, 10-5. Extremely lg R/C/D stk. Almost solid roast beef. Needs an entire day. NIMS. Not strictly a bksp. *RC writes "The real reason he dislikes this place is not because it is a shop, but because he was in a looney bin round here."*

AYR, SCOTLAND

The new bksp in the High Street has some s/h bks upstairs.

BANGOR

BANGOR BOOKS, 122 High Street, Bangor, Gwynned, Wales. 0248 352659. Mon-Sat, 9.30-5. Clsd Wed in winter. Med size R/C stk av cal cnd and prices.

BANGOR, NORTHERN IRELAND

THE OTHER BOOKSHOP, 4 Dufferin Avenue, Bangor, Northern Ireland. 0247 458778. Mon-Sat, 10-5. Med size R/C stk. Emphon pbks and remainders. Av cal cnd and prices.

ALMOST IDENTICAL TO THE OTHER BOOKSHOP*, 30 Dufferin Avenue, Bangor. No phone. As ab.

BARNARD CASTLE, CO. DURHAM

There is a s/h bksp but it was NV in the last year. There used to be two and one has closed down and there are differing reports of which one it is, but neither were great.

BARNSTAPLE

TARKA BOOKS, 121 Boutport Street, Devon. 0271 74997. Tues-Sat, 10-5. Med size R/C stk av cal cnd and prices.

BARNSTAPLE, DEVON

ROBERTS AND YOUNG, Gammon Walk, Barnstaple, North Devon. 0271 23591. Mon-Sat, 9-5. Med size R/C stk av cal cnd and prices. NIMS. NV.

BARROW IN FURNESS

MOSTLY BOOKS, 247 Rawlinson Street, Barrow in Furness, Cumbria LA14 1DW. 0229 36808. Tues-Sat, 11-5. Clsd Thurs. Med size R/C/D stk spec in technical bks of an artistic nature.

BATH

ASPIDISTRA, 46 St James Street, Bath BA1 1UG. 0225 461948. Mon-Sat,10.30-4. Med size R/C stk keen on art. Av cal cnd and prices.

DEREK AND GLENDA WALLIS, 6 Chapel Row, Bath BA1 1HN. 0225 424677. Mon-Sat, 10-5.30. Lg R/C/D stk av cal cnd and prices. Emphon childrens and ill.

BANKES BOOKS, 5 Margarets Buildings, Bath, Avon BA12 1LP. 0225 444580. Mon-Sat,10-5. Med/lg C/D stk. Emphon antiquarian. Ab av cal cnd and prices.

BATH OLD BOOKS, 9C Margarets Buildings, Bath, Avon. 0225 422244. Mon-Sat, 9.30-5. Med/lg C/D stk ab av cal cnd and prices.

CAMDEN BOOKS, 146 Walcot Street, Bath, Avon BA1 5BL. 0225 461606. Mon-Sat, 10-5. Med/lg C/D stk ab av cal cnd and prices. Emphon Art.

BATH BOOK EXCHANGE, 35 Broad Street, Bath, Avon BA1 5LP. 0225 66214. Mon-Sat, 9-5. L 12.30-1.30. Small/med size low key R stk. Emphon pbks and remainders.

GEORGE BAYNTUN, Manvers Street, Bath, Avon BA1 1JW. 0225 466000. Mon-Fri, 9-5.30. L 1-2. Med size spec in decorative bindings. Bks to be photographed against. NIMS. In the basement is P.R.R. Rainsford which spec in art bks but appt required.

BECCLES

BESLEY'S BOOKS, 4 Blyburgate, Beccles, Suffolk NR34 9TA. 0502 7157642. Med size R/C/D stk av cal cnd and prices. TWC.

BEDFORD

RICHARD WILDMAN, 20 Mill Street, Bedford MK40 3HD 0234 43905. Tues-Sat, 12.6. Med size R/C stk av cal cnd and prices.

Another Bookshop opened on Aug 31 NV

BELFAST

MEWS ANTIQUES, 260 Antrim Road, Belfast. 0232 751319. Mon-Sat, 10-5. Antique shop with room of BTA R/C bks. Av cnd and prices.

VOLUME ONE, Unit 10, The Haymarket, Royal Avenue. BT1 1DT. No phone. Med size R/C stk NSOC av prices. Emphon pbks.

THE KNOWS HORRENDA BOOKSHOP*, 23 Lower North Street, Belfast. No phone. Mon-Sat, 10-5. Med size R/C stk av cal cnd. Emphon pbks and horror.

ARCADE BOOKS, 10-12 Gresham Street, Belfast, Northern Ireland BT1 1TN. 0232 438474. Mon-Sat, 10-5. Med size R/C stk. Emphon pbks.NSOC. Av prices.

BOOKSTORE*, 73 Union Street, Belfast BT1 2JG. 0232 24246. Mon-Sat, 10-5. Small/med size R stk bl av cal cnd and prices in MS as the NO NO BOOKSHOP.

ROMA RYAN,73 Dublin Road, Belfast BT2 7HF. 0232 242777. Mon-Sat, 11-5.30. Med size R/C stk av cal cnd and prices. Emphon Irish.

PROSPECT HOUSE BOOKS, 93 Dublin Road, Belfast BT2 2HF. 0232 245787. Mon-Sat, 11-5. Sat 4.45. Med/lg C/D stk ab av cal cnd and prices.

BOOKFINDERS, 47 University Road, Belfast, Northern Ireland BT2 1ND. 0232 228269. Mon-Sat, 11-5.30. Med size R/C stk. Emphon student acad. Av cal cnd and prices.

LEAVES BOOKSHOP, 84A Stranmillis Road, Belfast BT9 5AD. 0232 664600. Mon-Fri, 10.45-4, Sat 10-5. Med size R/C stk av cal cnd and prices. Emphon student and acad.

WELL READ, 171 Ormeau Road, Belfast, Northern Ireland. No phone. Mon-Sat, 10-6. Med size R stk av cal cnd and prices.
WORLD OF BOOKS, 329 Woodstock Road, Belfast, Northern Ireland. No phone. Med size R/C stk av cal cnd and prices. Emphon remainders and theology.

BELFORD, NORTHUMBRIA

THE BELFORD BOOKSHOP, Market Place, Belford, Northumbria. 066 85367. Mon-Sat, 10-5. Clsd Thurs. Med size R/C stk av cal cnd and prices.

BEVERLEY

EASTGATE BOOKSHOP, 11 Eastgate, Beverley HU17 0DW. 0482 868579. Mon-Sat, 10-5. Med size R/C stk av cal cnd and prices. Res stk of bks on Borneo.
ALEX ALEC SMITH, 31 Highgate, Beverley, North Humberside HU17 0DN. 0482 869453. Tues-Sat, 10-5. Med size R/C stk ab av cal cnd. Av prices. Keen on lit.

BEXHILL

SAM ROBINSON, Parkhurst Road (No no.), Bexhill. No phone. Mon-Sat, but can be somewhat erratic. R/C stk. A Clive Linklater Spec. NIMS.

BIDEFORD

RAINBOW, 19 Market Place, Bideford, Devon. 023 7478592. Mon-Sat, 10-5. L 1-2, ex Wed. Med size R/C stk av cal cnd and prices. NV. NIMS.
SCUDDERS, 11 Bridge Street, Bideford, Devon EX39 2EU. 023 727567. Mon-Sat, 9.30-5.30. Antique shop with BTA stk of bks.

BILLINGBOROUGH

ALAN REDMOND BOOKS,25 High Street, Billingborough, Lincs NG34 0QB. 0529 240215. Sat-Sun, 10-6. Med size R/C stk av cal cnd and prices.

BILLINGSHURST

BOOKS AND THINGS, 58-62 High Street, Billingshurst, West Sussex. RH14 9NY. 0403 815131. Mon-Sat, 9.30-5? Small R/C stk. Slightly Bookfairy. Av cal cnd and prices. NV.

BIRKENHEAD

THE WIRRAL BOOKSHOP, 325 Borough Road, Birkenhead, Merseyside. 051 6380160. Fri-Sat only, 10.30-5. Med size R/C stk silverfish Drif Special. NV but door stepped. BR. Birkenhead North. OOS, turn left and keep walking.

BIRMINGHAM AND WEST MIDLANDS

TAPLINS BOOKSHOP, 62 Station Road, Marston Green, West Midlands B37 7BI. 021 7796505. Tues-Sat, 11-5. Med size R/C stk ab av cal cnd av prices.
STEPHEN WYCHERLEY, 508 Bristol Road, Selly Oak, Birmingham B29 6DB. 021 4711006. Mon-Sat, 10.30-5.30. Clsd Wed. Med size C/D stk av cal cnd ab av prices. Res stks. TWC.
BIRMINGHAM BOOKSHOP, 567 Bristol Road, Selly Oak, Birmingham. B29 6AF. 021 4728556. Mon-Sat, 10-5. Med/lg R/C/D stk av cal cnd and prices.
BEECH BOOKS, 286 Oldbury Road, Rowley Regis, Birmingham B65 0JN. 021 5599822. Mon-Thurs, 11-4.30. Fri-Sat, 11-5. Med size R/C stk av cal cnd and prices.
CLENT BOOKS, 52 Summer Hill, Halesowen, West Midlands. 021 5500309. Mon-Sat, 10-4. Med size R/C stk av cal cnd and prices.
SIMMONS BOOKSHOP, 37 Lower High Street, Wednesbury, West Midlands. WS10 7AQ. 021-502 4622. Mon-Sat, 9.30-5.30. Thurs 2, Fri 7.30. Med/lg R/C stk av cal cnd and prices.

BLITZGEIST, 189 High Street, Harbourne, Birmingham BI7 9QD. 021 4264122. Mon-Sat, 10-6. Med/lg R/C stk ab av cal cnd av prices. T&D.

BISHOP'S CASTLE

YARBOROUGH HOUSE BOOKS, The Square, Bishop's Castle SY9 5BN. 0588 638318. Tues, Thur? Sun. Med size R/C stk, no fiction, av cal cnd and prices. NIMS. NV recently, by anybody as far as I can work out.

BLAIR ATHOLL

BLAIR ATHOLL BROWSE, Blair Atholl Station, Perthshire. 079 681530. Mon-Sun, 12-8. Small/med size R/C stk slightly touristy. Av cal cnd ab av prices.

BLAKENEY

ELKIN MATTHEWS, Cley Road (no no) Blakeney, Norfolk NR25 7NL. 0263 740475. BTR. Med size C/D stk av cal cnd and prices. NIMS not open regular hours.

BLANDFORD FORUM

SECOND READING BOOKSHOP, 7 Nightingale Court, Blandford Forum, Dorset DT11 7EB. Mon-Sat, 10-5. Wed 1. Med size R/C stk av cal cnd and prices.

DORSET BOOKSHOP, 69 East Street, Blandford Forum DT1 7DX. 0258 52256. Mon-Sat, 9.30-5.30. Wed 1. New bksp with R/C stk av cal cnd and prices.

BOOKS AND BYGONES, 69 Salisbury Street, Blandford Forum DT11 7DX. 0258 456407. Mon-Sat, 10-4.30. Antique shop with BTA stk of bks. NIMS seldom open, poss in training to become a full time bookdealer.

BLYTH

SKELTER, 11A Beaconsfield Street, Blyth, Northumbria. Tues-Fri, 4.30-6, Sat 10-5. Med size R/C stk low key good cnd av prices.

BOROUGHBRIDGE

BATES AND HINDMARCH, Fishergate, Boroughbridge YO5 9AL. 0423 324258. Mon-Sat, 10.30-5. Small/med R/C stk av cal cnd ab av prices. Keen on India and Travel.

BOSTON, LINCOLNSHIRE

PILGRIM BOOKS, 7 Red Lion Street, Boston, Lincolnshire. 0205 356931. Wed 9-4. Sat 9-5. V Rel. Med size R/C stk av cal cnd and prices.

BOURNEMOUTH

SIDNEY WRIGHT, 12 & 13 Royal Arcade, Bournemouth, Dorset. BH1 4EZ. 0202 397153. Mon-Sat, 9-5.30. New bksp with lg R/C stk av cal cnd and prices.

BOOKS AND MAPS, 122 Tuckton Road, Southbourne, Dorset. 0202 421379. Mon-Sat, 9.30-5.30. Med size R/C/D stk av cal cnd and prices.

ASHLEY BOOKSHOP, 30B Ashley Road, Bournemouth, Dorset. 0202 302499. Mon-Sat, 10-5.30. Lg R/C stk av cal cnd and prices.

H & S ROWAN, 459 Christchurch Road, Boscombe, Bournemouth. 0202 398820. Mon-Sat, 9-6. Med/lg R/C/D stk av cal cnd and prices.

YESTERDAYS BOOKS, 65-67 Bennet Road, Charminster, Bournemouth. BH8 8RH. 0202 302023. Med size R/C/D stk av cal cnd and prices. res stk Africa.

HOLDENHURST BOOKS, 275 Holdenhurst Road, Bournemouth, Dorset BH6 4EZ. 0202 397718. Mon-Sat, 10-5.30. Clsd Wed. Med size R/C stk av cal cnd and prices. Emphon motoring. TWC. P.Poss.

BRACKLEY

THE OLD HALL BOOKSHOP, 32 Market Place, Brackley, Northamptonshire NN13 5DP. Mon-Sat, 9.30-5.30. L 1-2. Lg R/C stk ab av cal cnd av prices. Keen on lit.

BRADFORD

See Bradford in Main Sequence.

BRADFORD ON AVON, WILTSHIRE

R & S OTWAY, Church Street, Bradford on Avon BA15 1LN. 02216 3885. Mon-Sat, 10-5.30. Clsd Wed. Med size R/C/D stk. Emphon mod 1sts, BTA cnd and v pleasant to be in. I had written a long peon of praise to this place but it seems to gone AWOL which is truly a pity. There is also another low key shop in the centre of town and the new Whitehall bksp has some s/h bks in the rear room by request.

BRAITHWAITE

BOOK COTTAGE, Braithwaite, Keswick, Cumbria CA12 5SY. 059 682275. BTR. Med size R stk av cal cnd and prices.

BRAUNTON, DEVON

BOOK CELLAR, East Street (No no) Braunton, North Devon. 0271 815061. Mon-Sat, 10-5. Clsd Tues. Med size R/C stk BTA. NIMS. NV.

BRECON

D.G & A.S. EVANS, 7 The Street, Brecon, Powys LD3 7LL. 0874 2714. Mon-Sat, 9-5. Clsd Wed 1. New bksp with med size R/C stk slightly low key av cnd and prices.

BRENTWOOD, ESSEX

THE BOOKEND, 38 Kings Road, Brentwood, Essex. No phone. Mon-Sat, 10-5. Thur 1. Med size R/C stk av cal cnd and prices. T.

BRIDGE OF ALLEN

BRIDGE OF ALLEN BOOKS, 2 Henderson Street, Bridge of Allen, Scotland. FK9 4HT. 0786 834483. Mon-Sat, 9.30-5.30. Med size C/D stk, emphon acad & Scottish History. Ab av cal cnd and prices.

BRIDGEND, WALES

BRIDGEND BOOK BARN, Unit 3 Stormy Down Industrial Estate, Stormy Down, Bridgend, Wales. 0656 745540. Mon-Sun, 10-5.30. Med size R/C stk. Emphon S/F pbks and Welsh. Av cal cnd and prices.

BRIDLINGTON

JL BOOK EXCHANGE, 72 Hildethorpe Road, Bridlington YO15 3BQ. 0262 601285. Summer 8.30-8.30. Every day. Winter 9-5, Mon-Sat. Small R stk av cal cnd and prices.

BRIDPORT

PIC'S BOOKSHOP, 11 South Street, Bridport, Dorset DT6 3NR. 0308 25689. Mon-Sat, 9.30-5. Thur 1. Med size R/C stk av cal cnd and prices.

BRIGHTLINGSEA

VICTORIA BOOKS, 22 Victoria Place, Brightlingsea, Essex CO7 9BX. 0206 302374. Mon-Sat, 10.30-4.30. Clsd Tues. Med size R/C stk av cal cnd and prices.

BRIGHTON

THE TRAFALGAR BOOKSHOP, 44 Trafalgar Street, Brighton BN1 4ED. 0273 684300. Mon-Fri, 10-6. Sat 5. Med/lg R/C/D stk av cal cnd and prices. Emphon Sports esp horseracing.

DEJA VU, 21 Walton Street, Brighton, East Sussex BN1 4ED. 0273 600400. Mon-Sat, 11-6. Med size spec in Occult and Esoteric. Ab av cal cnd and prices.

WAX FACTOR, 24 Trafalgar Street, Brighton. 0273 673744. Mon-Sat, 9.30-5.30. Record shop with some bks on pop music, the occult. Also pbks. NIMS too deafening.

COURTHOUSE BOOKSHOP, 181 Edward Street, Brighton, East Sussex BN2 2JB. 0273 600365. Mon-Sat, 10.30-4.30. Small R/C stk. Av cal cnd and prices

TALL STOREY'S, 88 St James Street, Brighton, East Sussex BN2 1TP. 0273 697381. Mon-Sat, 10-6. Med/lg R/C stk res D stk primarily left wing.

KEMPTOWN BOOKS, 91 St Georges Road, Brighton, East Sussex BN2 1EF. 0273 682110. Mon-Sat, 10.30-5.30. New bksp with small C stk. Emphon artistic. NIMS

HOLLEYMAN & TREACHER, 21A-22 Duke Street, Brighton BN1 1AB. 0273 28007. Mon-Sat, 9-5.30. Lg R/C/D stk av cal cnd and prices.

COLIN PAGE, 36 Duke Street, Brighton BN1 1AG. 0273 25954. Mon-Sat, 10-5.30. Med/lg R/C/D stk ab av cal cnd and prices. T.

N.F. BROOKES, 12A Queens Road, Brighton, East Sussex BN1 3WA. 0273 23105. Mon-Sat, 9.30-5.15. Sun 11-1.30. Lg R/C stk. Emphon remainders and foreign languages. Av cal cnd and prices.

BRISTOL

BRISTOL BOOKS,5 North Street, Bedminster, Bristol BS3 1EN. 0272 634716. Mon-Sat, 10-6. Small/med size R/C stk. Emphon pbks. Av cal cnd and prices.

BRISTOL BOOKS, 180B Cheltenham Road, Montpelier, Bristol BS6 5RB. 0272 245548. Mon-Sat, 10-6. Med size stk. Emphon pbks. Av cal cnd and prices.

THE WISE OWL BOOKSHOP, 26 Upper Maudlin Street, Bristol BS2 8DJ. 0272 262738. Mon-Sat, 10.30-5.30. Med/lg R/C stk. Emphon occult and Performing Arts. Av cal cnd and prices.

COTHAM HILL BOOKSHOP, 29A Cotham Hill, Bristol BS6 6JY. 0272 732344. Mon-Sat, 9.30-5.30. Med/lg R/C/D stk av cal cnd and prices. Emphon Art and Batsfords.

PATTERSON AND LIDDLE, 2C Chandos Road, Bristol BS6 6PE. 0272 731205. Mon-Sat, 10-6. Med size R/C/D stk av cal cnd and prices. Emphon Railways.

JOHN ROBERTS, 43 Triangle West, Bristol BS68 1ES. 0272 268368. Mon-Sat, 9-5. Med size R/C stk av cal cnd and prices. TWC.

UTA'S BOOKSHOP, 68 Park Row, Bristol BS1 5LE. ,0272 272996. Mon-Sat, 10-5.45. Small spec in acad pseud pbks av cal cnd and prices. NIMS.

GEORGE'S, 52 Park Street, Bristol BS1 5JN. 0272 276602. Mon-Sat, 9-5.30. Med/lg C/D stk ab av cal cnd and prices. Emphon Bibliography and Classics.

BRIXHAM

THE BOOK WARREN, 9A Bolton Street, Brixham, Devon. 08045 58531. Mon-Sat, 10-4.30. Clsd Wed in winter. Med size R/C stk av cal cnd and prices.

BROADSTAIRS

ALBION BOOKSHOP, 29 Albion Street, Broadstairs, Kent CT10 1IX. 0843 62876. Mon-Sat, 9.30-5.30. L 1-2. Lg R/C stk ave cal cnd and prices.

BROADWAY

STRATFORD TREVERS, 45 High Street, Broadway, Worcestershire WR12 7DP. 0386 853668. Mon-Sat, 9.30-5.15. L 1-2.15. Sun 2.15-5.30. Med/lg C stk ab av cal cnd and prices.

BROMLEY
See London.
BUNGAY
SCORPIO BOOKS, 1 Nethergate, Bungay, Suffolk NR35 1HE. 0986 5743. Thur, Fri, Sat, 10-1 & 2-5. Med size General stk spec in Aviation Military and Jazz. NIMS 5.
BURFORD, OXFORDSHIRE
THE COTSWOLD BOOKSHOP, High Street, Burford, Oxfordshire OX8 4QA. 099 382 3308. Mon-Sat, 9-dusk. Med size R/C stk av cal cnd and prices.
BURTON ON TRENT
THE NEEDWOOD BOOKSHOP, 55 New Street, Burton on Trent. 0283 41641. Mon-Sat, 9.30-5. V Rel. Med/lg R/C stk. Slightly Roast Beef Bookfairy, but well worth a look if you are in the area.
THE BRIDGE-END BOOKSHOP, 198 Bearwood Hill Road, Burton on Trent. 0283 46743. Mon-Sat, 9-5. Clsd am Thur. Med size R/C stk. Drif Special. Silverfish spec. Av prices
BURY ST. EDMUNDS
BURY BOOKSHOP, 28A Hatter Street, Bury St. Edmunds, Suffolk LF33 1NE. 0248 703107. Mon-Sat, 9.30-3. Rel. New bksp with med size R/C stk av cal cnd and prices.
BUXTON, DERBYSHIRE
HALL BANK BOOKSHOP, 9 Hall Bank, Buxton, Derbyshire SK17 6EW. 0298 70889. Mon-Sat, 10.30-5.30. Sun 2-4.30. BTR in winter. Med size R/C stk av cal cnd and prices. NIMS. NV. There is also another establishment in Buxton selling bks but NV either.
CAERNARVON
THE BALCONY BOOKSHOP, The Old Market Hall, Palace Street, Caernarvon, Gwynned, Wales. 0286 671152. Mon-Sat, 10.30-5. Winter 11-4.45. Clsd Thur. Med size R/C stk. Av cal cnd and prices. TWC.
CAISTOR, LINCOLNSHIRE
PLOUGH BOOKS, 19 Plough Hill, Caistor, Lincolnshire LN7 6UB. 0472 852073. Tues-Sat, 10.30-5. Sun 11-4. Med size R/C stk. Av cal cnd and prices. NV. NIMS.
CAMBOURNE, CORNWALL
VICTORIA GALLERY, 28 Gross Street, Cambourne TR14 8EX. 0209 719268. Mon-Sat, 10-5.30. Antique shop with med size R/C stk. BTA. NIMS. NV.
CAMBRIDGE
ALISTAIR AND GARON, 70 King Street, Cambridge CB1 1LN. 0228 62086. Mon-Sat, 9.30-6. Record shop with a small/med stk of R/C bks. Av cal cnd and prices. NIMS. NEB.
THE BOOKROOM, 13A St Elegius Street, Cambridge CB2 1HS. 0223 69694. Mon-Fri 9.30-5. Med size C stk. Av cal cnd and prices. NIMS mainly because I can never find the place.
C. DAVID, 3 St Edwards Passage, Cambridge CB2 3PJ. 0223 354619. Mon-Sat, 9.30-5. Rel. Med/lg C/D stk. Av cal cnd and prices.
THE HAUNTED BOOKSHOP, 9 St Edwards Passage, Cambridge CB2 3RJ. 0223 312913. Mon-Sat, 9.30-5.30. L 1-2. Med size C/D stk. Ab av cal cnd. Av prices. Emphon childrens.
GREEN STREET BOOKSHOP, 3 Green Street, Cambridge. 0223 67876. Mon-Fri, 9.15-5. Sat 9.30-4.30. Med/lg C/D stk. Emphon student acad. Ab av cal cnd and prices.
DEIGHTON BELL, 13, Trinity Street, Cambridge CB2 1TJ. 0223 353939. Mon-Sat, 9.30-5.30. Med/lg C/D stk. Ab av cal cnd and prices. Emphon lit bibliography, antiquarian and charm.

QUINTO, 34 Trinity Street, Cambridge. CB2 1TB. 0223 358279. Mon-Sat, 9-6. Med/lg R/.C stk. Av cal cnd and prices.
THE UNMAUDLIN BOOKSHOP, 12A Magdalene Street, Cambridge. 0223 62457. Mon-Sat, 10.30-6. Sun 2-5. Med size R/C stk. Av cal cnd and prices.

CANTERBURY

DAVID MILES, 37 Northgate, Canterbury, Kent CT1 1BL. 0227 464773. Mon-Sat, 10-5. Lg C/D stk. Ab av cal cnd and prices. Emphon childrens and ill.
BELL HARRY BOOKSHOP, 110 Northgate, Canterbury, Kent. 0227 453481. Wed, Fri & Sat, 10-5. L 1-2.15 sometimes. Med size R/C stk. Av cal cnd and prices.
THE CHAUCER BOOKSHOP, 6 Beer Cart Lane, Canterbury CT1 2NY. 0227 453912. Mon-Sat, 9.30-5.30. Med size R/C/D stk. Av cal cnd and prices.
STEPHEN THOMPSON, 7 Longport, Canterbury, Kent CT1 1TE. 0227 453013. Mon-Sat, 10-5. L 1-2.15. Med size R/C stk. Av cal cnd and prices.
PAUL HOLCOMBE, 5 North Lane, Canterbury CT2 7EB. 0227 457913. Mon 11-4. Tues clsd. Wed 10-4.30. Thur clsd. Fri & Sat, 10-5. Sun 12-4. Lg R/C stk. Emphon Scientific and Engineering. Av cal cnd and prices.

CARDIFF

CAPITAL BOOKSHOP, 27 Morgan Arcade, Cardiff CR1 2AF. 0222 388423. Mon-Sat, 10-5.30. Med/lg R/C stk. Ab av cal cnd. Av prices.
SECOND READING, Dickens Arcade, 9-11 Castle Street, Cardiff CF5 1FN. 0222 461404. Mon-Sat, 10-5.30. Med size R/C stk. Av cal cnd and prices. NIMS. NV owing to compilers incompetence.
ALBANY BOOKS, 206 City Road, Cardiff, Wales CF2 3JG. 0222 498802. Tues-Sat, 10-5.30. Med/lg R/C/D stk. Av cal cnd and prices. TWC.

CARLISLE

BOOKCASE, 17 Castle Street, Carlisle. 0228 445560. Mon-Sat. Med/lg R/C stock. Av cal cnd and prices.

CARMARTHEN

CARMARTHEN BOOKS, 1 St Mary's Street, Carmarthen, Dyfed. 0267 235462. Mon-Sat, 10-5. Clsd Thur. Med size R/C stk. Av cal cnd and prices. Keen on Welsh and Ill.

CARNFORTH

THE CARNFORTH BOOKSHOP, 38-42 Market Street, Carnforth, Lancashire LA5 9JE. 0524 734588. Mon-Sat, 9.30-5.30. Lg R/C stk. Av cal cnd and prices.

CARSHALTON

See London.

CARTMEL

PETER BAIN SMITH, Bank Court, Cartmel, Cumbria LA11 6QB. 044 854359. Everyday 11-6. Winter clsd Mon & Tues. Med/lg R/C stk. Keen on childrens bks.

CHANNEL ISLANDS

THESAURUS, 26 Burrar Street, St Helier, Jersey, Channel Islands. 0534 37045. Mon-Sat, 8.30-5.30. V lg R/C/D stk. Ab av cal cnd. Av prices. Bgns known. WAD. T&D. P poss (of aeroplanes only). NIMS. NV.
THESAURUS, 16 Tudor House, Mill Street, St Peters Port, Guernsey. 0481 202217. Mon-Sat, 10.30-5.30. Mon & Wed 1. Med size R/C/D stk. Av cal cnd and prices.
There are also some antiques shops with bks and pbks bksps.

CHARD

THE CHARD BOOKSHOP, 2 Pig Lane, Holyrood Street, Chard, Somerset. TA20 2AH. 0460 67046. Tues-Sat, 9.30-6. Small/med R/C stk. Av cal cnd and prices. Keen on Asia, Bookfairy. etgow. P poss.

CHELTENHAM, GLOUCESTERSHIRE

HEYNES BOOKSHOP, 49 Clarence Street, Cheltenham. 0242 515423. Mon-Sat, 10-5. Med/lg R/C stk. NSOC. Av cal. Ab av prices.

MICHAEL REYNER, 11 St Lukes Road, Cheltenham, Glos. 0242 512806. Thur-Sat, 10-5. Med size R/C stk. Emphon Cricket. Av cal cnd and prices.

ALAN HANCOX, 101 Promenade, Cheltenham, Glos. 0242 513204. Mon-Sat, 9.30-4.45. L 1-2.15. Rel. Wed 1. Med/lg R/C stk. Ab av cal cnd. Av prices. Keen on lit and arts.

CHEPSTOW, WALES

GLANCE BACK BOOKS, 17 Upper Church Street, Chepstow, Gwent. Phone unknown. Lg R/C stk. Av cal cnd and prices. NIMS. NV.

CHESTER

STOTHERT, 4 St Nicholas Street, Chester. 0244 40756. Mon-Sat, 9.30-5.30 L 1-2. Med size R/C stk. Av cal cnd and prices.

EARLS EYE BOOKS, B/15 Chester Market. 0244 319688. Mon-Sat, 10-6. BTA bookstall. NIMS.

CHICHESTER

THE CHICHESTER BOOKSHOP, 39 Southgate, Chichester, West Sussex PO15 1DP. 0243 785473. Mon-Sat, 9-5. Lg R/C/D stk. Av cal cnd and prices.

ST PETERS BOOKSHOP, St Peters Arcade, West Street, Chichester PO19 1QI. 0243 778477. Tues-Sat, 10.30-5.30 L 1.30-2.30. Small/med size R/C/D stk. Av cal cnd and prices.

CHILHAM

THE FORGE BOOKSHOP, The Street, Chilham, Kent. 0227 730267. Mon-Sat, 9.30-5.30. Small R/C stk. Av cal cnd. Keen on Gardening.

CHIPPING, SODBURY

BAILEY'S BOOKSHOP, 15 Horse Street, Chipping, Sodbury, Wilts BS17 6DA. 0454 513399. Mon-Sat, 9.30-5. Clsd Wed. Med size R/C stk. Av cal cnd and prices.

CHORLTON CUM HARDY, MANCHESTER

BRIAN BARLOW, 52 Beech Road, Chorlton Cum Hardy, Manchester M21 1EG. 061 9629646. Mon-Sat, 10-5.30. Ex Wed 1. Med size R/C stk. Av cal cnd and prices. Emphon pbks.

CHORLTON ON MEDLOCK, MANCHESTER

McGILL'S BOOKSHOP, 184 Oxford Road, Chorlton on Medlock, Manchester M13 8QQ. 061 2734736. Mon-Sat, 10.30-5.30. Med size R/C stk. Av cal cnd and prices. Emphon students bks.

CIRENCESTER

THOMPSON'S BOOKSHOP, Dunstall House, Park Street, Cirencester, Glos GL7 2BX. 0285 655239. Tues-Sat, 10-5. Med size R/C stk and spec Architecture stk. Ab av cal cnd and prices.

CLEETHORPES

PIK A BOOK, 203 Grimsby Road, Cleethorpes, South Humberside DN35 7HH. No phone. Mon-Sat, 10-5. Small R stk. Av cal cnd and prices.

LAFAYETTE BOOKSELLERS, 6 High Street, Cleethorpes DN35 8JN. 699244. Tues-Sat. R stk. Av cal cnd and prices. T.

CLEVEDON

CLEVEDON BOOKS, Cinema Building, Old Church Road, Clevedon BS21 5NN. 0272 872304. Tues-Sat. Clsd Wed 10.30-5.30. L 1-2.45. Med size R/C stk. Emphon Prints. Bl av cal cnd and ab av prices. NIMS. Out to Lunch.

There are rumours of a second newly opened shop in Clevedon, but no further details available.

COCKERMOUTH

WINKWORTH, 102 Main Street, Cockermouth, Cumbria. CA2 9LX. 0900 824984. Mon-Sat, 9-5. New bksp with med size R/C stk. Keen on local history. Av cal cnd and prices.

COGGESHALL

JOHN LEWIS, 35 Stoneham Street, Coggeshall, Essex CO6 1UH. 0376 61518. Med size spec stk. C stk of Maritime bks. NIMS. DT.2.

ELKIN MATTHEWS, 16 Stoneham Street, Coggeshall CO6 1TT. 0376 61730. Mon-Sat, 9-4.30. L 1-2. Clsd Wed. Med size C/D stk. Emphon childrens and ill. Ab av cal cnd and prices. WAD.

COLCHESTER

ALPHABET'S, 13 Trinity Street, Colchester, Essex CO1 1JN. 0206 572751. Mon-Sat, 10-5. Clsd Thur. Med size R/C stk. Bl av cal cnd. Ave prices. TWC.

GREYFRIARS BOOKS, 92B East Road, Colchester, Essex CO1 2QN. 0206 563138. Mon-Sat, 9.45-5.30. Med size R/C stk. Av cal cnd and prices.

CASTLE BOOKSHOP, 57 North Hill, Colchester, Essex CO1 1QR. 0206 577550. Mon-Sat, 9-5. V. Rel. Lg R/C/D stk. Av cal cnd and prices. TWC.

COLDSTREAM, SCOTLAND

A s/h bksp owned by GT Books of Edinburgh is about to open in Coldstream (August 1991). NFDA.

COLERAINE, NORTHERN IRELAND

THE IRISH DRIF SPECIAL*. Mac's Market, Railway Place, Coleraine. N Ireland 54024. Mon-Sat, 10.30-5.30. Med size R stock NSOC. Av cal and prices.

THE COLERAINE BOOKSHOP, 5 Stone Row, Coleraine, N Ireland. 0265 52557. Mon-Sat, 10-5. Clsd Thur. Med size R/C/D stk. Av cal cnd and prices.

COLNE, LANCASHIRE

S/h bksp in Colne. NV but alleged to be R/C stk slightly low key.

COLWYN BAY

BAY BOOKSHOP, 14 Seaview Road, Colwyn Bay, Clwyd LL29 8DG. 0492 531642. Mon-Sat, 9.30-5.30. Clsd Wed pm in winter. Med/lg R/C stk. Av cal cnd and prices.

COLWYN BOOKS, 66 Abergale Road, Colwyn Bay, Clywd LL29 7PP. 0492 530683. Mon-Sat, 9-5. Clsd Wed pm. Med size R/C stk. Av cal cnd and prices. TWC. P poss.

CONWAY

THE CONWAY BOOKSHOP*, 21 High Street, Conway, Gwynned, Wales LL26 0AA. 0492 592137. Mon-Sat, 10-6. Sun 11-1. Less in winter. Med size R/C stk. Av cal cnd and prices. TWC.

COTTINGHAM

THE COTTINGHAM BOOKSHOP, Cotta House, 169/171 Hallgate, Cottingham HU17 4BB. 0482 845567. Mon-Sat, 10-5. Med size R stk. Ab av cal cnd and prices.

COVENTRY

ARMSTRONG'S, 163 Sovereign Road, Coventry, West Midlands. 0203 714344. Mon-Sat, 10-5. L 1-2.30. Med size B&MC special. Av cal cnd and prices.

GOSFORD BOOKS, 116 Gosford Street, Gosford, Coventry, West Midlands CV1 5DL. 0203 20813. Mon-Sat, 10-5.30. Med size R/C stk. Av cal cnd and prices. Keen on Philosophy.

COWES, ISLE OF WIGHT

THE NEVER OPEN BOOKSHOP*, 65 High Street, Cowes, Isle of Wight. 0983 293598. Mon-Sat, 10-5. BTR. Med size R/C stk. Av cal cnd and prices.

CRANBROOK

THORNTON'S, The Street, Cranbrook TN17 2JD. 0580 712965. Apr-Oct, Tues-Sat, 11-6. Fri-Sat, winter 10-5.30. Med size R/C stk. Keen on Gardening. Av cal cnd and prices. NIMS Seasonal.

CRAYFORD, KENT

See London.

CREWE

COPNAL BOOKS, 16 Meredith Street, Crewe CW1 2PW. 0270 585622. Mon-Sat, 10-5.30. Med size R/C stk. Av cal cnd and prices. NV even though I spend half my life in Crewe I never seem to be there other than in the evening. I can however recommend the fish and chip by the station.

CRIEFF

STRATHERN ANTIQUES, 2 Comrie Street, Crieff, Perthshire PH7 4AY. 0764 4344. Mon-Sat, Ex Wed. Antique shop with BTA R/C stk but not worth visiting unless going to Crieff Cinema. NIMS.

CRIEFF CINEMA BOOKSHOP, High Street, Crieff, Perthshire, Scotland PH7 3AO. 0764 3673. Mon-Sat, 10-5. L 1-2. Lg R/C stk. Av cal cnd and prices. Rumoured to be closing down. NIMS.

CREWKERNE

COACH HOUSE BOOKS, 1 North Street, Somerset TA18 7AJ. 0460 74344. Mon-Sat, 10-6. Small spec C shop. Military History. Av cal cnd and prices.

OSCAR'S ANTIQUES, 13 Market Square, Crewkerne, Somerset. 0460 72718. Mon-Sat, 10-5. Unr Antique shop with med size R stk at D prices. NIMS. Not int enough.

THE BOOKSHOP, 17 Falkland Square, Crewkerne, Somerset TA18 7JB. 0460 76572. Tue-Sat, 10-5.45. Med size R/C stk. Av cal cnd and prices. A Drif Special.

CROMER, NORFOLK

BOOKWORMS, 9 New Street, Cromer, Norfolk NR27 9HF. 0263 515078. Mon-Sat, 10-5. Sun 2-5. Clsd Wed. Small/med size R/C stk. Ab av cal cnd. Av prices.

CROMFORD

SCARTHIN BOOKS, The Promenade, Scarthin, Cromford. DE4 3QF. 0629 823272. Mon-Sat, 10-6. L 1.30-2.30. Sun 12-6. Lg R/C nearly D stk. NSOC. No trade.

DARLINGTON

VOKES AND SON, 14 Bondgate, Darlington DL5 7JJ. Mon-Sat, 9-5.30. 0325 359790. Med size R/C/D stock. Av cal cnd and prices.

DAWLISH

THE OLD BOOKSHOP, Strand Hill, Dawlish, Devon. 0626 775177. Mon-Sat,10-5. Suns in summer. Med size R/D stk. Av cal cnd and prices.

DEAL

THE GOLDEN HIND, 85 Beach Street, Deal, Kent CT14 6JR. 0304 375086. Mon-Sat, 10-5.30. Sun 2-5.30. Med size R/C stk. Av cal cnd. Non av prices.

DEEPING ST JAMES

BRIDGE BOOKSHOP, 106 Church Street, Deeping St James, Peterborough PE6 8HE. 0778 343175. Mon-Sat, 10.30-5.30. Clsd Thur. Med size R/C stk. Av cal cnd and prices. Keen on local history.

DERBY

LAURA'S BOOKSHOP, 58 Osmaston Road, Derby DE1 3HZ. 0332 47094. Tues-Sat, 10-5.30. Clsd Wed. Med/lg R/C stk. Ab av cal cnd and prices. WAD.

DEVIZES

D'ARCY BOOKS, The Chequers, High Street, Devizes, Wiltshire SN10 1AT. 0380 726922. Mon-Sat, 10.30-5.30. Med/lg R/C stk. Ab av cal cnd and prices.

DINGWALL

DINGWALL ANTIQUES, 6 Church Street, Dingwall, Ross. IV15 9SB. This antique shop with bks has recently changed hands and was NV at time of publication.

DONCASTER

ATHENA BOOKS, 34 Imperial Crescent, Doncaster DN2 5BW. 0302 322913. Mon-Sat, 9-5. Med/lg spec in Military History. Ab av cal cnd. Av prices. TWC. P poss. NIMS spec.

DORKING

T.S HILL BOOKS, 122 South Street, Dorking, Surrey. RH24 2EU. 0306 886468. Mon-Sat, 10-5. Clsd Wed. Med size R/C stk. Av cal cnd and prices. TWC.

DOUGLAS, ISLE OF MAN

DON MULRYAN, 9 Duke Street, Douglas, Isle of Man. 0824 29660. Tues-Sat, 9.30-5. Clsd Tues. Med size R/C stk. Emphon local history. NIMS. NV.
There are also two antique shops with bks in Peel on the other side of the Island.

DRIFFIELD

THE DRIFFIELD BOOKSHOP, 21 Middle Street North, Driffield YO25 7SW. 0377 44210. Mon-Sat, 10-5.30. Thur 6.30. Fri 10-8. Med size R/C/D stk. Emphon Mod lit and S.F. Ab av cal cnd and prices.

DROITWICH

GRANT BOOKS, Victoria Square, (No no) Droitwich. 0905 778155. Med size spec in golf. Ab av cal cnd and prices. NIMS but does have some general bks.

DULVERTON

ROTHWELL AND DUNWORTH, 2 Bridge Street, Dulverton TA22 9HZ. 0398 23169. Mon-Sat, 10-5. L 1-2. Ex Thur. Med size R/C/D stk. Emphon hunting shooting and fishing.

DUNDEE

COLLECTORS CORNUCOPIA, 15 King Street, Dundee. 24946. Mon-Sat, 10-5. Clsd Wed. Med size primarily stamps with some bks and ephemera. Av cal cnd and prices. NIMS. NEB. See also Newport on Tay.

DUNKELD

DUNKELD ANTIQUES, Tay Terrace, Dunkeld, Perthshire PR8 0AD. 035 028832. Mon-Sat, 10.30-5.30. Sun 12-5.30. Med/lg antiques shop with BTA R/C bks. Av cnd. Ab av prices.

DURHAM

UNIVERSITY BOOKSHOP, 55/57 Saddler Street, Durham DH1 3ET. 091 3842095. Mon-Sat, 9.30-5. Med size R/C stk acad orientated. Av cal cnd and prices.

EAST GRINSTEAD

THE CAFE BOOKSHOP*, 27 High Street, East Grinstead RH19 3AW. 0342 322669. Mon-Sat, 9-5.30. New bksp with small low key R stk. Bl av cnd and prices. TWC. NIMS. Too small.

EAST LOOE

See Looe.

EAST MOLESLEY

See London.

EASTBOURNE

CAMMILA'S BOOKSHOP, 57 Grove Road, Eastbourne, East Sussex BN21 4TX. 0323 36001. Mon-Sat, 10-6. Lg R/C/D stk. Bl av cal cnd. Ab av prices.

RAYMOND SMITH, 30 South Street, Eastbourne, East Sussex. BN21 2PL. 0323 34128. Mon-Sat, 9-5.30. Clsd Wed. R/C stk. Av cal cnd and prices.

EDGWARE

See London.

EDINBURGH

BOOKFARE, 9 Victoria Street, Edinburgh EH1 2HG. 031 2259237. Mon-Sat, 10.30-5.30. Med size R/C stk. Av cal cnd and prices.

JAMES THIN, 53-59 South Bridge, Edinburgh EH1 1YS. 031 5566743. Mon-Sun, 9-10. Med size R/C stk. Av cal cnd and prices. Res stk of D bks.

GT BOOKS, 8 Drummond Street, Edinburgh. 031 5568032. Mon-Sat, 10-5. Med size shop with R/C stk but primarily remainders. Av cal cnd and prices.

PETER BELL, 68 Westport, Edinburgh EH1 2LD. 031 2290562. Mon-Sat 10.30-5.30. Med size C/D stk. Ab av cal cnd and prices. Emphon acad and female biography.

ARMCHAIR BOOKS, 72 Westport, Edinburgh EH6 8PD. 031 2251678. Mon-Sat, 10.30-5.30. Med size R/C stk. Av cal cnd and prices.

GRANT AND SHAW, 62 Westport, Edinburgh EH1 2LD. 031 2298393. BTR. Med size C/D stk. Av cal cnd and prices.

JAMES A. DICKSON, 12 Forest Road, Edinburgh EH1 2QN. 0312256937. Tues-Sat, 9.30-5.30. New bksp with spec stk of Religious bks. Av cal cnd and prices. TWC. NIMS. NEB.

McNAUGHTONS, 3A Haddington Place, Edinburgh, Scotland EH9 1HY. 031 5565897. Tues-Sat, 9.30-5.30. Med/lg C/D stk. Ab av cal cnd and prices.

TILL'S, 1 Hope Park Crescent, Edinburgh EH8 9NA. Mon-Fri, 12-7.30. Sat 11-6. Primarily film posters, otherwise a Book and Magazine C Special. NIMS not serious enough.

WESTPORT BOOKS, 151 Westport, Edinburgh, Scotland EH3 9DB. 031 2294431. Mon-Fri, 10.30-5.30. Sat 11-5. Med size R/C stk. Av cal cnd and prices. Emphon Music

ANDREW PRINGLE, 7 Dundas Street, Edinburgh EH3 6QB. 031 5569698. Mon-Fri, 9.30-5.30 L 12.30-1.30. Sat 10-1. Med/lg C/D stk. Ab av cal cnd. Av prices. Emphon lit and travel.

OLD GRINDLES, Spittal Street, Edinburgh ED3 0DY. 031 2297352. Mon-Sat, 9-9. Med size R/C/D stk. Av cal cnd and prices. Emphon lit. No trade discount.

CASTLE BOOKS, 204 Canongate, Edinburgh, Scotland EH8 8DQ. 031 5560624. Mon-Sat, 11-5. Sun in summer. Med size R/C stk. Av cal cnd and prices.

DUNDAS BOOKSHOP, 23A Dundas Street, Edinburgh EH3 6QQ. 031 5504591. Tues-Sat, 12-5.30. Med size R/C stk. Av cal cond and prices.

BROUGHTON BOOKS, 2A Broughton Place, Edinburgh EH1 3RX. 031 5531925. Mon-Fri, 12-6. Sat 10.30-5.30. Med size R/C stk. Av cal cnd and prices.

LATTON BOOKS, 3 Esksdie East, Mussleburgh EH21 7RU. 031 6653651. Mon-Sat 9-5. Wed 1. L 1-2. Med/lg R/C stk. Ab av cal cnd and prices.

EGHAM

See Englefield Green.

ELGIN

SPEY BOOKS, 105 High Street, Elgin, Scotland. Phone unknown. Hours unknown. Med size spec in Natural History and Scottish. Open Fri, Sat and Tues. BR. Elgin, OOS, turn left, turn right towards Church and attempt to walk straight ahead until you get to the second shopping street. Shop is upstairs. Nearest Aberdeen, Inverness. Blair Atholl. NIMS I have been there but I have not yet got in.

ELY, CAMBRIDGESHIRE

THE ELY BOOKSHOP, 11A St Mary's, Ely, Cambridgeshire CB7 4GS. 0753 681024. Mon-Sat, 10-3. Tues clsd. (longer in summer). Med size R/C stk. Av cal cnd and prices.

EMSWORTH

MARY HUBBARD, 10 South Street, Emsworth, Hampshire PO19 7EH. 0243 37794. Mon. Thurs-Sat, 10-5.30. Small R/C stk. Av cal cnd and prices.

THE BOOKSHOP, The Square, Emsworth, Hampshire PO30 7EJ. 0243 372617. Mon-Sat, 10-5.30. L 1-2.15. Clsd Wed 1. New bksp with small R stk. Bl av cal cnd and prices. NIMS too awful.

ENFIELD

See London.

ENGLEFIELD GREEN

BLACKLOCKS, 8 Victoria Street, Englefield Green, Surrey TW20 0JJ. 0704 434856. Mon-Sat, 9-5. Small R/C stk. Av cal cnd and prices.

EPPING

See London.

ETON

ETON ANTIQUE BOOKSHOP, 88 High Street, Eton, Berkshire SL4 6AP. 0753 855534. Mon-Sat, 10-5.30. Sun 12-6. Med size C/D stk. Av cal cnd. Ab av prices.

EVESHAM

BOOKWORMS, 81 Port Street, Evesham, Worcestershire. 0386 45509. Tues-Sat, 9.30-5. Med size R/C stk. Av cal. NSOC. Av prices.

EXETER

EXETER RARE BOOKS, 12A Guildhall Shopping Centre, Exeter. 0382 438021. Mon-Sat, 10-5. L 1-2. Med size C/D stk. Av cal cnd and prices.

DICKENS CENTENARY BOOKCASE, City Arcade, Fore Street, Exeter. 0392 431587. Mon-Sat, 10-5. Med size R/C stk. Av cal cnd and prices.

EYE, SUFFOLK

FAITH LEGG, The Guildhall Bookroom, Church Street, Eye IP35 7BD. 0379 870193. Fri-Sat, 10-5. Med size General stk plus spec in Embroidery and Crafts. NIMS 5.

FAKENHAM

THE TIN DRUM BOOKSHOP, 32 Oak Street, Fakenham, Norfolk NR21 9DY. 0328 864937. Mon-Sat, 10-6. Wed 1. Lg R/C/D stk. NSOC. Av prices.

FALMOUTH

BROWSER'S BOOKSHOP, 13 St George's Arcade, Falmouth, Cornwall. 0326 313464. Mon-Sun, 10-5. Med/lg R/C. Nearly D stk. Av cal cnd and prices. Keen on Nautical.

BOOKMARK, 94 High Street, Falmouth, Cornwall TR1 2AD. 0326 211252. Mon-Sat, 10-5. Rel. Med/lg R/C stk. Ab av cal cnd. Av prices. TWC.

TONY POWELL, 2 Old Brewery Yard, High Street, Falmouth, Cornwall. No phone. Mon-Sat, 10-4. Small/med size R/C stk. Slightly book and mag C. Av cnd. Ab av prices.

FARNBOROUGH

E.S. WICKS, 48 Peabody Road, Farnborough, Hampshire. 0252 544876. Mon-Sat, 9-5. Fri & Sat 5.30. Rel. Med/lg R/C stk. Av cal cnd and prices.

FARNBOROUGH BOOKSHOP & GALLERY, 28 Guildford Road, West Farnborough, Hampshire GU17 6PU. 0252 518033. Mon-Sat, 10-5. Med size R/C stk. Av cal cnd and prices. TWC. P poss. NIMS never open.

FARNHAM

BYGONES, 5A Castle Street, Farnham, Surrey GU9 7HT. 0252 737865. Tues-Sat, 10-5. Med size R/C/D stk. Av cal cnd and prices. TWC.

COBWEBS, 29 The Woolmead, East Street, Farnham, Surrey. 0252 734531. Mon-Sat, 10-5. Lg R/C stk. Ab av cal cnd and prices.

FAVERSHAM

THE FAVERSHAM BOOKSHOP, 1A Gatefield Street, Faversham, Kent ME13 8NX. 0795 532873. Mon-Sat, 10-5.30 L 1-2. Clsd Thur. No L Sat. Med size R/C stk. Av cal cnd and prices. Keen on Kipling.

FELIXSTOWE

THE TREASURE CHEST, 70 Hamilton Road, Felixstowe, Suffolk IP11 7AF. 0394 270717. Mon-Sat, 9-5.30. Med/lg R/C/D stk. Av cal cnd and prices. TWC

FOLKESTONE

G & D.J MARRIN, 149 Sandgate Road, Folkestone, Kent CT20 2DA. 0303 53036. Mon-Sat, 9.30-5.30. L 1-2.30. Med size R/C/D stk. Av cal cnd and prices. Emphon Local History and WW1.

FOWEY, CORNWALL

BOOKENDS, 4 South Street, Fowey, Cornwall PL25 1AR. 072 6833361. Mon-Sat, 9.30-6. L 1-2. Small/med size R/C stk. Av cal cnd and prices. NIMS. NV. There is also a rumour of another shop in this town.

FRAMLINGHAM

MRS. T. BELL, 19 Market Hill, Framlingham, Suffolk IP13 9BB. 0728 723406. Mon-Sat, 9.45-1, 2-4.30. Clsd Wed. Med size R stk. Av cal cnd and prices. T.

FROME

THE OLD CURIOSITY SHOP, 15 Catherine Hill, Frome BA11 1BZ. 0573 64482. Mon-Sat, 10-5. L 1-2. Clsd Thurs. Med/lg R/C/D stk. Roast Beef NSOC. Av prices. P poss.

GIGGLESWICK

OOST HORN BOOKS, Giggleswick (that believe it or not is the complete address). 072 923438. Tues-Sat, 10.30-5.30. Med

size R/C stk. Av cal cnd and prices. NIMS. NV.
See also Settle.

GLASGOW

COOPER HAY, 203 Bath Street, Glasgow G2 4HZ. 041 226 3074. Mon-Fri, 10-5. Sat 10-1. Med/lg C/D stk. Ab av cal cnd. Av prices.

CALEDONIA BOOKSHOP, 483 Great Western Road, Glasgow GT2 8EH. 041 3349663. Mon-Sat, 10.30-6. Med/lg size R/C stk. Ab av cal cnd and prices.

GILMOREHILL BOOKS, 43 Bank Street, Glasgow GI2 6NE. 041 3397504. Mon-Sat, 11-6. Med size R/C stk. Av cal cnd and prices.

VOLTAIRE & ROUSSEAU, 12 Otago Lane, Glasgow. GL1 7QI. 041 3391811. Mon-Sat, 11-6.30. Small R/C stk. Av cal cnd and prices.

ADAM'S BOOKS, 13 Battlefield Avenue, Glasgow. GL2 9HT. 041 6491314. Mon-Sat, 11-6. Med size R/C stk. Av cal cnd and prices.

WESTWORDS, 14 Newton Street, Greenock, Glasgow. 0475 892467. Mon-Sat, 9.30-5.30. Med size R/C stk. All Bl av cal cnd.

GLASTONBURY

DEJA VU, 17 High Street, Glastonbury, Somerset. 0272 600400. (Not Glastonbury). Mon-Sat 10.30-5. Seven days a week. Med size spec in Occult and Esoteric. Av cal cnd and prices. NIMS.

HADDONS BOOKSHOP, 30 Benedict Street, Glastonbury. 0458 31753. Mon-Sat, 9-5.30. Med size R/C stk. Av cal cnd and prices.

GLOSSOP, DERBYSHIRE

There is a fireplace shop in the High Street, which has a significant number of bks and a stall in the Antiques Market at the far end of the High Street. Both NV.

GLOUCESTER

QUAYSIDE BOOKSHOP, 2 Severn Road, Gloucester GL1 2LE. 0452 300422. Everyday 10.30-5.30. Med/lg R/C stk. Ab ava cal cnd and prices.

GODALMING

THE EUREKA BOOKSHOP, 19A Church Street, Godalming, Surrey GU1 1EL. 0843 426968. Mon-Fri, 10.30-3. Wed 1. Sat 10.30-5.30. Small R/C stk. Av cal cnd and prices.

NSF, 9 Queen Street, Godalming, Surrey. No phone. Mon-Sat, 10-4. Med size R stk. Emphon pbks. Av cal cnd and prices.

GOODRINGTON, PAIGNTON

BIDDY'S BOOKSHOP, 99 Dartmouth Road, Goodrington, Paignton, Devon. 0803 556151. Mon-Sun, 10-4.30. Much more in summer. Med size R/C stk low key. Good cnd. Av prices.

GOSFORTH

ARCHIE MILES, Beck Place, Gosforth, Cumbria CA20 1AT. 094 05792. Tues-Sat, 10-6. Sun 2-6. Med size C/D stk. Ab av cal cnd and prices. TWC.

GOSPORT

RICHARD MARTIN, 25 Stoke Road, Gosport, Hampshire PO12 1LS. 0705 520642. Tues-Sat, 10-5. L 1-2.15. Med size C stk. Emphon Maritime. Av cal cnd and prices.

GRAYS, ESSEX

KENDON'S (BOB GILBERT), 10 London Road, Grays, Essex. 0375 372187. (Home) Sats 9.30-5. Some Thur pm. Med size R/C stk. Av cal cnd and prices.

GREAT AYTON

THE GREAT AYTON BOOKSHOP, 17 High Street, Great Ayton, North Yorkshire. Tues-Sat, 10-5.30. Wed 2. Sun 2-5.30. Med size R/C stk. Av cal cnd and prices.

GREAT YARMOUTH

DAVID FERROW, 77 Howard Street South, Great Yarmouth NR30 1LN. 0493 843600. Mon-Fri, 9.30-5.30. L 1-2.30. Med/lg R/C/D stk. Av cal cnd. Ab av prices.

GREENOCK

See Glasgow.

GUERNSEY

See Channel Islands.

GUILDFORD, SURREY

THOMAS THORP, 170 High Street, Guildford GU1 3HP. 0483 62770. Mon-Sat, 9-5.30. Lg new shop with med size R/C stk which seem to be decreasing fast. NIMS see Guildford.

THOMAS TRAYLEN, 49-50 Quarry Street, Guildford GU1 3AA. 0483 572424. Mon-Sat, 9-5. Lg C/D stk. Ab av cal cnd and prices. Emphon roast beef. NIMS see above.

HADDINGTON

JEAN LAWSON, 3 Lodge Street, Haddington, Scotland. 062 0825851. Tues-Sat, 10-5. Clsd Thur. L 1-2. Small R/C stk. Emphon childrens. NIMS. NV.

HADLEIGH, ESSEX

THE IDLER, 71 High Street, Hadleigh, Suffolk. 0473 827752. Mon-Sat, 9.30-5.30. Wed 1. Small stk. Av cal cnd and prices. NIMS.

HALESOWEN

See Birmingham and West Midlands.

HALIFAX

THE COLLECTOR, 36 The Colonnade, Piece Hall, Halifax HX1 1RS. 0422 363893. Mon-Sat, 10-5.30. Clsd Wed, Thur. Open Sun pm. Med size spec in Military History. Ab av cal cnd. Av prices.

WEST RIDING BOOKS, 12 The Piece Hall, Halifax. No phone. Thur-Sun, 10.46-6. Med size R/C stk. Slightly low key.

THE SHOP FOR THE DERANGED LADDER CARRIER*, Piece Hall, Halifax. Phone unknown. Lg R/C nearly D stk. NSOC. Permanently expanding. Av prices.

HAMPTON, MIDDLESEX

See London

HANLEY

See Stoke on Trent.

HARBOURNE

See Birmingham and West Midlands.

HARPENDEN

BOOK CABIN, 379 Luton Road, Harpenden, Herts AL5 3NF. 058 2768581. Mon-Sat, 9.30-5. Med size C/D stk. Av cal cnd and prices. Emphon antiquarian. WAD.

HARROGATE

RIPON BOOKSHOP, 6 Station Bridge, Harrogate. 0423 501835. Mon-Sat, 10-5. Unr. Med size R/C stk. Roast Beef. Emphon Yorkshire. TWC. P diff.

THE HARROGATE BOOKSHOP, 29 Cheltenham Crescent, Harrogate. 0423 500479. Mon-Sat, 10-5.30. Rel. Med/lg R/C/D stk, solid roast beef, but with juniper sauce. Emphon music. WAD. Vetgow and v helpful.

J E COURTNEY, 5 Mount Parade, Harrogate. Tues-Sat, 0423 500341.10-5.30. Small C spec stk, emphon Maritime. Av cal, ab av cnd, av prices. TWC. P poss.

BOOKSTOP BOOKSHOP, 11 Mayfield Grove, Harrogate. 0423 505817. Mon-Sat, 10-5.30, Wed 1. Med size R/C stk, slightly lit. Keen on pbks, but worth a look. P poss.

HASLEMERE

THE HASLEMERE BOOKSHOP, 2 Causewayside, Haslemere, Surrey GU27 2JJ. 0428 52952. Mon-Sat, 9-5.15. New bksp with med size R/C stk. Av cal cnd and prices.

HASTINGS

HOWES BOOKSHOP, Trinity Hall, Braybrooke Terrace, Hastings, East Sussex TN14 1EG. 0424 423437. Mon-Fri, 9.30-5. Sat 9.30-1. V lg R/C/D stk. Ab av cal and cnd. Av prices. TWC.

JOHN WILBRAHAM, 16 George Street, Old Town, Hastings TN34 3EE. 0424 446413. Mon-Sat, 9.30-5.30. L 1-2. Clsd Wed. Rel. Med size R/C/D stk. Av cal cnd and prices. Emphon antiquarian.

OLD HASTINGS BOOKSHOP, 15 George Street, Hastings TN34 3EG. 0424 425989. Mon-Sat, 10-4. Clsd Wed. Med size R/C stk. Av cal cnd and prices.

TAMARISK, 80 High Street, Hastings, East Sussex TN34 3EL. 0424 420591. Mon-Sat, 10.30-5.30. L 1-2. No L Sat. Med size R/C stk. Emphon lit and music. Av cal cnd and prices.

See St Leonards.

HAVANT

BOOKENDS, 2 North Street, Havant, Hampshire PO9 1PR. 0795 470094. Mon-Sat, 9-5. Med size R/C stk. Av cal cnd and prices. TWC.

HAWES

KIT CALVERT, Market Place, Hawes, North Yorkshire. 0969 667667. Mon-Sat, 10-5. Sun 2-5. BTR in winter. Med size R/C stk. Ab av cal cnd and prices. NV.

HAY ON WYE

CASTLE BOOKS, 23 Castle Street, Hay on Wye HR5 5DF. 0497 820160. Mon-Sat, 9-6. Med size R/C stk. Av cal cnd and prices.

BOZ BOOKS, 13A Castle Street, Hay on Wye HR3 6AA. 0497 821277. Mon-Sat, 10-5. Med size C/D stk. Ab av cal. Av cnd. Ab av prices. Emphon Dickens.

RICHARD BOOTH'S BOOKSHOP, 44 Lion Street, Hay on Wye HR5 5AA. 0497 820322. Mon-Sun, 9-8. Lg R/C stk mainly low key. Low cnd. Ab av prices.

ADDYMAN BOOKS, 39 Lion Street, Hay on Wye HR3 5AD. 0497 821136. Mon-Sat, 10-6. Sun 12-6. Med size R/C/D stk. Av cal cnd and prices.

J. GEOFFREY ASPIN, 27 Castle Street, Hay on Wye HR3 5DF. 0497 820437. Mon-Sat, 10-5.30. Med size C/D bks. Ab av cal cnd and prices.

THE CHILDREN'S BOOKSHOP, Toll Cottage, Hay on Wye HR3 5EW. 0497 821083. Mon-Sat, 9-6. Sun. 5.30. Med size R/C stk slightly low key children's bks. Av cnd and prices.

HAY CASTLE BOOKSHOP, Hay on Wye HR3 5DL. 0497 820503. Mon-Sun, 10-5. Flavour of the month bookdealing.

THE HAY CINEMA BOOKSHOP, Castle Street, Hay on Wye HR3 5DF. 0497 820071. Mon-Sun, 10-6.30. V lg R/C/D stk. Bl av cal cnd. Ab av prices.

HAY ON WYE BOOKSELLERS, 14 High Town, Hay on Wye. 0497 820875. Mon-Sun, 9-5.30. Later Sun am. Lg R/C/D stk. Av cal cnd and prices.

THE POETRY BOOKSHOP, 22 Broad Street, Hay on Wye HE3 5BU. 0497 820305. Mon-Sat, 10-5.30 L 1-2. Med size spec in 20th

Century Poetry, the sort that only comes in bks an eighth of an inch wide. No thick stuff.

ROSE'S BOOKSHOP, 14 Broad Street, Hay on Wye. 0497 820018. Mon-Sun, 9.30-5.30. Sun 2.30. Med size R/C stk of childrens bks. Av cal cnd and prices.

MARK WESTWOOD BOOKS, High Town, Hay on Wye HR3 5AE. 0497 820068. Tues-Sat, 2.30-5. Med size C/D stk. Bookfairy. Emphon Science and Technical. Ab av cal cnd and prices. There are actually 18 shops in Hay on Wye. I burnt the other six entries as a token gesture. See MS.

HEBDEN BRIDGE

STAIRWAY BOOKS, 3 Albert Street, Hebden Bridge, HX7 8AH. 0422 845105. Mon-Sat, 11-5. Clsd Tues. Open Sun in summer. Med size R/C stk. Ab av cal cnd, av prices. T. NIMS. NV. Rumour of 2nd shop in Hebden Bridge.

HELENSBURGH

McCLAREN BOOKS, 91 West Clyde Street, Helensburgh, Glasgow. 0436 76453. Mon-Sat, 9.30-5.30. L 1-2. Clsd Wed. Med/lg spec Maritime stk. Ab av cal cnd and av prices. Also has good general stk.

HELMSLEY

RIEVAULX, 18 High Street, Helsley, North Yorkshire YO6 5AG. 0439 70912. Tues-Sat, 10.30-5.30. Sun 2-6. Med size C/D stk. Ab av cnd and prices. NIMS. NV.

HELMSLEY BOOKS, The Old Fire Station, Borogate, Helmsley YO6 5BN. 0439 70014. Mon-Sat, 10.30-5. Sun in summer. Med size R/C stk. Av cal cnd and prices. NIMS. NV.

HENLEY ON THAMES

THE ATTIC, 4 Station Road, Henley on Thames RG9 1AY. 0491 579107. Mon-Sat, 9.30-6. Sun 11-5. Med size R/C stk. Av cal cnd and prices.

RICHARD WAY, 54 Friday Street, Henley on Thames RG9 1AH. 0491 576663. Mon-Sat, 10-5.30. Med size R/C/D stk. Ab av cal cnd and prices. Emphon rowing.

HEREFORD

CHAPTERS, 17 Union Street, Hereford. No phone. Mon-Sat, 9-5. Sat 9.15. Med size Charity bksp with av cal cnd and prices.

THE HEREFORD BOOKSHOP, 24 Church Street, Hereford HR1 2LR. 0432 357617. Mon-Sat, 9.15-5.30. New bksp with upstairs room of R/C stk. Av cal cnd and prices.

PIERPOINT GALLERY, 24 Church Street, Hereford HR1 2LW. 0432 357617. Mon-Sat, 9.15-5.30. Med size R/C stk. Bl av cal cnd. Av prices.

HERNE BAY

PENDEES, 29 High Street, Herne Bay, Kent CT6 5LJ. 0227 374778. Mon-Sat, 9-5. Thur 1. Med size R/C stk. Bl av cal cnd. Av prices.

HERTFORD

OXFAM BOOKSHOP, 9 Station Road, Hertford. No phone. Mon-Sat, 10.30-4.30. Small R stk. Av cal cnd and prices.

CASTLE BOOKSHOP, 25 Castle Street, Hertford SG14 1HH. 0892 586537. Mon-Sat, 10-5. Clsd Thur. Med size R/C stk. Av cal cnd and prices. NIMS see Oxfam Hertford for explanation.

HEXHAM

HENCOTES BOOKS AND ANTIQUES, 8 Hencotes, Hexham, Northumberland NE46 0EJ. 0434 605971. Mon-Sat, 9.30-4.30. Thur 3. Med size low key R/C stk. Low prices.

HINCKLEY

THE READERS RETURN, 32-34 New Buildings, Hinckley, Leicestershire. 0455 61107. Mon-Sat, 10-5.30. Clsd Wed. Med size R/C stk. Bl av cal cnd, av prices. NIMS. NV.

HINDHEAD

BEACON HILL BOOKS, Beacon Hill Road (no no.), Hindhead, Surrey GU26 2AH. 0428 606783. Mon-Sat, 9-5. Med size R/C stk. Emphon Natural History. Primarily remainders. NIMS.

HITCHIN

ERIC T. MOORE, 24 Bridge Street, Hitchin, Hertfordshire SG5 2DC. 0662 450497. Mon-Sat, 9.30-5.30. L 1-2.15. Med/lg R/C stk. Av cal cnd and prices.

HOLT, NORFOLK

SIMON GOUGH, 5 Fish Street Hill, Holt, Norfolk. 026 3712650. Mon-Sat, 9.30-5.30. Med/lg C/D stk. Ab av cal cnd and prices. Emphon HSF.

HOLT, WALES

CASTLE BOOKSHOP, Castle Street, Holt, Clywd. LL13 9YW. 0829 270382. Mon-Sat, 10.30-6. Med size R/C stk. Emphon art. Av cal cnd and prices.

HOLYHEAD

ANGLESEY BOOKS, 1 Thomas Street, Holyhead, Anglesey, Gwynned LL65 1RR. 0407 760988. Mon-Sat, 10-4.30. Tues 1. Med size R/C stk. Ab av cal cnd. Av prices. Spec in mountaineering.

HONITON

BROCKWELL BOOKS, 174 High Street, Honiton, Devon. 0404 43460. Mon-Sat, 10-5.30. Med/lg R/C stk. Ab av cal cnd. Av prices.

G.M. WOODHEAD, 53 High Street, Honiton, Devon. 0404 42969. Mon-Sat, 10-5. L 1-2.15. L R stk. Bl av cal cnd. Av prices.

HORNCASTLE

JABBERWOCKY, 14 St Lawrence Street, Horncastle, Lincolnshire LN19 5BJ. 0507 522112. Mon ? Wed Sat 10-5. Med size R/C. Bl av cal cnd and prices.

TIM SMITH'S BOOKS, 12 North Street, Horncastle, Lincolnshire. 0507 527139. Mon ? Sat 10-5. Clsd Wed. Med size R/C stk. Av cal cnd and prices.

HORSHAM

THE HORSHAM BOOKSHOP, 4 Park Street, Horsham, West Sussex RH12 1DG. 0403 52187. Tues-Sat, 9.30-5.30. Med size R/C stk. Av cal cnd. Ab av prices.

MURRAY & KENNET, 102 Bishopric, Horsham, West Sussex. RH12 1QH. 0403 54817. Mon-Sat, 9-5.15. L 1.30-2.15. Clsd Thur. Med size R/C stk. Ab av cal cnd. Av prices. Emphon mod 1sts.

HOWDEN

New bksp with med size stks of R/C bks BTA cal cnd. Av prices. BR. Goole. OOS. Turn right towards town and turn right and bear right.

HUDDERSFIELD

ROBLINS, 18 Westgate, Huddersfield HD1 1NN. 0484 516793. Mon-Sat, 9.30-5.30. Med size R/C stk. Emphon pbks. B & MC. Av cnd and prices.

HULL

KAYE BOOKS, 15-17 Hepworth Arcade, Silver Street, Hull HU11 JU. 0482 26457. Mon-Sat, 10-4.30. Thur 3. Med size new shop with small stk of s/h. Av cal cnd and prices.

HUNGERFORD

BLAKEWAY BOOKS, 13 Bridge Street, Hungerford, Berkshire RG17 0EH. 0488 683581. Fri & Sat, 10-5. Also seems to be open most weekdays. Med size R/C stk. Av cal cnd and prices. NIMS.

HURSTPIERPOINT

CHIMERA BOOKS, 17 High Street, Hurstpierpoint BN6 9SB. 0273 832255. Mon-Sat, 9-5.30. Med size spec in Oriental Art. Ab av cal cnd and prices. NIMS spec.

HYTHE

THE OLD GALLERY BOOKSHOP, 125 High Street, Hythe, Kent. 0303 289339. Mon-Sat, 10-5. Med size R/C stk. Keen on Military History, local History and Transport.

ICKENHAM, MIDDLESEX.

See London.

ILFRACOMBE

FITZJOHN'S BOOKS, 44 Fore Street, Ilfracombe, Devon. 0271 866888. Mon-Sat, 10-5. Med size R/C stk. Emphon remainders. Av cal cnd and prices.

INVERNESS

HIGHLAND ANTIQUES, 15 Tomnahurich Street, Inverness, Scotland. 0463 231316. Mon-Sat, 10-5. Clsd Wed. Antique shop with BTA R/C stk. Emphon HSF. Av cal cnd and prices. TWC.

THE INVERNESS BOOKSHOP, 10 Bank Street, Inverness IV1 1QY. 0463 329947. Mon-Sat, 10-5.30. L R/C/D stk. Ab av cal cnd and prices. Emphon Scottish and lit.

IONA, SCOTLAND

THE IONA BOOKSHOP, The Old Printing House Building, Iona, Argyll, Scotland PA76 6SL. 068 17304. Shop open seven days a week in summer, by appointment in winter. I have tried several times to get to this shop but it is not poss to do it in less than 2 days. My dream is to have a photograph of myself taken outside it. I will have another go next year.

IPSWICH

CLAUDE COX, 3 & 5 Silent Street, Ipswich IP1 1TF. 0473 254776. Mon-Sat, 10-5. Clsd Wed. Med/lg R/C/D stk. Abav cal. Emphon Antiquarian and printing.

ISLE OF MAN

See Douglas.

ISLE OF WIGHT

See individual towns: Cowes, Newport, Ryde, St Helens, Totland, Ventnor, Yarmouth.

ISLEWORTH, MIDDLESEX

See London.

JERSEY

See Channel Islands.

JESMOND, TYNE & WEAR

See Newcastle.

KENDAL

KIRKLAND BOOKS, 68 Kirkland, Kendal, Cumbria. No phone. Mon-Sat, 10-5. Clsd Thur. Med size R/C stk. Av cal cnd and prices.

KESWICK

APPLEBY'S, 5 St John's Street, Keswick, Cumbria CA12 5AU. 07687 74054. Mon-Sat, 10-5. New shop with med size R/C stk. Av cal cnd and prices. Keen on cricket.

KING'S LYNN

THE DIAMOND BOOKSHOP, 1 The Diamond, King's Lynn, Norfolk. 0553 775230. Sats 11-3. Med size R/C stk. Av cal cnd and prices. Keen on music.

There is also a second more regularly open shop which has just moved.

KINGSBRIDGE

ROOM AT THE TOP, The Shambles, Market Arcade, Fore Street, Kingsbridge, Devon. 0548 856364. Mon-Sat, 9-4. Thur & Sat 12. Med size R/C/ nearly D stk. Av cal cnd and prices.

KINGTON

CASTLE HILL BOOKSHOP, 12 Church Street, Kington, Herefordshire HR5 3AZ. 0544 231195. Mon-Sat, 10-5.30. 2-5 Sun in summer. Med size R/C stk. Ab av cal cnd. Ab av prices. NIMS. NV.

ARROW BOOKS, 17 Duke Street, Kington, Herefordshire. 0544 230729. Mon-Sat, 10-5. Clsd Wed. Small/med R/C stk slightly roast beef. Av cnd and prices. BR. NIMS. NV recently.

KIRKBY LONSDALE

BECKHEAD BOOKS, 10 Beckhead, Kirkby Lonsdale, Cumbria LA6 2AY. 0468 71314. Mon-Sat, 10-5. Clsd Wed. Less in winter. Med size R/C stk. NSOC. Av prices. NV. NIMS.

KIRKALDY

BOOK ENDS, 449 High Street, Kircaldy, Scotland. 0592 205294. Tues-Sat, 10-5. Med size R/C stk. Av cal cnd and prices.

KIRKWALL

A & P STEADMAN, Unit 1 Halston Industrial Estate, Kirkwall, The Orkneys. 0856 5040. Mon-Sat, 9-4.45. Med size R/C stk. Emphon local History. NV.

KNIGHTON, WALES

THE BOOKSHOP, 2 Broad Street, Knighton LD7 1BL. 0547 520224. Mon-Sat, 9.30-5.30 Wed 1. Sat 4.30. New bksp with small low key stk of s/h. Av cnd and prices. NIMS. NV.

LAMPETER

WEST WALES BOOKS, Railway Hotel, Tregaron Road, Lampeter. 0570 423778. Mon-Sat, 10-6. Med size R/C stk. Av cal cnd and prices.

LANCASTER

ATTICUS, 26 King Street, Lancaster. 0524 381413. Mon-Sat, 10.30-5.30. Small/med R/C stk. Av cal cnd and prices. Emphon student acad bks.

McCORMACKS, 6 Rosemary Lane, Lancaster LA1 1NR. 0624 36405. Mon-Sat, 10-5. Clsd Wed. Med/lg C stk. Ab av cal cnd and prices.

LANCHESTER

THOMAS RARE BOOKS, 9 Station Road, County Durham DH7 0EX. 0207 529006. Tues-Fri, 1-5. Sat 9-5. Small stk. Ab av cal cnd and prices. Bookfairy. NV.

LANGPORT, SOMERSET

THE OLD BOOKSHOP, Bow Street, (No no.) Langport, Somerset TA10 8PQ. 0458 252644. Mon-Sat, 9-5.30. Small R/C stk. Av cal cnd and prices. ETF. NV.

LAUGHARNE

CORRAN BOOKS, King Street, Laugharne, Dyfed SA33 4SJ. 099 427444. Mon-Sat, 11-5, Sun 2-5 in summer. L R/C stk. Emphon Welsh Lit. Av cal cnd and prices.

LAVENHAM

R.G. ARCHER, 7 Water Street, Lavenham, Suffolk CO10 9RW. 0787 247229. Mon-Sat, 9-5. Sun 10-5. Med size R/C stk. Av cal cnd. NIMS.

LEATHERHEAD

BOOKWORM, 22 North Street, Leatherhead, Surrey KT22 7AT. Mon-Sat, 9.30-5.30. New bksp with small R/C stk. Av cal cnd and prices. It is not so much bookworm as silverfish. NIMS. Not good enough.

LEEK

THE LEEK BOOKSHOP, 76-78 Edward Street, Leek, Staffs. 0538 573591. Mon-Sat, 10-4. Clsd Thur. Med size R/C stk. Av cal cnd and prices.

THE VILLAGE BOOKSHOP, 17 Russell Street, Leek ST13 5JF. 0538 372092. Mon-Sat, 9.30-5. Thur 1. Med size R/C stk. Av cal cnd and prices.

There is another 3rd bksp in Leek, but none of the above have been visited. NIMS.

LEICESTER

CLARENDON BOOKS, 144 Park Road LE2 3AN. 0533 701856. Tues-Sat, 10-5. Sun pm. Med size R/C stk. Av cal cnd and prices.

BLACK CAT BOOKSHOP, Silver Arcade (No no.), Leicester. LE1 5FB. 0533 512756. Mon-Sat, 9.30-5. Med size R/C stk. Av cal cnd and prices.

FOREST BOOKS, 42 Silver Arcade, Leicester LE1 5FB. 0533 627171. Mon-Sat, 9.30-5. Med/lg R/C stk. Av cal and prices. Ab av int.

MAYNARD AND BRADLEY, 1 Royal Arcade, Silver Street, Leicester LE1 5XW. 0533 532712. Mon-Sat, 9.30-5.30. Sat 9. Med size R/C/D stk. Bookfairy. Emphon Local History.

TIN DRUM BOOKS, 68 Narborough Road, Leicester LE3 0BR. 0533 548236. Mon-Sat, 10-6. Med size R/C stk. Av cal cnd and prices. NIMS. Giopoc.

LEIGH ON SEA

LEIGH GALLERY BOOKS, 137 Leigh Road, Leigh on Sea, Essex. 0702 715427. Tues-Sat, 10-4.45. Med R/C stk. Av cal cnd and prices. TWC.

LEOMINSTER

MAINLY BOOKS, 7 School Lane, Leominster, Herefordshire HR6 8AA. 0568 5722. Mon-Sat, 9.30-6. Med size R/C stk. Av cal cnd and prices.

MINSTER BOOKS AND ANTIQUES, 4 Corn Square, Leominster, Herefordshire HR6 5AA. 0568 5397. Mon-Sat, 10-5. Small R stk in shop selling stamps. NIMS.

LETCHWORTH

DAVID'S BOOKSHOP, 7 Eastcheap, Letchworth, Hertfordshire SG6 3NF. 0462 686764. Mon-Sat, 9-6. Med size R/C stk. Av cal cnd and prices.

LEWES

A. J. CUMMING, 159? High Street, Lewes, East Sussex BN7 1KU. 0273 472319. Mon-Sat, 10-5. L 1-2. Med/lg C/D stk. Ab av cal cnd and prices. WAD.

15TH CENTURY BOOKSHOP, 99 High Street, Lewes BN7 1XH. 0273 474160. Mon-Sat, 10-5.30. Med/nearly lg R/C stk. NSOC. Ab av prices.

BOW WINDOWS BOOKSHOP, 128 High Street, Lewes. 0273 480780. Mon-Sat, 9-5. Med size C/D stk. Solid Roast Beef.

LEYBURN

WHITE BOAR ANTIQUES, Kirkgate, Middleham. 0969 23901. Mon-Sat, 10-5.30. Antique shop with BTA stk of R/C bks. Av cnd and prices. NV. NEB.

LEYLAND

GREAT GRANDFATHERS, 832 Towngate, Leyland, Lancashire PR5 1LR. 0772 622262. Tues-Sat, 9.30-5.30. Clsd Wed. Med/lg R/C/D stk. Av cal cnd and prices.

LICHFIELD

THE STAFFS BOOKSHOP, 6 Dam Street, Lichfield, Staffordshire WS13 6AA. 0543 264093. Mon-Sat, 9.30-5.30. L R/C/D stk. Ab av cal cnd and prices. Emphon childrens and ill. WAD. There is a second shop nearby - NV.

LINCOLN

READERS REST, 13-14 Steep Hill, Lincoln LN2 1LT. 0522 543217. Mon-Sat, 9.30-5. Some Suns. Med size R/C stk. Av cal cnd and prices.

ELIZABETH NELSON, Eastgate Antiques Centre, Eastgate, Lincoln. 0522 34816. Mon-Sat, 9.30-5.30. Med size C bks on collecting. Ab av.

HARLEQUIN, 20-22 Steep Hill, Lincoln. 0522 22589. Mon-Sat, 10.30-5. L 1-2.30. Med/lg R/C stk. Av cal cnd and prices.

LITTLEBOROUGH, GREATER MANCHESTER

GEORGE KELSALL, 22 Church Street, Littleborough, Greater Manchester DL15 9AA. 0706 70244. Mon-Sat, 10-5.30. Clsd Tues. New bksp with med size R/C/D stk. Ab av cal cnd and prices.

LIVERPOOL

HENRY BOON, 32 Berry Street, Liverpool. 051 7094501. Mon-Sat, 10-5. Med size R/C stk. Av cal cnd and prices

REID OF LIVERPOOL, 105 Mount Pleasant,Liverpool L5 5AT.051 7092312. Mon-Sat, 10.30-6. Med/lg R/C/D stk. Av cal cnd and prices.

HAZLEDEAN BOOKSHOP, 61 Renshaw Street, Liverpool LL1 2SJ. 051 7088780. Mon-Sat, 12-6. Totally Unr. The owner of this shop is not keen on D or writers and yet in the window were three bks by Mr. Iain Sinclair, who is both a bookdealer and a writer. I appear as a character in one of these bks. I was unable to work out whether I was welcome as a work of fiction, but not in reality.

THE OUT OF PRINT BOOKSHOP, 97 Renshaw Street, Liverpool L1 2FP. 051 7089700. Mon-Sat, 10-5. Med size R/C stk. Ab av cal cnd and prices.

LLANDLOES

THE GREAT OAK BOOKSHOP, 35 Great Oak Street, Llandloes, Powys SY18 6BW. 05512 2959. Tues-Sat, 10-6. Med size R/C stk. Av cal cnd and prices. Also sells tapes and records. NIMS. NV.

LLANDUDNO

DAVID HUGHES, 21 Madoc Street, Llandudno, Gwynned, Wales LL65. 0492 77700. Mon-Sat, 10.30-5. L 1-2.30. L R/C stk. Ab av int, bl av cnd. Ab av prices.

LLANRWST

PROSPECT BOOKS AND PRINTS, 18 Denbigh Street, Llanrwst, Gwynned, Wales LL26 0AA. 0492 640111. Mon-Sat, 9-5. Med size C/D stk. Av cal cnd and prices. Emphon HSF.

TOWN INDEX LONDON

London is defined as anywhere within the M25 orbital motorway. Please note that the areas are named after the most obvious location and not the official name; this means that it is called The Charing Cross Road and not Soho or Westminster.

ALDWYCH

THE ECONOMISTS BOOKSHOP, Clare Street, London WC2A 2AB. 071 4058643. Mon-Sat, 10-5. New bksp with small spec stk of s/h economics bks. Av cal cnd and prices.

ARNOS GROVE

DENIS CAINE, 343 Bowes Road, London N11 1AA. 081 3484888. Mon-Sat, 10-5. Med size R/C stk. Av cal cnd and prices.

BALHAM

MY BACK PAGES, 879 Balham Station Road, Balham SW12. 081 7694851. Mon-Sat, 10.30-7.30. Rel. Med/lg R/C stk. Av cal cnd. Emphon remainders. Av prices.
Now have shop in Tooting.

BAYSWATER

BAYSWATER BOOKS, 27A, Craven Terrace, London W2 3EL. 071 4027398. Mon-Sat, 11-7. Small General stk. Av cal cnd and prices.

BELSIZE PARK

VILLAGE BOOKSHOP, 41 Belsize Lane, London NW3. 071 7943180. Med size R/C stk. Av cal NSOC. Av prices.

BLACKHEATH

BOOKSHOP BLACKHEATH, 74 Tranquil Vale, Blackheath, London SE3 0BN. 081 8524786. Mon-Sat, 9.30-5. Med/lg R/C stk. Av cal cnd and prices.

STUDIO BOOKS, 2 Montpelier Vale, London SE3 1TA. 081 3189666. Tues-Sat, 11-6. Med/lg R/C stk. Av cal cnd and prices.

BLOOMSBURY

MARCHMONT BOOKSHOP, 39 Burton Street, London WC1H 9AL. 071 3877989. Mon-Fri, 11-6.30. Med size R/C stk. Av cal cnd and prices.

COLLINGE AND CLARKE, 13 Leigh Street, London WC1H 8EW. 071 3877105. Mon-Sat, 11-6.30. Sat 3.30. Med size C/D stk spec in Private Press. Emphon art and History. Av cal cnd and prices.

WORLD OF BOOKS, Bloomsbury Way (No no.), Adjacent Royal Hotel. Mon-Sat, 11-7. Newly opened R/C stk. Emphon History. Av cal cnd and prices. NFDA.

SKOOB 2 BOOKS, 15 Sicilian Avenue, London WC1A 2QH. 071 4043063. Mon-Sat, 10.30-6.30. L R/C stk. Av cal cnd and prices. Emphon acad text and lit.

DILLONS, 82 Gower Street, London WC2E 6EQ. 071 6361577. Mon-Fri, 9.30-7.30. Sat 5.30. L C/D stk acad orientated. Ab av cal cnd and prices.

ROBERT CONNELLY, 31/35 Great Ormond Street, London WC1N 3HZ. 071 4301294. Mon-Fri, 12-6. Small spec stk devoted to Medical and Scientific bks. Ab av cal cnd and prices. A consultancy rather than a general practioner.

FREW MACKENZIE, 106 Great Russell Street, London WC1B 3HA. 071 5802311. Mon-Fri, 10-6. Sat 10-2. Med size C/D stk. Ab av cal cnd and prices. Emphon antqrn, bindings and sets.

MUSEUM BOOKSHOP, 36 Great Russell Street, London WC1E 3PP. 071 5804086. Mon-Fri, 10-5.30. Sat 11-5.30. Med size spec in Archeology. Ab av cal cnd and prices.

GREAT RUSSELL STREET BOOKS, 44 Great Russell Street, London WC1B 3PA. 071 6377635. Tues-Fri, 10.30-5.30. Sat 12-3. Med size C/D stk. Av cal cnd and prices. Emphon antiquarian, prints.

FINE BOOKS ORIENTAL, 46 Great Russell Street, London WC1B 3PE. 071 8362865. Mon-Fri, 9.30-5.30. Med/lg spec in Middle East and Oriental. Ab av cal cnd. Av prices.

CHECK BOOKS, 31 Museum Street, London WC1A 1LH. 071 6375862. Mon-Sat 10.30-6. Sun 12-6. Med/lg C/D stk. Ab av cal cnd and prices. Emphon Travel, Art and Mod 1sts. TWC.

ULYSSES 40 Museum Street, London WC1 1LP. 071 8311600. Open as CHECK BOOKS opposite. About to open spec in Mod 1sts editions, ill and Private Press.

COLLETS CHINESE BOOKSHOP, 40 Great Russell Street, London WC1B 3PJ. 071 5807538. Mon-Sat, 9.45-5.30. New bksp with small s/h spec stk of Chinese bks. NIMS spec.

BLOOMSBURY RARE BOOKS, 29 Museum Street, London WC1A 1LH. 071 6366206. Mon-Sat, 10.30-6. Sun 12-6. Med size C/D stk. Emphon antiquarian and bindings. Av cal cnd and prices. TWC.

ATLANTIS, 48 Museum Street, London WC1A 1LE. 071 406 2120. Med size spec shop of Esoteric and Occult. Av cal cnd and prices.

VANBRUGH RARE BOOKS, 40A Museum Street, London WC1. 071 4040748. Mon-Sat, 10-5.30. Small spec stk of antiquarian and bks on wine. Ab av cal cnd. Av prices.

BALLANTYNE AND DATE, 38 Museum Street, London WC1A 1LP. 071 2424249. Med size C/D stk. Ab av cal cnd and prices. Emphon Industrial History and Art.

LOUIS BONDY, 16 Little Russell Street, London WC1A 2HN. 071 4052733. Mon-Fri, 10.30-6.30. Sat 10.30-5.30. Small C/D stk. Ab av cal. Av cnd and prices. Emphon Caricature, Miniatures.

SKOOB TWO, 19 Bury Place, Bloomsbury, London WC1A 2JH. 071 4050030. Mon? Sat 10.30-6.30. Med size R/C stk of Occult Acad bks. Ave cnd and prices.

DAVID MAYOU, 2 Pied Bull Yard, Bury Place, London WC1A 2JR. 071 4301227. Med size spec C/D stk Mod 1sts and Churchill. Ab av cal cnd and prices. Rumoured closing.

CENTRAL BOOKS, 37 Grays Inn Road, London WC1X 8PS. 071 2426166. Mon-Fri, 10-6. Sat 5. New bksp with small back room of left wing political lit. Av cal cnd. Ab av prices. NIMS too small.

GAY'S THE WORD, 66 Marchmont Street, London WC1N 1AB. 071 2787654. Mon-Sat, 11-7. Sun 2-6. Med size new bksp spec in Homosexual bks. Mainly new. V small s/h stk. NIMS.

There are now s/h bks in the basement of HOUSMAN'S in the Caledonian Road. King's Cross end.

BOND STREET

SARAH BADDIEL GRAYS TWO, Davies Mews, London W1. 071 4081239. Mon-Fri, 10-6. Small stall spec in golf. NIMS Spec.

CAISSIA BOOKS, A18/A19 Grays Antique Market, 1-7 Davies Mews, London W1Y 1AA. 071 6293644. Med sized spec in Chess. Ab av cal cnd and prices. NIMS Spec.

OFFSTAGE, 37 Chalk Farm Road, London NW1 8AJ. 071 4854996. Tues-Sat, 10-5.30. Sun 2-5.30. New bksp with v small theatrical stk. NIMS. D3.

TOSSIE STICKLE, 77 Regents Park Road, London. NW1. Mon-Sat, 11.30-5. Antique shop with small stk of s/h bks. Av cal cnd and prices. NIMS. D3.

BROMLEY

THE BROMLEY BOOKSHOP, 39 High Street, Bromley, Kent BR1 1LE. 081 3130242. Mon-Sat, 10-5. Med size R/C stk. Av cal cnd and prices.

CAMBERWELL

CAMBERWELL BOOKSHOP, 28 Camberwell Grove, London SE5 8RE. 081 7011839. Tues-Sat, 10-6. Med size spec in Art Reference and Design. Av cal cnd and prices.

CARSHALTON

THE COYDON BOOKSHOP, 304 Carshalton Road, London SM5 3QB. 081 6436857. Mon-Sat, 10.30-5.30. Med/lg R/C stk. Av cal cnd and prices.

CHALK FARM

WALDEN BOOKS, 38 Harmood Street, London NW1 8DP. 071 2678146. Thur-Sun, 10.30-6.30. Med size R/C stk. Av cal cnd and prices.

CHARING CROSS

REG & PHILIP REMINGTON, 18 Cecil Court, Charing Cross Road, London. WC2N 4HE. 071 8369771. Mon-Sat, 10-5. Med size spec in Travel and Topography. Ab av cal cnd and prices.

PLEASURES OF PAST TIMES, 11 Cecil Court, Charing Cross Road, London. 071 8361142. Mon-Fri, 11-5.45. L 2.30-3.30. Med size spec in Performing Arts. Ab av cal cnd and prices.

MARCHPANE, 16 Cecil Court, London WC2N 4HE. Mon-Sat, 11-7. Med size spec in childrens bks. Av cal cnd and prices.

H.M. FLETCHER, 27 Cecil Court, Charing Cross Road, London WC2H 4EZ. 071 8362865. Mon-Fri, 10-5. Med size R/C/D stk. Av cal cnd and prices. TWC.

ANN CREED, 22 Cecil Court, Charing Cross Road, London WC2N 4HE. 071 6367757. Mon-Sat, 10-7. Rel. Med/lg spec in Art Reference & Design. Ab av cal cnd and prices.

THE CLEARING HOUSE, 10 Cecil Court, Charing Cross Road, London WC2N 4HE. No phone. Mon-Sun, 9-9. Med size R/C stk all £1.50 each.

WATKINS, 10-21 Cecil Court, Charing Cross Road, London WC2N 4EZ. 071 8362182. Mon-Sat, 10-6. Med size new bksp with spec stk of s/h Occult and Esoteric. Av cal cnd and prices.

FRANCES EDWARDES, 13 Great Newport Street, London WC2H 7JA. 071 3797669. Mon-Sat, 10.30-7. Med size spec in Military History. Av cal. Bl av cnd. Ab av prices.

DANCE BOOKS, 9 Cecil Court, Charing Cross Road, London WC2N 4EZ. 071 836 2314. Mon-Sat, 11-7. Med size spec in Dance, but I have never worked out which are the s/h bks.

E.C NOLAN, 1 Cecil Court, Charing Cross Road, London WC2N 4EZ. 071 4972328. Small spec stk BTR in basement of print dealers. NIMS excuse 2.

ZENO, 6 Denmark Street, London WC2H 8LP. 071 836 2522. Mon-Sat, 9.30-5.30. Sat 5. Med size spec in Greek bks. NIMS.

ALAN BRETT, 24 Cecil Court, London WC2 4HE. 071 8368222. Mon-Fri, 9.30-5. Sat 9-5. Med sized spec in prints and ill bks. Libricide. NIMS Spec.

BELL BOOK AND RADMELL, 4 Cecil Court, Charing Cross Road, London WC2M 4HE. 071 8365888. Mon-Fri 10-5.30. Med size spec in mod 1sts. Ab av cal cnd and prices. NIMS Spec.

PORDES, 58-60 Charing Cross Road, London WC2H 0BB. 071 8369031. Mon-Sat 10-7. Med size R/C stk. Av cal cnd and prices. Emphon remainders.

SHIPLEY, 70 Charing Cross Road, London WC2H 0BB. 071 8964872. Mon-Sat. Claim to be a s/h Art dealer, but I have never been able to work out which are the s/h bks. NIMS.

THE TRAVELLERS BOOKSHOP, 23 Cecil Court, Charing Cross Road, London WC2N 4EZ. 071 8369152. Mon? Sat 10-6.30. Med size spec in Baedeckers. Ab av cal cnd and prices.

ANY AMOUNT OF BOOKS, 62 Charing Cross Road, London WC2H 0BB. 071 240 8140. Mon-Sat, 10.30-7.30. Med size R/C/D stk. Av cal cnd and prices.

ADELAIDE BOOK CENTRE, 9 Adelaide Street, London WC2. 071 8366502. Mon-Sun, 12-8. Med size R/C stk. Bl av cal cnd. Ab av prices.

PAUL HILTON, 14 Cecil Court, Charing Cross Road, London W2N 4EE. Phone unknown. Mon-Sat, 10-7. Med size R/C/D stk. Av cal cnd and prices. Emphon lit.

TRAVIS & EMERY, 17 Cecil Court, London WC2N 4EZ. 071 2402129. Mon-Fri, 10-6. Sat 1. Rel. Med size spec in classical music. Ab av cal cnd and prices.

MURDER ONE, 71-73 Charing Cross Road, London WC2. 071 4972210. Mon-Sat, 10-7. New bksp with lg spec stk of True crime and detective fiction. Ab av cal cnd and prices.

CHEAM

THE WHITEHALL BOOKSHOP, 45 The Broadway, Cheam, Surrey. 081 6438272. Med size R/C stk. Av cal cnd and prices. Recently changed hands and already much improved.

CHISWICK

FAIRCROSS BOOKS, 166 Thames Road, Strand On The Green, London W4. 081 9941912. Mon-Sun, 10.30-5.30. Med size R/C stk in Antiques shop. Ab av cal cnd and prices for antique shop.

W. FOSTER, 183 Chiswick High Road, London W4. 081 9952768. Mon-Sat, 10.30-5.30. Med size R/C/D stk. Ab av cal cnd. Av prices. Trade discounts over £50.00.

THE CITY

WILDY AND SON, Lincoln's Inn Archway, Carey Street, London. WC2A 3JD. Mon-Fri, 8.45-5.15. 071 2425778. Spec shop of Law bks. Ab av cal cnd. Av prices. NIMS.

CLARKE HALL, 7 Bride Court, Bride Lane EC4Y 8DU. 071 3534116. Mon-Fri, 10.30-6.30. Med size R/C/D stk. Av cal cnd and prices. Emphon Mod 1sts. ill and Samuel Johnson.

ASH RARE BOOKS, 25 Royal Exchange, London EC3V 3LP. 071 6262665. Mon-Fri, 10-5.30. Small C stk. Ab av cal cnd and prices. Emphon prints.

FARRINGDON ROAD BOOKSTALLS, London EC1. Mon-Fri, 11-3. Sat 10-12. The Legend lives. Tube: Farringdon Road, OOS, turn right and right.

COVENT GARDEN

BERTRAM ROTA, 9-11 Langley Court, Long Acre, London WC2H 9RX. 071 8360723. Mon-Fri, 9.30-5.30. Med size spec in Mod 1sts and lit. Ab av cal cnd and prices.

CRAYFORD

DARTFORD HEATH BOOKS, Farm Buildings, Maiden Lane, Crayford, Kent. 0322 550601. Thur & Fri only. 10.30-5. Small R/C stk. Emphon archaeology. NIMS. Not open enough.

CROUCH END

CROUCH END BOOKSHOP, 60 Crouch End Hill, London N8 8AG. 081 3488968. Mon-Sat, 9-6. New bksp with small R/C stk. Av cal cnd and prices.

EALING

G.L. GREEN, 104 Pitshanger Lane, London W5 1QX. 081 9946454. Wed-Sat, 10-5. Spec in Maritime bks. Ab av cal cnd and prices. NIMS Spec.

EARLS COURT

RESPONSE, 300 Brompton Road, London SW5 9JE. 071 3704606. Mon-Sat, 12. 7. Small R stk. Bl av cal cnd. Ab av prices. No T.

EARLSFIELD

BOOKCELLAR, 404 Garret Lane, Earlsfield, London SW18. 081 9446458. Mon-Sat, 10-6. Med size R/C stk slightly remaindery. Av cal cnd and prices. TWC.

EAST MOLESEY

THE MOLE BOOKSHOP, 81 Walton Road, East Molesey, Surrey KT8 0DP. 071 4813467. Sats only. Med size R/C stk. Av cal cnd and prices.

BROWSERS, 74 Walton Road, East Molesey, Surrey. 081 9783565. Tues-Sat, 10-5. Clsd Wed. Small R stk. Av cal cnd and prices.

EDGWARE

THE TWO JAYS, 14 Whitchurch Lane, Middlesex. HA6 6JZ. 081 9521349. Tues, Wed, Fri, Sat, 10-5. Med size R/C/D stk. Av cal cnd and prices.

ELEPHANT AND CASTLE

MY BACK PAGES, Elephant and Castle Shopping Centre, London. SE1. 081 7694851. Mon-Sat, 10.30-6.30. Med size R/C stk. Emphon pbks. Av cal cnd and prices.

ENFIELD

THE ENFIELD BOOKSHOP, 36 Gordon Road, Enfield, Middlesex EN2 0AN. Tues-Sat, 10-5. Clsd Thurs. Med size R/C stk. Av cal cnd and prices.

LISA MATTHEWS, 213 Garret Lane, Wandsworth, London SW18 4DS. 081 877 0783. Med size R/C stk. Emphon detective fiction. Av cal. NSOC. Adventurous prices.

EPPING

BROWSERS BOOKSHOP, 9 Station Road, Epping, Essex CM16 4HA. 081 5084086. Mon, Tues, Fri, Sat 10-5. Med size R/C stk. Ab av cal cnd and prices.

EUSTON

FLINDERS, 10 Woburn Walk, London WC1H 0JL. 071 3886080. Mon-Fri. Med size spec in Australiana. Av cal cnd and prices. NIMS. 4. Spec shop. There is not much I can say about spec shops unless they are really bad. As I know nothing about Australia, I am in no position to comment.

FINCHLEY

MANOR HOUSE BOOKS, 80 East End Road, London N20 8HR. 071 4454293. Mon-Thurs, 10-4. Sun 10-2. New bksp with small spec stk of Judaica. Ab av cal cnd. Av prices. NIMS. NV.

FRIERN BARNET

THE HISTORY BOOKSHOP, 2 The Broadway, Freirn Barnet Road, London N11. 081 3618326. Now by appointment only. NIMS.

FULHAM

THE CONSTANT READER, 627 Fulham Road, London SW6 5DQ. 071 7310218. Mon-Sat, 10.30-6.30. Med/lg R/C stk. Av cal cnd not av prices. TWC.

GLOUCESTER ROAD

THE GLOUCESTER ROAD BOOKSHOP, 123 Gloucester Road, London SW7 4TS. 071 3703503. Mon-Fri, 8.30-10.30. Sat & Sun 10.30-6.30. Lg R/C stk. Av cal cnd and prices.

GREENWICH

MARITIME BOOKS, 23 Nelson Road, London SE10 9JB. 081 8531727. Mon-Sat, 10-6. Med size spec in Maritime bks. Ab av cal cnd and prices.

ROGERS TURNER, 27 Nelson Road, London SE10. 081 8531727. Mon-Sat, 10-6. Med size C/D stk spec in Clocks, Science and German. Ab av cal cnd and prices.

MARCET BOOKS, 4A Nelson Road, London. SE10. 081 8535408. Mon-Sun 10.30-5.30. Med size R/C stk. Emphon Maritime. Av cal cnd and prices.

SOUTH LONDON BOOKCENTRE, 18-19 Stockwell Street, Greenwich, London SE10. 081 2532151. Wed, Thur, 10-6. Sat & Sun, 9-5. Rel. Lg R/C stk mini bookfair. Av cal cnd and prices.

SPREAD EAGLE BOOKS, 8 Nevada Street, Greenwich, London SE10. 081 305 1666. Mon-Sun, 10.30-5. L 1-2.30. Med size R/C stk. Av cal cnd and prices.

HACKNEY

ARCADY, 59 Wilton Way, Hackney, London E8. Thur-Sat, 11-6. Sun 3-6. Med size R/C stk. Av cal cnd and prices. Keen on entertainment.

HAMPSTEAD

KEITH FAWKES, 1-3 Flask Walk, Hampstead, London NW3. 071 436 0614. Mon-Sat, 10-5.30. Med size R/C stk. Av cal cnd and prices.

HAMPTON

IAN SHERIDAN, 34 Thames Street, Hampton, Middlesex. 081 9791704. Mon-Sun,10-7. Lg R/C stk. NSOC. Av cal. Over av prices.

HAMPTON CHARITY BOOKSHOP, Hampton Station, Middlesex. No phone. Mon-Sun, 10-4. Small R stk. Av cal cnd and prices.

HIGHBURY

G.W WALFORD, 15, Calabria Road, Highbury Fields, London N5 1JB. 071 226 5682. Suffers from The William Rees Mogg syndrome you can only go in if you are the right sort of customer and no indication is given about how you learn to be the right sort of customer. Needless to say they are proud members of the ABA.

HIGHBURY CORNER

FANTASY CENTRE, 157 Holloway Road, London N7 8LX. 071 6079433. Mon-Sat, 10-6. Sat 5. Med size spec in SF and Weird Fiction. Ab av cal cnd and prices.

HIGHGATE

FISHER AND SPERR, 46 Highgate High Street, London. N6 5JH. 071 3807244. Mon-Sat, 10.30-5.30. L 1-2. Med/lg R/C/D stk. Av cal cnd. Ab av prices.

RIPPING YARNS, 355 Archway Road, Highgate, London N6. 071 341 6111. Mon-Sat, 10.30-5.30. Sat 5. Sun 11-4. Med/lg R/C stk. Av cal. NSOC. Ab av prices.

BONAVENTURE, 259 Archway Road, Highgate, London N6 5BS. 071 3412545. Wed-Sat, 10.30-6. Med size R/C stk. Av cal. NSOC. Av prices.

HOLLAND PARK

BERNARD SHAPERO, 80 Holland Park Avenue, London W11 3RE. 071 4930876. Mon-Fri, 10-7. Sat 6. Lg C/D stk. Ab av cal cnd and prices. Emphon plate bks.

ICKENHAM

THE HAYES BOOKSHOP, 6 Glebe Avenue, Ickenham, Middlesex. UB10 8FB. 08956 37725. Mon-Sat, 9.30-5.30. Med size R/C stk. Ab av cal cnd. Bl av prices.

ILFORD

TERRY'S, 26 Chapel Road, Ilford, Essex IG1 2AH. 081 4782850. Mon-Sat, 10-4. Wed 2. Clsd Thur. Small R/C stk primarily pbks. Av cal cnd. Ab av prices.

ISLEWORTH

CHATOR'S MOTORING BOOKSELLER, 8 South Street, Isleworth, Middlesex. 081 5495144. Mon-Sat 9-5.30. Wed 1. Med size spec in motoring. New & s/h. Bl av cal cnd. Av prices.

ISLINGTON

BOUTLE & KING, 23 Arlington Way, London EC1R 1UY, 071 278 4497. Mon-Sat, 10.30-6. Med size R/C/D stk, av cal, cnd & prices. Keen on Lefties.

UPPER STREET BOOKSHOP, 182 Upper Street, London N1 1RQ. 071 3593785. Tues-Sat, 10-6. Med size R/C stk. Emphon Architecture and Entertainment.

KEW GARDENS

LLOYDS, 9 Mortlake Terreace, Kew TW9 3DT. 081 9403512. Mon-Sat, 10-5.30. Clsd Wed. Spec. Gardening bksp with med size General stk. Av cal cnd and prices.

KING'S ROAD

THORNTON'S, 634 Kings Road, London SW6. 071 7366181. Mon-Sat, 10-5.45. Med/lg R/C/D stk. Av cal cnd and prices. Emphon Religious bks.

CHELSEA RARE BOOKS, 313 Kings Road, London SW3 5EP. 071 3510950. Mon-Sat, 10-6. Med size C/D stk. Ab av cal cnd and prices.

HARRINGTON BROTHERS, 253 Kings Road, London SW3 5EL. 071 8233449. Mon-Sat, 10-6. Lg C/D stk Plate bks, Voyages Natural History, Sets.

BARBARA STONE, Antiquarius, 135 Kings Road, London SW3 4PW. 071 3510963. Mon-Sat, 10.30-5.30. Lg stall childrens and ill bks. Ab av cal cnd and prices.

KINGSTON

DERRICK NIGHTINGALE, 32 Coombe Road, Kingston. KT2 7AQ. 081 5495144. Mon-Sat, 9.30-5.30. Wed 9. Med size R/C/D stk. Av cal cnd and prices. Emphon lit.

KNIGHTSBRIDGE

The Old Newspaper and Ephemera Shop, 37 Kinnerton Street, London SW1X 8ED. 071 2357788. Mon-Fri, 10-5. Thurs 8. Rel. Spec in ephemera.

MARBLE ARCH

HOSAIN'S, 25 Connaught Street, London W2 2AY. 071 2627900. Tues-Fri, 10.30-5.30. Sat 1.030-1. Med size spec Indian and Middle Eastern travel bks. Av cal cnd and prices.

MARYLEBONE

SPCK, Holy Trinity Church, Marylebone Road, London. NW1 4DU. 071 3875282. Mon-Thur, 9-5.30. Fri. 5. Rel. V lg spec stk of Theology. Ab av cal cnd. Av prices. Tube Great Portland Street, OOS opp.

THE BOOKING HALL, 7 Charlotte Place, London W1 1AQ. 071 2552123. Mon-Fri, 11-7, Sat 10-5. Small spec in Railway lit. NIMS. NOB.

STEPHEN FOSTER, 95 Bell Street, London NW1 6TB. 071 7240876. Tues-Sat, 10.30-6. Rel. Med size R/C/D stk. Av cal cnd and prices.

BIBLIOPOLA, Alfie's Antiques Market, 13-25, Church Street, London. NW8. 071 7247231. Tues-Sat, 10-6. Med size spec in Antiquarian, childrens and ill. Ab av cal cnd and prices.

ARCHIVE BOOKSTORE, 63 Bell Street, London NW1 6TB. 071 4028212. Med size R/C stk. Av cal cnd. Ab av prices. Emphon antiquarian and sheet music.

MAYFAIR

MAGGS BROS., 50 Berkeley Square, London W1X 6EL. 071 4934160. Mon-Fri, 9.30-5. Lg C/D stk. Ab av cal cnd and prices. Military History, Antiquarian, English Lit, Autographs and Letters. Fine bindings. Ill bks. Not a bksp, more a collection of superlatives. Heavy men, in heavy overcoats, spending heavy money in a heavy atmosphere.

SOTHERANS, 3-5 Sackville Street, London W1 2DP. 071 7340308. Mon-Fri, 9.30-5.30. Sat am. V Rel. Lg C/D stk. Ab av cal cnd and prices. WAD. T ABA only.

M & R GLENDALE, 9A New Cavendish Street, London W1M 7RN. 071 4875348. Mon-Fri, 10-6. Med size C/D stk. Emphon Juvenile, entertainment, games. Ab av cal cnd and prices. TWC.

HEYWOOD HILL, 10 Curzon Street, Mayfair, London W1Y 7FJ. 071 6290674. Mon-Fri, 9.30-5.30. Sat 9-12.30. Med size R/C/D stk. Av cal cnd and prices.

Newly opened THE QUEEN STREET BOOKSHOP, Mayfair. Adjacent to HEYWOOD HILL. Mon-Fri, 10-5. Upmarket C shop. Libricide. Leatherwear and Plate bks. Ab av cnd and cal.

NOTTING HILL GATE

MUSIC AND VIDEO EXHANGE BOOKSHOP, 56 Notting Hill Gate, London W11. 071 2298420. Mon-Sun, 10-8. Med size R/C stk. Av cal cnd and prices.

NOTTING HILL BOOKS, 132 Palace Gardens Terrace, London W8. 071 7275988. Mon-Sat, 10.15-6. Thur 1. New bksp with small R/C stk. Av cal cnd and prices. NIMS. Too small.

MELLOR & BAXTER, 121 Kensington Church Street, London W8 7LP. 071 2292033. Med size C/D stk of leatherwear and bindings. Av cal cnd and prices.

OSTERLEY

THE OSTERLEY BOOKSHOP, 168A Thornbury Road, Osterley, London TW7 4QE, 081 5606206. Mon-Sun, 10.30-5.30, Sun 4.45. Med size R/C stk av cal, cnd prices. No T.

PIMLICO

BOOKS OF ASIA, 47 Moreton Street, London. SW1V 2NY. 071 8216544. Tues-Sat, 10-6. Med/lg spec stk. India, South East Asia, Middle East and the Pacific. Ab av cal cnd and prices.

PORTOBELLO ROAD

The following bookstalls open on a Sat only. The phone numbers are home phone numbers. The order in which they are listed is the best order in which to visit them all.

S. BILTCLIFFE, 289 Portobello Road, W11. 071 7405326.

KAY BOOKS, 291 Westbourne Grove, London W11. 071 6407779.

D. ALTMAN, 291 Westbourne Grove, London W11. 071 6377635.

B. BAILEY, 113 Portobello Road, London W11. 071 2291629.

FEM POEL, 113 Portobello Road, London W11. 071 7312736.

DEMETZY BOOKS, 113 Portobello Road, W11. 0993 702209.

R. BARKER, 284 Westbourne Grove, London W11. 0716724024.

L. CHRISTIE, 282 Westbourne Grove, London W11. 071 6724024.
H. TRUSCOTT, 139 Portobello Road, London W11. 0403 730554.
BOOKS AND THINGS, 157 Portobello Road, W11. 071 3705593.
J. LASSALE, 146 Portobello Road, London W11. 071 6077121.
QUADRILLE, 146 Portobello Road, London W11. 081 4509008.

PURLEY

PREDOMINANTLY PRINTED, 339 Brighton Road, Purley, Surrey. 081 6671671. Mon-Sat, 10-5. Med size spec in Ephemera. Av cal cnd and prices.

RICHMOND

THE RICHMOND BOOKSHOP, 20 Red Lion Street, Richmond TW9 1RW. 081 9405512. Fri & Sat only, 9.30-6. Med size R/C stk. Emphon remaindery bks. Av cal cnd and prices. NIMS. NOE & Summer blight.

HOUBEN, 2 Church Court, Richmond TW9 1JR. 081 9401055. Mon-Sat, 10-5. New bksp with small R/C stk. Av cal cnd and prices. TWC.

BALDUR BOOKSHOP, 44 Hill Rise, Richmond, Surrey TW10 6UB. 0819401214. Mon-Sat, 9.30-5.30. Clsd Wed. Med size R/C stk. Av cal cnd and prices.

ST. JAMES

SIMS REED, 58 Jermyn Street, London SW1 6LX. 071 4938468. Mon-Fri, 10-6.30. Med size spec in Art reference. Ab av cal cnd and prices. Office shop. NIMS.

THOMAS HENEAGE, 42 Duke Street, London SW1Y 6DT. 071 7203158. Mon-Fri, 10-6. Sat 10-2. Lg spec Art Reference stk. Ab av cal cnd and prices.

SHEEN

VANDELEUR, 69 Sheen Lane, London SE14. 0818786837. BTR. Med size C/D stk. Ab av cal cnd and prices. NIMS. NOE and rumoured to be up for sale.

SOHO

QUARITCH, 5-8 Lower John Street, London W1R 4AU. 071 7342983. Mon-Fri, 9.30-5.30. Lg spec in Antiquarian, Natural History, Science. Ab av cal cnd and prices. NIMS. The William Rees Mogg excuse.

STAMFORD HILL

PENDLEBURY'S, Church House, Portland Road, Stamford Hill, London N16 7HJ. 081 8094922. Mon-Sat, 9.30-5. Sat 1. Med size spec in Theology. Av cal cnd and prices.

STOKE NEWINGTON

VORTEX, 139-141 Stoke Newington Church Street, London N16. 071 2546516. Mon-Fri, 11-6. Sat 10.30-6. Sun 12.30-6. Med size R/C stk. Bl av cal cnd and prices.

CIRCA, 144 Stoke Newington Church Street, London N16. 071 2499775. Mon-Fri, 12.30-6.30. Sat 11.30-6. Small spec in acad pbks. Ab av cal cnd and prices.

STRATFORD

K. SCOTT, 27 Romford Road, Stratford, London E15. 081 5191593. Mon-Sat, 9-5.30. Med size R/C stk. Av cal cnd and prices. Emphon Remainders.

STREATHAM

J.G. BOOKS, 27 Streatham Vale, London SW16. 081 7644669. Mon-Fri, 10-6. L 1-4. Clsd Wed. Sat 10-5. Small spec stk of bks on Lizards and Snakes. Av cal cnd and prices. NIMS spec.

VILLAGE BOOKS, 17 Shrubbery Road, London SW16 2AL. 081 6772667. Mon-Sat, 10.30-7. Clsd Wed. Rel. New bksp with small R/C stk. Av cal cnd and prices. TWC.SWISS COTTAGE

FITZJOHN'S BOOKS, Northways Parade, College Crescent, Swiss Cottage, London NW3. 071 7229864. Mon-Sat, 11-6. Med size R/C stk primarily remainders.

SYDENHAM

KIRKDALE BOOKSHOP, 272 Kirkdale, London SE26 4RS. 081 7784701. Mon-Sat, 9.30-5.30. Clsd Wed. Med size R/C stk in new bksp. Av cal cnd and prices.

HILLYERS, 301 Sydenham Road, London SE26. 081 7786361. Mon-Sat, 8.30-4. Sat 2, Clsd Wed. Antique shop with small R/C stk. Av cal cnd and prices. NIMS too small & boring.

THAMES DITTON

ELIZABETH GANT, 52 High Street, Thames Ditton, Surrey KT7 0BA. 081 3987484. Mon-Sat, 10.30-5.30. Clsd Wed. Med size R/C stk. Emphon childrens and ill. Ab av cal cnd and prices.

ROBIN BOOKS, 6 High Street, Thames Ditton, Surrey KT7 0RY. 081 8990962. Mon-Sat, 10-5.30. Wed clsd. Med/lg R/C stk. Emphon childrens and ill. Av cal. Bl av cnd. Ab av prices. TWC.

TWICKENHAM

ANTHONY HALL, 30 Staines Road, Twickenham TW2 5AU. 081 8982636. Mon-Sat, 9-5.30. Wed 1. Med size spec shop Russia & East European. Ab av cal cnd and prices.

MARION PITMAN, 29 Hampton Road, Twickenham TW2 5QE. 081 8987165. Med size R/C stk. Bl av cnd cal. Av prices.

UXBRIDGE

T.H BARNARD, 11 Windsor Street, Uxbridge UB8 1AB. 0895 58054. Mon-Sat, 9-5. Wed 1. Med/lg R/C stk. Av cal cnd and prices.

WALTHAMSTOW

RAYMOND PORT, Antique City Market, Unit 4, 98 Wood Street, London E17 3HX. 081 5204032. Mon-Sat, 9.30-5. Med size R/C stk. Av cal cnd and prices.

THE SPORTING BOOKSHOP, Antique City Market, Unit 13, 98 Wood Street, London E17 3HX. 081 5264032. Mon-Sat, 9.30-5.30. Med size spec in sports bks. Av cal cnd and prices. TWC.

NORMAN LORD, Antique City Market, Unit 3, 98 Wood Street, London E17 3HX. 081 5208300. Mon-Sat, 10-5. Clsd Thur. Med size R/C stk. Av cal cnd and prices. Emphon Performing Arts.

PSYCHIC SENSE, Antique City Market, Unit 1, 98 Wood Street, Walthamstow, London E17 3HX. 081 5204032. Mon-Sat, 9.30-5. Med size spec in Esoteric and Occult. Av cal cnd and prices.

WATERLOO

There are a small number of bookstalls mainly selling pbks outside of the National Theatre in the afternoon in summer.

WATERLOO STATION BOOKSHOP*, 29 Tenison Road, London. 071. Mon-Sat, 10.30-6.30. Med size R/C stk emphon remainders.

SECONDHAND BOOKS, 20 The Cut, London. SE1. 071 6339652. Wed-Sat, 11-7. Med size R/C stk ave cal cnd prices. Emphon remainders.

WELLING

FALCONWOOD TRANSPORT & MILITARY BOOKSHOP, 5 Falconwood Parade Green, Welling, Kent DA16 2PL. 081 3038291. Thur-Sat, 9.30-5.30. Med size spec Transport. NIMS. NOE. Spec and name too long.

WEST DULWICH

COLLECTED WORKS, 3 Melbourne Terrace, London SE22 8RE. 081 2994199. Mon-Sat, 10-6. Clsd Wed. Med size R/C stk. Av cal cnd and prices. Emphon mod 1sts.

WHETSTONE

WHETSTONE BOOKS, 368 Oakleigh Road North, London N20 0SF. 081 3688338. Mon-Sat, 10-3.30. Sat 10-5. Med size R/C stk. Av cal cnd and prices.

WILLESDEN GREEN

GABRIELS, 47 Walm Lane, London NW2 4QU. 081 4512047. Med size R stk. Av cal cnd and prices.

WIMBLEDON

BOOKS AND LYRICS, Unit 6 Merton Abbey Mills, South Wimbledon, London SW19. 081 5430625. Tues? Sun.11-6. Rel. Med/lg R/C/D stk. Av cal cnd and prices. Low key.

PSEUD BOOKS, Merton Abbey Mills, Wimbledon. SW19 2RD. 081 5430625. Sat & Sun only. Small shop with precious lit intellectual stk. See BOOKS AND LYRICS on Northern Line.

TLON BOOKS, Merton Abbey Mills, Wimbledon SW19 2RD. Sat & Sun, 10-6. and Thur L. Small R stk. Av cal cnd and prices.

LONDONDERRY, NORTHERN IRELAND

BOOK BARGAINS, 47 Spencer Road, Northern Ireland. Mon-Sat, 10-5. L 1-3. Med size R/C stk. Emphon pbks. Av cal cnd and prices.

THE UPPER DECK BOOKSHOP, Carlisle Road, Londonderry. No phone. Mon-Sat, 10-5. Clsd Tues. Med size R stk. NSOC. Av prices.

LOOE

THE OLD HALL BOOKSHOP, Shutta Road, East Looe, Cornwall PL13 1BJ. 03036 3700. Mon-Sat, 10-5.30. Med size R/C/D stk. Av cal cnd and prices.

LOUGHBOROUGH, LEICESTERSHIRE

SPARROW HILL BOOKS, 3 Sparrow Hill, Loughborough, Leicestershire LE11 1ET. 0509 239879. Thur-Sat, 10-5. Med size R/C stk. Av cal cnd and prices.

LOUTH, LINCOLNSHIRE

There are two shops. Neither of which has been visited, but are said to be similar to the shops in Horncastle.

LOWESTOFT

JOHN ROLPH, Manor House, Pakefield Street, Lowestoft NH35 0HT. 0502 572039. Tues-Sat, 11-5. L 1-2.30. Clsd Mon & Thur. Med size R/C stk. Av cal cnd and prices.

LUDLOW

BOOKS AND CHATTELS, 107 Corve Street, Ludlow, Shropshire SY4 1DJ. 0584 876191. Mon-Sat, 11-6. Clsd Thur. Med size R/C stk. Ab av cal cnd and prices. NIMS. NV. ETF.

20TH CENTURY BOOKS, 188 Corve Street SY8 2PG. 0584 874441. Mon-Sat, 10-5. BTR ring on Sats. Med size R/C/D stk. Av cal cnd and prices. NIMS. NV which may have been a mistake as there are rumours of other shops in Ludlow.

I think there should be a 3rd shop in Ludlow. d.

LYME REGIS

MARINE WORKSHOP BOOKSHOP, The Cobb, Lyme Regis, Dorset DT7 3JF. 029 742499. Every day, 10-5. Small/med size R/C stk. Bl av cal cnd. Av prices. NIMS rumoured to be closing. Rumoured closing and I think 2nd shop missed. NFDA.

LYMINGTON

HUGHES & SMEETH, 9 Gosport Street, Lymington, Hampshire SO14 9OG. 0590 76324. Mon-Sat, 9.30-5. Med size R/C stk. Av cal cnd and prices. TWC. Emphon Maritime.

TRIANGLE BOOKS, 70 High Street, Lymington, Hampshire. Mon-Sat, 10-5. Med size R/C stk. Ab av cal cnd. Av prices.

LYNTON, DEVON

Antique shop with bks.

LYTHAM ST. ANNES

THE BOOKSHOP, 26 St Andrews Street, Lytham St Annes. Lancs. 728278. Mon-Sat, 10-5.30. Med size new bksp with basement of s/h R/C stk. Av cal cnd and prices.

MACCLESFIELD

BRIDGEWATER BOOKS, 28 Sunderland Street, Macclesfield SK11 6JL. 0625 24763. Mon-Sat, 9-5. Clsd Wed. New bksp with small/med size R/C stk. Av cal cnd and prices.

Second shop, NFDA. Med size C/D stk. Bookfairy. BR Macclesfield. OOS, Straight ahead, Up steep, cobbled hill and keeping to right. Turn left at Town Hall, cross to paved zone and continue for one third of mile and SIOL on corner.

MACHYNLLETH

THE DYFI VALLEY BOOKSHOP, 6 Doll Street, Machynlleth, Wales SY20 8NN. 0654 703849. Mon-Sat, 10-6. L 12.30-1.30. Clsd Thur. Med size R/C stk. Av cal cnd and prices.

MALDON

ALL BOOKS, 2 Mill Road, Maldon, Essex. 0621 856214. Mon-Sat. Clsd Wed. Sun 2-6. Med R stk. Av cal cnd and prices.

MALMESBURY

BATSTONE BOOKS, 12 Gloucester Street, Malmesbury, Wilts SN10 0SA. 066 823072. Small R/C stk. Av cal cnd and prices. Keen on Occult.

MALVERN, HEREFORD & WORCESTERSHIRE

THE MALVERN BOOKSHOP, 7 Abbey Road, Malvern WR14 3ES. 0684 575915. Mon-Sat, 9.15-5. Clsd Wed. Med size R/C stk. Av cal cnd and prices.

PRIORY BOOKS, Church Walk (No no.), Malvern. 06845 560258. Tues-Sat, 10-5. L 12.45-2. Med size R/C stk. Av cal cnd and prices.

MANCHESTER

See also: Altrincham, Chorlton Cum Hardy, Chorlton On Medlock, Hale, Littleborough, Oldham, Prestwich, Ramsbottom, Rochdale, Romilley, Stockport.

FENNEL BOOKSHOP, 23 Fennel Street, Manchester M4 1DU. 061 8353759. Mon-Sat, 10-5.30. Med/lg R/C stk. Ab av cal cnd. Av prices.

GIBBS BOOKSHOP, 10 Charlotte Street, Manchester M1 4FL. 061 2367179. Mon-Sat, 9.30-5.30. Med size R/C/D stk. Av cal cnd and prices.

E.J. MORTERN, Warburton Street, Didsbury, Manchester M20 0RA. 061 4457629. Mon-Sat, 10-5.30. Primarily a new bksp with a small stk of R/C bks. Av cal cnd and prices. NV and NIMS

PARAMOUNT BOOK EXCHANGE, Shudehill, Manchester M4 2AF. 061 8349509. Mon-Sun, 9-7. Med size R/C stk. Av cal cnd and prices.

MANSFIELD

THE BOOKSHELF, 16 Albert Street, Mansfield NG18 1EB. 0623

648231. Mon-Sat, 9.30-5. Clsd Wed. Med size R/C stk. Av cal cnd and prices. NIMS. NV.

MARLBOROUGH, WILTS

THE ANTIQUE AND BOOK COLLECTOR, Katherine House, The Parade, Marlborough, Wiltshire SN8 1NE. 0672 514040. Mon-Sat, 9.45-5.30. Med/lg C/D stk. Av cal cnd and prices.

THE MARLBOROUGH BOOKSHOP, 6 Kingsbury Street, Marlborough, Wiltshire SN8 1NE. 0672 54074. Mon-Sat, 9.45-5. Print shop with backroom of Sporting and ill bks. Av cal cnd. Ab av prices.

MILITARY PARADE BOOKSHOP, The Parade, Marlborough, Wiltshire SN8 1NE. 0672 5156470. Mon-Sat, 10-5. Small size spec in Military History. Av cal cnd and prices. NIMS spec.

MARSTON GREEN

See Birmingham.

MATLOCK, DERBYSHIRE

THE BOOKCELLAR, Dale Road (No no.), Matlock, Derbyshire. 0629 57644. Mon-Sat, 9.30-5.30. Med size R/C stk. Ab av cal cnd. Av prices.

JARVIS BOOKS, 57 Smedley Street East, Matlock, Derbyshire. 0629 55322. Mon-Sat, 9.30-5.30. Med/lg stk. Ab av cal cnd. Emphon mountaineering.

MIDHURST

BROWSE AWHILE, The Mini Market, Grange Road (No no.) Midhurst GU29 9LT. 073 0815425. Tues-Fri, 11-4. Sat 9.30-5. Clsd Wed. Small Bookfairy type stk. Av cal cnd and prices. NIMS. I cannot stand the twee name. It is diff to find despite being a one street town. The hours are too complicated to remember. The whole place has that intimidating atmosphere that antiques markets engender, and it's miles from a railway station.

RC: *The truth is one of his major creditors lives in Midhurst.*

MINEHEAD

ALCOMBE BOOKS, 26 Alcombe Road, Minehead, Somerset. TA24 6AZ. 0643 3425. Mon-Sat, 10-5. Ex Wed & Sat. Med size R/C stk. Av cal cnd and prices.

MOLD, WALES.

Bookstall in Market most days. NV.

MONMOUTH

BRIAN STEVENS, 1 Church Street, Monmouth NP5 3BX. 0600 3701. Mon-Sat, 10-5. L 1-2. Clsd Thur. Med size R/C stk. Av cal cnd and prices.

MONTROSE

THE MONTROSE BOOKSHOP, 91 Murray Street, Montrose DD10 8JZ. 0674 73382. Tues-Sat, 10-4. Clsd Wed. Med size R/C stk slightly low key. Av cnd and prices.

MORTON IN MARSH

FOUR SHIRE BOOKSHOP, 17 High Street, Morton in Marsh, Gloucs GL56 0AF. 0608 51451. Mon-Sat, 11-5. Med size R/C stk. Av cal cnd and prices. Keen on needlework.

NAILSWORTH

VALENTINES BOOKS, Old Market, Nailsworth, Gloucestershire GL6 0DU. 045 3832483. Mon-Sat, 9-5.30. Med size R/C stk. Av cal cnd and prices.

NANTWICH, CHESHIRE

GUIDEMASTER BOOKS, 81 Welsh Row, Nantwich, Cheshire. 0270 629108. Open every day, 10-duskish. Med size R/C stk. Ave cal cnd and prices.

NEW MILTON

BOOKS AND THINGS, 99 Old Milton Road, New Milton, Hampshire BH25 6DN. 0425 617521. Mon-Sat, 9.30-5.30. Clsd Wed. Med size R/C stock. Av cal cnd. Ab av prices.

NEWBURGH, SCOTLAND

THE NEWBURGH BOOKSHOP*, 150 High Street, Newburgh, Fife. 073 885301. Tues, Fri & Sat, 10-5 in summer only. Small R stk. Av cal cnd and prices. NIMS. NEE.

NEWBURY, BERKSHIRE

INVICTA BOOKSHOP, 8 Cromwell Place, Friar Street, Newbury, Reading RG1 1DT. 0635 31176. Mon-Sat, 9.30-5.30. Med/lg R/C stk. Ab av cal cnd and prices.

NEWCASTLE UNDER LYME

POMES PENY EACH, 63 High Street, Wolstanton, Newcastle under Lyme ST5 0ER. 0782 636729. Mon-Sat, 9.30-6. Med size R/C stk. Emphon on lit and Mod 1sts. Ab av cal cnd, av prices.

NEWCASTLE UPON TYNE

THE NEWCASTLE BOOKSHOP, 1 Side, Newcastle NE1 3JE. 091 2615380. Tues-Sat, 10-5. Med size R/C/D stk. Av cal cnd and prices.

ROBERT STEEDMAN, 8 Gray Street, Newcastle NE1 6EE. 091 2326561. Mon-Fri, 9-5. Sat 12.30. Med size C/D stk. Ab av cal cnd and prices.

BAY BOOKS, 10A Norman Road, Monkseaton, Whitley Bay, Newcastle. 091 2514448. Mon, Thur? Sat, 10.30-5. Med size pbks some hardbacks. Av cal, ab av cnd and prices.

BEWICK BOOKS, 14 Clayton Road, Jesmond, Newcastle NE2 4RP. 091 2812711. Mon-Sat, 10.30-4. Med size antique shop with bks. Av cal cnd and prices.

OLIVER'S BOOKSHOP, 48A Whitley Road, Whitley Bay, Newcastle NE25 2NP. 091 2513552. Mon-Sat, 11-5. Clsd Wed. Rel. Med size R/C stk. Ab av cal cnd and prices.

DAVIS BOOKS, 140 Westgate Road, Newcastle. 091 2814580. Mon-Sat, 10-5. New bksp with med/lg R/C stk. Av cal cnd and prices.

AVENUE BOOKS, Land of Green Ginger, Front Street, Tynemouth. 091 2575836. Med size R/C stk. Keen on Natural History. Av cal cnd and prices.

NORTH SHIELDS BOOKS, 7 Kirkton Park Terrace, North Shields. 091 2961918. Mon-Sat, 11-5.30. Med size R/C stk. Av cal cnd and prices.

KEEL ROW BOOKS, 11 Fenwick Terrace, Preston, North Shields NE29 0LY. 091 2960664. The hours are unbelievable. Lg R/C stk. Bl av cal cnd. Ab av prices.

NEWENT

COBWEBS, 8/10 Church Street, Newent, Gloucestershire GL18 1PP. 0531 821734. Mon-Sat, 9-5. L 1-2. Clsd Wed. Med/lg R/C stk. Av cal cnd and prices.

NEWPORT, ISLE OF WIGHT

MR. MICAWBER, 61 Pyle Street, Newport, Isle of Wight. 0983 525320. Mon-Sat, 10-5.30. New Remainder shop with small/med size R/C stk. Av cal cnd and prices.

NEWPORT, WALES

CARNINGLI CENTRE, East Street, Newport, Dyfed, Wales SA42 0ST. 0239 820724. Mon-Sat, 9.30-5. Clsd Wed 1. Med size R stk. Ab av cal cnd. Av prices.

NEWPORT ON TAY

MAIR WILKES, 3 St Marys Lane, Newport on Tay, Fife DD6 6AW. 0382 542352. Sat only or by appointment. Lg C/D stk. Ab av cal cnd. Av prices. Emphon Psychology and Scottish.

NEWPORT PAGNELL, BUCKINGHAMSHIRE

KEN'S, 29 High Street, Newport Pagnell ME16 8AR. 0908 610003. Mon-Sat, 9.30-5. Med/lg R/C/D stk. Emphon Ephemera. Ab av cal cnd. Av prices.

NEWTON ABBOT

LINDY'S, 58 Queen Street, Newton Abbot, Devon TQ12 2BZ. 0626 63221. Mon-Sat, 9.30-5. Thur 1. Med/lg R/C stk. Ab av cal cnd. Av prices. Emphon Ephemera and Theology.

NORTHAMPTON

WOOTAN BILLINGHAM, 70 St Giles Street, Northampton NN1 4AW. 0604 34531. Mon-Sat, 10-5. Med size R/C stk. Av cal cnd and prices.

OCCULTIQUE, 73 Kettering Road, Northampton NN1 4AW. 0604 27727. Mon-Sat, 10-5. Med size spec in Occult. Av cal cnd and prices.

ABINGTON BOOKS, 327 Wellingborough Road, Northampton NN1 4EW. 0604 32933. Mon-Sat, 9-5. Med size R/C stk. Av cal cnd and prices.

NORTHFIELD, BIRMINGHAM

NORTHFIELD BOOKSHOP AND FURNISHINGS, 51-53, Church Road, Northfield. 021 477 7704. Mon-Sat, 9.30-4.30. Wed 1. Med size R/C stk. Bl av cal cnd and prices.

NORWICH

THE TOMBLAND BOOKSHOP, 8 Tombland, Norwich NR3 1HP. 0603 760610. Med/lg R/C/D stk. Ab av cal cnd and prices.

ST MICHAEL AT PLEA BOOKSHOP, Bank Olain, Norwich, Norfolk. 0603 619266. Mon-Sat, 9.30-5. Small/med size R/C stk. Emphon Local History. Av cal cnd and prices.

THE MOVIE SHOP, 11 St Gregorys Alley, Norwich, Norfolk NR2 1ER. 0603 615239. Mon-Sat, 10-5. Mainly film bks but some other R/C/D stk. Not strong on cnd. Av cal and prices.

HENRY COLLINSON, Bagley Court, Pottergale, Norwich. 0603 66348. (Home). Mon-Sat, 8.30-5.30. Camera shop with BTA R/C stk. Av cnd and prices.

SCIENTIFIC ANGLIAN, 30 St Benedict Street, Norwich NR2 4AC. 0663 624079. Mon-Sat, 10-5.30. Clsd Mon & Thur am. Later opening in winter. Med/lg R/C stk. Av cal. NSOC. Av prices.

TRISTRAM AND JULIA HULL, 72 St Benedicts Street, Norwich NR7 4AH. 0603 624890. Tues-Sat, 10-5.30 L 1-2. Clsd Thur. Med size C/D stk. Emphon art and design, esp printing. Ab av cal cnd and prices.

PETER CROWE, 75 Upper St Giles Street, Norwich NR21 1AD. 0603 624800. Mon-Sat,9.30-5.30. Lg R/C/D stk. Av cal cnd and prices.

J.R. & H.E ELLIS, 53 Giles Street, Norwich NR2 1NR. 0603 623679. Mon-Sat,8-5.30. Med/lg R/C stk. Av cal. Ab av cnd. Av prices. Slightly remaindery.

NORTHWICH

CASTLE BOOK CENTRE, 85 Chester Road, Northwich, Cheshire. 0606 781269. Mon-Sat, 10-5.30. Wed 4.30. Med size R/C stk. Av cal cnd and prices.

NOTTINGHAM

GEOFF BLORE'S BOOKSHOP, 484 Mansfield Road, Nottingham. NG5 2BF. 0602 691441. Mon-Sat, 10.30-5. Med/lg R/C stk. Ab av cal cnd. Av prices.

JERMY AND WESTERMANN, 203 Mansfield Road, Nottingham NG1 3PS. 0602 474522. Mon-Sat, 11-5 Med/lg R/C/D stk. Ab av cal cnd. Av prices. About to change hands.

MAYNARD AND BRADLEY, 30 Friar Street, Nottingham. 0602 484824. Mon-Sat, 9.30-5.30. Sat 9. Med size R/C stk. Av cal cnd and prices.

OAKHAM

COUNTY BOOKSHOP, 343 Northgate, Oakham, Rutland LE15 6QS. 0572 722403. Mon-Sat, 10.30-5. Med size R/C stk. Av cal cnd and prices.

OLDHAM

MOORLAND BOOKS, Unit 20 Alexandra Craft Centre, High Street, Uppermill, Oldham. OL3 6HV. 0457 871306. Wed-Sat, 11-4. Later Sat and Sun. Med size R/C stk. Av cal cnd and prices. Better than it sounds.

ORMSKIRK

MERE BOOKS, 48 Southport Road, Ormkirk, Lancashire L39 1QB. 0695 77570. Mon-Fri, 9.30-5.30. Med size R/C stk. Av cal cnd. Low prices.

OSTERLEY

See London.

OSWESTRY

NEWGATE BOOKS, 59 Church Street, Oswestry SY11 2SZ. 0691 650178. Tues-Sat, 9.30-5. Clsd Thur. Med size R/C stk. Slightly HSF Roast Beef but can be well worth a look, but also I did not manage it. NIMS. NV and very unsure if it is still there.

OTFORD

THE DARENTH BOOKSHOP, 8 High Street, Otford, Kent TN14 5PQ. 09592 2430. Mon-Sat, 9-5. Clsd Wed. New bksp with med size R/C stk. Emphon Local History. Av cal cnd. Ab av prices. NIMS too small.

OXFORD

THE LITTLE BOOKSHOP, Covered Market, High Street, Oxford. 0865 591176. Mon-Sat, 10-5. Small/med size R/C stk. Bl av cal cnd. Ab av prices.

WATERFIELD'S, 36 Park End Street, Oxford. OX1 1HJ. 0865 721809. Mon-Sat, 9.30-5.30. Lg R/C stk. Ab av cal cnd and prices. Emphon arts.

THE OXFAM BOOKSHOP, 56 St Giles Street, Oxford OX1 3LU. 0865 310145. Mon-Sat, 10-5. Med size BTA charity shop.

THE CLASSICS BOOKSHOP, 3 Turl Street, Oxford OX1 3DQ. 0865 726466. Mon-Sat, 10-5.30. Med size spec in Classics. (i.e. Latin, Greek, Archeology and Ancient History). Av cal, ab av cnd and prices.

THE BOOKSHOP, Oxford Antiques Centre, 27 Park End Street, Oxford. 0865 521075. Tues-Sat, 10-5.30. Med size R/C stk. Av cal cnd and prices.

TITLES, 15 Turl Street, Oxford. OX1 3DQ. 0865 727928. Mon-Sat, 9.30-5.30. Med size C/D stk. Av av cal cnd and prices.

NINER AND HILL, 43 High Street, Oxford OX1 4AP. 0865 726195. Mon-Sat, 10-5.30. Small/med size C/D stk. Ab av cal cnd and prices.

SANDERS, 104 High Street, Oxford OX1 4BW. 0865 242590. Mon-Sat, 9-5.15. L 1-2.15. Print shop with upstairs room of C bks. Av cal cnd and prices. NIMS. Print shop.

BLACKWELLS 48-51 Broad Street, Oxford OX1 3BQ. 0865 792792. Lg C/D stk. V acad. Ab av cal cnd and prices.

THORNTONS, 11 Broad Street, Oxford OX1 3DQ. 0865 242939. Mon-Sat, 9.30-5.30. V lg acad C stk. Ab av cal cnd and prices.

PADSTOW

STRAND BOOKS, 4 The Strand, Padstow, Cornwall PI28 8AZ. No phone. Mon-Sat, 9-5. + in summer. Clsd Wed 1. Med size R/C stk. NSOC. Av cal. Ab av prices.

PAIGNTON, DEVON

THE POCKET BOOKSHOP, 159 Winner Street, Paignton, Devon. TQ3 3BP 0803 529804. Mon-Sat, 10.30-6 + in summer. Med size R/C stk. Ab av cal cnd, av prices. T. P. poss.

PAISLEY, GLASGOW

WORDSWORTH, 14 Johnston Street, Paisley PA1 1KG. 041 8877303. Mon-Sat, 10.15-5.30. Med size R/C stk. Bl av cal cnd and prices.

PENN

THE COTTAGE BOOKSHOP, Elm Road, Penn, Buckinghamshire HP10 8LB. 049 4812631. Tues-Sat, 10-5. L 1-2.15. Rel. V lg R stk. Ab av cal, av cnd and low prices.

PENRITH

ST ANDREWS BOOKSHOP, St Andrews View (No no.), Penrith, Cumbria CA11 7YF. 0768 64455. Mon-Sat, 9-5. Wed 1. New bksp with med size s/h C stk. Av cal cnd and prices. Keen on Natural History and Ornithology.

PENZANCE

ARGANTE, 1 Princes Street, Penzance, Cornwall PL18 2NL. No phone. Mon-Sat, 9-5. Med size R/C stk. Slightly low key. Av cnd and prices.

PENZANCE RARE BOOKS, 43 Causewayhead, Penzance TR18 2BS. 0735 62140. Mon-Sat, 9-5.30. Med/lg R/C stk. Av cal cnd and prices.

THE BOOK CELLAR, 7 Chapel Street, Penzance, Cornwall. 0736 60320. Mon-Sat, 10-5. Antique shop with basement of BTA R/C bks. Av cnd and prices. NIMS too few.

PERSHORE

IAN K. PUGH, 40 Bridge Street, Pershore, Worcestershire. 0386 552681. Mon-Sat, 10-5. Clsd Thur. Med size R/C/D stk. Av cal cnd. Ab av prices.

PERTH

PERTH BOOKSHOP, 3A Abbot Street, Perth, Scotland PH2 0EB. 0738 33970. Mon-Sat, 10-5. Clsd Wed. Clsd Sat 1 in winter. Small/med size C/dealerish stk. Ab av cal cnd. Av prices.

PETERBOROUGH

OLD SOKE BOOKS, 68 Burghley Road, Peterborough PE1 2QE. 0733 64147. Fri & Sat, 10-5. Med size R/C/D stk. Av cal cnd and prices. ETGOW. P. diff.

T.V. COLES, 961 Lincoln Road, Peterborough PE4. 0733 77268. Mon-Sat, 10-5. Clsd Wed. Med size R/C stk. Slightly low key. Keen on Military History.

PETERSFIELD

THE PETERSFIELD BOOKSHOP, 16A Chapel Street, Petersfield, Hampshire. 0730 63438. Mon-Sat, 9-5.30. Lg R/C/D stk. Av cal cnd and prices.

PETWORTH

BOOKROOM, Petworth Antiques Market, East Street, Petworth GU28 0AB. 0798 42073. Mon-Sat, 10-5.30. Small touristy stk. Keen on leatherware. NIMS. Too small

PLYMOUTH

BARBICAN BOOKSHOP, 46 South Side Street, Barbican, Plymouth. 0752 664957. Mon-Sat, 10.30-5.30. Med size R/C stk. Bl av cal, av cnd and prices. TWC.

CORNERSTONE BOOKS, New Street Antiques Centre, The Barbican, Plymouth. 0752 661165. Mon-Sat, 10-5. Med size R/C stk. Ab av cal cnd and prices.

POLESWORTH

G & J CHESTERS, 19 Bridge Street, Polesworth, Staffordshire. R78 1DR. 0827 894743. Mon-Sat, 9.30-5.30. Wed clsd. Open until 9 Thur. Med/lg C/D bks. Ab av cal cnd, av prices. Emphon Local Topography and acad.

POOLE

POOLE BOOKSHOP, 106 Indoor Market, High Street, Poole, Dorset. No phone. Mon-Sat, 9-5. Med size R stk primarily pbks. Low key (i.e. not penguins) ETF in High Street.

PORTSMOUTH

See Southsea.

PRESTON

THE BOOK HOUSE, 65/67 Fylde Road, Preston, Lancashire PR1 2XQ. 0772 201576. Mon-Sat, 10-5.30. Med size R/C student acad stk. Av cal cnd and prices.

HALEWOOD AND SONS, 68 Friargate, Preston, Lancashire PR1 2AT. 0772 52603. Mon-Sat, 9.15-5.30. Rel. Lg C/D stk. Ab av cal cnd and prices. Res stk.

BOOKS FOR EVERYBODY, 13 Lowthian Street, Preston, Lancashire. PR1 2EP. Mon-Sat, 10-5. Small R stk. Keen on childrens and pbks.

PRESTWICH

BROWZERS BOOKSHOP, 14 Warwick Street, Prestwich, Manchester. 061 7980626. Mon-Sat, 10-5. Clsd Wed. Med size R/C stk. Av cal cnd and prices.

PUDDLETOWN

THE ANTIQUE MAP AND BOOKSTORE, 32 High Street, Puddletown, Dorset DT2 8RU. 0305 848633. Mon-Sat, 9-5. Med size C/D stk. Ab av cal cnd and prices. Keen on Hardy. Distinctly Bookfairy. NIMS you have to ring a bell to get in.

PULBOROUGH

SUSSEX BOOKS, 42A Lower Street, Pulborough, West Sussex. RH20 2BW. 079 823030. Mon-Sat, 10-5.30. Clsd Wed pm. Small R/C. Touristy. NIMS.

RAMSBOTTOM

LITTLE HOLCOMBE BOOKS, 52 Bridge Street,Ramsbottom, Greater Manchester BL0 9AW. 070 6825322. Mon-Sat, 9.30-5. Wed 1. Med size R/C stk. Av cal cnd and prices. Emphon childrens.

RAMSGATE

WINDMILL BARGAIN BOOKS, 20 Grange Road, Ramsgate, Kent CT11. 0843 591334. Mon-Sat, 9-5.30. Small R stk. Av cal cnd and low prices.

MICHAELS BOOKSHOP, 72 Kings Street, Ramsgate, Kent CT11 8NY. 0843 589500. Mon-Sat, 9.30-5.30. Remainder shop with med size R/C stk. Av cal cnd and prices.

THE OLD RAMSGATE BOOKSHOP, 1 Windmill Parade, Grange Road, Ramsgate CT11 9ND. 0843 586377. Mon-Sat, 10-5. Clsd Thur pm. Med/lg R/C stk. Low key, av cnd, low prices.

RAVENSTONEDALE

THE BOOKHOUSE, Grey Garth, Ravenstonedale, Nr. Kirkby Stephen CA17 4NQ. 058 73634. Mon-Sun, 9-8. Med size R/C/D stk. Emphon Industrial Industry. Av cal cnd and prices. NV.

READING

VICTORIA BOOKS, Eldon Terrace, Reading, Berkshire RG1 4DX. 0734 500303. Mon-Fri, 10-5. Clsd Wed. Small R/C stk. Av cal cnd and prices. NIMS because I have never made it in. Keegans now solely remainders.

REDCAR

REDCAR BOOKSHOP, 39 Lord Street, Redcar, North Yorkshire TS10 3HN. 0642 486122. Tues-Sat, 10-5. Clsd Thur. Med size R stk. Av cal cnd, bl av prices.

REIGATE

REIGATE GALLERIES, 45A Bell Street, Reigate, Surrey RH2 7AG. 0737 246055. Mon-Sat, 9.30-5.30. Wed 1. Rel. Med size R/C stk. Av cal cnd and prices.

RHOS POINT

RHOS POINT BOOKS, 85 The Promenade, Rhos on Sea, Clwyd, Wales. 0492 45236. Summer every day, 9.30-5.30. Less in winter. Small size R/C stk. Ab av cal, bl av cnd, av prices.

RICHMOND, SURREY

See London.

RICHMOND, YORKSHIRE

FIVE OWLS BOOKSHOP, 26 Victoria Road, Richmond, Yorkshire. 0748 3648. Sat 10.30-5. L (can you believe it?) 12.30-2.30. Med size R/C stk. Av cal cnd and prices. Wins the prize for the most customer orientated bksp in Britain. NV.

Such was my ire with these pathetic opening hours that I stormed off in a chauffeur driven huff and missed another shop in the basement by the Church in the square in Richmond, which by all accounts (and there have been several, regarding my gross incompetence) is a Drif Special. It contains a small R/C stk. NSOC., and is best for Dwarfs.

RIPON

ST MARGARET'S BOOKSHOP, 10/11 Kirkgate, Ripon. 0765 2877. Mon-Sat, 10-5. Clsd Wed 1. New bksp with small R/C stk. Av cal cnd and prices. NV, not enough bks.

ROCHDALE

THE ROCHDALE BOOKSHOP, 399 Oldham Road, Rochdale OL16 5LN. 0706 31136. Sats only and occasionally open weekdays. Med/lg C/D stk. Ab av cal, av cnd and prices. NIMS. Not open enough.

ROCHESTER

BAGGINS BOOK BAZAAR, 19 High Street, Rochester, Kent ME1 1QB. 0634 811651. Mon-Sun, 10-6. V lg R/C/D stk. Bl av cal cnd and prices. TWC.

HEARTS OF OAK BOOKSHOP, 63 High Street, Rochester, Kent. 0634 41851. Mon-Sun, 10-6. Med/lg spec shop. Military History, Transport, Maritime, Aviation. Bl av cal cnd and prices.

ROMILLEY, CHESHIRE

ROMILLEY LITTLE BOOKSHOP, 1 Hill Street, Romilley, Manchester SK6 2AH. 061 4274853. (Home). Not sure about times. Med size R/C stk. Av cal cnd and prices.

ROMSEY

RUSKINS, 27 Bell Street, Romsey, Hampshire SO51 8GY. 0794 523881. Mon-Sat, 9.30-5.30. New bksp with med size BTA s/h stk, emphon F. Nightingale. NIMS. NV.

ROSS ON WYE

ROSS OLD BOOKS AND PRINT SHOP, 51-52, High Street, Ross on Wye, HR9 5HH. 0989 67458. Mon-Sat, 10-5. Med size R/C/D stk. Av cal cnd and prices.

ROWLEY REGIS, WEST MIDLANDS

See Birmingham.

RUTHIN

SPREAD EAGLE BOOKS, 3 Upper Clwyd Street, Ruthin, Wales LL15 1HY. 08242 3840. Mon-Sat, 9.30-5.30. New bksp with small R/C stk. Av cal cnd and prices. NIMS. NV.

RYDE, ISLE OF WIGHT

HERITAGE BOOKS, 7 Cross Street, Ryde, Isle of Wight PO3 2AD. 0983 62933. Mon-Sat, 10-5. Med/lg R/C/D stk. Av cal cnd and prices.

RYE

ANTHONY NEVILLE, 15 Market Square, Rye, East Sussex. TN31 7LA. 0797 224552. Mon-Sat, 10-5.30. Clsd Tues. Med size C/D stk. Ab av cal cnd and prices. TWC.

LANDGATE BOOKS, Hilders Cliff, Rye, East Sussex. 0797 222280. Wed-Sat, 10-5. Med size R/C stk. Av cal cnd and prices.

ST ALBANS

PATON BOOKS, 32-34, Holywell Street, St Albans AL3 4LR. 0727 65576. Tues-Sat, 9-5. New bksp with lg room of R/C stk. Av cal cnd and prices.

THOMAS THORPE, 9 George Street, St Albans, Hertfordshire AL3 4ER. 0727 65576. Tues-Sat, 9.30-5.30. Med/lg C/D stk. Ab av cal cnd and prices.

OXFAM BOOKSHOP, The Street with No Name, St Albans, Hertfordshire. No Phone. Mon-Sat, 10.30-4.30. Med size BTA charity bksp.

ST ANDREWS

BOUQUINISTE, 31 Market Square, St Andrews, Fife, Scotland KY16 9NS. 0334 76724. Mon-Sat, 10-5. Clsd Thur in winter. Med size R/C stk. Av cal cnd and prices.

BILLSONS OF ST ANDREWS, 15 Greyfriars Gardens, St Andrews, Fife, Scotland KY16 9DE. 0334 75063. Thur-Sun, 2.30-5. Small C/D stk spec in Scottish.

McILLREAVEY, 57 South Street, St Andrews, Fife, Scotland KY16 9QR. 0334 72487. Mon-Sat, 9.30-5.30. Lg C/D stk, emphon lit and Scottish. Bookfairy. Ab av cal cnd and prices.

BOOKO BOOKS, South Street (No no.), St Andrews, Fife. Mon-Sun, 9-9. 0334 76738. Med size R/C stk. Bl av cal cnd and prices. Emphon novels.

QUARTO BOOKSHOP, 8 Golf Place, St Andrews, Fife, Scotland KY16 9JA. 0334 74616. Mon-Sat, 9.30-5.30. L 1-2.15. Med size R/C stk. Av cal cnd and prices. TWC.

ST COLUMB MAJOR

COLLECTORS CORNER, 7 Bank Street, St Columb Major, Cornwall TH9 5AT. 0637 889715. Mon-Sat, 10-5. Med size R/C stk.Av cal cnd and prices.

ST HELENS, ISLE OF WIGHT

MOTHER GOOSE BOOKSHOP, Upper Green Road, St Helens, Isle of Wight PO33 1XB. 0983 873897. Mon-Sat, 11.30-10. L 1-7.30. Med size R/C stk. Av cal cnd and prices.

ST IVES

THE MIRROR AND THE LAMP, 1 St Andrews Street, St Ives, Cornwall TR26 1AH. No phone. Tues, Wed, Fri and Sat, 1-6. Small stk of poetry and art.

SALISBURY

D.M. BEACH, 52 High Street, Salisbury SP1 2EG. 0722 333801. Mon-Sat, 9-5.30. Med/lg R/C stk. Av cal cnd and prices.

JOHN AND JUDITH HEAD, 88 Crane Street, Salisbury SP1 2QD. 0722 27706. Mon-Fri, 10-5. Lg spec shop in Hunting, Shooting and Fishing. Ab av cal cnd and prices.

SALTBURN

SALTBURN BOOKSHOP, 3 Amber Street, Saltburn, Cleveland TS10 1DT. 0207 23335. Wed-Sat, 11-5. L 1-2. Med size R/C stk. Low key, av cnd and prices.

SANDOWN

ARMSTRONGS, 14a York Road, Sandown, Isle of Wight. 0983 406226. Small R stk. Bl av cal cnd and prices. NIMS. Too bad. Possibly the worst bksp in Britain.

SANDWICH

STRAND BOOKS, 21 Strand Street, Sandwich, Kent CT13 9DX. 0304 611948. Mon-Sat, 10-5.30 L 1-2.15. Clsd Wed. Small/med size R stk. Ab av prices. Av cnd.

SCARBOROUGH

SCARBOROUGH BOOKS, 55 Castle Road, Scarborough YO11 1BH. 0723 388813. Mon-Sat, 10-5. Sun in summer. Med size R/C stk. Av cal cnd and prices. Keen on Esoteric.

BAR BOOKSHOP, Chapman's Yard, Waterhouse Lane, Scarborough YO11 1DP. 0723 500141. Thur, Fri & Sat, 10-5. Med size R/C stk, emphon esoteric. Av cal cnd and prices.

SEAFORD

THE BARN COLLECTORS MARKET, Church Lane, Seaford, East Sussex. 0323 890010. Tues, Thur, Sat 10-4.30. Med/lg R/C stk. Av cal. NSOC. Av prices. TWC.

SEDBERGH

R.F.G HOLLETT & SON, 6 Finkle Street, Sedbergh LA10 5BZ. 05396 20298. Mon-Sat, 10-5. L 12-1.15. Med/lg C/D stk. Ab av cal cnd, way ab av prices. Also has res stk way ab. T. NIMS. I'm too poor to even go through the door.

SHAFTESBURY

THE BOOK IN HAND, 17 Bell Street, Shaftesbury, Dorset SP7 8AR. No phone. Mon-Sat, 10-4.30. L 1-2. Less in winter. Med size R/C stk. Ab av cal cnd, ave prices.

SHERBOURNE

CHAPTER HOUSE BOOKSHOP AND GALLERY, Trendle Street (No no.) Sherbourne, Dorset DT9 3NT. 0935 816262. Mon-Sat, 10-5.30. L 1-2. Med/lg size R/C stk. Av cal cnd and prices.

BOOKLORE, 2 Hound Street, Sherbourne DT9 3AA. 0939 814191. Mon-Sat, 9.30-5. Wed 1. New bksp with small R/C stk. Av cal cnd and prices. NIMS.

SWAN GALLERY, 51 Cheap Street, Sherbourne, Dorset. 0935 814465. Mon-Sat, 10-5.30. Print Gallery with med size Bookfairy stk of bks. Av cal cnd and prices. ETF in main street. NIMS.

SHERINGHAM, NORFOLK

PETER'S BOOKSHOP, 19 St Peters Street, Sheringham, Norfolk NR26 8QY. 0263 823008. Summer Mon-Sun, 10-6. Winter clsd Sun, Mon and Wed. Lg R/C stk. NSOC. Av cal and prices.

SHREWSBURY

CANDLE LANE BOOKS, 28 Princess Street, Shrewsbury, Shropshire SY1 1LW. 0743 65301. Mon-Sat, 9.30-5. Rel. Lg R/C/D stk, emphon HSF. Av cal cnd and prices. TWC.

QUARRY BOOKS, 24 Claremont, Shrewsbury SY1 1RD. 0722 61404. Mon-Sat, 9.30-5.30. Med/lg R/C stk. Ab av cal cnd and prices.

SIDMOUTH

SIDMOUTH OLD BOOKS, 12 Temple Street, Sidmouth, Devon EX10 9LY. 0395 514461. Mon-Sat, 10-5. Med size R/D stk. Av cal cnd and prices.

SITTINGBOURNE

See Cranbrook, Kent.

SKIPTON

CHILTON BOOKS, 49 Belmont Bridge, Skipton. Mon-Sat, 10-5. Clsd Tues. Med size R/C stk, av cal cnd and prices. Currently up for sale.

THE BOX OF DELIGHTS, 25 Otley Street, Mon-Sat, 11-5.30. Clsd Tues & Thur. Med size C/D stk, ab av cal, emphon ill & childrens. More than av imagination shown in stk and sometimes prices. WAD. P poss.

SLEAFORD

WESTGATE BOOKSHOP, 45 Westgate, Sleaford, Lincolnshire NG34 7PU. 0525 304276. Mon-Sat, 10-5. Clsd Thur. Med size R stk. Av cal cnd and prices.

SNETTISHAM

TORC BOOKS, 9 Hall Road, Snettisham, Norfolk. PE31 7LY. 0485 54188. Sats 10-6. and BTR. Med size R/C stk. Av cal cnd and prices.

SOMERTON

SIMON'S BOOKS, Broad Street (No no.), Somerton. 0458 72343. Tues-Sat, 10-5.30. Med size R/C stk. Av cal cnd and prices.

SOUTHAMPTON

H.M. GILBERT, 2 Portland Street, Southampton, Hampshire. 0705 226420. Mon-Sat, 8.30-5.30. Lg R/C stk. Av cal cnd and prices.

NORTHAM BOOKS, 30 Northam Road, Southampton SO1. No phone. Wed-Sat, 10-5. Med/lg R/C stk. Av cal cnd and ab av prices.

SOUTHEND ON SEA

ATTICUS BOOKS, 20 Alexandria Street, Southend On Sea, Essex. SS1 1BJ. 0702 353630. Sats only. Small/med R/C stk. Av cal cnd and prices.

SOUTHPORT

ANTHONY PARKINSON, 359 Lord Street, Southport PR8 1NH. 0704 47016. Mon-Sun, 10.30-5. Med size R/C stk. Slightly low key. Av cal cnd and prices.

BROADHURST, 5-7, Market Square, Southport, Merseyside PR8 1HD. 0704 32064. Mon-Sat, 9-5.30 ex Tues. Lg R/C/D stk. Ab av cal cnd and prices. WAD.

BRYAN KERNAGHAN, 53 Wayfarers Arcade, Southport PR8 1NT. 0704 546329. Mon-Sat, 10-5. Med size R/C/D stk. Ab av cal cnd and prices. WAD. T. P diff.

SOUTHSEA

BOOK ACADEMY, 13 Marion Road, Southsea, Hampshire PO5 2AT. 0702 816632. Mon-Sat, 9-5. Rel. Med size R/C stk. Av cal. NSOC. Av prices. Res stk of religious bks.

ADELPHI BOOKS, 1 Albert Road, Southsea, Hampshire PO5 2SE. No phone. Tues-Fri, 11.30-4.30. Sat 10-5. Med size R/C stk. Av cal cnd and prices.

STAR BOOKSHOP, 69 Fawcett Road, Southsea, Hampshire PO4 0DR. 0705 737077. Tues-Sat, 12-6.30. Sat 11-6. Med/lg R/C/D stk. Av cal cnd and prices.

MILLERS BOOKS AND PRINTS, 55 Fawcett Road, Southsea PO4 0DA. 0705 755796. Tues-Sat, 11-6. Clsd Wed. Med size R/C stk.Av cal cnd and prices.

SOUTHWOLD
PLEASURES, 36 East Street, Southwold, Suffolk IP18 6EJ. 0702 723776. Mon-Sat, 10-5. L 1-2.30. Summer. Less in Winter. Med size R/C stk. Av cal cnd and prices. T.

STAFFORD
ROBERT A. PICKEN, 11 Goal Road, Stafford ST11 3AN. 0785 53425. Mon-Sat, 10.30-5.30. Wed clsd. Rel. Small/med size R/C stk. Av cal cnd and prices.

STIRLING
CORN EXCHANGE BOOKSHOP, 53 King Street, Stirling FK8 1DN. 0786 73112. Mon-Fri, 10-3. L 1-2 Clsd. Sat 10-5. Med size R/C stk. Bl av can cnd and prices.
THE STIRLING BOOKSHOP, 30 Spittal Street, Stirling FK8 1DV. 0876 81771. Mon-Sat, 10-5. Lg R/C/D stk. Ab av cal cnd and prices.

STOCKPORT
GRENVILLE STREET BOOKSHOP, 105 Grenville Street, Stockport, Cheshire SK3 8ET. 061 471 1909. Tues-Sat, 10-6. Med/lg R/C/D stk, emphon travel. Av cal cnd and prices.
THE HEATONS BOOKSHOP, 13 School Lane, Heaton Chapel, Stockport, Cheshire. 061 4315905. Mon-Sat, 10.30-4.30. Med size R/C stk, emphon acad and scholarly technical bks.

STOCKTON
BARNARD GALLERY, 2 Theatre Yard, Stockton, Cleveland TW18 5NL. 0642 616203. Tues-Fri, 10-4. Sat 10-5.30. Clsd Thur. Med size R/C stk. Low key. Av cnd, low prices.

STOKE ON TRENT
ANTIQUARIAN BOOK CENTRE, 30-32, Hope Street, Hanley, Stoke On Trent. 0762 261352. Mon-Sat, 10-5.30. Med size R/C stk. Av cal cnd and prices. Keen on ceramic and technical.

STOKESLEY
THE STOKESLEY BOOKSHOP, 63 High Street, Stokesley, Cleveland TS9 5BQ. 0642 712514. Mon-Sat, 10-5. Med size R/C stk.Av cal cnd and prices.

STORNOWAY
THE STORNOWAY BOOKSHOP*, Bells Road, Stornoway, Hebrides. Med size R/C stk. Av cal cnd and prices. NIMS. NV.

STOW ON THE WOLD
BOOKBOX, Sheep Street, Stow on the Wold, Gloucestershire GL54 1AA. 0451 31214. Mon-Sat, 10-5. BTR in winter. Med/lg R/C stk. Ab av cal cnd and prices.

STRATFORD ON AVON
ROBERT VAUGHAN, 20 Chapel Street, Stratford on Avon CV37 6EP. 0793 527364. Mon-Sat, 9.30-5.30. Med size C/D stk, emphon Shakespeare. Ab av cal cnd and prices.
CHAUCER HEAD BOOKSHOP, 21 Chapel Street, Stratford Upon Avon CV37 6EP. 0789 415691. Mon-Sat, 10-5.30. Sun 1-5. Med size R/C stk. Ab av cal cnd, av prices.
PAPER MOON BOOKS, 4 Sheep Street, Stratford Upon Avon. 0789 297249. Mon-Sat, 10-5.30. V lg bookstall. Ab av cal cnd and prices. Tourist orientated.

STROUD
IMPRINT, 31 High Street, Stroud, Gloucestershire. GL5 1AS. Mon-Sast, 10-5.30. Med size R/C stk, emphon entertainment. Ab av cal cnd and av prices. TWC.
ALAN AND JOAN TUCKER, Station Road, Stroud, Gloucestershire. GL5 3AF. 0453 764768. Mon-Sat, 10-5. L 12.30-1.30. Clsd Thur. New bksp with BTA R/C stk. Av cnd and prices.

STURMINSTER NEWTON

STOUR BOOKS, Bridge Street, Sturminster Newton, Dorset. 0258 73561. Mon-Sat, 10-4.30. Clsd all day Tues and 1 Wed & Sat. Small R/C stk primarily childrens and ill. Av cal cnd and ab av prices. NIMS. It is bad enough having to cope with shops closing on a Wed and Thur, but to have to put up with one that closes on a Tues is asking a little much. In honour of this shop, no shop that closes on a Tues will be allowed in the MS. This will be known as the Sturminster Newton Excuse.

SUDBURY

SUFFOLK RARE BOOKS, 7 New Street, Sudbury, Suffolk CO10 6JH. 0787 72075. Tues, Thur, Fri & Sat, 10.30-4.30. Med size R/C/D stk. Av cal cnd and prices. T.

SUNDERLAND

There are two shops but you would have to be schizophrenic to want to visit them.

SWANAGE

ANTIQUARIAN AND SECONDHAND BOOKS, 55 High Street, Swanage, Dorset. 424088. Mon-Sat, 10-5. Med/lg R/C stk. Av cal cnd and prices. TWC.

SWANSEA

DYLAN'S, Salubrious Passage, Swansea, West Glamorgan, Wales. SA1 3RT. 0792 655255. Mon-Sat, 10-5. Lg R/C/D stk. Ab av cal cnd and prices. Emphon unusual bks and Welsh subjects. T.

THE OLD BOOK MART, 37 St Helens Road, Swansea, Wales. SA1 4AY. 0792 474919. Mon-Sat, 10-5. Med size R/C stk, emphon remainders and Occult. Av cal cnd and prices.

RC writes: What happened to Ralph the Book? d. dunno.

SWAY

BEAGLE BOOKS, 1 Middle Road, Sway, Hampshire SO41 6AI. 0590 683421. Mon-Fri, 10-4. Clsd Wed. L 1-2. Sat 9-1. Small C stk, emphon Natural History. Av cal cnd and prices.

SWINDON

VICTORIA BOOKSHOP, 30 Wood Street, Swindon SN1 4AB. 0793 480178. Mon-Sat, 9-5.30. Med/lg stk. Av cal cnd and prices.

TAUNTON

STAPLEGROVE BOOKSHOP, 19 Staplegrove Road, Taunton, Somerset TA1 3PF. 0823 336450. Mon-Sat, 10-5. Med size R/C stk. Av cal cnd and prices.

ROTHWELL AND DUNWORTH, 14 Paul Street, Taunton, Somerset. 0823 82476. Mon-Sat, 11-5.15. Sat 1. Med size R/C/D stk. Keen on cricket.

TEIGNMOUTH

THE BOOKWORM, 26 Regent Street, Teignmouth, Devon. 0626 775177. Mon-Sat, 10.30-6.30. More in summer. Med size R/C stk. Slightly low key. Av cnd and prices.

TENBY

ALBATROSS BOOKSHOP, 1 Bridge Street, Tenby, Dyfed. 0834 2113. BTR. Hours subject to enormous change. Med size R/C stk. Av cal cnd and prices. Emphon Ornithology. NIMS. NV.

TEWKESBURY

WAYFARER BOOKS, 19 Church Street, Tewkesbury, Gloucestershire. 0684 293337. Mon-Sat, 10-5. Med size R/C stk. Av cal cnd and prices.

THIRSK

HAMBLETON BOOKSHOP, 43 Market Place, Thirsk, North Yorkshire YO7 1HA. 0845 22343. Mon-Sat, 9.30-5. Clsd Wed during winter. New bksp wiht med size R/C stk. Keen on geology. Av cal cnd and prices.

TIVERTON

THE ANGEL HILL BOOKSHOP, 17 Angel Hill, Tiverton, North Devon. 0884 257783. Mon-Sat, 10-5. R/C stk, emphon esoteric. ETF. NV.

TODMORDEN, LANCASHIRE

BORDER BOOKSHOP, 63 Halifax Road, Todmorden, Lancs. 0706 814721. Mon-Sat, 10-5. Clsd Tues. L R/C stk. Ab av cal cnd av prices. NV. The Sturminster Newton excuse.

There is also a second newly opened shop in Todmorden. Also NV.

TOTLAND, ISLE OF WIGHT

SKLARROF, Craglea, The Broadway, Totland, Isle of Wight. 0983 754960. Mon-Sat, 10-5. Sun in summer. Clsd Wed. Med size R/C/D stk. Ab av cal cnd and prices. Emphon M Peeke, Mod 1sts and signed bks. TWC.

TOTNES

PEDLARS PACK, 4 The Palins, Totnes, Devon. 0803 35944. Mon-Sat, 9-5. Med/lg C/D stk. Av cal cnd and prices. TWC. P. poss.

THE BOOKSHOP, 72 Fore Street, Totnes, Devon. 0803 864088. Mon-Sat, 9.30-5.30. Thur 1. Rel. Med size R/C stk, emphon remainders. Av cal cnd and prices. TWC. P. diff.

TRURO

JUST BOOKS, 9 Pindar Mews, Truro, Cornwall TR1 2UX. 087 42532. Mon-Sat, 10-5. Clsd Thur. Med size R/C stk. Av cal cnd and prices. TWC.

TUNBRIDGE WELLS

HALL'S BOOKSHOP, 20 Chapel Place, Tunbridge Wells TN1 1YQ. 0872 27842. Mon-Sat, 9.30-5. Med/lg R/C/D stk. Av cal cnd and prices.

TWICKENHAM

See London.

TYWYN

TOWN AND GOWN BOOKSHOP, 9 Seafront Arcade, Tywyn, Gwynned LL36 0DG. 0341 250542. Every day during summer BTR in winter. Med size R stk. Low key. NIMS. NV.

ULVERSTON

THE OLD STORYTELLERS BOOKSHOP, 11 Fountain Street, Ulverston, Cumbria. LA12 7EQ. 022996123. Tues-Sat, 10-5.30. Clsd Wed. Med/lg R/C stk. Av cal cnd and prices. Emphon Local History.

UPPINGHAM

GOLDMARK BOOKS, Orange Street, Uppingham, Rutland LE15 9SQ. 0572 822694. Mon-Sat, 9-5. Med/lg R/C stk. Av cal cnd and prices.

NOT JUST BOOKS, Market Place, Uppingham, Rutland LE15 9QH. 0572 821306. Mon-Sat, 9.30-5.30. Med/lg R stk. Av cal cnd, highish prices.

THE RUTLAND BOOKSHOP, 13 High Street West, Uppingham. 0572 833450. Tues-Sat, 11-5.30. L 1-2.15. Med size R/C stk HSF. Av cal cnd and prices.

UXBRIDGE

See London.

VENTNOR

THE VENTNOR BOOKSHOP, 19 Pier Street, Ventnor, Isle of Wight PO38 1ST. 0083 853706. Mon-Sat, 10-5. Clsd Wed & Thur. Med size R/C/D stk. Ab av cal cnd and prices.

WALLINGFORD

TOBY ENGLISH, Lamb Arcade, Wallingford, Oxfordshire OX10 0BS. 0491 36389. Mon-Sat, 10-4.30. Med/lg R/C/D stk. Keen on SF and Fantasy. Ab av cal cnd and prices.

WALSINGHAM

PILGRIMS PROGRESS, 51 High Street, Walsingham, Norfolk NR22. 032 820399. Mon-Sun 7.30-7.30 Summer. Winter 2-5. Med size R/C stk. Av cal cnd and prices. NV. I should have gone there but the last time I visited the place I thought it was a miracle that I got away without being bored to death by the owner, and I do not have enough faith to believe that it could happen twice.

WAREHAM

ST JOHNS HILL BOOKS, 2 St Johns Hill, Wareham, Dorset. 092 952577. Tues, Thur, Sat, 10-5. Med size R/C stk. Av cal cnd and prices. NIMS not open enough and rumoured to be up for sale.

WAYTOWN

HARE AND HOUNDS PUB, Waytown, Dorset DT6 5DQ. 030888203. Every day 11-30-2.30 and 5.30-10.30- Med size R/C/D stk. Av cal cnd and prices.

WEDNESBURY

SIMMONS BOOKSHOP, 37 Lower High Street, Wednesbury, West Midlands WS10 7AQ. 021 5024622. Mon-Sat, 9-5.30. Clsd Thur 2. Open Fri evening 7.30 Med/lg R/C stk, emphon fiction, NSOC, av cal, low prices.

WELLINGBOROUGH

THE PARK BOOKSHOP, 12 Park Road, Wellingborough, Northamptonshire NN8 4PG. 0933 222592. Mon-Sat, 10-5. Med size R/C stk. Av cal cnd and prices.

WELLS

COURTYARD BOOKS, Old Palace Yard, Priory Road, Wells, Somerset. 0749 07112. Mon-Sat, 10-5. Med/lg R/C bks. Ab av cal, av cnd and prices.

WELLS NEXT SEA, NORFOLK

COOK, 65 Snaithe Street, Wells Next Sea, Norfolk NR23 1AN. 0328 710419. Mon-Sun, 10-5. Less in winter. Small R stk, ab av cal cnd, av prices.

WEST KIRBY

BOOKENDS, 4 Hilbre Road, West Kirby, Merseyside L48 7HD. 051 6256389. Mon-Sat, 10-4. L 1-2. Med size R/C stk. Av cal cnd and prices.

WEST MALLING

FOXED AND BOUND, 8 West Street, West Malling, Kent ME19 8QU. 0732 847886. Tues-Sat, 10-5. Med size R/C stk. Av cal cnd, ab av prices. Emphon Biography, folklore and childrens.

WESTCLIFFE ON SEA

BARRIE ELLEN, 262 London Road, Westcliffe on Sea, Essex. SS9 7JR. 0702 338763. Mon-Sat, 9.30-5.30. Clsd Wed. Med size R/C stk, emphon chess. Av cal cnd and prices. TWC.

WESTERHAM

ALAN TAYLOR SMITH BOOKS, 4 The Grange, High Street, Westerham, Kent TN16 1AH. 0959 61100. Mon-Sat, 10-5. Med size R/C stk. Av cal cnd, ab av prices.

WESTLETON

CHAPEL BOOKS, Westleton, Suffolk IP17 3AA. 072873 616. Usually opens seven days a week. 11-6 in summer, but always Sat & Sun at least. Med size R/C stk. Av cal cnd and prices. T.

WESTON SUPERMARE

STERLING BOOKS, 43A Locking Road, Weston Supermare, Avon BS23 3DG. 0934 625056. Mon-Sat, 9-6. L 1-2. Clsd Thur. Lg R/C/D stk. Ab av cal cnd and prices.

SEVERN BOOKS, 48 Severn Road, Weston Supermare BS23 1DT. 0934 635589. Mon? Sat 10-5. Sun in summer. Med size R/C stk. Av cal cnd and prices.

MANNA BOOKS, 30 Orchard Street, Weston Supermare BS23 1BQ. 0934 626228. Mon-Sat, 10-5. Clsd Wed. Med size R/C stk, emphon alternative and esoteric. Av cal cnd and prices.

WETHERBY

WORDS AND MUSIC, Church Street, Wetherby, Yorkshire. 0937 66009. Mon-Sat, 10-5.30. Clsd Wed. Med size R/C stk. Av cal cnd, ab av prices. NV. NIMS.

WEYMOUTH

QUEST BOOKS, 13A Cove Street, Weymouth, Dorset. 0305 789142. Mon-Sat, 10.30-5.30. L 1-2. Small R stk. Av cal cnd and prices.

BOOKS AFLOAT, 66 Park Street, Weymouth, Dorset DT4 7DE. 0305 779774. Tues-Sat, 9.30-5.30. Med size R/C stk. Spec in maritime. Ab av cal cnd, av prices.

WHITCHURCH

BARN BOOKS, Pear Tree Farm, Norbury, Whitchurch, Shropshire SY13. 0948 3742. Fri 2-6, Sat 10-6. Sun 2-6. Med size R/C stk mainly rural bks. NV. NIMS.
Second shop in High Street NV.

WHITEHAVEN

MICHAEL MOON, 41-43 Roper Street, Whitehaven, Cumbria CA25 7BS. 0948 82936. Mon-Sat, 9.30-5. V lg R/C/D stk. Ab av cal cnd and prices.

WHITSTABLE

BOOKS AND PIECES, 48 Oxford Road, Whitstable, Kent. No phone. Mon-Sat, 10-5. Wed pm clsd. Small/med size R nearly C stk. Av cal cnd and prices.

WIGAN

THE BOOK HOUSE, 8 The Wiend, Wigan, Lancashire. 0942 44648. Mon-Sat, 10.30-5.30. Med size R/C stk. Av cal cnd and prices.

WILLITON

BLACKMORES BOOKSHOP, 6 High Street, Williton, Somerset TA4 4NW. 0984 32227. Mon-Sat, 9-5.30, ex Sat 1. Primarily a cafe with books. I liked the coffee. NV.

WINCHESTER

PETER M. DALY, 10A Jewry Street, Winchester SO23 8EZ. 0962 67732. Wed, Fri, Sat, 10-5. L 1-2 Sat. Small/med R/C/D stk, emphon Natural History, mountaineering, travel. Av cal cnd and prices.

GILBERTS, 19 The Square, Winchester SO23 9BY. 0962 53932. Mon-Sat, 9-5.30. New bksp with med size R/C stk. Av cal cnd and prices.

BOOKS AND THINGS, 50 Stockbridge Road, Winchester SO22 6EL. Mon-Sat, 12-5.30. Sat 10. Med size R/C stk. Av cal cnd, bl av prices. Emphon pbks.

WINGHAM

LLOYDS, 27 High Street, Wingham, Kent CT3 1AW. 0227 720774. Mon-Sat, 9.30-5. L 1-2.15. Med size R/C stk. Av cal cnd and prices.

WITHAM

BALDWIN'S BOOKS, Fossil Hall, Boars Tye Road, Siver End, Witham, Essex CM8 3QA. 0376 83502. BTR Spec in Geology, paleontogy, and archeology. NIMS. Diatribe 3.

WIVELSCOMBE

WIVEY BOOKS, 1 High Street, Wivelscombe, Somerset. 0984 23506. Some dispute about the opening hours, best to ring. Med size R/C stk. Almost a Drif Special. Av cal cnd and prices. NV.

WOLVERHAMPTON

BERRY STREET BOOKSHOP, 35 Berry Street, Wolverhampton. 0902 28939. Mon-Fri, 10-5. Med size R/C stk. Low key, av cnd and prices.

BOOKSTACK, 53 Bath Road, Wolverhampton, West Midlands. WV1 4EL. Mon-Sat, 11-5. Rel. Med/lg R/C stk. Av cal. NSOC. Av prices. TWC.

WOODBRIDGE

BLAKES, 88 The Thoroughfare, Woodbridge, Suffolk IP13 1AL. 0394 380382. Mon? Sat 9.30-5. Med size R/C stk. Av cal cnd and prices.

WOODSTOCK

THE WOODSTOCK BOOKSHOP, 3 Market Place, Woodstock, Oxfordshire OX7 1SY. 0999 811005. Mon-Sat, 10-5. L 1-2. Med size C/D stk spec in OUP bks. Ab av cal cnd and prices.

THE AFTERNOON BOOKSHOP, 21 Oxford Street, Woodstock, Oxfordshire OX7 1TN. 0999 813445. Mon-Sat, 12-5. Small C shop. Ab av cal cnd, av prices.

WOOLER

THE WOOLER BOOKSHOP, High Street, Wooler, Northumberland. No phone. Mon-Sat, 10-5. Med size R/C stk. NSOC. Strange pricing. ETF. Nearest Newcastle. NIMS.

WORCESTER

ANDREW BOYLE, 21 Friar Street, Worcester WR1 2NA. 0905 611700. Med size C/D stk, emphon childrens bks. Not strictly a bksp and it is also rumoured to be closing down.

HOLBOURNE BOOKS, 67 Upper Tything, Worcester WR1 1JX. 0905 27824. Mon-Sat, 10-5. Med/lg R/C/D stk. Av cal cnd and prices.

GRADUATE BOOKS AND RECORDS, 65 Sidbury, Worcester WH1 2HU. 0905 723959. Mon-Sat, 10.30-5.30. Med size R/C stk in Record shop. Av cal cnd and prices. NIMS. NEB.

WORTHING

BADGERS, 8-10 Gratwicke Road, Worthing, West Sussex BN11 3BS. 0903 211816. Mon-Sat, 9.15-6. Lg R/C stk, emphon Occult. Av cal cnd and prices.

KIM'S BOOKSHOP, 33 West Buildings, Worthing, West Sussex BN11 3BS. 0903 206202. Mon-Sat, 10-5.15. Med/lg R/C stk. Ab av cal cnd, av prices. Keen on Natural History and Orchids.

THE STEYNE BOOKSHOP, 5 High Street, Worthing, West Sussex BN11 1NY. 0903 206216. Mon-Sat, 10-5.30. L R/C/D stk. Av cal cnd and prices.

WREXHAM

GLYN'S BOOKS, 1 Overton Arcade, High Street, Wrexham LL13 8LL. 0978 355797. Mon-Sat, 10-5. Med size R/C stk. Av cal cnd and prices. Emphon Mod 1sts.

WYMONDHAM

A.C. & M. THOMPSON, 1 Town Green, Wymondham, Norfolk NR18 0PN. 0953 602244. Mon-Sat, 10.15-5. Rel. Med size R/C stk. Av cal, ab av con, av prices.

TURRET HOUSE BOOKS, 27 Middleton Street, Wymondham, Norfolk NR18 0AB. 0953 603642. Mon-Sat, 9-6. Med size spec in Science and Microscope bks. Some General bks. Av cal cnd and prices.

YARMOUTH, ISLE OF WIGHT

THE OUT TO LUNCH BOOKSHOP*, High Street (No no.), Yarmouth, Isle of Wight. 0983760851. Fri, Sat 10-4. L 12.30- 1.30. Sun 1-4. Med size R/C stk, emphon Natural History. Av cal cnd and prices. T.

YORK

JACK DUNCANS, 36 Fossgate, York YO1 7TF. 0904 941389. Mon-Sat, 10-5.30. Lg C/D stk. Ab av cal cnd and prices. Emphon Music & lit.

SPELMANS, 70 Micklegate, York YO1 1LP. 0904 624414. Mon-Sat, 9-5.30. Med size R/C/D stk. Ab av cal cnd and prices.

O'FLYNN, 35 Micklegate, York YO1 1JH. 0904 641404. Mon-Sat, 9-6. Med/lg R/C stk, emphon prints. Av cal, NSOC, ab av prices.

THE MINSTERGATES BOOKSHOP, 8 Minstergates, York YO1 2HL. 0904 621812. Mon-Sat, 10-5.30. Rel. Med size R/C stk. Av cal cnd and prices. Keen on folklore.

TAIKOO BOOKS, 29 High Petergate, York YO1 2HP. 0904 413711. Med size spec in Foreign Travel and Topography. V high cal cnd, av prices.

YOXFORD

YOXFORD BOOKSHOP, High Street (No no.), Suffolk. 073 877309. BTR. Small/med size R stk. Av cal cnd and prices. T.

FN: Only those SPCK's with a significant number of secondhand books have been included, the number and quality of the rest seems to be declining fast.

The shops listed in this subject index are those which genuinely have enough books in that particular subject to merit a visit. Those shops which are hopeless in the subject which they claim to specialise in are omitted and some shops which would not claim to have a particular specialisation are included. Thus the bookshop in Moreton in Marsh claims to have a specialisation in Needlework, but you are as likely to find a needlework book you want there as you are to find a pair of socks without a hole when you really wish to impress somebody. But the shop in Beccles which would not claim to have a poetry section is included in that classification. Not only because it does have a significant number of books but because the entire shop is poetry itself.

ARCHITECTURE (The only shop dealing solely in Architecture is Thompsons of Cirencester, but several Art bksps also have worthwhile stocks).

ART (By far the best Art bksp in Britain is Ann Creed of Charing Cross Road, known to her detractors as Ann Greed, but it is imposs to have a successful spec shop and have low prices.)
LONDON: THOMAS HENEAGE/CHECK BOOKS/BALLANTYNE & DATE/ CAMBERWELL BKSP; **BRISTOL**: COTHAM HILL; **NEWCASTLE**: THE NEWCASTLE BKSP; **HOLT**: CASTLE BKSP; **EDINBURGH**: MCNAUGHTONS.

AUSTRALIA
LONDON: FLINDERS

BATSFORDS
BRISTOL: COTHAM HILL BKSP

BAEDECKERS
LONDON: THE TRAVELLERS BKSP

BIBLIOGRAPHY
LONDON: MAGGS **HASTINGS**: THE HOWES; **BRISTOL**: GEORGES; **CAMBRIDGE**: DEIGHTON BELL; **IPSWICH**: CLAUDE COX.

BIOGRAPHY
WEST MALLING: FOXED AND BOUND

BINDINGS (see leatherware)

CARICATURE
LONDON: BONDY

CERAMICS
STOKE ON TRENT: ANTIQUARIAN BOOK CENTRE

CHESS
WESTCLIFFE ON SEA: BARRY ELLEN; **LONDON**: CAISSIA

CHILDRENS BOOKS (That is bks that adults buy for themselves not children)
CANTERBURY: DAVID MILES; **LICHFIELD**: THE STAFFS BKSP; **CAMBRIDGE**: THE HAUNTED BKSP; **LONDON**: MARCHPANE/ELIZABETH GANT/RIPPING YARNS/ROBIN BOOKS/PLEASURES OF PASTIMES; **RAMSBOTTOM**: LITTLE HOLCOMBE BKS

(And the CHILDREN'S BOOKSHOP, Hay on Wye, which is the only shop I have ever seen any children in).

CHINESE
LONDON: COLLETTS; (see also travel)

CHURCHILL
WESTERHAM: ALAN TAYLOR SMITH

CLASSICS
LONDON: THE MUSEUM BKSP; **HASTINGS**: THE HOWES; **BRISTOL**: GEORGES; **OXFORD**: THE CLASSICS BKSP.

COOKERY
ARUNDEL: THE ARUNDEL BKSP.

CLOCKS
LONDON: ROGERS TURNER

CRICKET
THE HORSHAM BKSP; **LONDON**: THE SPORTING BKSP; **KESWICK**: APPLEBYS; **CHELTENHAM**: MICHAEL REYNER.

CRIME
LONDON: MURDER ONE

DETECTIVE FICTION
LONDON: MURDER ONE and LISA MATTHEWS

DICKENS
HAY ON WYE: BOZ BOOKS

drif specials (In no drif special order).
GRAYS: BOB GILBERT; **LOWESTOFT**: JOHN ROLPH; **WESTLETON**: CHAPEL BKS; **SLEAFORD**: WESTGATE BKSP; **BIRMINGHAM**: THE NORTHFIELD BKSP; BEECH BKS; **LEICESTER**: CLARENDON BKS; **HEXHAM**: HENCOTES; **IOW**: GOLDEN HOURS BKSP; **ALTON**: THE ALTON S/H BKS; **SEAFORD**: BARN COLLECTORS MKT; **CREWKERNE**: the d'constructed bksp; **ST ANDREWS**: BOOK 0 BOOKS; **LONDON**: THE OSTERLEY BKSP; WORDS & MUSIC.

EIRE (You try finding a bksp in Eire without books on Eire)

EPHEMERA
LONDON: THE OLD NEWSPAPER & EPHEMERA SHOP/PREDOMINANTLY PRINTED; **NEWPORT PAGNELL**: KEN'S; **NEWTON ABBOT**: LINDY'S.

ESSEX
GRAYS: BOB GILBERT.

ETHNIC ART
LONDON: BOOKS OF ASIA.

FIRST EDITIONS
LONDON: BELL, BOOK & RADMALL/CHECK BKS/CHARLOTTE ROBINSON/ BERTRAM ROTA; **BRADFORD ON AVON**: WHITE HILL BKS; **LIVERPOOL**: HAZLEDENE BKS.

FISHING
SALISBURY: JOHN & JUDITH HEAD.

GOLF
LONDON: BADDIEL and THE SPORTING BKSP; **DROITWICH**: GRANT BOOKS.

GREEK
LONDON: ZENO

HISTORY
LONDON: DILLONS; **TUNBRIDGE WELLS**: HALLS; **HASTINGS**: THE HOWES; **BRISTOL**: GEORGES; **EDINBURGH**: PETER BELL.

HOMOSEXUAL
LONDON: GAYS THE WORD

HUNTING, SHOOTING & FISHING
ABERGEVENNY: LOCKYER; **DULVERTON**: ROTHWELL & DUNWORTH; **SALISBURY**: JOHN & JUDITH HEAD; **NEW ALRESFORD**: NEW ALRESFORD BKSP.

ILLUSTRATED
LONDON: BALLANTYNE & DATE/MAGGS BROTHERS/HENEAGE/ROBIN BKS; **CAMBRIDGE**: THE HAUNTED BKSP; **BRIGHTON**: COLIN PAGE; **BRISTOL**: COTHAM HILL; **GLASGOW**: COOPER HAY; **EDINBURGH**: MCNAUGHTONS; **CANTERBURY**: DAVID MILES; **LITCHFIELD**: THE STAFFS BKSP.

JAZZ
BUNGAY: SCORPIO BKS; **EDINBURGH**: LATTO BKS.

SAMUEL JOHNSON
LONDON: CLARKE HALL; **LITCHFIELD**: THE STAFFS BKSP.

KIPLING
THE FAVERSHAM BKSP.

LAW
LONDON: WILDY & SONS.

LEFT WING POLITICS
LONDON: BOUTLE & KING/CENTRAL BOOKS; **CAMBRIDGE**: IAN PATTERSON.

LITERATURE (Modern)
LONDON: CHARING CROSS BKSP/DILLONS/BELL BOOK & RADMALL/ CHARLOTTE ROBINSON/ GLOUCESTER RD BKSP/CHECK BKS/ BALLANTYNE & DATE; **CANTERBURY**: CHAUCER HEAD BKSP; **HASTINGS**: THE HOWES; **BRIGHTON**: TALL STOREYS; **PORTSMOUTH**: THE STAR BKSP; **BRISTOL**: COTHAM HILL and GEORGES; **CHELTENHAM**: HANCOCKS; **LIVERPOOL**: HAZLEDENE; **SOUTHPORT**: BROADHURSTS; **GLASGOW**: CALEDONIA BKS; **EDINBURGH**: OLD GRINDLES; **INVERNESS**: THE INVERNESS BKSP.

MARITIME
LONDON: THE MARITIME BKSP/MR GREEN; **ROCHESTER**: HEARTS OF OAK; **COLCHESTER**: ALPHABET BKS; **HARROGATE**: COURTNEY; **GOSPORT**: RICHARD MARTIN; **WEYMOUTH**: BOOKS AFLOAT; **HELENSBURGH**: MCLAREN BKS; **NEWCASTLE U TYNE**: FRANK SMITH.

MEDICAL
LONDON: ROBERT CONNOLLY

MILITARY HISTORY
LONDON: MAGGS BROTHERS; **DONCASTER**: ATHENA BKS; **HALIFAX**: THE COLLECTOR; **MARLBOROUGH**: THE MILITARY PARADE BKSP.

MINATURE BOOKS
LONDON: LOUIS BONDY; **GLASGOW**: COOPER HAY.

MINERALOGY
COLCHESTER: GREYFRIARS BOOKS; **MARK'S TAY**: BALDWINS BKS.

MOUNTAINEERING

HOLYHEAD: HOLYHEAD BKS; **MATLOCK**: JARVIS BKS; **EAST MOLESEY**: MOLE BKSP; **GIGGLESWICK**: POST HORN BKSP; **YORK**: TAIKOO; **INVERNESS**: THE INVERNESS BKSP.

MUSIC

LONDON: TRAVIS & EMERY/ARCHIVE; **OXFORD**: BLACKWELLS; **LEICESTER**: FOREST BKS; **MALVERN**: THE MALVERN BKSP; **BRISTOL**: THE WISE OWL BKSP.

NATURAL HISTORY

LONDON: SOTHERANS/J G BOOKS; **MALVERN**: THE MALVERN BKSP; **PERSHORE**: IAN PUGH; **WORTHING**: KIM'S BKS; **SWAY**: EAGLE BKS; **BECCLES**: BESLEYS BKS; **NORTHWICH**: FOREST BKS; **RAMSBOTTOM**: LITTLE HOLCOMBE BKS.

NEWSPAPERS & MAGAZINES

LONDON: THE OLD NEWSPAPER & EPHEMERA SHOP; **CHESTERFIELD**: TILLEY'S; **NEWPORT PAGNELL**: KEN'S; **NEWTON ABBOT**: LINDY'S; **SHEFFIELD**: TILLEY'S.

OCCULT

LONDON: WATKINS/ATLANTIS/SKOOB 2; **BRIGHTON**: DEJA VU; **WORTHING**: BADGERS BKSP; **SWANSEA**: THE OLD BOOK MART; **BRISTOL**: WISE OWL; **NORTHAMPTON**: OCCULTIQUE; **SCARBOROUGH**: SCARBOROUGH BKSP.

ORCHIDS

WORTHING: KIM'S.

ORIENTAL

LONDON: BOOKS OF ASIA/CHECK BKS/FINE BOOKS ORIENTAL; **YORK**: TAIKOO; **BRIGHTON**: COLIN PAGE (see also travel).

ORNITHOLOGY

LONDON: SOTHERANS; **PENRITH**: ST ANDREWS BKSP; **NEWCASTLE**: AVENUE BKSP

OXFORD UNIVERSITY PRESS

THE WOODSTOCK BKSP

PACIFIC

LONDON: BOOKS OF ASIA.

PERFORMING ARTS

LONDON: PLEASURES OF PASTIMES/UPPER STREET BKSP/SOUTH LONDON BK CTR/NORMAN LORD; **STRATFORD ON AVON**: ROBERT VAUGHAN; **HAY ON WYE**: THE PERFORMING ARTS BKSP.

PHILOSPHY

COVENTRY: GOSFORD BKS; **TIVERTON**: ANGEL HILL BKSP; **OXFORD**: BLACKWELLS/WATERFIELDS; **NEWCASTLE**: OLIVERS.

PLATE BOOKS

LONDON: HARRINGTONS/QUEEN STREET BKSP/BERNARD SHAPIRO/BRIAN BAILEY/ALAN BRETT; **LEWES**: ANDREW CUMMING; **BRIGHTON**: COLIN PAGE; **SOUTHPORT**: KERNAGHANS and BROADHURST; **GLASGOW**: COOPER HAY; **EDINBURGH**: MCNAUGHTONS; **NEWCASTLE**: STEEDMANS; **GREAT YARMOUTH**: FERROW; **NORWICH**: CROW; **IPSWICH**: CLAUDE COX.

POETRY (see all mod 1sts and literature shops)
BECCLES: BESLEY; **HAY ON WYE:** THE POETRY BKSP.

PRIVATE PRESS
LONDON: MAGGS BROTHERS/CHECK BKS/BALLANTYNE & DATE/ COLLINGE & CLARKE.

PSYCHOLOGY
NEWPORT ON TAY: MAIR WILKES.

RAILWAYS
LONDON: BALLANTYNE & DATE; **BRISTOL:** PATTERSON & LIDDLE; **MARLBOROUGH:** THE ANTIQUE & BOOK COLLECTOR.

ROWING
HENLEY ON THAMES: RICHARD WAY.

RUSSIA
LONDON: ANTHONY HALL.

SCIENCE AND TECHNOLOGY
LONDON: ROGERS TURNER/ROBERT CONNOLLY; **WYMONDHAM:** TURRET HOUSE BOOKS; **HAY ON WYE:** MARK WESTWARDS; **CANTERBURY:** PAUL HOLCOMBE.

SCIENCE FICTION & FANTASY
LONDON: THE FANTASY CENTRE/ BOOKMARK; **WALLINGFORD:** TOBY ENGLISH; **DRIFFIELD:** THE DRIFFIELD BKSP.

SCOTLAND (you try finding a Scottish bksp without books on Scotland!)

SHAKESPEARE
STRATFORD ON AVON: ROBERT VAUGHAN

SIGNED BOOKS
LONDON: MAGGS; **IOW:** SKLARROF (see 1st ed dealers).

SNAKES & LIZARDS
LONDON: J G BOOKS.

SOCCER
LONDON: BOOKMARK/THE SPORTING BKSP.

SOUTH EAST ASIA
LONDON: BOOKS OF ASIA

STEINER (RUDOLPH)
FALMOUTH: BOOKMARK

THEOLOGY
LONDON: SPCK/JOHN THORNTON; **DURHAM:** THE BARBICAN BKRM; **EDINBURGH:** JAMES DICKSON; **GLASTONBURY:** HADDONS BKSP; **RYDE:** HERITAGE BKS; **NEWTON ABBOT:** LINDY'S; **BURTON ON TRENT:** NEEDWOOD BKSP; **WALSINGHAM:** PILGRIM'S PROGRESS; **OXFORD:** THORNTONS; **DARLINGTON:** VOKES & SON; **BELFAST:** WORLD OF BKS. (if you are interested in theology, you would be unlikely to be interested in most of the provincial SPCKs)

TRAVEL

LONDON: CHECK BKS/SOTHERANS/REMINGTONS/THE TRAVELLER'S BKSP/BERNARD SHAPIRO; **MARLBOROUGH**: THE ANTIQUE & BK COLLECTOR; **LEWES**: ANDREW CUMMINGS; **BRIGHTON**: COLIN PAGE; **PRESTON**: PRESTON BOOK CO; **GUILDFORD**: THORP/TRAYLEN'S; **VENTNOR**: THE VENTNOR BKSP; **BRISTOL**: GEORGES; **BATH**: BANKES; **SOUTHPORT**: BROADHURST and KERNAGHAN; **LIVERPOOL**: REIDS; **INVERNESS**: THE INVERNESS BKSP.

WALES (You try finding a bksp that doesn't go in for Welsh bks in Wales)

WINE

LONDON: VANBRUGH RARE BOOKS.

(See pages 117/118)

Dear Miss Manners,   12th Sept. 1991

I have taken your wonderful advice, oh why didn't I write to you sooner. I finished the book in less than a fortnight, I know that that was longer than you thought such a small thing should take, but I would have just died if I had not had a break at the hairdressers. You know how we girls are. But now I have another tiny problem which I just know that only you will be able to solve for me.

I rang that lovely little Barry Shaw on 31st August and told him of my magnificent work, and, that I would be 'coming out' on 1st October (well that might be an exaggeration, I got my Chargé d'Affaires to ring him) it is so difficult to get good servants these days, and I was unable to remonstrate when she said that she had no idea who Mr. Shaw was (I don't think she had a good upbringing, she comes from somewhere north of Charing Cross, I think its Marylebone or Regents Park, its one of those funny places where they're always 'hotting' or holding riots.

"Everybody who counts knows that he is the editor of the Bookdealer Magazine, the trade journal which always comes out weakly" I said.

Dear Miss Manners I know you cannot solve the servant problem (I find it reassuring to know that the editor of the Bookdealer and I share the same difficulties). But please, Miss Manners, could you tell me when I might be able to expect a mention in Mr. Shaw's publication.

The Tsarina of all the Charing Cross Roads
Rightful Ruler of the East, Hackney [not North London]

(Miss Manners replies,

Listen you brazen hussy, everybody knows you're a total fraud, always dressing things up - not least yourself, Mr. Shaw has better things to do than spend his time haunting secondhand bookshops, unlike you who uses everybody else's shop as a personal office. Mr Shaw has never been seen in a Secondhand bookshop least of all the Charing Cross Road where he might bump into such low lifers as yourself, and worse have to look at books. He should be given the Helen Hanff Award for not sullying them. Mr Shaw is an important person with immense tact. That is why he left strict instructions that no mention of your tuppeny ha'penny publication (£9.99 indeed!) should be made until he returned from holiday. And I don't doubt when he does return that he will be overburdened with producing snippets about important bookdealers. (Dead ones).

After all, he did notice you when you stopped producing your alleged guide book. Judging by the way you look I'd say he'll be getting round to noticing you again soon. But even when you are dead, I can fully understand why he does not want to tell his readers the truth. It could kill them.

Yours in Disgust,
Miss Manners.

PS: And don't think I haven't heard of your reply when the PBFA asked for its money back - hours of laughter is no way for anybody to respond to a morally justified request.)

FORGOTTEN BUT NOT GONE

F H BELL — **Morecambe**
124 Heysham Road, Morecambe, Lancs. 0524 420769
Mon-Sat, 10-5, EC Wed & Sat.
Med size R/C stk. Drif Special. T & Disc. Etgow, well WAD. BR Morecambe, OOS, turn left and right and left towards Heysham, SIOR approx. 1 mile, above Knitting Wool Shop.

THE STUDIO BOOKSHOP — **New Alresford**
17 Broad Street, New Alresford, Hampshire SO24 9AW. 0962 732188. **Mon-Sat, 10-5, EC Wed.**
Med/lg R/C/D stk, emphon HSF. ETF in centre of town. BR Winchester (NAST 10 miles).

HELGATO — **St Leonards**
121 Bohemia Road, St Leonards, E Sussex. 0424 423049.
Mon-Sat, 10-5, clsd Wed
Med size C/D stk, emphon ill & design bks. Ab av cal, cnd, av prices. Etgow. P.poss. Directions as Bookmans Halt, same road, see Hastings in Main Sequence.

HELLENIC BOOK SERVICES — **London**
91 Fortress Road, London NW5 1AG. 071 267 9499.
Mon-Sat, 9.30-6
New bksp with spec stk of s/h Greek bks. NV. Tube: Kentish Town, OOS turn right and bear right up hill, SIOL.

***THE FLYING SCOTSMAN BKSP** — **London**
Schlater Street (no No.), Bethnal Green, London E1. No Tel.
Sunday mornings only!
In this London the people of the abyss meet the sea wolf. This iron heel makes John Barleycorn seem like the daughter of the snows.

They call him the Flying Scotsman, but in truth he is the dirty British coaster. This marine store beggars description, even the Silverfish have thrown in the fin. This is not so much the bksp of the greasy spoon as that of the well oiled. My own definition of condition is 'with cover good', 'without cover bad' - the flying Scotsmans' is 'without cover good', 'without any pages, not quite so good'.

There are other bkstls in Club Row Market on a Sunday morning. BR Liverpool Street, OOS turn left into Shoreditch, turn right into Bethnal Green Road and follow through into market.

THE BLUE RIDER — **Mere**
Salisbury Street (no No.), Wiltshire BA12 6HE. 0747 860593
Mon-Sat, 9.30-5, L 1-2, clsd Wed
Med size R/C stk, keen on mod 1sts. NV, but not for want of trying. I had a bodyguard, a chauffeur, a lot of determination and most surprisingly of all, tons of money, but I picked the wrong day. In ten years of trying I have never once got into this shop.

POTTERTON BOOKS — **Sessay**
The Old Rectory, Sessay, Thirsk YO7 3LZ. 0845 401 218.
Mon-Fri, 9-5
Med size spec stk, arts, crafts and design. NV but judging from catalogues, very high cal and even higher prices. BR Thirsk, OOS turn right and keep walking for 12 miles.

***THE QUEEN STREET MAYFAIR BOOKSHOP** **London**
18 Queen Street, London W1X 8JN. 071 629 0532
Mon-Fri, 10-5, Rel
Med size D/C stk, libracide and lthrwr, plate bks. Ab av cal, cnd and prices. From Hayward Hill (London - see Main sequence), OOSH turn right and right.
RC Writes
Next door to Hayward Hill the proprietor of the above shop used be an ex chauffeur of the skinhead guerrilla who only discovered this place by accident after leaving the best barbers in London. He was so shocked at the prices that he reeled round the corner only to discover that Charlie Russell was an even greater scalper.

Hoylake

RC writes
That swine he always accuses me of being drunk. He forced me to spend a day driving to Hoylake in search of a shop. Whilst I went off for some much needed sustenance, he spent 3 hours yakking to the owner and we then drove back to London only to discover that he had lost the details. According to him you come out of Hoylake Station, turn right, turn left and there is an old public toilets (trust him to remember that, and inside the bookshop are R/C/D bks - ab av cnd, av prices. I can't understand it, I never saw a veggie restaurant in Hoylake.

On Thursdays only there is a secondhand book market at Camden Passage. Primarily pbks, but it does have the Flying Scotsman, (see above) in a less hungover state.

Penn
Opp the Cottage bksp is a plate bookdealers.

CHARLOTTE ROBINSON **London**
35 Gt. Pulteney Street, London W1
Mon-Fri, 11-6
Med size C/D stk, bookfairy, keen on mod 1sts, ill and childrens. Ab av cal, cnd and prices. BR Piccadilly, OOS on Shaftesbury Ave exit, cont up Shaftesbury Av, left into Gt Windmill St and left at Brewer St, and second right.

ADDENDUM

PAGES: 75, 83, 86, 95,
96, 108, 119,
195, 246, 252,
262, 265, 268,
291, 302, 306,
103, 246, 251,
245,

BOOK FINDERS. *
AVIATION △.

ADDENDUM

Barstable Books.
(R J Carpenter)
28, Ravensbourne Dr
Chelmsford, Essex
CM1. 2SJ.
(T/No 58649)

HP BookFinders. *
M. E. EARL.
18 Fullers Field
Great Milton, Oxford,
OX9. 7PJ.
0844- 278141
0831 - 124106.

MRS LEAVER. *
27, Salisbury Ave,
Cheltenham, Glouc.
GL51 5BT.

Frank Smith △
100, Heaton Road
N.U.T.
(aviation & Marine).

The Old Book & Print Shop.
43 Park Street,
Old Hatfield, Hatfield.
Herts. AL9. 5BA.
0707 - 274200/270007.

Brian Cocks. △
18, Woodgate, Helpston,
Peterborough. PE6. 7ED.
0733 - 252791.

Richard Pike. △
39, Highview Way.
Patcham, Brighton
Sx. BN1. 8WS.

Falconwood Transport △
& Military Bookshop.
5, Falconwood Parade
The Green, Welling, Kent.
DA16 2PL.
081-303-8291.

Patterson & Liddle. △
10, Margaret Bldgs.
Brock Street
Bath. BA1. 2LP.
0225 - 426722. (10 - 5.30)

Keegans Bookshop. △
Merchants Place
Friar Street
Reading. RG1. 1DT. 0734-587253

ADDENDUM

Fletcher Aviation Ltd. ∆
Dept AM. Po Box 347.
Camberley, Sy.
GU15. 4GB.

AeroMart Aviation books.
48, Marlborough Rd.
Ipswich. IP4. 5BA.

Premier Books & Prints.
65, High Town, Luton.
LU2. 0BW. 611991.

The Eagle Bookshop.
103, Castle Road
Bedford. 01234-269 2[illegible]

Brian Cocks
18 Woodgate,
Helpston
Peterborough
PE6. 7ED.
01733-252791.

Soldridge Books.
Soldridge House
Alton, Hants.
GU34 5JF.
01420-562811.

Cirrus Aviation B[illegible]
North Lodge,
Wakefield Road
Swillington, Lee[ds]
LS26 8DT
01132-862907.

Robert Hunn & Co.
Station House.
Stamford, Lincs
PE9. 2JN.
01780-766266.

ADDENDUM

ADDENDUM

ADDENDUM

ADDENDUM